THE INCA WORLD

THE INCA WORLD
ANCIENT PEOPLE AND PLACES

ART • ARCHITECTURE • RELIGION • EVERYDAY LIFE • CULTURE

**THE NATIVE CIVILIZATIONS OF THE ANDES AND SOUTH AMERICA
EXPLORED IN 500 PAINTINGS, DRAWINGS AND PHOTOGRAPHS**

Dr DAVID M JONES

LORENZ BOOKS

CONTENTS

INTRODUCTION

The Inca Empire was the culmination of thousands of years of cultural evolution, the end product of gradual developments from small farming villages to cities with large populations and sophisticated political, economic and religious organization.

THE ANDEAN AREA

The vast continent of South America, nearly separate geologically and geographically, never formed a single cultural unit. Its inhabitants developed at different paces, although cultures in large areas were aware of and interactive with each other through trade, political alliance, conquest and the diffusion of ideas.

The ancient cultures that archaeologists call 'civilizations' (urban-based societies with centralized political organization and advanced technology) were confined to the Andes mountains and adjacent western coastal valleys and deserts. Sophisticated societies and beliefs were also developed by other South American peoples, but they did not build monumental ceremonial centres or cities, or, for the most part, develop technology of the same complexity or variety as Andean cultures, or establish kingdoms and empires.

Below: Andean foothills, typical upland valley terrain and Mount Illimani, Bolivia.

This book concentrates on the 'Andean Area', where civilizations evolved in the sierras and adjacent foothills and coastal regions, north to south from the present-day Colombian–Ecuadorian border to the northern half of Chile and east to west from the Amazonian Rainforest to the Pacific.

CIVILIZED CONTACTS

The Andean Area is a nuclear region where civilization emerged independently. Other nuclear regions were Mesopotamia, Egypt, north-western India, China, Southeast Asia and Mesoamerica. Ancient Andeans had no direct knowledge of or contact with the peoples of any of these other regions. There is no substantiated confirmation in written records, or any unequivocal archaeological evidence, to prove that sustained contact existed between the Old World and the New before 1492.

There is equally no evidence to suggest the Incas were aware of the Aztec Empire or Maya city-states in Mesoamerica.

By the 1520s, Inca traders were travelling up the north-west coast, making contact and trading with sophisticated metallurgy-producing 'chiefdoms' in north-western South America. Likewise, in the early 16th century, Aztecs traded at the international emporium of Xicalango in the Yucatán Peninsula, and were on the

Above: Inca maize planting in August (yupuy quilla, soil turning) depicted in Poma de Ayala's Nueva Corónica, *c.1615.*

verge of invading the Maya city-states. The two empires might eventually have met, and the consequences would undoubtedly have been interesting.

WHAT IS CIVILIZATION?

Civilization is an elusive term. Much has been written in an attempt to define it, to list its essential characteristics. Standard dictionary definitions help little, for they tend to state that civilization is the 'opposite of barbarism', and that it involves the arts and refinement of culture. The end product – cultures with cities and a high level of sophisticated technology – seems obvious. Civilization is recognizable when full-blown. But it is the point at which civilization can be said to arrive that is so difficult to perceive and define.

'Laundry lists' of criteria by which civilization can be defined have been made. They include: size, rulership, cities, domesticated animals and plants, irrigation agriculture, social organization (which includes individuals who do not participate in or contribute directly to subsistence), writing, a monetary system, a state army,

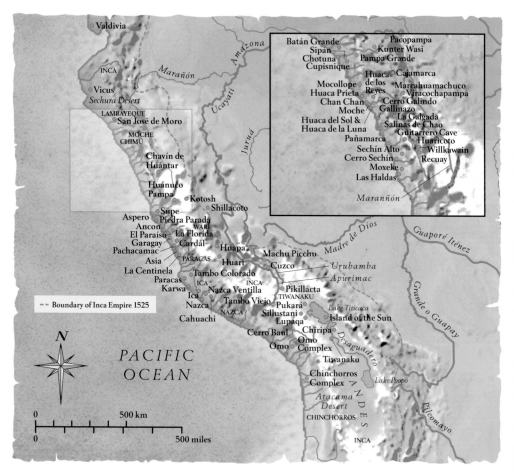

Valdivia
INCA
Vicus
Sechura Desert
LAMBAYEQUE
San José de Moro
MOCHE
CHIMÚ
Chavín de
Huántar
Huánuco
Pampa
Kotosh
Shillacoto
Supe
Aspero
Ancon
Piedra Parada
WARI
El Paraíso
La Florida
Garagay
Cardál
Pachacamac
Huapa
Asia
PARACAS
Huari
Machu Picchu
Cuzco
Urubamba
Apurimac
La Centinela
Tambo Colorado
Paracas
INCA
Karwa
ICA
Nazca
Ventilla
Pikillacta
Ica
TIWANAKU
Tambo Viejo
Nazca
Pukará
Cahuachi
NAZCA
Sillustani
Lupaqa
Cerro Baul
Chiripa
Island of the Sun
Omo
Omo
Complex
Tiwanaku
Chinchorros
Complex
Lake Poopó
*Atacama
Desert*
CHINCHORROS
INCA

-- Boundary of Inca Empire 1525

*PACIFIC
OCEAN*

N

0   500 km
0   500 miles

Batán Grande
Pacopampa
Sipán
Kunter Wasi
Chotuna
Pampa Grande
Cupisnique
Huaca
Cajamarca
Mocollope
de los
Reyes
Marcahuamachuco
Huaca Prieta
Viracochapampa
Chan Chan
Cerro Galindo
Moche
Gallinazo
Huaca del Sol &
La Galgada
Huaca de la Luna
Salinas de Chao
Pañamarca
Guitarrero Cave
Sechín Alto
Huaricoto
Cerro Sechín
Willkawain
Moxeke
Recuay
Las Haldas
Maranñón

Above: Map of the Andean Area, showing sites, of all periods, discussed in the text.

a road system and a certain level of technological sophistication with specialized craftspeople. Yet every nuclear area listed above lacked one or more of these criteria.

ANDEAN CIVILIZATION
The Andean Area is vast. Within it, long-distance communication was a major feature of its civilization. Communication was also long-lived, for as each successive culture developed, it was based on the developments that preceded it.

Pre-Inca Andean city-states, kingdoms and empires evolved, based on maize and potato agriculture and on the herding of camelids (llamas, alpacas and vicuñas). The range of contrasting landscapes was immense in the Andean Area – from coastal plains and deserts, to inland valleys, to sierra basins and plateaux, to high pampas grasslands, to eastern mountain slopes descending to Amazonian rainforests.

A key factor in Andean cultural development and endurance was access to and control of water, which became important

not only functionally, but also religiously. Geographical contrast fostered and nurtured the development of sophisticated agriculture based on complex irrigation technologies and a wide variety of crops, both within and between lowland and highland regions. These developments fostered economic specialization, enabling cultures to develop social hierarchies and complex divisions and distributions of labour and rulership. They also developed

trading contacts across long distances, and religious beliefs and structures, both theoretical and architectural.

LEGACY
The sophisticated technologies developed in Andean civilization came to be sponsored by the state. Rulers and the religious hierarchy required large-scale production of exquisite ceramics, textiles and jewellery as statements of social status, state power and religious devotion.

Sadly, these precious archaeological objects attract the interest and greed of modern collectors as much as they do scholars seeking the knowledge such objects can reveal. Since the Spanish Conquest, a legacy of illicit digging for monetary gain and exclusive ownership has fostered trade in antiquities fed by looting on a grand scale.

Undisturbed archaeological evidence, from the humblest building to the elite tombs of Sipán, provides the best source of information about everyday culture and conspicuous consumption of precious objects in their social and ritual contexts. Robbed from the ground by looters, and of its cultural context, it is lost forever.

Below: Highland plateau among the Cordillera de los Frailes, Bolivia.

THE SOURCES

Scholars have three sources of information about the Incas and their predecessors: historical documents, archaeological evidence, and anthropological or ethnological information about Andean peoples.

Written sources are particularly relevant for our picture of Inca society, but the principal sources of knowledge for pre-Inca civilization come from archaeology and anthropology. Artefacts and structures are direct evidence of what ancient Andeans made and used. But the manner of their use and what social, political, economic and religious meanings they have must be interpreted.

For pre-Inca cultures there is almost no historical evidence. Inca records of the peoples they conquered (for example the Chimú Kingdom that began before the Inca Empire and was contemporary to the early Inca), written down after the Spanish Conquest, are subject to Inca imperial views. However, comparison of pre-Inca archaeological evidence with Inca materials and history can reveal similarities that enable scholars to suggest that Inca social, political, economic and religious practices and beliefs were the end results of much earlier developments of these themes.

Above: Totora-reed boats on Lake Titicaca. Design has changed little since ancient times, but modern cloth sails mean less labour.

ARCHAEOLOGICAL PROJECTIONS

In combination with archaeology, much of what we gain from written sources about the Incas and their contemporaries can be 'projected' into the past, as a way of interpreting and understanding pre-Inca civilization and cultures.

Archaeology comprises methods of recovery, analytical procedures and reasoning to reconstruct as much as possible about the nature of people's lives in past cultures. Archaeological evidence is viable wherever and whenever historical evidence does not exist, or does not document groups or aspects of a people or culture. In addition to excavating and collecting artefacts (any object or remains made by humans or left as the result of their activities), archaeologists carefully record their contexts – the positions and relationships between artefacts and the soil in which they are found.

Contexts enable archaeologists to date objects and structures in relationship to each other, to see similarities and differences between types of artefacts, and thus deduce their uses, technology, and social and economic relationships between peoples and cultures. Artefacts, contexts and relationships also enable archaeologists to offer explanations of how cultures functioned, from straightforward deductions about manufacturing technology, to conclusions about trade and reasoned speculation about political relationships and religious beliefs.

DATING

Historical sources normally give dates for the events being recorded, although these are not always accurate. Until 1949 archaeological evidence, unless it could be linked to a historical source, could not be given calendar dates, only dates relative to other archaeological evidence (before, after or at the same time as). Such relative dating was determined by association in the same stratigraphic layer of earth, or in a layer above (later than) or below (earlier than) another artefact. This is true whether the artefact concerned is something small, such as a hand tool, or large, such as the foundation walls of a temple.

Below: Inca farmers tending maize seedlings in irrigated fields in January when the rain came, or qhapaq raymi quilla – the month of feasting, depicted in Poma de Ayala's Nueva Corónica, c.1615.

Above: A Moche stirrup-spout effigy bottle modelled as the head of an apparently blind man.

Science has discovered several radiometric ways to determine absolute dates for archaeological materials. Two principal methods are radiocarbon dating and dendrochronology (tree-ring dating). The former is the main method for Andean ancient history because its limits (back to about 50,000 years ago) are well within the range of human occupation of the Andean Area. The latter was developed from the early decades of the 20th century but is of no use in Andean cultures because most of the wood used in Andean architecture has not survived, and a tree-ring sequence is not available for the region.

CAUTION

Archaeological evidence has drawbacks. Many human activities produce no physical objects or traces. For example, languages, religious beliefs or social relationships usually leave no direct remains and can only be deduced from related artefacts (e.g. written sources, idols in a temple, burial practices or the nature of house plans). Many organic materials are destroyed by natural decay (such as wood, fibre, bones and plant materials), although some natural conditions (extreme dryness, burning or lack of air) sometimes preserve organic materials. Humans themselves often destroy their own artefacts through use, abandonment or war.

ANTHROPOLOGY

Ethnological information about contemporary Andean people can provide insight into ancient cultures. Because the landscape in remote Andean regions has changed little since Inca times, some ancient traditions and technology have survived, particularly agricultural methods. Observations of contemporary society can help in the interpretation of otherwise puzzling archaeological remains or historical descriptions, through direct parallels or as models for comparison.

One of the major characteristics of Andean civilization appears to be longevity of technology, cultural practices, social organization and religious belief, which are recognizably different in detail to distinguish diverse peoples and nations through time.

The direct observations of Felipe Guaman Poma de Ayala and the sources used by Bernabé Cobo were the first ethnographies. Later explorers and travellers added to and confirmed many 16th-century records when they recorded native practices. Joining a French expedition to

Above: Professor John Howland Rowe of the University of California at Berkeley at the ruins of the Palace of Emperor Huyana Capac at Quisphuanca, Peru.

South America in the late 1730s, Antonio Juan de Ulloa recorded contemporary Andean practices.

Later, Alexander von Humboldt travelled throughout the Americas and recorded his observations on natural history and geology, ethnology and archaeology. His *Political Essay on the Kingdom of New Spain* (1811) and *Researches Concerning the Institutions and Monuments of the Ancient Inhabitants of America* (1814) were monumental works, and his lectures back in Europe brought South America and its peoples into public awareness.

Below: An alpaca herd grazing in the highland Valle de Coloa, Bolivia.

DISCOVERING THE INCAS AND THEIR PREDECESSORS

Awareness of ancient civilizations in the New World began to increase in the late 18th and 19th centuries as excavations and the collecting of antiquities developed. Primitive excavations were undertaken in Europe and the Americas. Scholars began to re-examine colonial records, old maps and the objects taken back to Europe by the conquistadors and surviving in ancient graves. Sadly, then and now, the antiquities black market encourages looting, and the ancient sites of South America are riddled with *huaqueros'* (tomb robbers') pits.

The archaeologists and anthropologists of the time began to ask serious questions about the past, and when the ancient historians failed them, or, in the New World, simply did not exist, they began to use archaeology and ethnology to seek their own answers. Their early efforts went little beyond recognition, recording and description of ancient objects and sites. Gradually, however, their growing knowledge led to fieldwork designed to answer specific questions about the rise of civilization in the ancient Andes, and to address the 'problem' of the very presence of white people in the New World prior to the arrival of Europeans.

Modern archaeologists and anthropologists developed sophisticated techniques and reasoning during the 20th century to explore Andean civilizations, and continue their quest into the 21st century.

Left: Archaeologists cleaning the base of one of the many temple tombs at Sipán in the Lambayeque Valley, Peru.

NATIVE AND SPANISH SOURCES

Much of European knowledge about native Andeans was biased according to the viewpoint and nationality of the author of any written source. Early sources are mostly limited to information about the Incas, and authors throughout the later 16th and 17th centuries often copied from earlier writers, so reinforcing their views.

NATIVE RECORD-KEEPING

Neither the Incas nor any earlier Andean civilization developed writing. The Incas did, however, invent a system of record keeping called the *quipu*. This was a system of knot tying and colour coding, kept by trained court officials called *quipucamayoqs*. Records were kept as bundles of llama wool threads, suspended from a main thread or rod. The types, colours and sequences of knots, the directions of tying and other details served as tabulations of the numbers and types of goods collected as imperial taxes, and also as statistics on peoples of the empire, their populations, movements and tax quotas.

Below: The Incas and Spaniards were curious about each other. Asked what the Spaniard eats, the reply is 'gold' (Poma de Ayala, Nueva Corónica, c.1615).

Much information in early Spanish sources comes from consultations with *quipucamayoqs*. For example, in the 1560s and 1570s Sarmiento de Gamboa interviewed more than 100 *quipucamayoqs* to compile an Inca history for the viceroy of Peru; and in 1608 Melchior Carlos Inca, a claimant of the Inca throne, compiled the *Relación de los Quipucamayoqs* using the testimonies of four elderly *quipucamayoqs* recorded in 1542.

A second group of record-keepers, called *amautas*, were court historians who memorized the deeds of the emperors, ancient legends and religious information, which they passed down through generations of *amautas*. They, too, provided information for Spanish sources.

Finally, Inca priests had a detailed knowledge of the gods and their relationships, and of ceremony and ritual. They knew the sacred sites and pathways (*ceques*), and the movements of the sun, moon, Venus, Pleiades and Milky Way. Local priests knew their sacred sites (*huacas*), of which there were thousands throughout the empire.

SPANISH RECORDS

The only written records, therefore, date from after the Spanish Conquest. They include: Spanish conquistador accounts; records of the Catholic clergy as they converted native Andeans to Christianity; records of Spanish administrative officials as they organized their conquered subjects for labour and taxation; legal documents of colonial court actions; and personal letters and histories written by native and Spanish individuals to describe their own lives and views, or to summarize Inca religion and history. These sources reveal much information about Inca daily life, social and political organization and religious beliefs.

First-hand accounts based on direct observation at the time of writing are known as primary sources. Chief among these is the native Felipe Guaman Poma

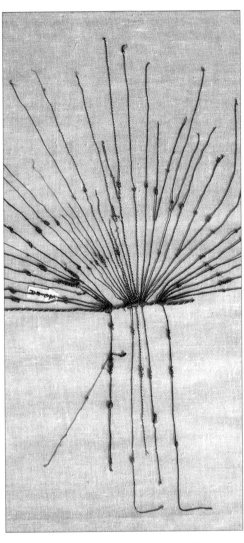

Above: A typical Inca quipu *of tied and dyed knotting, used as a record and memory aid by Inca record-keepers.*

de Ayala's *El Premier Nueva Corónica y Buen Gobierno*, written 1584–1615. He describes Inca life in great detail, protests to the king of Spain about the treatment of the Incas and graphically represents Inca life and religion in 398 drawings.

By contrast, works written by authors using the information in primary sources are known as secondary sources. A principal secondary source is Father Bernabé Cobo's *Historia del Nuevo Mundo* (1653), which includes *Inca Religion and Customs*. Cobo used the works of, among others, Juan Polo de Ondegardo (1560s and 70s), from which he completed the list of Cuzco shrines and *ceques*, and Garcilasco de la Vega ('El Inca'), son of a conquistador and Inca princess, who wrote a commentary on the Inca imperial household and a general history of the Spanish Conquest. Cobo's monumental 20-year work is considered the most balanced and comprehensive early account of Inca history and religion.

APPROACH WITH CAUTION

Such records must be used with caution, however. Each writer, native or Spaniard, was writing from his own cultural point of view and did not fully understand the institutions and social structure of the other. Each inevitably interpreted information about the other from his own viewpoint.

For example, however comprehensive Poma de Ayala's nearly 1,200-page compilation is, his family, originally from

Below: After Pizarro's treachery and capture of Atahualpa at Cajamarca there followed many fierce battles between Inca armies and the Spaniards, here against Francisco Hernández Girón (Poma de Ayala, c.1615).

Above: A 16th-century Spanish caravel sailing for the New World. The caravel was a fast and easily manoeuvrable ship with a gently sloping bow and a single stern castle.

Huanuco in the Central Highlands, had been forcibly relocated by the Incas to Huamango (Ayacucho). In addition, members of his family served as *quipucamayoqs* and he himself converted to Christianity and became an interpreter for Spanish administrative and ecclesiastical inspectors. He therefore bore a grudge against the Incas, abhorred the persistence of Andean religious practices, and at the same time protested about the brutality of Spanish treatment of his fellow natives (frequently shown in his depictions).

Incas and Spaniards both had ulterior motives for their conquests and considered themselves a superior race. As a result, they sometimes deliberately falsified their accounts to justify their actions. In particular, the main source for Spanish chroniclers was the Incas themselves, more specifically the Inca ruling class. So information about ordinary Incas and their contemporaries (both elite and common citizens), and about pre-Inca cultures were doubly filtered: first through the

Inca elite's preconceptions (in the primary source) and later through Spanish opinions (in the secondary source).

Another note of caution that must be added is the vagueness that pervades places and names in Inca and Spanish writings. Provinces, towns and peoples listed by one traveller differ from those listed by another travelling the same route. There were also widespread movements of peoples over the centuries and by the Incas themselves.

Despite these drawbacks, scholars generally think that the basic events in Inca history were more accurately recorded the closer they occurred to the Spanish Conquest. Also that, by comparing and contrasting several sources describing the same events or information about Inca society, truthful information can be extracted.

EXPLORERS AND THE FIRST ARCHAEOLOGISTS

Early Spanish writings primarily concern the Incas, which leaves our principal source of information about pre-Inca Andean civilization to be archaeology. Until the material remains of ancient sites were explored and excavated there was much speculation but little substance to writings about ancient Andean cultures.

ARCHAEOLOGICAL EXPLORERS

Alexander von Humboldt was the first scholar seriously to consider reasons for the presence of humans in the New World and to attempt to make a record of the ancient ruins he saw in the Andes. He was a pioneer, struggling to separate observation and description from speculation and interpretation.

The first dedicated report on ancient Andean antiquities was that of Mariano Edward de Rivero and John James von Tschudi in 1841. Inspired by antiquarian activities and publications in Europe and North America, Rivero had been appointed director of Peru's national museum in Lima, where antiquities from all over Peru were collected. The two made a systematic record of what was known.

William Prescott's *History of the Conquest of Peru* (1847) did much to inspire enthusiasm for ancient Andean civilization, but by and large did not consider archaeological material. Johann Tschudi's five-volume *Reisen durch Süd Amerika* (1869) and Ephraim G. Squier's *Peru: Incidents of Travel and Exploration in the Land of the Incas* (1877) echo the travels of John Stephens and Frederick Catherwood in Mesoamerica.

These and other early attempts to write about ancient Andean civilization lacked a methodological approach to relate the archaeological materials and ruins to contexts. It was soon realized that the ruins themselves must be explored beyond mere descriptions of their surface remains, and that study of ancient Andean artefacts must go further than collection from looted tombs and description.

THE FIRST EXCAVATORS

One of the earliest deliberate excavations was undertaken by Alphons Stübel and Wilhelm Reiss. At the ancient cemetery of Ancón, north of Lima, they excavated unlooted tombs containing mummy

Above: An early 20th-century photograph of the 'Sun Gate' at Tiwanaku shows it cracked and collapsing. The entire gateway is actually a single monolithic carved block, now repaired.

bundles, thus gaining primary information on burial practices and their contents in context. They published their finds and interpretations in three volumes in *The Necropolis of Ancón in Peru* between 1880 and 1887.

Similarly, Adolph Bandelier carried out excavations of Tiwanaku sites on the islands in the Titicaca Basin, which he published in 1910, and at Tiwanaku itself in 1911. On the Island of the Sun in Titicaca, at the site of Chucaripupata, he found gold, silver, bronze and copper artefacts, including a golden mask, near the sacred rock of Titikala.

The work of Stübel and Reiss inspired a young fellow German, Max Uhle. After studying philology, Uhle switched to archaeology and ethnography and became curator at the Dresden Museum. He met Stübel and collaborated with him to publish *Die Ruinenstätte von Tiahuanaco* in 1892, based on the records and photographs Stübel had made at Tiwanaku. Uhle began his own fieldwork in Peru in the same year and continued until 1912. He was the first to apply the archaeological principles of stratigraphy (assessing

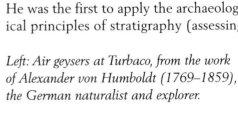

Left: Air geysers at Turbaco, from the work of Alexander von Humboldt (1769–1859), the German naturalist and explorer.

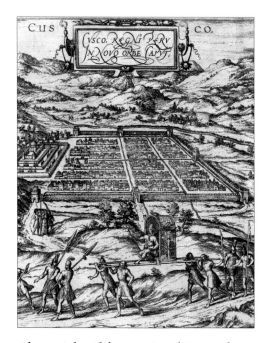

Above: A fanciful engraving of Cuzco, the Inca capital, by the German cartographer Georg Braun, 1594. Pizarro called it "the most noble and great city" when he entered it on 23 March 1534.

the chronology of finds from their positions in the earth) in his excavations. With his knowledge of Inca and Tiwanaku pottery types, his excavations at Pachacamac on the Peruvian coast enabled him to construct the first pre-Inca chronology of ancient Andean ceramics. Knowing that Inca pottery was dated to the 15th and 16th centuries, and that the Incas revered the monuments of ancient Tiwanaku, he reasoned that Tiwanaku ceramics pre-dated the Incas. The pottery he excavated at Pachacamac was often found in the same layers as Inca pottery, but showed no stylistic influence from Tiwanaku. He reasoned that it must be intermediate in date between the two. This was the beginning of 30 years of excavation and analysis in Peru, Bolivia, Ecuador and Chile, during which he used the relative dating method of seriation to provide a chronology of ancient Andean ceramic styles that basically remains valid today.

A 20TH-CENTURY EXPLORER
Adventurous exploration, however, had not ended. Prescott had inspired many, including Hiram Bingham. Young Bingham had gone to Peru in 1911 on a romantic dream. "Archaeology lies

outside my field and I know very little about the Incas, except the fascinating story told by Prescott in his famous *Conquest of Peru*", he declared to the Peruvian Prefect whose *Departamento* he wanted to explore.

Inca imperial Machu Picchu became 'lost' after the Spanish Conquest only because of its remote location. (Colonial records refer to the site and local people knew it well.) Although Bingham always claimed that he wandered by chance up the newly opened road from Cuzco to the north-west towards the Amazon, in fact, Melchor Artega, a local farmer, described the site to Bingham when he and his team arrived in the Urubamba Valley. Artega, Sergeant Carrasco, Bingham's Quechua translator, and a boy even acted as guides. Nevertheless it was Bingham who brought the spectacular find to the attention of the Western world and solved the 'mystery' of the famous site. To his credit, he did not stop there,

Below: A classic view of the Machu Picchu ruins, the Inca imperial retreat and sacred city in the remote Andes north-west of Cuzco.

Above: Alexander von Humboldt, explorer, geographer, naturalist and lecturer, the first person to make a thorough scientific exploration of the Andes, including its archaeological ruins.

but continued to explore, and in his single summer season made several more discoveries of remote Inca sites.

Bingham's 'discovery' of Machu Picchu, for better or worse, will remain one of the most important events in the annals of Andean archaeology, and it made him a celebrity: he became an Ivy League professor, an Air Force hero and was elected to the US Senate.

20TH-CENTURY ARCHAEOLOGY AND BEYOND

The early 20th century was an age of discovery, large-scale excavation and development of scientific archaeology. Grand multi-disciplinary research programmes were undertaken in the Andes, and Alfred Kroeber and John Rowe of the University of California, Berkeley, refined and expanded Max Uhle's chronological scheme, defining the Periods and Horizons of Andean prehistory. The discovery of radiocarbon dating by Willard Libby enabled calendar dates to be fixed at many sites.

GRAND PROJECTS

Universities, museums and research organizations with enormous resources funded large-scale survey projects and excavations through multiple field seasons. Archaeologists began to ask specific questions about Andean civilization and to undertake work designed to answer them. They went beyond exploration and description to analysis and interpretation,

Below: An adobe brick-lined Nazca shaft tomb, used for the repeated deposition of honoured elite – part of the cult of ancestor worship.

not only of the detailed prehistoric Andean events but also of mechanisms and explanations of why domestication occurred, and why cities arose.

Increasing collections of pottery, metalwork, textiles and other materials prompted the development of methods for conserving and restoring them. This work provided increasingly sophisticated information, making possible complex interpretations that went beyond technology to provide explanations about ancient religion, politics and social structure.

Julio Tello, a native Peruvian, studied archaeology and anthropology at Harvard University, followed by a lifelong career, beginning in the 1920s, investigating the origins of Andean civilization through excavations at the Paracas cemeteries, Sechín Alto and Chavín de Huántar. With Kroeber, he established the Institute of Andean Research in Lima in 1939.

The Second World War only briefly interrupted such studies. Scholars in the 1950s and 1960s extended the reach of projects to all periods of Andean prehistory, until the huge amount of discovery and interpretation required collation and

Above: Moche Huaca del Sol, made of millions of adobe mud bricks. In plan it formed a thick-armed cross, largely destroyed by Spaniards looking for buried treasure.

systemization. In 1969 the Peruvian archaeologist Luis Lumbreras produced the first great synthesis of Peruvian prehistory, *The Peoples and Cultures of Ancient Peru* (translated into English by Betty Meggers in 1974); and in 1971 Gordon Willey published the second volume of his monumental *An Introduction to American Archaeology: South America*.

The increasing fieldwork and accelerating pace of analysis and interpretation during the later 20th and 21st centuries required renewed synthesis. Most notable is Michael Moseley's *The Incas and their Ancestors: The Archaeology of Peru*, published in 1992, then revised in 2001.

REVOLUTION?

A 'revolution' dubbed 'New Archaeology' in the 1960s and 70s applied wider theoretical concepts to archaeological data. Scholars increasingly questioned the system of methods and principles that were used in archaeology and posed deeper questions about alleged cultural universals. This healthy internal analysis happily did not deter fieldwork and data accumulation through excavations and field surveys continued. Archaeologists continue to ask wide questions as well as conduct detailed analysis and interpretation

in specific areas and specialized topics, so expanding our overall understanding of Andean prehistory.

LINES OF ENQUIRY

The Nazca lines have fascinated generations. In the 1940s, Paul and Rose Kosok expounded their theory that the lines were astronomically motivated. Maria Reiche, inspired by the Kosoks, became 'queen of the pampa' and devoted her life to the astronomical cause. Her particular contribution was the extensive mapping of lines, especially the figures. Neither the Kosoks nor Reiche, however, could prove their astronomical theories with convincing statistical evidence.

In the 1970s and 80s, the archaeo-astronomer Frank Aveni conducted the most extensive survey and study of Nazca geoglyphs yet made. He found no statistically significant correlations or directional correlations. Instead, he found 62 nodes from which lines radiated, and discovered there are many generations of lines, earlier ones crossing older ones, concluding that they were for ritual processions, made over generations for specific occasions.

SHAKEN REVELATIONS

In 1950, an earthquake flattened much of Cuzco, including the Dominican church and monastery. Reconstruction of the monastery provided an opportunity to investigate the Coricancha temple beneath, so priority was given to exposing the Inca remains.

Above: Archaeologists of the Instituto Nacional de Cultura uncover the skeleton of one of 72 Inca battle victims in a mass burial at Puruchuco, a suburb of Lima.

Excavations in the monastery plaza revealed an Inca cobblestone floor and wall foundations on the southern and northern sides. With John Rowe's map based on colonial documents, excavators Oscar Ladrón de Guevera and Raymundo Béjar Navarro, together with architectural historians Graziano Gasparini and Luise Margolies, were able to plan and illustrate the appearance of the sacred temple. Much of the monastery ruins were removed and the Coricancha complex was reconstructed, as seen today.

CONTINUED DISCOVERIES

Despite the wealth of Andean metalwork, ceramics and textiles in museums, there is no greater treasure than a collection of such artefacts found *in situ*. The discovery of unlooted Moche tombs at Sipán in the Lambayeque Valley in the late 1980s by Walter Alva and Susana Meneses was just that. Having heard about a *huaquero* raid on the Sipán pyramid, the police in turn raided the robbers' house and recovered artefacts the robbers had taken. The

Left: Ruins of part of the Kalasasaya sacred temple compound at Tiwanaku, Bolivia. They have since been re-erected and the compound partly reconstructed.

police chief then phoned Alva, and under armed guard he and Meneses excavated the low platform at the foot of the pyramid, where they discovered six burial levels, including the fabulously rich tombs of the Lord of Sipán, a Moche priest and the Old Lord of Sipán.

In 2002, the ironically named shanty-town of Tupac Amaru (last 'Inca' emperor, 1571–2) on Lima's outskirts was being cleared for redevelopment. Following modern practice, archaeological investigations preceded, during which an Inca cemetery of up to 10,000 burials was discovered. Some 2,000 burials of men, women and children were recovered, together with 60,000 artefacts, including 40 elite mummy bundles with 'false heads', some with wigs! These finds – everyday items, utensils and food, personal valuables – are being analysed. Their value for the reconstruction of Inca burial practices and everyday life are incalculable.

Even more recently, in 2007, a remarkable discovery was made in the Puruchuco suburb of Lima: a mass grave of 72 bodies killed in battle in 1536. The skull of one drew immediate attention: it was of a young Inca warrior, and it had two round holes in it. Near it was a small plug of bone with musket-ball markings, and electron microscopy detected traces of lead in the skull! It was the first time that evidence of death by gunshot – an Inca shot by a Spaniard – had ever been found in the Americas.

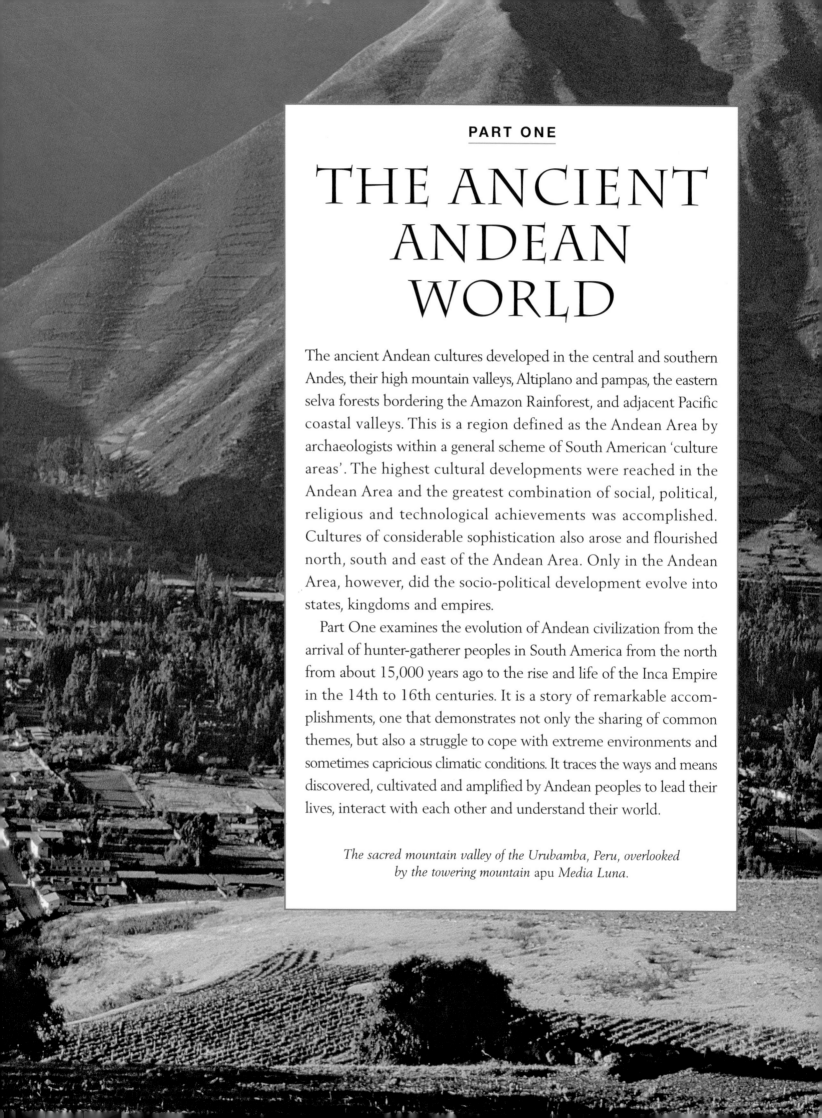

PART ONE

THE ANCIENT ANDEAN WORLD

The ancient Andean cultures developed in the central and southern Andes, their high mountain valleys, Altiplano and pampas, the eastern selva forests bordering the Amazon Rainforest, and adjacent Pacific coastal valleys. This is a region defined as the Andean Area by archaeologists within a general scheme of South American 'culture areas'. The highest cultural developments were reached in the Andean Area and the greatest combination of social, political, religious and technological achievements was accomplished. Cultures of considerable sophistication also arose and flourished north, south and east of the Andean Area. Only in the Andean Area, however, did the socio-political development evolve into states, kingdoms and empires.

Part One examines the evolution of Andean civilization from the arrival of hunter-gatherer peoples in South America from the north from about 15,000 years ago to the rise and life of the Inca Empire in the 14th to 16th centuries. It is a story of remarkable accomplishments, one that demonstrates not only the sharing of common themes, but also a struggle to cope with extreme environments and sometimes capricious climatic conditions. It traces the ways and means discovered, cultivated and amplified by Andean peoples to lead their lives, interact with each other and understand their world.

The sacred mountain valley of the Urubamba, Peru, overlooked by the towering mountain apu *Media Luna.*

TIMELINE OF THE INCAS AND THEIR ANCESTORS

CHRONOLOGY OF ANDEAN AREA CIVILIZATION

The chronology of the Andean Area is complex. Archaeologists have developed a scheme based on technological achievements and on changing political organization through time, from the first arrival of humans in the area (15,000–3500BC) to the conquest of the Inca Empire by Francisco Pizarro in 1532. The pace of technological development varied in different regions within the Andean Area, especially in early periods in its history. The development of lasting and strong contact between regions, however, spread both technology and ideas and led to regions depending on each other to some degree. Sometimes this interdependence was due to large areas being under the control of one 'authority', while at other times the unifying link was religious or based on trade/technology.

The principal chronological scheme for the Andean Area comprises a sequence of eight time units: five Periods and three Horizons. Periods are defined as times when political unity across regions was less consolidated. Smaller areas were controlled by city-states, sometimes in loose groupings,

perhaps sharing religious beliefs despite having different political views. The Horizons, by contrast, were times when much larger political units were formed. These units exercised political, economic and religious control over extended areas, usually including different types of terrain rather than being confined to coastal valley groups or sierra city-states.

Different scholars give various dates for the beginnings and endings of the Periods and Horizons, and no two books on Andean civilization give exactly the same dates. The durations of Periods and

Above: The walled royal compounds of the Chimú capital Chan Chan.

Horizons also vary from one region to another within the Andean Area, and the charts have increased in complexity as authors have divided the Andean Area into coastal, sierra and Altiplano regions, or even into north, central and southern coastal regions and north, central and southern highland regions. The dates given here are a compilation from several sources, thus avoiding any anomalies in any specific sources.

CHRONOLOGICAL PERIOD	DATES	PRINCIPAL CULTURES
Lithic / Archaic Period	15,000–3500BC	spread of peoples into the Andean Area hunter-gatherer cultures
Preceramic / Formative Period (Cotton Preceramic)	3500–1800BC	early agriculture and first ceremonial centres
Initial Period	1800–750BC	U-shaped ceremonial centres, platform mounds and sunken courts
Early Horizon	750–200BC	Chavín, Paracas, Pukará (Yaya-Mama) cults
Early Intermediate Period	200BC–AD600	Moche, Nazca and Titicaca Basin confederacies
Middle Horizon	AD600–1000	Wari and Tiwanaku empires
Late Intermediate Period	AD1000–1400	Chimú and Inca empires
Late Horizon	AD1400–1532	Inca Empire and Spanish Conquest

LITHIC / ARCHAIC PERIOD (15,000–3500 BC)

Above: View from the Cuz del Condor showing the mountains and valleys of Peru.

Ice-free corridors open up across the Bering Strait *c*.40,000 to *c*.20,000 years ago, but there is no evidence that humans entered the New World until the late stages of this time period.

c.20,000 BC Migrating hunter-gatherers, using stone-, bone-, wood- and shell-tool technologies, probably entered the New World from north-east Asia.

from *c*.15,000 years ago Palaeoindians migrated south and east to populate North and South America, reaching Monte Verde in southern Chile *c*.14,850 years ago.

c.8500–5000 BC Andean and Altiplano hunter-gatherers occupy cave and rock shelter sites in the Andes (e.g. Pachamachay, Guitarrero, Tres Ventanas and Toquepala caves). Evidence of tending of hemp-like fibre, medicinal plants, herbs and wild tubers.

c.6000 BC–*c*.5500 BC The first true monumental structures, two long parallel mounds, are built at Nanchoc, a late Archaic Period valley in the Zana Valley, north-west Peru.

by 5000 BC plant domestication, as opposed to tending wild plants, is truly underway in the highlands.

c.5000 BC The Chinchorros peoples make the first deliberately mummified burials in the Atacama Desert.

PRECERAMIC / FORMATIVE PERIOD (3500–1800 BC)

Above: Alpaca grazing in the Valle de Coloa. Camelids were herded c.3500–1800 BC.

This period is sometimes also called the Cotton Preceramic.

c.3500–1800 BC True plant domestication of cotton, squashes, gourds, beans, maize, potatoes, sweet potatoes and chillies. Llamas and other camelids herded on the Altiplano.

c.3500 BC Valdivians found Real Alto.

c.3200 BC First ceramics made by Valdivian farmers in coastal Ecuador.

by 3000 BC the full range of major food plants is grown in the highlands and the guinea pig is bred for meat.

c.3000 BC Coastal villages such as Huaca Prieta flourish, producing early textiles.

c.2700 BC Early northern coastal civic-ceremonial centres at Aspero – Huaca de los Idolos and Huaca de los Sacrificios.

by 2500 BC the llama and alpaca have been truly domesticated.

c.2500 BC Clay figurines at Huaca de los Idolos, Aspero.

c.2500–2000 BC Large raised mound platforms constructed at El Paraíso, La Galagada and Kotosh.

c.2000 BC Carved gourds at Huaca Prieta. Earliest coastal and highland pottery. Loom and heddle weaving begins.

INITIAL PERIOD (1800–750 BC)

Above: The U-shaped ceremonial centre of Chavín de Huántar began c.900 BC.

Spread of pottery, irrigation agriculture, monumental architecture, religious processions and ritual decapitation.

from *c*.1800 BC Sophisticated irrigation systems developed in coastal oases, valleys, the highlands and Altiplano.

c.1800 BC Construction at Moxeke includes colossal adobe heads.

c.1750 BC Builders at La Florida bring the first pottery to this region.

c.1500 BC Cerro Sechín flourishes as a major highland town.

c.1500 BC Earliest Andean gold foil made at Waywaka, Peruvian highlands.

c.1459–1150 BC Hammered gold and copper foil at Mina Perdida, coastal Peru.

c.1400–1200 BC Sechín Alto becomes the largest U-shaped civic-ceremonial centre in the New World.

c.1300 BC The five platform mounds at Cardál are erected.

c.1200 BC Carved lines of warriors at Cerro Sechín show regional conflict.

c.1000 BC The El Paraíso Tradition flourishes in the Rimac Valley.

c.900 BC Earliest U-shaped ceremonial complex at Chavín de Huántar begins.

EARLY HORIZON
(750–200BC)

Above: The Paracas Peninsula, which was a necropolis site for several settlements.

Religious cults develop around Chavín de Huántar and Pukará. Decapitation, hallucinogenic drug use and ancestor worship become widespread.

*c.*800BC Sechín Alto abandoned as a ceremonial centre.

from *c.*750BC The Old Temple at Chavín established as a cult centre. Influence of the Lanzón deity and the Staff Deity spreads. The Paracas Peninsula serves as a necropolis site, and the Oculate Being is depicted on textiles and ceramics.

*c.*500BC Construction of the New Temple at Chavín de Huántar begins.

*c.*500BC Earliest known fired-clay discs for pottery vessel making, Paracas.

*c.*400–200BC The Old Temple at Chavín enlarged to create the New Temple. The Chavín Cult spreads, especially at Kuntur Wasi and Karwa (Paracas).

*c.*400BC Annual rainfall levels fall in the Titicaca Basin. Pukará becomes centre of the Yaya-Mama Cult.

*c.*350 to 200BC Highland regional conflict evident in fortress-building in the Santa, Casma and Nepeña valleys.

*c.*250BC Beginning of the first settlement at Tiwanaku in the Titicaca Basin.

*c.*200BC Influence of Chavín Cult wanes.

EARLY INTERMEDIATE PERIOD
(200BC–AD600)

Above: Construction of the Moche Huaca del Sol began c.AD100.

Cohesion of the Chavín Cult disintegrates, and several regional chiefdoms develop in the coastal and mountain valleys.

*c.*100BC Rise of the Nazca in the southern Peruvian coastal valleys and Cahuachi founded.

*c.*AD100 Burial of the Old Lord of Sipán in Lambayeque Valley.

*c.*AD100 Sacred ceremonial centre of Cahuachi dominates the Nazca area.

*c.*1st century AD Moche dynasty founded in the northern coastal valleys.

*c.*AD100 Construction of first temple platforms at Huaca del Sol and Huaca de la Luna at Moche begins.

*c.*AD250 Construction of first temple at Pachacamac and start of the Pachacamac Cult. Major construction of temple platforms at Tiwanaku begins.

*c.*AD300 Burial of the Lord of Sipán in Lambayeque Valley.

AD300–550 Several Moche regional cities founded at Huancaco, Pamapa de los Incas, Pañamarca and Mocollope.

*c.*AD500 The Moche ceremonial platforms of the Huacas del Sol and de la Luna were the largest in the area.

*c.*AD700 Moche/Nazca power wanes.

MIDDLE HORIZON
(AD600–1000)

Above: View of wall and monolithic stelae, Semi-Subterranean Court, Tiwanaku.

Much of the Andean Area unified in two empires: Tiwanaku in the south and Wari in the north.

*c.*AD200 Major phase of monumental construction begins at Tiwanaku.

*c.*AD250 Settlement at Huari founded.

*c.*AD300 Major construction of central ceremonial plaza at Tiwanaku begins.

*c.*AD400–750 Elite residential quarters at Tiwanaku built. Tiwanaku colonies established at San Pedro Atacama, Omo and in the Cochabamba Valley.

*c.*AD500 Major construction at Huari and beginning of domination of the central highlands by the Wari Empire.

*c.*AD550 Pampa Grande flourishes, ruled by Sicán Lords.

by *c.*AD600 the cities of Huari and Tiwanaku dominate the highlands, building empires in the central and highlands Altiplano, respectively.

*c.*AD650 Wari city of Pikillacta founded, and Wari colonies established at Jincamocco, Azángaro, Viracochapampa and Marca Huamachuco.

*c.*AD750–1000 Third major phase of palace building begins at Tiwanaku.

*c.*AD850–900 Pikillacta abandoned.

LATE INTERMEDIATE PERIOD (AD1000–1400)

Above: View of present-day Cuzco and the Cuzco Valley where the Incas settled.

An era of political break-up is characterized by the rise of new city-states, including Lambayeque, Chimú and Pachacamac, the Colla and Lupaka kingdoms, and numerous city-states in the central and southern Andean valleys.

*c.*AD900–950 Rise of the Lambayeque-Sicán state in northern coastal Peru. Burial of the Sicán Lords at Lambayeque. Sicán capital city at Batán Grande.

*c.*AD950 Sediments of Lake Titicaca show evidence of decreased rainfall and start of a long period of drought leading to the eventual demise of Tiwanaku.

*c.*AD900 Chan Chan, capital of the Chimú, founded in the Moche Valley.

*c.*AD1000 Tiwanaku and Wari empires wane as regional political rivalry reasserts itself.

*c.*AD1000 Huari city-state abandoned.

*c.*1100 The Incas under Manco Capac, migrate into the Cuzco Valley, found Cuzco and establish the Inca dynasty.

*c.*1250 City of Tiwanaku abandoned, perhaps because of changes in climate.

*c.*1300 Sinchi Roca becomes the first emperor to use the title Sapa Inca.

*c.*1350 The Chimú conquer the Lambayeque-Sicán peoples.

LATE HORIZON (AD1400–1532)

Above: Inca stonework is distinctive in style and among the finest in the world.

In little more than 130 years the Incas build a huge empire, from Colombia to mid-Chile and from the rainforest to the Pacific and establish an imperial cult centred on Inti, the sun god, whose representative on Earth was the Sapa Inca.

*c.*1425 Viracocha, the eighth ruler, begins the Inca conquests and domination of the Cuzco Valley.

1438 Pachacuti Inca Yupanqui defeats the Chancas to dominate the Cuzco Valley and begin the expansion of the Inca Empire both within and outside the valley.

1438–71 Pachacuti begins his rebuilding of Cuzco as the imperial capital to the plan of a crouching puma, with the fortress and sun temple of Sacsahuaman forming the puma's head.

*c.*1450 Pachacuti establishes the city of Machu Picchu.

*c.*1462 Pachacuti begins the conquest of the Kingdom of Chimú.

1471 The Incas conquer the Kingdom of Chimú.

1471–93 Inca Tupac Yupanqui expands the empire west and south, doubling its size – north as far as the present-day Ecuador–Colombia border and south into the Titicaca Basin.

Above: The city of Machu Picchu, founded by Pachacuti c.1450.

1493–1526 Huayna Capac consolidates the empire, building fortresses, road systems, storage redistribution and religious precincts throughout the provinces. The provincial city of Qenqo is founded.

1526 Huayna Capac dies of smallpox without an agreed successor.

1526–32 Huayna Capac's son Huáscar seizes the throne but is challenged by his brother Atahualpa. A six-year civil war ends in the capture of Huáscar.

1530 Inca Empire at its greatest extent, and the largest territory in the world.

1532 Francisco Pizarro lands with a small Spanish army on the north coast of the Inca Empire and marches to meet Atahualpa at Cajamarca. He exploits the disruption of the civil war to play one claimant against the other.

1532 The Spaniards defeat the Incas at the Battle of Cajamarca and capture Atahualpa, holding him for ransom.

1533 Atahualpa condemned in a rigged Spanish trial and executed for adultery and idolatry.

1535 Francisco Pizarro founds Lima as his capital in Spanish Peru.

1541 Pizarro assassinated in his palace at Lima by Almagro and his associates.

CHAPTER ONE

LIVING IN THE LANDSCAPE

The diverse landscapes of South America were created by geological processes, and the varied fauna and flora developed as a result of biological evolution. South America includes multiple environmental and ecological zones. Its fauna and flora evolved independently from about 175 million years ago in the middle Jurassic Period, after the super-continent of Pangaea (Antarctica, Australia, India, Africa, Eurasia, and North and South America) began to divide into today's continents. Through remote periods of physical isolation from North America, the flora and fauna of the continent evolved into unique groups and species, which were later mutually exchanged with North America when the landmasses were ultimately reconnected. This combination of events created the landscapes and plant and animal life encountered by the first human migrants into South America as the great Ice Ages of the northern hemisphere ended.

Social evolution created the ultimate sophistication of Andean civilization, which enabled the Incas to create an empire that controlled the largest territory in the world at the time of the Spanish arrival in the New World.

This chapter describes both these worlds – the physical and the socio-political – as they were when an intrepid and determined group of men from the Old World reached the New World of the South American continent in a second episode of migration. This time, it was a clash of urban empires.

Left: The upper Urubamba–Vilcanote River, Peru, a sacred mountain valley whose rich soils are especially productive.

LANDSCAPES OF THE ANDEAN AREA

South America has evolved animal and plant species unique to its regions owing to long periods of physical isolation from North America. Towards the end of the Pliocene Epoch, *c.*3 million years ago, the Central American ridge re-emerged above sea level to reunite North and South America, creating a land bridge for their long-separated mammals.

GEOGRAPHICAL REGIONS

South America includes several major ecological and environmental regions that merge into each other across the breadth and length of the continent: the great western coastal deserts, pierced by scores of oases valleys and their rivers flowing into the Pacific Ocean; the Andean mountain range, winding the entire length of the continent, 7,500km (4,660 miles) from the Caribbean to Tierra del Fuego; the more gradual descent of the eastern Andes; the high Altiplano between the two Andean cordilleras and pampas to the south and east; and the huge Amazon Basin. There are also the rich maritime seascapes of the Pacific, Atlantic and Caribbean coastal waters.

Prehistorians subdivide the continent into zones of cultural development, each characterized by distinct archaeological

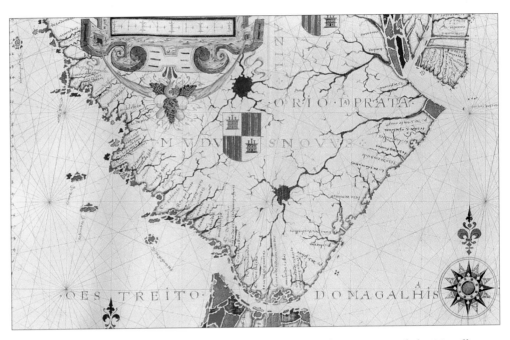

evidence and levels of technological and socio-political achievement. None of these zones was culturally isolated, and inter-relationships between zones were never static, but changed through time. The zone with which this book is concerned is the Andean Area. It comprises, west to east, the Pacific coast to the Amazonian Rainforest, and, north to south, roughly the modern Colombian–Ecuadorian border to the northern half of Chile.

Above: South America and the Magellan Straits from the Hydrographic Atlas *of 1571 by Fernan Vaz Dourado.*

THE ANDEAN AREA

The Andean Area is remarkable for its contrasting landscapes, both geographical and cultural. It includes the world's driest deserts, such as the Sechura in northern Peru–Ecuador, the Nazca in central Peru and the Atacama in northern Chile; some of the world's highest mountains, with peaks of more than 7,000m (23,000ft); and some of the lushest rainforests along the eastern edge of the Amazon Basin.

Climatic conditions vary greatly within the zone. El Niño events disrupt weather patterns and marine cycles about every four to ten years, reversing normal patterns by creating floods in coastal regions and drought in the mountains and Altiplano. Throughout Andean history there were

intermittent periods of prolonged drought, coinciding with the cultural periods defined by archaeologists. Evidence from glacial ice cores and lake sediments show sustained drought periods occurring *c.*2200–1900BC, 900–800BC, 400–200BC, AD1–300, AD562–95 and

Below: The Atacama Desert, northern Chile, is one of the driest places on Earth – high and dry, with sparse, tough vegetation.

Below: An Andean mountain peak, Mount Huayna Potosi, Bolivia, with abundant snow most of the year, from which flow waters to make mountain valleys fertile.

Above: Lush Amazonian rainforests flank the eastern Andes. The Incas considered their inhabitants to be subhuman.

AD1100–1450; and intervening wetter periods *c.*AD400–500, AD900–1000 and 1500–1700.

There was also great cultural variation. People developed distinct responses to different landscapes and environments, and distinct cultures. They evolved from wandering hunter-gatherers to early village farming communities as they selected and nurtured certain plants and animals into domestication. Finally, as they developed and mastered increasingly sophisticated socio-political and technological techniques, they evolved into civilizations with spreading towns and cities, kingdoms and even empires.

CIVILIZATION

Archaeologists are involved in never-ending examination and discussion of what defines civilization and what stimulates its development. Civilization of the highest calibre was attained in the Andean Area, and it evolved in part in response to the challenges presented by its varied landscapes.

Its Pacific coasts are the world's richest fishing grounds, the consequence of the cold Humboldt Current that sweeps up from Antarctica and brings huge fish shoals and migrating sea mammals, as well as nurturing rich coastal shellfish and bird populations. There is such abundance that the earliest inhabitants could support large village populations mostly reliant

Right: A high Andean lake valley, the Laguna Colorado, Bolivia, provided abundant flamingos to be hunted.

on the foreshore and near offshore waters for their livings. The river valleys descending from the western Andean foothills to the coastal plains have rich soils on which early peoples learned to practise increasingly intense and sophisticated irrigation agriculture. Similarly, in high Andean valleys and the Altiplano, people graduated from simple rainfall agriculture to increasingly intense cultivation using raised fields, hillside terracing and irrigation systems. On the rich grasslands of the southern Andean plateaux, people developed pastoralism with the domestication of the llama and alpaca.

INTERREGIONAL RELATIONS

These developments in agriculture, which led to trading between different regions, and the technological and socio-political advances they stimulated, enabled populations to increase, so that larger towns and cities came into being. Remarkable throughout Andean prehistory is the continuity of contact between the different regions, beginning from the earliest times, as proved by the discovery of products and raw materials from different regions in the others.

There was exchange between the highlands and lowlands in both physical objects and ideas. For example, coastal

Above: Vast high grasslands of the southern Andean Altiplano provided an ideal environment for llama and alpaca herding.

products, such as oyster shells, were regarded as exotic treasures among mountain cultures. Reciprocally, early coastal textiles were made of the cotton grown locally, and of llama wool traded from Altiplano herders. People also borrowed and exchanged artistic expressions and symbolism between regions. This is demonstrated by the spread of the Chavín Staff Deity from the central highlands to southern desert coasts and the Altiplano; by the recognition by coastal peoples of the sacredness of the mountains, no doubt fostered by a realization that mountains were the ultimate source of their water, and their construction of man-made 'mountains' in the form of huge pyramidal platforms; and by the representation of rainforest animals such as monkeys and caymans in Nazca lines and in Chavín stone sculpture.

27

PLANTS IN THE ANDEAN AREA

Tens of thousands of plant species evolved in South America: grasses and reeds; tropical and western forest trees; cacti; fungi; herbal plants and flowers; and a variety of wild edible fruits and vegetables. Different environments within the Andean Area provided a rich diversity and potential cultigens. Microclimates created by altitude change and latitude provided pockets and refuges for different species.

VEGETATION REGIONS
The Pacific coastal environment is one of the world's richest. Oxygen- and nutrient-rich cold currents support the trillions of phytoplankton that form the base of the coastal food chain. Small fishes feed on these microscopic plants, and are fed upon by predatory fishes, and so on up the food chain. Inland, the coastal plain from Ecuador to northern Chile includes vast expanses of almost barren desert.

The Andes include four vegetation zones: tropical, subtropical, south temperate

and *paramo* (between high *puna* grassland and the snowline). Vegetation in the coastal valleys that punctuate the coastal plain changes up-valley as altitude increases.

The western Andean slopes are characterized by temperate forests, found from near sea level to the tree-line. The lower altitudes have broadleaf evergreen trees, while higher up conifers dominate. Species include the algarrobo, lengas, podocarps, the monkey puzzle and cypresses. Dry forests of the southern Bolivian and northern Argentinian Altiplano feature trees of the pea family, together with vast grasslands, known as *puna*, and a large number of cacti species.

As the eastern Andes, known as selva or *montaña*, descend to the Amazon Basin, they are forested by evergreen trees from *c*.3,000m (10,000ft) and lower, to merge with the tropical rainforest. A host of herbal and medicinal plants include the coca (*Erythroxylon coca*), which became so important in Andean religion and in general use to combat high-altitude fatigue and increase stamina.

CULTIVATED PLANTS
Of the vast number of native species, less than 1 per cent was domesticated by ancient Andeans. Discussions of Andean plants important to civilization ultimately focus on this small percentage of cultigens.

The 23 principal pre-Hispanic cultivated species became domesticated through selective tending. Early agriculture relied on run-off water (especially in coastal valleys) and rainfall (especially in the Andes), until irrigation, terracing and raised-field agriculture were developed as means of increasing yields and areas under cultivation.

Left: The interdependence of highland and lowland, east and west, are exemplified in this Chancay carved wooden club – a rainforest monkey holding a maize cob, an essential early domesticated food plant.

Above: Tambopata Reserve, Peru – misty, forested regions of the eastern Andes, known as selva or montaña *– provided valuable herbs and medicinal plants.*

Altitudinal growing ranges of the domestic plants vary, and their distribution across environmental zones stimulated exchange. It is argued that the wild ranges of most cultigens were extended as humans nurtured those species that seemed most promising and able to provide sustainable yields.

Altitude and latitude (and thus temperature and rainfall) affect both cultivation and distribution. Andean

*Below: Quinoa (*Chanopodium quinoa*) was, alongside the potato and maize, one of the earliest and essential domesticated Andean food plants.*

domesticated plants can be grouped by their altitudinal ranges – see the fact box below. An extreme example is the ulluco (an edible tuber), which grows at 3,700–3,830m (12,180–12,560ft).

Less than 20 per cent of these crops grow well at altitudes above 3,000m (10,000ft), while 90 per cent thrive up to 1,000m (3,300ft). It is significant that the mainstays of the ancient Andean diet – maize, potatoes and common beans – can be cultivated at the widest possible range of altitudes. The many cultigens of lower altitude, which formed a complementary role to the classic trio in daily lowland and highland diet, were thus an important part of lowland–highland exchange. The staple diet was supplemented by gathering wild and semi-domesticated fruits and nuts, including cashews, pumpkins, palmettos, pineapples, sour cherries, custard apples, cactus fruits, elderberries and an ancient variety of banana. Wild herbs were gathered for seasoning.

DRUGS, TOOLS AND BUILDINGS

In addition to edible plants, medicinal and hallucinogenic plants played an important role in curing illness and for shamanistic trance inducement. Coca was cultivated, but the hallucinogenic mescaline of the San Pedro cactus and many hallucinogenic mushrooms from the tropical forests were also gathered and traded widely. Maize was used for the fermentation of *chicha* beer, the common drink in weak form and used in stronger form in religious ceremony.

Andean trees provided wood for weapons and tools, such as arrow and spear shafts, the *atl-atl* (spear-thrower) and hardwood war clubs. Tools included the foot-plough, sod-breaking club and hoe handle. Coca snuff pallets and drinking cups (*keros*) were also of wood. Algarrobo tree trunks provided pillars and rafters in early Spanish Colonial buildings, preserving an architectural style depicted in numerous Moche ceramic models.

Cane and totora reeds from riverbanks and the shores of Lake Titicaca and other lakes were extensively used for thatching and for fishing craft. Reeds were also used to make flutes and panpipes.

Most textiles for clothing and llama packs were made of cotton and wool. Cotton was indispensable among coastal peoples for fishing gear (nets, line and bindings), while wild fibrous plants

Above: Cacti in Salar de Uyruni Isla Pescado, Bolivia, one of many micro-habitats in the southern Andean Altiplano.

provided the rough twine and cordage needed for rope, baskets and containers, sandals and sleeping mats. The cultivated gourd, which preceded pottery for containers, continued to be used throughout pre-Hispanic times for fishing floats as well.

ANDEAN DOMESTICATED PLANTS BY ALTITUDINAL RANGES

Up to 1,000m (3,300ft)
- arracachas (a tuberous root plant) (850–956m/2,790–3,140ft)
- bottle gourds (850–956m/2,790–3,140ft)
- two varieties of chilli peppers (2–1,000m/6.56–3,300ft and 385–1,000m/1,263–3,300ft)
- guavas (28–1,000m/92–3,300ft)
- lima beans (28–1,000m/92–3,300ft)
- peanuts (46–1,000m/151–3,300ft)
- three varieties of squash (850–969m/2,790–3,179ft, 385–1,000m/ 1,263–3,300ft and 28–1,000m/ 92–3,300ft)
- sweet potatoes (28–1,000m/ 92–3,300ft)
- tobacco (57–1,000m/187–3,300ft)

Just over 1,000m (3,300ft)
- cotton (329–1,006m/1,079–3,300ft)
- manioc (46–1,006m/150–3,300ft)

Middle range
- avocados (320–1,750m/1,049–5,741ft)
- coca (450–1,200m/1,476–3,937ft)
- oca (850–1,700m/2,790–5,577ft)

Very wide range
- beans (2–3,700m/6½–12,140ft)
- maize (2–3,350m/6½–10,990ft)
- potatoes (2–3,830m/6½–12,565ft)
- quinoa (28–3,878m/92–12,720ft)
- mashwa (an edible tuber) (850–3,700m/2,788–12,140ft)
- ulluco (an edible tuber) (3,700–3,830m/12,180–12,560ft)

ANIMALS IN THE ANDEAN AREA

The differing environments within the Andean Area supported a large variety of animal species. As with plants, micro-environments fostered the development of species native to different regions. Remarkable traits of Andean Area fauna are their adaptations to the rarefied air of the mountains and their survival in barren desert environments. Ancient Andean peoples also knew of and revered animals from outside the Andean Area.

FOOD SUPPLIES

The earliest Andean hunter-gatherers would still have had mastodons (the larger mammoths had never reached South America), wild horse and ground sloths to hunt. When these became extinct *c*.8,000BC, large game animals such as deer (white-tailed, brocket and heumul), the llama and other camelids (vicuña and guanaco) were supplemented

Below: The camelid llama, originally a migrant from the north into temperate South America, once domesticated, provided wool and meat. It was a beast of burden and a sacred symbol to ancient Andeans.

by smaller game such as guinea pigs, viscachas (large burrowing rodents), skunk and fowl.

In contrast, coastal peoples hunted sea mammals (sea lions, seals and whales), supplemented by large and small fish, sea birds and a host of foreshore invertebrates, from molluscs to lobsters and crabs to clams and other shellfish. The principal sources of animal protein after the Lithic and Preceramic periods was provided by coastal fishing and sea mammal hunting, and by fishing in Lake Titicaca and similar high lakes. Fish are scarce in Andean highland rivers.

FOOD CHAINS

The marine animal food chain starts with the smaller fish – especially anchovies and sardines – that feed on phytoplankton, and moves up through ocean birds to sea mammals and, ultimately, humans. There are also shallow-water and foreshore invertebrate herbivores and their attendant predators, from mussels and shellfish to crabs, shorebirds, sea mammals and man.

Inland and in the mountains the ultimate predator is the mountain lion or puma, and in the rainforest and lowlands the jaguar; other top predators are raptors. The chain descends down through increasingly smaller animals to the invertebrates that feed on soil and other detritus.

MIGRATION

There are about 600 mammalian species in South America, dominated by rodents and bats, most of which live in the rainforests. Likewise with birds: the overwhelming variety are tropical; a second group are the western sea and coastal birds; and a third the temperate forest avians and the Andean species, including condors, hawks and the harpy eagle.

The emergence of the Central American land bridge at the end of Pliocene epoch enabled the migration of mammals in both directions between South and North America.

Above: Native burdens were exemplified in Poma de Ayala's Nueva Corónica, *c.1615 by symbolic characterization. The royal administrator is a serpent, the itinerant Spaniard a jaguar, the* encomendero *labour and land-holder a (non-native) lion, the parish priest a fox, the notary a cat, and the native governor a rodent.*

Into temperate South America came smilodons (sabretooth cats), wild horses, spectacled bears, tapirs, llamas, peccaries, foxes, rats and mice. Into the tropics came heteromyid rodents, squirrels and shrews.

From south to north temperate environments went giant ground sloths, armadillos, glyptodons (armadillo-like but larger), porcupines and didelphis rodents; and to tropical areas went cebid monkeys, tree sloths, anteaters, and agouti and paca rodents.

North–south migrants added to these existing native mammals, including a wealth of rodents (including the guinea pig), monkeys, bats and the jaguar, as well as a huge number of bird species, reptiles, amphibians and invertebrates. The greatest varieties of all groups are native to the Amazonian Basin, outside the Andean Area.

Right: The revered jaguar (and its mountain cousin the puma) provided a symbol of strength and cunning to Andean warriors and priests.

DOMESTICATED ANIMALS

As with plants, only a few animals were domesticated: llamas, alpacas, guinea pigs, ducks and dogs. The domestication process was gradual, beginning with the deliberate selection and concentrated tending of these species. The main highland sources of meat were guinea pigs and ducks, although llama and deer were also eaten. Hunting, however, had become the pursuit of the elite in a culture whose staple diet was provided by cultivated plant foods.

The llama is one of three South American camelids: llamas, guanacos and vicuñas. The llama is the domesticated variety of the guanaco, which remained wild and was sometimes hunted for its meat, as was the vicuña. A fourth camelid, the alpaca, was also domesticated or semi-domesticated, but it is uncertain if the breed is the result of descent from the guanaco, or a guanaco/vicuña hybrid. Llamas and alpacas, fully domesticated by *c.*2500BC, were herded in great flocks, principally for their wool and as pack animals, but also for ritual sacrifice, divination and meat. Their bones were valuable for tool-making and their dung for fertilizer.

Below: An 18th-century watercolour of the guinea pig, an early Andean domesticated rodent, which provided a readily available meat source and still does today.

Guinea pigs were domesticated as early as the late Preceramic Period, but this is evident less from anatomical differences to wild relatives than from what appear to be hutches. Hunting of wild guinea pigs for meat no doubt continued. In later pre-Hispanic times the guinea pig was also used in religious ceremony, divination and curing. Ducks were raised for food and eggs; dogs as hunting companions and food.

REVERED ANIMALS

As well as llamas and guinea pigs, several other native Andean and non-native animals were highly revered and used in ritual and prophecy. The flights and habits of condors, hawks and eagles were carefully observed for divination. Indeed, observation of the mobbing and killing of an eagle by buzzards during ceremonies to honour the sun god Inti were regarded by Inca priests as foretelling the coming fall of the empire. The early twined cloth from Preceramic Huaca Prieta features an eagle with outspread wings and a snake inside its stomach.

The puma and its lowland cousin the jaguar also feature in the earliest Andean art. Use of the jaguar in monumental stone sculpture and portable objects in the Chavín Cult right through to the plan of Inca Cuzco in the form of a crouching puma demonstrate its enduring importance.

As well as the jaguar, monkeys, the cayman (South American freshwater alligator), serpents and a great variety of colourful rainforest birds were especially revered for their powers, cleverness and (in the case of the birds) feathers. All feature repeatedly in Andean art in religious contexts and demonstrate long-distance communication between highlands and lowlands.

THE INCA EMPIRE AT PIZARRO'S ARRIVAL

From humble beginnings as one tribe among several in the Cuzco Valley, the Incas rapidly expanded the territory in their control. Their conquests were few in the first few centuries after the founding ruler Manco Capac had established rule in Cuzco. Even by about 1400, Inca territory comprised only the valleys adjacent to the Cuzco Valley in the Urubamba and Apurimac river drainages.

GREAT EXPANSION

From the reign of Pachacuti Inca Yupanqui (tenth emperor, 1438–71) and his successors, however, the Inca emperors embarked on continuous campaigns to subdue the known world. Inca belief taught them that they were destined to rule, and in fewer than 100 years they ruled the largest empire ever created in

Below: Chan Chan, the capital of the Kingdom of the Chimú, was a serious rival to the late 15th-century expanding Inca Empire until it fell to Inca Pachacuti and his son and heir Tupac Yupanqui in 1471.

the Americas. It stretched from the modern borders of Ecuador and Colombia to more than halfway down the coast of modern Chile (4,200km/2,600 miles; equivalent in distance of roughly Spain to Moscow).

Their empire was long and narrow, however (only c.650km/400 miles at its greatest east–west width), and confined to regions familiar to them. The Incas were among a long line of cultures that had spread their control of economic resources in the Andes and western coastal lowlands. Their armies were well equipped and disciplined, and were trained to fight on such terrain in pitched battles, during which two armies were amassed and thrown at each other to 'slug it out' until one force broke ranks and fled or laid down their arms in defeat. Indeed, in many cases, as Inca reputation for fighting skills and fierceness, and the seeming inevitability of conquest, spread, many nations (kingdoms and city-states) did not resist, but surrendered without battle and proceeded to negotiate the best deal they could make.

*Above: An Inca post-runner or messenger (*chasqui*) depicted in Poma de Ayala's* Nueva Corónica, *c.1615.*

AMAZONIAN FAILURE

The Incas attempted to expand east into the Amazon Rainforest. Their armies, however, were in unfamiliar terrain and

faced an enemy who fought unconventionally. In the Amazon, the Incas were not confronting organized states, ruled in a manner similar to the long-developed structures in the Andes. Instead, Amazonian peoples lived in small groups with local chiefs; rather than fight, they simply disappeared into the forest and remained illusive.

The products of the rainforest were obtainable by barter, so there was no reason for the Incas to conquer the land except for the motive of dominating the known world. But they ruled almost all the people whom they considered civilized, and the Amazonians could easily be dismissed as subhuman and therefore incapable of participating in the imperial state structure.

ADMINISTRATIVE GENIUS

A large factor in Inca success was the way in which they treated conquered peoples. Inca provincial governors were placed in charge of the four great divisions of the empire – the four quarters of Tahuantinsuyu – conceived to mimic the four world directions: Antisuyu (north-east), Chinchaysuyu (north-west), Cuntisuyu (south-west) and Collasuyu (south-east). But local rulers and chiefs were normally treated with courtesy and kept in place,

Below: Manco Capac, legendary leader of the Inca people and 'founder' of the empire, depicted in an 18th-century genealogy.

where they were allowed to maintain local control. Their sons were taken as house captives to Cuzco, where they were indoctrinated with Inca values; and their daughters were also taken and indoctrinated – some would be offered as pawns for marriages of alliance with other rulers, though others would be sacrificed.

The genius of the Inca Empire was its administrative organization. Inca civil and economic control was simple in concept and followed developments that had evolved over the past 3,000 years of pre-Hispanic Andean civilization. There was an incremental structure of civic control based on decimal multiples of households, with each higher-ranking official being in charge of ten times more households. Like their concept of the cosmos as a series of layers, this structure presented everyone with a clear line of responsibility from one level to the next.

SOCIAL ORGANIZATION

The Incas intensified and formalized social practices that were ingrained in Andean peoples from early times – the idea of reciprocal obligations and of co-operation with one's kin group of relatives, both blood and by marriage, known as the *ayllu*.

While there was no monetary system, there were taxes and obligations to the state, called the *mit'a*, that amounted to the same thing. Every individual owed labour to the Inca state, which through the *mit'a* was fulfilled by the household rather than by each individual. This left

Above: Huánuca Pampa was typical of Inca regional cities and a great storehouse for the redistribution of imperial tax goods.

the household intact and able to fulfil its obligation at home while some member fulfilled *mit'a* service. Quotas of produce (agricultural or textile) were collected into storehouses for redistribution according to need. In this way the Incas ensured that all their subjects had the necessities of life and so largely forestalled rebellion.

Some rebellions did occur, however, and these were dealt with swiftly. Rebellious groups were moved wholesale to distant provinces, where, in unfamiliar territory and among strangers, they were isolated from their secure social structure. In addition, loyal groups were moved into potentially rebellious areas to keep control. The Inca administrators' skill was in indoctrinating people into a system against which it was futile to resist, and which was in most cases familiar.

All land theoretically belonged to the Inca emperor. It was divided into three parts, the produce of which was given to: the emperor and his household, the Inca state religion and the people themselves. The Incas expanded the land under production, rejuvenating old and constructing new terraces and raised fields. They built provincial storehouse capitals, linked by a road system that made it easy to move goods, and armies, throughout the empire. And they created a messenger service to keep the emperor and his governors informed. This was the empire 'discovered' by Francisco Pizarro.

CIVIL WAR: FALL OF THE INCA EMPIRE

By the early 16th century, the Incas ruled almost all the civilized peoples of South America. The twelfth emperor, Huayna Capac (1493–1526), ruled a stable empire, which he was still expanding. He had gone on campaign to the northern provinces to quell an outbreak of rebellion in the recently subdued Quito province.

STILL EXPANDING

The Incas were aware of the wealth of the gold- and silver-working cultures to the north of the empire. Though not quite the urban civilizations of the Andean Area – many lacked the tradition of stone architecture and conurbation – Colombian metalworking cultures were sophisticated chiefdoms with loose confederations of political power. Whether they would have been easily incorporated into the Inca imperial structure will never be known, however, for in the very year (1526) of Francisco Pizarro's second expedition to the north-west coast of South America,

Below: Hatun Rumiyoc Street, Cuzco, showing the wall of the royal palaces of Inca Roca.

Huayna Capac died of a mysterious disease, as did his chosen heir, Ninancuyuchi. The illness was smallpox, which had been introduced by the Spaniards into Mesoamerica and spread south, ravaging the native populations as it did so because they had no resistance to it.

Huayna Capac's and his heir's deaths were a significant blow to the stability of the empire, which was functioning smoothly despite the very recent acquisition of some territories. Huayna Capac had, in fact, inherited most of the empire he ruled intact and had spent most of his campaign consolidating his inheritance and strengthening the infrastructure. He was particularly engaged in building Inca towns in the northern part of the empire.

DISARRAY AND DISRUPTION

The smooth inheritance that had previously been the case was in disarray. Without a living designated heir, the imperial household was in confusion. Huayna Capac had more than a score of sons, one of whom, Atahualpa, was on campaign with him, while another, Huáscar, he had left in Cuzco as one of four governors. Members of the

Above: The Inca civil war was breaking up the empire when the Spaniards arrived. Camac Inca leads his Inca troops (from Poma de Ayala's Nueva Corónica, *c.1615).*

imperial household quickly divided into factions, each with its own interpretation of what Huayna Capac's intentions had been. They questioned whether Huayna Capac had in fact truly or properly anointed Ninancuyuchi. Huáscar's faction naturally claimed that Huayna Capac intended him to inherit, while Atahualpa's faction claimed that Huayna Capac would have wanted Atahualpa to use his control of the army to take control and maintain the security of the empire in its time of crisis over the succession.

In such unprecedented circumstances, Huáscar seized the throne. At first Atahualpa acknowledged him, but when a local chief spread a rumour that Atahualpa was plotting against Huáscar, the latter declared his half-brother an enemy and traitor and civil war ensued.

The war lasted six years before Atahualpa was finally victorious and had captured and imprisoned Huáscar.

Above: Inca emperor Huayna Capac, 12th Sapa Inca, who died of smallpox, setting off the Inca civil war. From an 18th-century 'Cuzco School' Inca genealogy.

EFFECTS ON THE PEOPLE

The effects of these events on the structure of the empire must have been immense, and the speed of the expansion of the empire would now take its toll. With the imperial armies engaged in fighting each other, recently conquered peoples, especially those far from Cuzco, could cease to acknowledge imperial rule and take back local power.

Soldiers in the army of one or other faction, or people who lived where the fighting between the brothers occurred, would have been directly affected by the war, but most ordinary subjects would have simply carried on making a living. The social structure was, at their level, intact and their households and kinship obligations still operative.

While the events of the civil war were unfolding, there is no evidence of widespread rebellion, just as there was no such outbreak after Atahualpa was executed in 1533. Clearly there was an ingrained inertia in ordinary Andean lives to simply get on with daily routine and lie low. The burdens imposed on them by the Incas – such as the labour tax, textile quotas, the Quechua language and the precedence of the imperial state religion on Inti over local gods – were temporarily relieved, but so too was the structure of the redistribution of goods.

External factors also had an effect, and the spread of smallpox was undoubtedly of more immediate concern. It devastated the peoples in the area that had been the northern Kingdom of Chimú shortly after the outbreak that had killed Huayna Capac and Ninancuyuchi.

At the same time, the disruption of the world into which many had been born must have been psychologically devastating. General religious belief among Andean peoples acknowledged the arbitrary power of the gods, and the death of their emperor by such a mysterious disease must have been regarded as divine retribution for something he and they had done.

A PLANNED BREAK-UP?

Some sources indicate that Huayna Capac had planned to divide the empire among several sons. He was disturbed by a prophecy that the empire was ending and that he was the last of the Inca dynasty. He told his sons that Inti had informed him that the demise of the Inca would come with the arrival of powerful foreigners and that the priests had foretold all: a new moon had appeared with three halos, which they said represented the death of Inti, war among his descendants and the break-up of the empire. Some scholars even think that the Inca Empire was over-extended and would not have been able to sustain its unwieldy size – that it was effectively self-dividing by 1526.

Below: Sapa Inca Atahualpa, who challenged the heir designate, Huáscar, when their father Huayna Capac died. From an 18th-century 'Cuzco School' Inca genealogy.

PIZARRO'S CONQUEST

Pizarro's three expeditions (1524–5, 1526–7 and 1531–3) to north-west South America seemed to be the fulfilment of the priests' prophecy. He made his first contact with Inca subjects in 1526, when he encountered a balsa trading raft with two traders from the Inca subject port of Tumbes, laden with gold and silver objects and textiles. The traders described the cities and wealth of the empire to Pizarro.

CLASH OF CULTURES

When Francisco Pizarro began his final expedition, he carried in his head visions of the fabulous civilizations and riches of Mesoamerica. He also projected the confidence and superior attitude of Europeans of the 16th century towards other cultures. Although he undoubtedly appreciated the sophistication of the Inca

Below: Rebellious uprisings were dealt with severely by the Spaniards, shown in an execution scene by the Flemish Theodore de Bry in his Historia Americae *(1602).*

Empire when he saw it himself – how else could it have built the great cities and amassed the riches he saw? – he also held in contempt foreign peoples whose religious beliefs were regarded as heathen and whose political and military abilities were regarded as inferior. The irony is that the Incas, in many respects, felt the same about the peoples they had themselves only recently conquered. Both the Spaniards and the Incas held their peoples and cultures as the pinnacle of social, political and technological achievement. Their abiding philosophy was that they were destined and entitled to rule the known world.

MULTIPLE FACTORS

Despite the obvious disruption of the civil war, what really brought the Inca Empire to its knees? By the time Pizarro arrived on the borders of the empire, Atahualpa had won and was in the process of reconsolidating Inca administrative structure and institutions. The

Above: Francisco Pizarro (1475–1541), Spanish foundling, illiterate pig herder, adventurer and conqueror of the Inca Empire.

empire was weakened, but Atahualpa still had his army, which was vastly superior in numbers to Pizarro's force.

The factors that ensured Pizarro's victory over the Inca are varied.

Despite their seemingly perfect world, in which everyone got what he or she needed, the imperial household was clearly becoming overburdened and demanding a large proportion of the empire's resources. There were also problems with the imperial succession: with so many potential heirs from multiple wives, there were bound to be court intrigues and contestations of legitimacy.

The empire was still expanding north when the Spaniards arrived, and their huge southern acquisitions beyond the Titicaca Basin were very recent. The peoples of many provinces simply bided their time through the civil war. Many must have resented their recent subjugation but were still in awe of Inca power and in fear of the strange events taking place.

The succession to the throne was not fully decided. Many Inca nobility still opposed Atahualpa even though he had

defeated Huáscar. When he occupied Cuzco, Atahualpa ordered the provincial governors and chief administrators to attend him in the capital. Many were of Huáscar's royal *panaca* lineage. Atahualpa committed acts of sacrilege by ordering them put to death, and, further, by ordering the burning of the mummy of Tupac Yupanqui, Huayna Capac's predecessor and ancestor of the *panaca*. These acts not only effectively eliminated potential claimants to the throne, but also broke the imperial line and contradicted the very concept of the Inca world, so fulfilling Huayna Capac's prophecy.

The coincidence of Huayna Capac's death by smallpox and the ensuing civil war can only be labelled a quirk of historical fate. What Pizarro did to seize the opportunity is, however, down to the audacity and character of the man himself and of his Spanish companions. He took advantage of the Inca's own road

Below: Pizarro demanded a room full of gold as ransom for Sapa Inca Atahualpa. This fanciful depiction includes un-Inca classical columns and a medieval chair.

Above: This modern interpretation of the Sapa Inca Atahualpa meeting Pizarro in 1532 in Cajamarca captures something of his alleged haughty nature and elevated importance.

system to move quickly into the heart of the empire, meeting with little resistance. Realizing the disruptive influence of the civil war, he was quick to exploit Atahualpa's hesitation to confront him. He also declared his intentions to be peaceful, possibly to ally himself with one side. He was astute enough to assess the Inca state of mind and to take advantage of their religious beliefs and the prediction of their demise. And he was simply bold and knew that at his age and at this stage of his 'career' the stakes were high and that he must not lose the opportunity.

He was right in most respects. The atrocious acts by Atahualpa against Inca world concepts left his subjects in a stupor. They had seen Atahualpa's hesitancy to challenge Pizarro and witnessed his weakness when captured and his orders to strip the empire of its wealth to ransom himself. They had underestimated the superiority of Spanish technology, misread Pizarro's motives and were unprepared for the psychological impact of ambush – a most un-Inca act. After the ambush and capture of Atahualpa, many finally rebelled, welcoming and joining the Spaniards to throw off the burdens of Inca rule.

DIVINE FATE

The psychological impact of the small-pox epidemic cannot be underestimated. During Huayna Capac's illness, traders from the northern borders reported to him the appearance of bearded strangers in strange ships and reminded him of his priests' prophecy of the end of the Incas. In the Andean belief in the arbitrary power of the gods, it was unambiguous that the disease was divine wrath. The appearance of people who were immune to it made them ready to accept the prophecy, divine approval of the new-comers and the fate of their civilization. Francisco Pizarro himself died a relatively young, supposedly rich, man, murdered by the hands of his own countrymen.

Finally, it must be said that reverence for their local landscape and many ancient beliefs endure today alongside Christian faith as proof of the quiet resilience of ordinary Andeans.

Below: Post-conquest rivalry among the Spanish conquistadors is exemplified in this unsympathetic caricature of Pizarro by 18th-century artist James Gillray.

CHAPTER TWO

FROM VILLAGES TO CITIES

The development of Andean civilization is divided by archaeologists into a series of defined time periods. This is for organizational convenience, for in reality such divisions are false because they are too rigid and because Andean ancient societies evolved continuously as they adapted to their times.

Through periods of climatic change, population increases and political upheavals, Andean peoples developed social, economic and technological structures and expertise. They slowly accumulated layers of social and political sophistication and religious complexity, moving from bands of hunter-gatherers through the more sedentary lifestyles of agriculturalists to the complicated lives of urban citizens.

As societies increased their ability to produce the essentials of life, more and more people were able to have jobs that were not linked with food production. In this way, specialists were able to increase in number and skill. True urbanism was achieved when the juxtaposition of political, bureaucratic and economic activities balanced and intervened between religious and domestic life. Technical skills and full-time specialization – in crafts or politics or religion – can be sustained only if the economic structure can support them, and the attainment of this balance is the hallmark of urban civilization. This chapter outlines the sweep of Andean prehistory from the first peopling of the continent to the Inca Empire.

Left: The sun temple ruins at the Inca royal estates at Rosaspata in the Vilcabamba Mountains, Peru.

THE FIRST ARRIVALS

People (modern *Homo sapiens*) migrated into the New World from the far north-eastern reaches of Asia during the final stages of the last great global Ice Age (the end of the Pleistocene Period), from at least 15,000 years ago. The archaeological evidence for this migration is scattered and comes from land sites in North, Central and South America. Geological evidence shows us that the world sea level at this time was lower by about 100m (330ft), because much water was still frozen in ice sheets and glaciers. A huge ice sheet covered most of the northern half of the North American continent, extending south from the Arctic.

MIGRATION ROUTES
The lower sea level created a land bridge across the Bering Strait, and the general chronological and geographical distribution of the evidence for the arrival and spread of hunter-gatherer peoples indicates they took this route into the New World. They followed an ice-free corridor that opened up in the western half of the continent between the Cordilleran and Laurentian (or Laurentide) ice sheets,

Below: A Moche moulded red-ware effigy jar, c.400AD. The face reveals 'typical' features of Andean peoples.

Above: Early migrants into South America encountered harsh environments such as the Atacama Desert of northern Chile.

migrating from the north-west to the south-east. As they found ice-free lands south of the ice fields, they spread east, west and south. They found the continent to have a vast larder of long-established animals and plants, most of them indigenously evolved species, and some large game animals (or their immediate ancestors) that had probably migrated from Asia during earlier breaks (interstadials) in the ice sheets – for example the Columbian mammoth, or American mastodon.

This conventional reconstruction of events has been challenged and modified in recent decades. It seems logical to assume that migration also took place by sea along a western coastal route. Island- and coastal-hopping in pursuit of sea mammals lacks direct evidence, which presumably lies beneath the water off the present coastlines. Another recent theory argues that there was also an earlier migration across the ice floes of the North Atlantic into north-eastern North America. This argument is based on conclusions about similarities between the European Solutrian lithic culture of south-western France, dated 22,000–16,500 years ago,

and the Clovis stone point tradition of North America, dated about 10,000 years ago. This theory is rigorously disputed.

MIGRATION GROUPS
Molecular biology, DNA and blood-group evidence shows that these New World immigrants descend from three or four distinct populations, revealing there were several incidents of migration into North America. Those peoples who continued into South America, however, descend from only one of these biological groups.

Below: An imaginative painting showing how the first migrants into the New World from north-east Asia followed game across the land bridge created across the Bering Strait during lowered sea levels in the late Ice Age.

The rate of migration is also a point of controversy and can only be guessed. Nevertheless, the earliest indisputable date for human occupation in South America comes from Monte Verde, southern Chile, about 14,850 years ago (averaged from more than a dozen radiocarbon dates), showing that the pace was rapid, or that early evidence from farther north remains to be found.

MONTE VERDE

At Monte Verde, a group of people lived for a season or two on the banks of a small creek. Eventually, their settlement was abandoned and covered by a peat layer deposited by the river. Their settlement comprised crude wooden-plank or log-floored pole- and hide-walled rectangular huts. There were at least 12 contiguous rooms or huts arranged in two parallel rows. Within them and around the site were found remains of wild potatoes and other plant remains, animal bones (including mastodon) and wooden and stone tools: wooden spears, digging sticks, three wooden mortars, stone scrapers (including three with wooden handles) and egg-sized pebbles, some grooved, believed to be sling and bolas stones. There were also clay-lined hearths for cooking and one human footprint preserved in the peat.

Separate from the dwellings was a single, 3 x 4m (10 x 13ft), Y-plan structure made of a sand-and-gravel floor, and two rows of wooden poles with hide walls forming the arms. The rear of the hut was

Left: Early hunter-gatherers left examples of their art on rock, as here in a depiction of a snake hunt in Zamora, Ecuador.

raised, and the open area between the arms had several clay-lined braziers and the remains of animal hides, burnt reeds, seeds and medicinal plants, including chewed leaves. Other hearths, piles of wood, artefacts, and plant and animal remains were scattered around the structure. Clearly this was a building for special purposes.

SCARCE EVIDENCE

Such rare preservation demonstrates the scarce nature of the evidence for early lithic cultures in the Andean Area. This Archaic or Lithic Period lasted down to about 7,000–5,000 years ago in different areas of the Andes. Lithic sites

and surface artefacts have been found throughout South America, including Brazil, Argentina and Uruguay, and the tip of Tierra del Fuego. Finds of lithic artefacts and occupation remains become more widespread after about 7,000 years ago. The varied terrains occupied gave rise to different artefact styles, including adaptations to the mountain environments, where several fluted projectile point styles were used in hunting horse, sloth and other animals, and to several coastal traditions along the Pacific coast, where bone harpoons were used to hunt maritime mammals.

Below: An essential New World hunting tool – and later weapon in war – was the atl-atl. *Two hunters are poised to hurl their spears with* atl-atls *at vicuñas on a Nazca pot.*

PRECERAMIC VILLAGES

The persistence of lithic-using hunter-gatherer cultures varied in different regions of the Andean Area, and there are few hard facts about exactly where and how the domestication of plants and animals took place in the Andes and western coastal valleys. Increasing heavy exploitation and reliance on certain species appears to have led to plant tending, which, after many generations – both of human populations and of the plants themselves – led to modifications to enhance the species and its yield.

DOMESTICATION – THE THEORY

There are some tens of thousands of plants and animal species in South America, but less than 1 per cent of these have been domesticated. It is argued that in regions where a species thrives and is abundant in its natural environment there is little reason for humans to tend or otherwise try to manipulate it, since they can simply gather it as needed. However, in marginal areas of a species' habitat, there is a need to nurture it if there is to be

Below: Llamas provided many products for early peoples in South America. As well as hunted quarry, they soon became domesticated as herded flocks in the Altiplano.

sufficient for human use, especially if the population in an area is increasing. Species found outside their known native regions can thus be regarded as 'domesticated'.

There are changes in environmental conditions and climate over short distances within the Andean Area, especially with altitude change. Thus even small movements of a species into a new environment introduced human selection as well as natural selection. It is believed that constant 'experiments' of this nature by an increasing human population brought domestication to selected food crops and fixed human reliance on a small number of species. At first they were able to exploit these crops in naturally watered soils; later, in an extension of the experiment, they grew them in soils to which they could bring water through irrigation schemes.

Significantly, however, the earliest known domesticated plants come from Guitarrero Cave, northern Peru, from c.8000BC. Fibre-plant remains dominate the Guitarrero assemblage (used for sandals, clothing, cordage, bedding mats and mesh sacks), but there were also specimens of domesticated beans and chilli pepper, both *not* native to the region and therefore probably cultivated there.

Above: One of the earliest uses of clay was for unfired figurines, such as this model of a woman from the early Valdivian culture in Ecuador, c.3500–1500BC.

The increased reliability of selected cultivated food sources also made it possible for people to congregate in larger settlements and to remain there permanently, rather than having to move through the seasons to exploit food sources in their own native environments. Gradually, both in lowland coastal and highland valleys, the number and sizes of settlements grew.

LATE PRECERAMIC ECONOMICS

Three elements form the foundations of the economic developments that characterize the late Preceramic Period in Andean prehistory. These are: the intensive exploitation of maritime resources at coastal settlements; the use of floodplain irrigation in coastal valleys and rainfall agriculture in highland valleys, for early agriculture; and long-distance trade. The last of these elements established, from the earliest times of

Above: A painting from the Mollopunko caves, northern Peru, c.5000BC appears to show a llama being led or tethered with a rope, an indication of early semi-domestication.

permanent settlement, an Andean tradition of reciprocal exchange between highland and lowland communities.

The richness of maritime resources on the Pacific coast made it possible for coastal peoples to live in large settlements mostly supported by maritime food sources. Sites have deep middens of accumulated shellfish, crustacean, fish and sea mammal remains. Until the late Preceramic and into the Initial Period, grown foods were only a marginal part of the diet, but nevertheless included squash, beans, chillies and two introductions to the coast (potatoes and maize) by c.2000BC. Such is the scene at sites up and down the coast, such as Huaca Prieta and Salinas de Chao on the northern coast, Aspero and Piedra Parada on the central coastal, and El Paraíso and Otuma on the southern coast.

Such intense exploitation of maritime resources, however, would not have been possible without a source of cotton for nets and fishing line and gourds for floats. Both these plants are not native to coast

environments, and were introduced from tropical regions to the east and north, where they were domesticated early on.

HIGHLAND CHANGES

Similar changes took place in the highlands. Annual precipitation of 5 to 6 months not only supported a rich natural flora but also appears to have provided hunter-gatherer peoples with several intermontane-valley species that became the staples of their diet: potatoes, maize and beans, and a host of other tubers,

grains and legumes. There was also meat, including deer, vicuña and guanaco (which remained wild), and the llama, alpaca and guinea pig, all of which show cultural and anatomical signs of domestication by the end of the Preceramic Period.

Plant domestication was underway by 5000BC in the highlands. By about 3000BC most of the full range of food plants capable of being grown in highland valleys had been adopted. Similarly, the guinea pig was bred as a domestic meat source, although anatomical evidence at this early date is insufficient to determine how far true domestication had proceeded. The domestication of the llama and alpaca, herded on the grasslands of the Altiplano, took place gradually over 2,000 years and was complete by c.25,000BC.

Such was the scene at the beginning of the Initial Period at sites such as La Galgada and Huaricoto in the northern highlands, Kotosh and Shillacoto in the central highlands, and Ondores farther south.

Below: Fishing became another important ancient Andean economy. The Aymara still use traditional totora-reed boats to fish on Lake Titcaca on the border of Bolivia–Peru.

THE INITIAL PERIOD

Beginning *c.*2000BC in the Andean Area, the Initial Period was a time of tremendous technological advancements and accomplishments. First, there was a flowering of textile technique and art when the simpler techniques of fibre twining and looping began to be replaced by cloth woven on heddle looms; second, the first ceramics began to be made in the Andean Area; and third, there was growth in monumental architecture building.

WEAVERS AND POTTERS

The invention of weaving using a heddle loom enabled the mass production of cloth. It went hand in hand with developments

Below: A terracotta figurine (c.2300BC) from the Valdivian culture of coastal Ecuador, some of the earliest pottery in the Andes.

in farming and pastoralism. As the farming of greater areas of land produced increased yields in cotton, and the expansion of llama herding in upland regions increased the availability of wool, so the innovation from simpler techniques meant that more textiles could be produced by specialists.

The first ceramics in South America were made, from *c.*3200BC, in the extreme north of the Andean Area by the early farmers of Valdivia on the coast of Ecuador. Pottery of a slightly later date (*c.*3000BC) was produced outside the Andean Area by people at Puerto Hormiga, on the Caribbean coast of Colombia.

For both weaving and pottery making, labour became more concentrated and specialists became possible. The increase in large building projects also fostered the development of social organization that featured specialists in two fields: those who planned and built them, and those who ran them. As some members of society concentrated their skills in agricultural production, so increasing the agricultural yields achievable by fewer farmers, other people were able to devote more of their time to ceramic production and weaving.

SPECIALISTS

No doubt the bulk of the population was not particularly specialized, and the majority of people probably continued to spend most of their time in agriculture, herding and other subsistence pursuits. But the increasingly greater availability of food for less effort inevitably gave people more time to vary their daily lives and to pursue craft activities beyond the purely useful. As a result, forms and varieties of decoration increased and regional styles developed. Thematic motifs reflecting religious belief became incorporated into ceramics and textiles, and special pieces were made for burials.

Together with an increasingly sophisticated evolution in religious beliefs, these innovations and developments themselves

Above: Irrigation techniques using narrow channels to route water into fields, developed by the earliest farmers, continued to be used until Inca times, as here at Tipon, near Cuzco.

became interwoven, on the basis that ceramic production and decoration, textile styles and decoration, and architectural construction were never separate thematically. Religious motivation and the demonstration of religious themes were always incorporated into Andean technological production and architectural form.

PUBLIC ARCHITECTURE

Perhaps these reconfigurations of social structure and time management are most dramatically represented in the expansion of monumental architecture. The size and planning of monumental architecture mirrors religious concepts in mimicking the sacred landscape and in orientation to the sources of sacred waters. Form also reflects what are assumed to be beliefs in Mother Earth and Father Sky deities.

Two classic forms were developed: the platform mound and the sunken court. Platforms supported single or multiple rooms. Often the two forms, plus subsidiary platforms, were combined in complexes forming a U shape. These forms established the traditions that would prevail through the Initial Period and into the Early Horizon.

INLAND MIGRATION

Settlement patterns also changed. Increases in agricultural production were in part made possible by shifting settlement to areas with greater expanses of better-watered lands. The largest centres of population shifted systematically inland in the central and northern coasts of the

Below: Fertile flatland was at a premium in the mountain valleys, so extensive terracing was used to create thousands of narrow fields, as here in Colca Canyon, Peru.

Andean Area. Settlements along the shoreline were abandoned in favour of richer-soiled valley mouths and lower valleys, where river water was more accessible. Maritime resources were not abandoned, but the dependence on agricultural crops by these coastal populations brought important shifts in emphasis and must have had profound effects on the organization and scheduling of their daily lives. Where formerly they lived on the seafront and brought agricultural produce to their settlements, they now began to live in towns among their fields and to travel to the seaside to collect shellfish or embark on fishing and sea mammal hunts.

The reasons for these changes are debated. From the late Preceramic Period, coastal settlements that were predominantly reliant on maritime resources had also incorporated newly domesticated food crops into their economy. But they had been reliant on small satellite settlements

Above: An Inca farmer tapping an irrigation channel to water the maize crop in November (a dry month), depicted in Poma de Ayala's Nueva Corónica, *c.1615.*

in the lower river valleys for agricultural produce, which might imply at least a rudimentary kind of irrigation.

What began in the Initial Period, and what in fact partly defines the period, is the development of much more substantial irrigation works, tapping the rivers with channels to run water into the fields. One reason might have been population growth and consequent pressure on resources. It is certain, however, that the abundant maritime resources would have been able to support even larger populations than our present archaeological knowledge shows us. We also know that there were small environmental changes in the coastlines that left some settlements more isolated from the sea. But these shifts were gradual and subtle.

What seems the best explanation includes both these factors, plus social and economic relationships that had developed in rudimentary fashion in the late Preceramic Period simultaneously. A combination of changing dietary preferences, increased success in farming, socio-political rivalry to control the best resources, and shifting patterns of work as these agricultural 'discoveries' were made seems to be a more plausible cause for both changing settlement patterns and the artistic, architectural and religious enhancements of the Initial Period.

THE EARLY HORIZON

The Early Horizon is defined as a period of cultural cohesion across large regions of the Andean Area, comprising northern and southern spheres. These spheres were not mutually exclusive: there were relationships, trade and influence between their communities, maintaining already-developed Andean cultural traditions of long-distance trade between highlands and lowlands.

INITIAL PERIOD TRADITIONS

The Initial Period flowering in monumental architecture developed into several regional traditions, both coastal and highland, and served the first Andean religious cults. These developments formed the basis of much more wide-spread Early Horizon traditions.

The classic form was the U-shaped complex, comprising a central mound, wings forming a U, and sunken courts. Many platforms supported complexes of small adjoining or individual rooms. These forms established the traditions that prevailed throughout the Initial Period and into the Early Horizon.

Sunken courts (called *plazas hundidas*) were one tradition. They were usually part of a complex with platforms mounds, but could be on their own. A second tradition, called Kotosh, featured a one-roomed enclosure for intimate worship.

Two further traditions, Supe and El Paraíso, show a new order of magnitude and organization. Earlier ceremonial complexes are more modest in size and are usually associated with domestic remains, indicating that they were built by their local communities. Complexes of the Supe and El Paraíso traditions, however, are larger, more complex and varied, and lack evidence that they were surrounded by immediate residential populations. They appear to be the earliest complexes that were built and maintained as centres for religious worship for regions of communities. The El Paraíso U-shaped ceremonial centre is a representative example of such a complex, associated with irrigation agriculture and dominating the Rimac Valley on the central southern Peruvian coast. The largest U-shaped complex ever built was Sechín Alto in the Casma Valley.

At the same time, the Chiripa Tradition developed in the Titicaca Basin. This consisted of symmetrical arrangements of one-roomed buildings around a square sunken court atop a low platform. The type-site is Chiripa on the southern Titicaca lakeshore, with 16 buildings around its sunken court.

SOCIAL ORGANIZATION

The strong association of monumental architecture in ceremonial complexes serving regions and irrigation agriculture indicates that kinship relations between communities formed strong links. This was an important Initial Period/Early Horizon development that endured throughout the rest of Andean prehistory.

It seems likely that linked communities and shared religious traditions strengthened social systems of communal labour,

Left: Chavín de Huánta united Andean and coastal people in the name of religion – the flanking columns of the Black and White Portal of the New Temple show an eagle (female) and a hawk (male), early examples of duality.

Above: 20th-century archaeologists at work at Chiripa Pata, a pre-Tiwanaku site with a massive temple.

co-operative administration between communities of irrigation works and water rights, perhaps collective land ownership and entitlement to shared resources. Lineage groups were probably moiety-based (two intermarriageable family groups of a descent lineage) from this early period (defined by the *ayllu* in Inca times).

EARLY HORIZON CULTS
These coastal and southern ceremonial centres waned and were eventually abandoned in the early centuries of the 1st millennium BC. In their places arose even stronger, more widespread religious traditions. Two spheres of development can be identified: a northern sphere dominated by the site of Chavín de Huántar and its religious cult, and a southern sphere, slightly more diversified, but with strong religious cults called Pukará–Yaya-Mama in the Titicaca Basin and the Paracas Oculate Being along the southern coast.

CHAVÍN DE HUÁNTAR
With the abandonment of Sechín Alto and other coastal centres, the beliefs and administrative organization associated with U-shaped and sunken-court complexes endured in the highlands. The small, unimposing site of Chavín de Huántar took up the mantle of regional religious focus. Settlement began c.900BC at the confluence of the Mosna and Wacheksa rivers, a site apparently deliberately chosen to take advantage of access to western coasts, mountains and eastern

tropical lowlands. The Castillo temple was a classic U-shaped form, although the platform is not high. It endured about 700 years, including phases with an Old Temple and a New Temple, first with a circular sunken court and later with a square one. The ceremonial core was less than a tenth the size of Sechín Alto.

The Castillo appears to have been a cult centre and pilgrimage site for almost the entire Andean Area. Its success can be attributed to established long-distance trade, the spread of Chavín symbolism on portable objects and the integration of llama-herding with irrigation agriculture. While Yaya-Mama and Oculate Being imagery were confined to their respective southern spheres, Chavín's appeal cut across old social boundaries and regionalism, and its universality is demonstrated by the appearance of the Staff Deity as far south as Karwa on

Below: The Oculate Being in his human form, wearing a Paracas-style golden diadem and holding a trophy-headed snake.

Above: Ancestor worship as seen in a Paracas burial tomb containing mummy bundles wrapped around the elite person's body.

the Paracas Peninsula, and of Chavín symbolism on stone sculptures at Pacopampa and Kuntur Wasi in the northern highlands.

The spread of Chavín religious symbolism was extraordinary. Arising at the end of a drought period that caused abandonment of the coastal centres, it catered to coastal and mountain deities alike. Its religious symbolism embraced general concepts of dualism, and earthly and celestial deities represented on a succession of huge stone idols, as well as smaller objects with representations of the Staff Being as both male and female, a feline-serpentine image and a great cayman idol. It is significant that none of the animals or plants on Chavín's stone carvings is native to its highland location.

PUKARÁ AND PARACAS
As the importance of Chiripa waned, so Pukará, north of Lake Titicaca, and about a dozen other sites north and south of the lake, became centres for the Yaya-Mama Cult. Its symbolism was the duality of male and female figures carved on opposite sides of stone stelae. The cult flourished at the same time as Chavín through the middle centuries of the 1st millennium BC.

On the southern coast, the settlement of Paracas represents a third Early Horizon cult, with its extraordinarily rich cemeteries serving regional communities. The principal deity here was the Oculate Being, colourfully represented on textiles and pottery as a wide-eyed, flying sky deity.

THE EARLY INTERMEDIATE PERIOD

Chavín de Huántar was not the capital of a state, but rather a place of religious focus, and the cultural coherence that defines the Early Horizon was religion. While the inhabitants of other cult centres, such as Karwa, Kotosh, Huaricoto, Pacopampa and Kuntur Wasi, clearly felt religious allegiance to the Castillo temple, there is no evidence of political control at sites with Chavín Cult art. There is no identifiable state administrative architecture or other evidence of other than local regional community government and social arrangements.

THE END OF CHAVÍN

Although the demise of Chavín de Huántar and its cult was sudden, the reasons are obscure. Monumental construction in northern and central Peru came to an abrupt end in the 3rd century BC. The centuries either side of the Early Horizon–Early Intermediate Period were plagued by drought. Scholars attribute Chavín's end to an inability to maintain stability and the redistribution of resources during such stressful times.

Below: The capital of the Moche state featured a huge ceremonial centre, including the Huaca del Sol and, shown here, the Huaca de la Luna temple mounds.

Perhaps the length of its success was due to an acceptance of fate and to a focus on religious faith to counter hard times.

THRESHOLD OF URBANISM

Chavín de Huántar and its influence brought Andean civilization to the brink of urbanism, but lacked a truly urban appearance. Its economic life, including the support of craft specialists, was centred on its religion and ceremony.

The abrupt deflation of such strong cultic and artistic coherence brought social withdrawal. Hard times caused greater competition and many centres were abandoned, while others became impoverished. Squatters, for example, occupied the circular sunken plaza at Chavín de Huántar. There were population shifts to hilltop fortresses on both the coast and in the highlands.

With climatic improvement, the best lands were occupied and population increased. Highland peoples combined terraced and raised-field agriculture with mountain pastoralism, while desert coastal peoples built extensive irrigation systems to water the valley bottoms. But once the easily exploited lands were filled, competition was again inevitable. Intermittent periods of drought again punctuated the first few centuries AD.

Above: The Early Intermediate Period Kingdom of the Moche was the Andean Area's earliest state in northern coastal Peru, established through military conquest, exemplified by this effigy pot of a Moche war leader.

Unlike in the Initial Period and Early Horizon, Early Intermediate residential communities outnumbered purely ceremonial ones, and were larger. Although many settlements were fortified, often on hilltops and ridges, undefended settlements were the norm, and small villages filled the valley bottoms.

POLITICAL AND SOCIAL CHANGE

There was a shift from religious cultism to political rule by powerful elites. The political shift was from the powerful

Right: Nazca religious practice featured thousands of individual lines and ground figures – geoglyphs – across some 640 sq km (425 sq miles) of desert floor, forming ritual pathways, such as the famous hummingbird figure.

influence of priests to rule by *curacas* (a noble or kingly class distinguished by wealth and power) in the name of the gods. Ceremonial structures were built by the rulers, who marshalled the labour of their 'subjects'.

The civilizations of the Moche in the northern coastal valleys and of the Nazca in the southern coastal deserts demonstrate these changes most clearly. Both developed and flourished from the beginning of the 1st millennium to about AD700. Other nodes of political power were in the Rimac Valley of the central coast (the Lima culture) and several highland states.

INCREASE IN URBANISM

The settlements of these cultures are characterized not only by their greater size but also by the variation of their architecture. Ceremonial centres were still distinct, and sometimes separate, but they were now surrounded by or linked (twinned) with residential areas developed with regular planning. Buildings reflected activities, showing administrative,

craft specialization and domestic functions. Residence sizes and decoration reveal variations in wealth and status – the birth of socio-economic classes.

Religious overtones in philosophic outlook were still a driving force in people's day-to-day existence, and religious symbolism still dominated art, but the juxtaposition of political, bureaucratic and economic activities, and their intervention between religious and domestic life, form the complexity of parts that define urbanism. These developments were in place throughout the Andes by about AD500.

SPECIALIZATION

Each of these regions produced distinctive ceramics, metalwork and textiles. The renown of Moche craftsmanship rests especially in the quality and quantity of its metallurgists, whereas the potters and weavers of Nazca, where the desiccated conditions of the desert have preserved textiles in particular, possessed an expertise achievable only by specialization. Technical skill and full-time specialization are

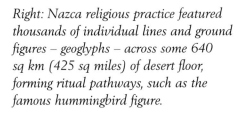

Left: Contemporary to the Moche, the Nazca peoples of southern coastal Peru formed a loose confederation of states. Much wealth was represented by their exquisite, colourful textiles, such as this hat, especially associated with ancestor worship and burial.

hallmarks of urbanism. Such practices can be sustained only if the economic structure can support them. There was state sponsorship of crafts, and objects were commissioned by the elite and made specifically for occasions, such as elite burial.

Battle scenes are a frequent Nazca and Moche artistic theme. Particular to Moche culture was a state specialization in ritual combat. Selected boys – the job might even have been hereditary – were trained from an early age to participate in gladiatorial contests with religious overtones. Moche ceramics depict some of these individuals in series of portrait vessels that show them through their lives, revealing those who were successful enough to last until they became the sacrificial victims when their skills waned and they lost their contests.

Particular to Nazca were its ground drawings: animals, plants and geometric shapes outlined on the desert surface were ritual pathways, binding society with religious ceremony.

Representative of these developments are the cities of Moche surrounding the ceremonial mounds of Huaca del Sol and Huaca de la Luna, Gallinazo, Sipán, Pampa Grande and Pañamarca in the northern coastal valleys; Pachacamac and Maranga in the central coast; and the twinned Cahuachi and Ventilla cites in the Nazca Valley. In the northern highlands were Cajamarca, Marca Huamachuco, Recuay and Wilkawain; Huarpa to the south; and in the Altiplano, Omo and the rise of Tiwanaku.

THE MIDDLE HORIZON

The Middle Horizon is defined as a further period of increased unity across regions. Precedents had been set in the later Early Intermediate Period with the evolution of more secular political regimes, albeit of city-states ruling small territories. The difference is in the underlying reasons for cross-regional unity: in the Early Horizon it was religion, while in the Middle Horizon it was politics, economy and military conquest.

MOCHE AND NAZCA

The closest thing to a large area under single rule in the Early Intermediate Period was the Moche Kingdom in the northern coastal valleys. Even this state, however, was characterized by semi-independent rulers from one valley to the next. The Moche were a seafaring people who pursued conquest from one

Below: A kero *drinking cup in the form of an effigy vessel – a puma head – also with a stylized beast and many typical Tiwanaku angular motifs.*

Above: Pikillacta's substantial stone walls formed the regimented town plan of the Wari highland provincial capital near Cuzco.

valley to another by sea invasion, as generations of the sons of kings sought new territories when valleys risked becoming overcrowded. The Moche shifted their centre of power from south to north, from Moche in the Moche Valley to Sipán, and later to Pampa Grande, in the Lambayeque Valley, in the 5th–6th centuries AD. By contrast, the Nazca culture was characterized by what appears to be a loose grouping of city-states.

RISE OF EMPIRES

Moche power collapsed and the Nazca and highland city-states waned with the rise of two civilizations that effectively split the Andean Area between them. They were the Wari and the Tiwanaku. Both expanded through military conquest and colonization. Each had a recognized imperial capital: Huari in a south-central highland intermontane valley between the Huamanga and Huanta basins, and Tiwanku near the southern shores of Lake Titicaca.

From AD650 the political states established by these two civilizations raised the socio-political level of Andean civilization to a new degree of urbanism and state control that in their turn provided models for later powers such as the Chimú and the Inca.

Above: The Wari provincial town near Ayacyucho, Peru, shows modular, angular, slab-like stone wall architecture.

SHARED RELIGION, DIFFERENT POLITICS

Wari and Tiwanaku religious symbolism was largely similar. Their rulers and people worshipped the same mountain gods, although they represented them in different media. The focus was on the Staff Deity, represented in imagery similar to that of the Chavín Cult, and which had been so widespread in the Early Horizon. Both Wari and Tiwanaku built in megalithic styles, but large-scale stone statuary was a particular Tiwanaku artistic and religious expression (and one that impressed the Incas centuries later, because it survived, standing silently among the ruins of the ancient city when Inca armies entered the Titicaca Basin).

The differing origins of the two capitals reflect different bases of each empire's power. Tiwanaku had been settled much earlier and had been part of the Early Horizon cult of Pukará–Yaya-Mama. It was thus steeped in religious cult practice. By about AD200 major building was under way and the city soon became the focus of Titicaca Basin religion and power. Tiwanaku representation of the Staff Deity on the Gateway of the Sun can be viewed as taking up the mantle of Chavín de Huántar.

Huari's rise was much later. A small settlement began to expand rapidly at the end of the 5th century AD. Within 100

Above: Tiwanaku, capital of the southern Andean Middle Horizon empire, features numerous enclosed ceremonial compounds at the heart of the city, including the Semi-Subterranean Temple Court, whose walls have sculptured decapitated heads and whose steps lead up to the gateway to the Kalasasaya sacred compound.

Below: The so-called 'monk', one of several colossal stone statues at Tiwanaku, stands in the Kalasasaya sacred compound.

years it was a dominant political power in the south-central highlands and began to expand through military conquest.

ADMINISTRATION AND COLONIZATION

Both empires grew as they took and exercised control of larger areas, each expanding north and south. They met at the La Raya Pass south of Cuzco, and in the upper Moquegua Valley, and there established their borders, under the watchful eyes of Wari garrisons at Pikillacta and Cerro Baúl. There seems to be less evidence of overt militarism at Tiwanaku, while the regimentation of Wari sites appears more martial. Evidence of violence is present in both, however, including stone sculptures of decapitated heads.

In both regimes, their provincial cities and holdings were linked by roads and trade connections, indicating the control of resources. One of Wari's earliest established provincial capitals, Viracochapampa, was 700km (435 miles) north, indicating direct control. This Wari infrastructure was later rejuvenated and improved by the Incas.

Wari expansion appears to have been stimulated by economic tension. To stay in power, Wari rulers needed to secure and control resources. They established deliberate agricultural colonies, such as Jincamocco and Azángaros, and provincial capitals at Viracochapampa and Pikillacta, all in the mid-7th century AD.

Tiwanaku colonization was different. It had a strong agricultural base in the Titicaca Basin, and within this heartland its control was direct. Farther afield control was through trade, for example to San Pedro de Atacama 700km (435 miles) south in northern Chile. Actual colonization by Tiwanaku was closer to home – for example at Omo, west, in the lowland Moquegua Valley, and in the Cochabamba Valley, east, in both cases in sparsely occupied areas – to secure resources they could not grow in the Titicaca Basin.

PATTERNS OF CONTINUITY

These alternative configurations of state organization reflect the path of Andean civilization nicely. The Chavín Cult had introduced widespread religious cohesion despite relative autonomy in local political and social arrangements. Fragmentation of cohesion in the Early Intermediate Period had more to do with the cessation of Chavín influence than with changes in local-level politics or day-to-day life.

The different beginnings and evolutions of these two Middle Horizon empires reflect both elements: imperial state political control from a military base in the case of Wari, similar to Moche expansion, and the centralized cult status and economic basis of Tiwanaku control.

THE LATE INTERMEDIATE PERIOD

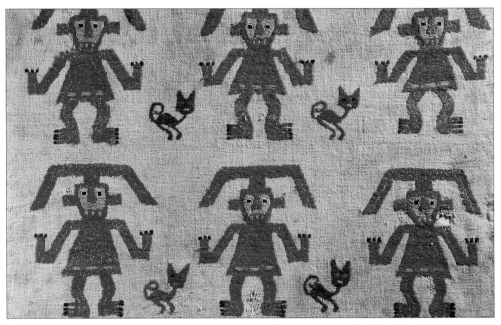

Wari and Tiwanaku powers waned swiftly in the final century of the 1st millennium AD. Reasons for the collapse of states are forever debated, but it seems that both empires may have become over-extended. As they colonized areas to secure resources, they no doubt raised resentment among some of their subjects. Abandonment of many of their provincial cities appears to have been sudden.

There is also climatic evidence. Data in cores taken from the Quelccaya icecap and from Lake Titicaca sediments show that rainfall decreased from c.AD950 and introduced a new, prolonged period of drought. The lake level dropped several metres (yards) and effectively ended the easy irrigation of raised-field agriculture.

Increased tension, failed crops, social unrest and the breakdown of trade links – all must have contributed to the swift declines of both capitals and their provincial settlements.

FRAGMENTATION AND WARFARE
Once again Andean societies withdrew into their local economies. As had been the case in the Early Intermediate Period, political and macro-social regimes fragmented into city-states, and for roughly the next 400 years local leaders seized power.

Left: A gold and jade repoussé decorated kero *drinking cup, with Staff Being-like imagery of a Sicán Lord, shows the richness of elite north coastal Peru Lambayeque tableware.*

With the Late Intermediate Period we come to the threshold of recorded history. Spanish chroniclers, transcribing the histories narrated to them by Inca and other native informants in the early 16th century, describe the period just preceding the rise of the Inca Empire as one of intense warfare between competing 'tribes' or ethnic groups. Strong, warlike leaders were called *sinchis* and they built many hilltop fortifications called pukarás, as shown in the archaeological record.

The Inca themselves, in their battles with neighbours in the Cuzco Valley, were participants towards the end of these developments, and indeed their second ruler (12th century) was named Sinchi Roca.

COASTAL STATES
Settlement patterns changed again as people isolated themselves in their local mountain valleys, often living in, or building for retreating to, fortresses overlooking their agricultural lands. Cultural initiatives

Above: A Chimú finely woven textile exhibits repeated figures wearing elaborate 'ceremonial' headgear and large earrings, plus felines.

and the focus of political power returned to the coast with the abandonment of Huari and Tiwanaku.

The traces of Moche culture that lingered in the northern coastal valleys were picked up by leaders living there, perhaps inspired by the visible ruins of the great Moche platform mounds. Following only brief domination by Wari, the Lambayeque-Sicán rulers established a capital at Batán Grande in the La Leche Valley. Like the Moche, they were renowned for their superb metallurgy, known from the royal burials discovered in the capital. Their kingdom was eventually incorporated by the Chimú.

On the central coast, several city-states arose as focuses of local power: the Chancay, Ichma, Cerro Azul and Chincha, all throwing off Wari rule. And the long-established city and pilgrimage oracle of Pachacamac in the Lurin Valley enjoyed a building boom that established it as the premier religious centre along the coast and to the stressed inland communities as well.

Above: A characteristic Chimú polished black effigy vessel or stirrup-spout bottle features a seated priest or elite person seated at a 'throne'.

On the southern coast, the Ica emerged to rule in the Nazca region, while farther south the Chiribaya people emerged from the power vacuum left when the Tiwanaku abandoned the Moquegua Valley.

Highland peoples are less identifiable archaeologically, although many tribal names were recorded from Inca informants. This is partly because they left no substantial legacy of monumental architecture or art, as did their coastal counterparts, before the Incas conquered the highlands.

To combat reduced rainfall and thus a fall in agricultural productivity, people were forced to concentrate on their local situation and to move to higher, moister elevations and into the wetter, eastern Cordillera. Increased use of terracing was necessary to grow sufficient crops. Competition fostered class separations, as the *chullpa* stone tower burials of the elite show.

Around Lake Titicaca, internecine rivalry resulted in the formation of a loose kingdom of seven confederated capitals or city-states.

CULTURAL DIVERGENCE

Fragmentation was not only political and social. Although art and architecture shared basic technology, approaches and subject matter, inheriting long developments in Andean civilization, the styles became regional: Sicán, Chimú, Chancay, Ica and Chiribaya. Architecture continued to be 'additive', and textiles, ceramics and metalwork mass-produced, standardized and prone to the use of repetitive patterns. Nevertheless, there were distinctive regional styles that can be identified with ethnic groups, both in the highlands and on the coast, the latter

Below: Labyrinthine corridors, compounds and storage rooms are formed within poured-mud, sculpted walls at the Chimú capital of Chan Chan.

Above: The poured-mud walls of Huaca el Dragón, a Chimú temple near the capital Chan Chan has rows of bas-relief warriors surrounding the 'rainbow' sculpture.

area being better documented archaeologically thanks to a return by Andeans, perhaps in their troubled times, to religion. Interestingly, the styles of these coastal peoples are recognized in the offerings they brought to the oracle city of Pachacamac.

Increased emphasis on social hierarchies and the accumulation of wealth by social class and individuals were the result of competition for resources. Elites show a voracious appetite for collecting and hoarding luxury goods. Regimented social control became a hallmark of late Andean social structure.

CHIMÚ

Around AD900 a new city was founded opposite the great Huaca del Sol and de la Luna. This was Chan Chan of the Chimú, which became the capital of the largest kingdom ever seen in the area, subsuming Lambayeque-Sicán culture after invasion *c.*1350. Its rulers, like the Moche, looked to the sea rather than to the highlands for their economic base. They invaded the adjacent valleys and eventually held the peoples of the valleys as far south as Lima in a tightly controlled administrative state. Before their conquest by the Inca, the rulers of Chimú collected huge wealth and created an imperial bureaucracy within their sprawling capital.

THE LATE HORIZON

The conquest of the Chimú Kingdom by the Incas in *c.*1462–70 marks a final episode of the Late Intermediate Period, mainly as a convenient historical date. Other scholars prefer to use 1438, the traditional date for the defeat of the Chancas by Pachacuti, the tenth Inca ruler of Cuzco.

By definition, the Late Horizon was a time of uniformity after a period of diversity. The meteoric rise of the Incas spans the two periods, and a date at which this was achieved to mark the end of the 'period' and the beginning of the 'horizon' is a moot point.

Below: An Inca-style geometric design embellishes this silver dish – tableware for nobles or for ritual offerings – from Ica in the Inca western suyu-quarter of Cuntisuyu.

LEGACY

The legacy of political and social fragmentation in the Late Intermediate Period highland valleys aided the Incas when they began to expand beyond the Cuzco Valley. Their forces frequently met weak or no organized opposition from people in farming communities still recovering from times of drought.

In the central sierra, however, they met stiff resistance from the highland group of city-states called Wanka (or Huanca), in the region of Lake Junin and the Mantaro, Tarma and Chanchamayo rivers. These peoples were primarily llama herders and had not adopted intensive maize agriculture until *c.*AD1000. They built fortified hilltop towns and resisted the Inca armies fiercely, no doubt

Above: Typical Inca close-fitting stonework in a trapezoidal, double-recessed niche with capstone arch in a Cuzco wall.

helped by their knowledge of the terrain. In the end, however, they were defeated by Pachacuti.

The Inca regime was the inheritor of all that came before it. Characteristic of the Inca Empire, above all else, is the Incas' incorporation of the political, social, religious and military cultures of their predecessors. The special talent of the Incas was in their expansion and intensification of these Andean practices.

ACHIEVEMENT

The Incas conquered an empire, albeit fleetingly, that was the largest territory in the world *c.*1530. Over the peoples of their empire they imposed, again only fleetingly, a level of uniformity that had never before existed in the Andean world. The uniformity, however, was less in art and architecture than in the organization of people's activities and social structure. They built extensively, but did not replace existing settlements by rebuilding them, and encouraged local crafts to continue, organizing the produce into their highly controlled economic bureaucracy.

Inca genius lay in their abilities to organize, incorporate and manipulate, and in their engineering. Inca power was expressed especially in their stonework: they rebuilt Cuzco and built provincial administrative capitals with walls of perfectly fitted monolithic blocks.

The Incas rejuvenated, improved and expanded on the roads and way stations built by the Wari and Tiwanaku throughout the central and southern highlands. And they incorporated many Wari outposts. The Incas' own road network comprised more than 33,000km (20,000 miles) of routes linking their capitals and fortresses. Likewise they exploited, extended and increased the terracing and raised-field systems of highland and Altiplano peoples, and expanded irrigation systems, in the never-ending need to increase production for expanding populations.

From the Wari they also copied the practice of relocating people to exploit resources. And they adopted the Wari use

Below: An Inca chicha *'beer' jar with typical geometric decoration.*

of the *quipu*, the string and knot system that served as a means of recording administrative essentials and statistics.

THE INCA MESSAGE

The Incas approached politics, social organization and art in terms of standardization and set units. While Inca standard shapes and patterns were imposed, aspects such as different colours marked regional and tribal identities.

In contrast to the intricate technology and exquisite beauty in much of the art and architecture of pre-Inca cultures, Inca art is more geometrically regular and less iconographic. Things Inca seem minimalist and utilitarian by contrast to the art of other Andean cultures. (Sadly, most Inca metalwork and sculpture, and much of their textiles and ceramics, were destroyed by the Spaniards.) Spreading their culture over newly conquered peoples was more to do with giving an impression of imposing power than imposing a new or complex symbolism. The sheer amount and bulk of Inca architecture and its road system, all of which served its bureaucratic organization and social control, was the message.

Even Inca religion was practical. In the late 14th and 15th centuries they increasingly pushed the imperial state cult of Inti, emphasizing that the Sapa Inca was

Above: To feed the huge population of the empire, the Incas made extensive terracing wherever possible to extend agricultural lands, as here at Moray near Cuzco.

the direct descendant of the sun. But they also left local religious belief in place, absorbed local belief into their own and continuously rewrote their history or left it vague with multiple versions and interpretations, to incorporate regional beliefs into the state mythology. The Incas did not challenge the obvious importance and influence of the Pachacamac oracle, but insisted on adding to the importance of the ancient pilgrimage city by building a temple to Inti there to add to the city's importance within the empire.

The imposition of Inca control was total in principal, but practical in application. As long as tribute in produced goods was paid and the labour tax obligation met, the imperial household was satisfied. They reciprocated, albeit non-symmetrically, with the redistribution of their subjects' produce such that all received what they needed.

The Incas generally improved the lives of their subjects and brought peace after their conquests, which was surely better than the continual warfare and competition over resources, both access to them and control over their movements and distribution, that had gone before.

CHAPTER THREE

BUILDING AN EMPIRE

The Inca Empire was forged in under 100 years, but the cultural development that preceded it took over 2,000 years. The Incas are recognizable archaeologically by a distinctive artefact assemblage, artistic expressions and architecture by *c.*AD1200.

The widespread exchange of traded items and ideas from the Preceramic and Initial periods coincided with the beginnings of monumental architecture at coastal and highland sites. The occurrence of common commodities, exotic items and artistic imagery reveals the beginnings of pan-Andean concepts that endured for the rest of Andean prehistory up to Inca times.

The Inca Empire brought a unity never before seen in the Andes over such a large area. Inca unity, however, was not based on imposed cultural uniformity. The Incas encouraged the regional diversity among their subjects, utilizing their cultural and artistic differences. At the same time, they controlled their movements, regulated the distribution of goods and wealth within an imperial economy, and imposed an all-inclusive religious conformity. They left their subjects in no doubt as to who was in control, and that resisting imperial rule was futile.

Four major concepts underlay the ancient Andean worldview: 'collectivity', 'reciprocity', 'transformation' and 'essence'. The names are words applied by modern anthropologists, but the ideas they represent would have been instantly recognizable to ancient Andeans. These ideas underpin everything from the most overarching institutions to the smallest details in ancient Andean art.

Left: When the Incas took over the pilgrimage shrine at Pachacamac, they built their own Temple of the Moon there.

CULTURAL UNITY (COLLECTIVITY)

The concept of collectivity is the idea of corporate thinking. From early times, Andean cultures thought in co-operative terms. People undertook activities that required collective and co-operative efforts, and the organization necessary to achieve agreed goals. Collectivity's underlying basis is that the group is more important than the individual, and in turn that the individual is looked after by the group. The idea involved every member of society in a web of responsibility to contribute to the whole.

Early tools were probably made by most individuals, or within small family groups. As populations increased and lived together in greater numbers, however, those more skilled in different materials or tasks could specialize in them. Specialists could then exchange each other's products or efforts.

By the time of the Inca Empire, and its immediate predecessors, the presence of specialists is known from descriptions of Inca society and its kinship and state structures. Archaeological evidence of similar structures and products in earlier cultures shows Inca culture was the culmination of many earlier developments.

Above and below: Religious themes and economic interdependence spread across vast areas from high lakeland valleys such as the Lake of the Incas (above) to dry landscapes such as the Atacama Desert (below).

This recognition of signs of collective thinking means that the general idea of these cultural features can be projected back to the earliest times. Certainly, many imperial constructs of Wari and Tiwanaku civilization are evident in Inca culture.

COTTON GROWING

The earliest coastal fishing villages reliant on marine resources fostered communities in which each member contributed a part. Fishermen and shore collectors required both intra- and inter-group co-operation, and the collections of both groups were pooled and redistributed within the community.

Cotton fibre was essential for tools for exploiting the marine environment – for nets, line, traps and bags – as well as for clothing and other household items. An increased reliance on cotton, and presumably a growing population needing clothes, led to it eventually being grown as a crop, so securing more control over supply.

Preceramic Period fishing villages dotted along the Pacific coast cultivated fertile flatlands in nearby lower river valleys to grow cotton for use in textiles. Similarly, the domestication of food plants and a few animals also fostered, and must have been achieved originally by, communal effort in highland valleys. Whether common or individual, fields needed watering and tending, and the development of irrigation systems and terracing to exploit more land required collective labour and co-operative use.

Above: This Chancay textile shows several characteristics of unity: figures in a Staff Being-like stance, angular geometric patterns and a monkey figure from the rainforest.

CO-OPERATION IN ADVERSITY

Although marine resources and agricultural production could be abundant, variations in climate and weather could bring cycles of drought or El Niño events, creating times of acute stress. In addition, the general harshness of some Andean Area environments – drought and unproductive years, desert and mountain terrains, each of which had limitations as to what resources were available or could be grown there – caused chronic stress. The people had to adapt socially to meet the demands of these environmental conditions.

The storage and redistribution of food within a community, so evident in Inca society, developed much earlier to supply individual specialists with food and drink, while they supplied artistic, political and religious expertise. Communal co-operation produced sustenance, tools and clothing, and sustained spiritual needs.

MONUMENTAL CO-OPERATION

The construction of monumental architecture in the Preceramic and Initial periods shows corporate effort on another level. It reveals the existence of inequality within the social structure. When large groups of people undertake communal, labour-intensive projects, some individuals need to organize and direct the enterprise. Such leaders need to exercise power among individuals, and thus authority becomes unequally distributed.

Further, the isolated nature of early monumental complexes – for they were not residential places – suggests that they served the towns and villages of the regions around them. Their shapes – pyramidal platforms supporting holy buildings and enclosed spaces clearly meant for crowd assembly – and the artefacts associated with them – figurines and stone sculptures regarded as idols representing deities, the finest ceramics and textiles, and imported items – show that their purpose was for the worship of religious ideas and accepted deities.

Taken together, these features reveal the birth of corporate thinking within and between communities, and of religious concepts that shared widespread acceptance.

ARTISTIC COLLECTIVITY

Collectivity in ancient Andean art can be seen through a certain emphasis on sameness. The limited number of basic ceramic forms, for example, shows conservatism through time, despite details of cultural style that make it possible to identify places and times of manufacture. In all artistic media there is a de-emphasis on portraiture and individual historical detail in favour of an emphasis on common types.

Deities and the general portrayal of them reveals a similar conservatism in the use of Staff Deity figures, and serpentine, feline, severed-head and other imagery. Both real-life and supernatural imagery focuses on roles rather than on individuals, portraying acts and practices rather than specific events linked to known individuals. The detailed decorations on ceramics, textiles and metalwork often concentrate on continuous and repetitive patterning and are often abstract.

Below: The ancient shape of the kero *cup changed little from Nazca to Inca times, and geometric designs perpetuated over millennia.*

TRADE AND MUTUAL OBLIGATION

A second fundamental Andean concept, reciprocity, becomes apparent early in cultures in their long-distance trade and the care taken in burials. It is linked to collectivity in a form of partnership in social structure, economy and art.

OBSIDIAN AND WOOD
Economically, reciprocity involves the exchange of resources. Exotic materials from the highlands were sought by lowland peoples, and vice versa. The exchange of goods is well demonstrated, both archaeologically and in Inca history.

Archaeological evidence shows that reciprocal exchange between lowlands and highlands began in the Preceramic Period, starting an economic pattern that prevailed throughout Andean prehistory. The full range of early highland–lowland exchange is still unknown, but from earliest times it included raw materials, food and finished artefacts. For example, obsidian (a natural volcanic glass used to make cutting blades, scrapers and projectile points) occurs only in highland areas above 4,000m (13,000ft), yet small quantities were found at most Preceramic and Initial Period coastal sites

(e.g. Ancón, Asia, Aspero and Otuma) from at least 3000BC. The closest obsidian source to Aspero is Quispisisa in the south-central Peruvian highlands, 385km (240 miles) to the south-east.

Similarly, wooden thresholds in doorways at coastal Río Seco were made from trees that grow in the highlands between 1,450m and 3,000m (4,800ft and 10,000ft). The strength of these exchange links is revealed by the fact that neither obsidian nor wood is essential in a coastal economy, yet they were preferred to local materials.

FROM FISH TO FEATHERS
Fish and salt were naturally lacking in the carbohydrate-dominated diet of highland peoples, yet not only are Pacific fish bones and shells found at all Preceramic highland sites with monumental public architecture, but there is also evidence of a trade in salt with coastal sites, where salt-making was carried out in large stone mortars.

Importation of thorny oyster shells both to highland and coastal sites reveals that exotic items from the fringes of the Andean Area were also sought. So, too, does the trade in tropical rainforest bird feathers, imported to highland and coastal sites across the Andes.

Maize, first domesticated in lowland river valleys, was soon found to grow from virtually sea level to 3,350m (more than 10,000ft), and so was added to the highland cuisine. Reciprocally, the discovery of potatoes, oca and ulluco (two other tubers) at some fishing villages reveals that coastal peoples also sought highland foods.

CLOTH AND IDEAS
Manufactured goods were also exchanged. Llama wool from the pampas grasslands was sought by coastal Early Horizon

Left: A Paracas culture wool poncho depicts characteristic Paracas repetitious figures, in wool imported from the llama-herding peoples of the Altiplano.

Paracas and later Nazca weavers to work with alongside cotton for mummy burial wraps. Farther north, cloth at Initial Period Galgada bears designs similar to those on textiles from coastal Huaca Prieta and Asia. And a distinctive stone bead with convex faces on both sides and two parallel drilled holes has been found at both coastal (e.g. Aspero and Bandurria) and highland (e.g. La Galgada and Huaritcoto) sites.

The exchange of objects and commodities also brought the spread of ideas. Similar artistic imagery is the principal sign of this, but the spread of maize and potato growing is another, if more mundane, example. Serpentine, feline, crustacean and avian imagery was used on gourds, ceramics and textiles from the earliest times, spreading among coastal and highland peoples and enduring through time.

KIN AND SOCIAL OBLIGATION

At the same time, the links brought by contact and trade forged personal and communal alliances. Intermarriage was

Below: A Chancay feather headdress exemplifies trade for colourful tropical birds from the eastern rainforests across the Andes to the western coasts.

Above: The early development of weaving led to trade in cotton and llama wool between lowlands and highlands (woman weaving, as depicted by Poma de Ayala, c.1615).

bound to take place, and the resultant blood ties between highland and lowland groups brought reciprocal obligations.

Kinship relations became extremely important in Andean society and are documented for the Late Intermediate Period and Late Horizon as the *ayllu* system. In Inca society the *ayllu* defined a community bound by kinship and territory. The *ayllu* social unit was also defined in political, ritual and economic terms: it could be a band of people or faction, or a state or ethnic group.

The operative force was that each member of the *ayllu* owed other members of the group, and the group as a whole, obligations in labour, food and goods, protection and social ceremony in exchanges to assure the group's cohesion and continuity. These blood relationships extended across generations.

Each *ayllu* could trace its origins back to founding ancestors, and mummified ancestors were honoured and regarded as sacred to the point of including them in community religious ritual and involving them in community decisions. On ceremonial occasions and religious festivals, the mummies were fed and consulted on agricultural and social matters.

Furthermore, there were obligatory relationships between individuals and *ayllus*, on the one

hand, and the state on the other. In Inca times this was demonstrated by the *mit'a* taxation system, a binding agreement of expected produce or labour delivered or performed by *ayllu* members for the state (in the Inca case, for the emperor and imperial household) and for the state religious organization. This dual structure meant that *ayllu* members had to cooperate in selecting some of their members to perform labours for the state, while other members performed tasks within the *ayllu*, including tasks that would have been undertaken by the missing members while on *mit'a* service.

Below: Preservation of the dead by mummification and wrapping in multiple layers of woven textiles, began the practice of ancestor worship that endured from Chinchorros and Paracas to Inca times.

LIVING IN A TRIPARTITE WORLD

Like collectivity and reciprocity, transformation and essence are also related concepts.

LEVELS OF EXISTENCE

Ancient Andeans regarded the universe and existence as consisting of multiple levels. The Inca tripartite realms of living world, world above and world below described by Spanish writers recorded a belief that began in the Preceramic and Initial periods and was shown in temple architecture. Platform mounds, temple rooms and enclosed spaces and sunken courtyards are facsimiles of this conceptual world: sky gods and earth goddesses are symbolized by pyramids and sunken enclosures. The world in which humans encounter and interact with the gods comprises the temples and ceremonial courts and plazas. All levels connected and interacted. Each was vital to the existence of the other two.

TRANSFORMATION

It is thought that processions through temple buildings were symbolic movements from the realm of the womb (the sunken courtyard) to the realm of the sky atop the platform. From the platform, or within an exclusive temple, priests were able to interact with the gods on behalf of the people, transforming the will of the gods to the world of the Earth.

Much Initial Period sculpture appears to show priestly or shamanic transformation in another way, too. As well as being a conduit between the gods and living people, shamanic trance, achieved with the aid of hallucinogenic substances, made priests vehicles between the different levels of the Andean world.

At Preceramic Huaca Prieta, a kind of transformation can be seen in the textile image of two crabs, linked by their tails on one side, and the other halves of whose tails transform into serpents. But it is in the Initial Period that Andean artisans began to

Above: Transformation is implied by the scarification and feline-like nose of this stone trophy head from Chavín de Huántar, and by its presumably drug-induced stare.

show humans in states of transformation. A mud sculpture at Moxeke depicts a caped priest emanating snakes, and painted adobe friezes at Garagay appear to depict transformation from human into insect. Condor markings on the faces of the Mina Perdida fibre figurines provide another example.

JAGUARS AND STONE WARRIORS

One of the most graphic depictions of transformation, however, is at Early Horizon Chavín de Huántar, after which sculptures and ceramic modelling frequently show humans in states of trance or midway between human and beast. At Chavín de Huántar, transformation from human to jaguar is shown in a series of sculptured stone heads on the walls of the New Temple. Other human-to-animal transformations were worked into Paracas and Nazca textiles.

The importance of the concept carried through to Inca times. At the moment of near defeat by the Chanca (traditionally dated 1438), Pachacuti Inca Yupanqui

Left: This clay model of a Moche priest in a state of prayer with joined hands (note the reciprocal hands on his headpiece) appears to be in a state of trance, probably induced by ritual chanting and drugs.

called upon field stones for help, where-upon the stones transformed themselves into warriors to secure Inca victory, then changed back. Ever after, the stones were honoured as a sacred *huaca*.

ESSENCE

Uniting the concepts of collectivity, duality and transformation, essence embodied Andean preference for 'symbolic reality' over appearance. Symbolism represented reality, even if hidden by outward appearance. It was less important for an image to be seen than for it to exist for its own sake. Whether or not it was being seen, an object existed, and, more importantly, what it represented also existed.

This idea was extended to the dismissal of the need for a human audience in some religious rituals. These took place in the

Below: Shamans were important figures in cultures through the Andean Area, depicted here in clay by Bahía culture (c.500BC–AD500), Manabi in Ecuador.

intimate confines of exclusive temples or in hidden chambers within temple mounds, enabling priests to control what the mass of people in the plaza witnessed. Thus, what the priests said or interpreted was the essence of what it was necessary for the common populace to know. And such practices simultaneously under-scored religious control and the idea that humans formed only one part in the Andean worldview.

With exceptions in Moche art, there was little recognition of individuals; rather, even where individuals were depicted, the essence of the depiction was the action performed by the person. Individuals were only a part in the whole and were subservient to the theme of the work.

SYMBOLIC CHARACTERIZATION

The paramount importance of symbolism was that it enabled Andean craftsmen to represent the character of a deity or religious concept with features that were commonly recognized. This imagery then spread through different religious cults and endured for great periods of time. So, although cultural styles are distinguishable in different Andean areas, and from different periods of history, many common feline, avian, serpentine, arachnid,

Above: The sunken court of the New Temple at Chavín de Huántar continued the tradition of large enclosures for worshippers in front of temple platforms, on which priests performed religious ceremonies.

plant and other symbols and features continued to be used from the Early to the Late Horizon.

Essence explains why Andean potters used moulds to make thousands of identical pieces, mostly restricted to a handful of shapes; why metallurgists sometimes painted over the metal, or hid base metals beneath gilding or plate; why elite individuals had their tombs filled with products made primarily for their eventual inhumation; and why weavers executed such elaborate patterns that the subject became illegible but remained true to its supernatural subject matter.

The transformation of procession along Nazca lines, too, retained the essence of its making, for it was not necessary to see the figure in its entirety at once – only to experience the symbolism and meaning of the procession. Essence also explains the seclusion of some idols within hidden chambers while others were on public display. Control of the symbolism was in the hands of the priests.

THE ANDEAN WORLDVIEW

Concepts of universality, continuity through life and death, and a cosmic cycle were all encompassed in the Andean worldview. The development of such views in some ways mirrors the actual evolution of Andean civilization.

BIRTH OF STATES

Changes in Andean society through 'horizons' and 'periods' reflect the nature of these developments through time periods characterized by cycles of greater and less political unity. Periods of political fragmentation were followed by times of political unity, then were replaced in turn by renewed fragmentation. Throughout these periods of waxing and waning political unification and break-up, however, there were certain universal developments that persisted or endured despite the political organization.

Religious concepts that developed in the Initial Period and the Early Horizon continued through centuries and millennia,

Below: Inca religion focused increasingly on the supremacy of the sun, Inti, and Viracocha. When the Incas conquered Pachacamac, they incorporated the shrine into their state religion, but demonstrated their authority by building their own Temple of the Sun there.

and formed a backbone of fundamental and universal concepts for Andean pre-Hispanic cultural development. Social structures involving relations between kinship groups and between highland and lowland peoples continued and provided a stabilizing structure that enabled society to continue at local levels, whoever ruled.

A NATURAL ANALOGUE

Nature itself seemed to comply, and perhaps suggested the idea of cycles to Andean minds. Andean peoples, even as they expanded and refined their levels of social and political organization, remained close to the landscape. This closeness is reflected in the ways in which they moulded the landscape with their irrigation systems and terracing, carved boulders into shapes mimicking the land, and regarded springs, rivers and stone formations as sacred *huacas*.

Life on the land was a repetitious cycle from one generation to another. The germination, growth and death of plants and animals and their coincidence with the seasons formed a backdrop for Andean religious philosophy. The analogy of the cycle of life from an encased, moist plant seed, to a tender young shoot, then a sturdy stem yielding its fruits, to the failing stalk

Above: Coya Mama, representing the moon, married her brother Maco Capac. 18th-century 'Cuzco School' genealogy of Inca emperors.

and, finally, withering plant seems obvious. The seasons and periodic occurrence of drought and floods, as El Niño events altered the Andean weather patterns, provided yet another analogy.

This relationship between ancient Andeans and their philosophical outlook can be called 'ecological'. Because they

Left: The Sillustani chullpas *near Puno, Lake Titicaca, were repeatedly re-opened for new mummy burials by the elite of the 13th-century Collao state.*

The long-lived oracle site of Pachacamac on the Peruvian coast represents another legendary constancy. Named after the worship of the coastal creator god, the pilgrimage centre endured for more than a thousand years, into the Late Horizon, and its ruins remain a sacred site today.

By contrast, in the ancient north coastal kingdom of Lambayeque-Sicán, Fempellec, twelfth in the dynastic succession founded by Naymlap, attempted to remove the sacred idol of Yampalec from its temple to another city. He was thwarted and executed by his priests in order to maintain political and religious continuity.

Below: Lloque Yupanqui, legendary 12th or 13th-century third Inca emperor and direct descendant in the ayllu *kinship founded by Manca Capac, depicted in an 18th-century 'Cuzco School' genealogy of Inca emperors.*

perceived their environment as sacred, they believed they were on Earth not to exploit it, but rather to enjoy its benefits through the grace of the gods. Andeans did not see themselves as the centre or focus of the world, but only as one group among all living things – including animals, plants and the stars. It was through the concessions and indulgence of the gods, who are universal and constant, that people were able to use their fellow living beings in life.

CONSCIOUS CONTINUITY

The cyclical nature and renewal of life represented continuity itself. Conscious political and social actions and decisions by Andean peoples and leaders also reflect this concept.

Ancestor worship, which appears to have begun as early as the Chinchorros and La Paloma peoples some 6,000 years ago, continued in the selection of special individuals and the attempts to bury them in a way that preserved their essence and linked them to the present. By the Late Intermediate Period and Late Horizon, the regular re-opening of *chullpas* in the Titicaca region to bring out the dead, and the special storage and inclusion of *mallquis* mummies in Chimú and Inca ceremony, had brought the association into physical presence.

The *ayllu* kinship structure and requirements of reciprocity strengthen continuity because both giver and receiver know what is required and what can be expected. Based on the worship of *ayllu* ancestors, the Inca imperial succession exemplifies the idea of continuity in being, theoretically, decided according to accepted precedence and formula.

Both the foundation of the Inca state and its succession were grounded in the legendary band of brother and sister founders, premier among whom was Manco Capac, who became first emperor. In theory, each subsequent Inca emperor was a direct descendant of Manco and his sister-wife Mama Ocllo. Significantly, at a crucial moment in Inca history, Yupanqui, son of Viracocha (eighth Inca emperor), defeated the Chanca, who threatened to conquer Cuzco when Viracocha fled the city, and took the name Pachacuti (literally 'revolution' or 'turning over or around'). The Incas themselves thus recognized both continuity of rulership and a cycle of change when Pachacuti began his reign after his father, named after the creator god, had admitted defeat. The god Viracocha, however, remained supreme in the Inca pantheon.

RELIGIOUS CONTINUITY

Perhaps the most obvious indication of Andean continuity is shown in the evolution of its religion, and is prominently visible in its art and architecture.

EARLY TRADITIONS
Early ceremonial centres, and the development of religious traditions at coastal U-shaped structures, and as complex clusters of rooms and temples on platforms in southern highland regions, show prescient Andean religious focus. They also demonstrate the establishment of architectural forms that remained in use throughout pre-Hispanic Andean civilization.

Likewise the serpentine, feline, avian and arachnid imagery so prominent in early ceramics, murals and sculpture continued to flourish regardless of political power structures. It seems that Andean consistency was lodged in its religion and expressed through artistic imagery.

CHAVÍN
The most celebrated and long-lived religious cult of pre-Hispanic Andean civilization was that of Pachacamac. The model of the Pachacamac Cult is used to characterize the Chavín Cult of the Early Horizon.

Chavín de Huántar, a relatively small U-shaped ceremonial centre established in the late Initial Period, appears unprepossessing compared to many much

Below: The long-lived pilgrimage shrine of Pachacamac, centred on the temple mound and oracle of the supreme god Pachacamac.

larger earlier and contemporary U-shaped ceremonial complexes. Its location, however, appears to have been deliberately chosen to command routes between coastal and mountain valleys.

Chavín's success and longevity are indisputably shown by the complexity of its temples and the expense devoted to their enlargement. The New Temple, built from *c.*500BC, more than doubled the size of the original complex and incorporated the older parts rather than abandoning them. A second temple was built, forming a larger U-shape, and a second sunken court, this time rectangular rather than circular. The complex plazas were capable of holding 1,500 worshippers, and there is evidence that the accommodations for priests and cult artisans increased in number and area.

The spread of the cult was through its religious imagery rather than by imitating its architecture, for no such complex, labyrinthine temple interior was built anywhere else. During the half millennium from *c.*500BC, Chavín feline imagery spread throughout the northern and central Andes and as far south as Karwa near Paracas in the southern coastal deserts.

Above: The New Temple – the deliberately located ceremonial site of Chavín de Huántar – began the Andean tradition of universal religion and pilgrimage shrines.

Chavín's principal deities formed the core of what must have been a widespread, uniform religion that transcended local political arrangements. The Staff Being became a universal image of divinity and could be either male or female. Jaguar and cayman imagery on Chavín de Huántar's monumental stone architecture and statuary reveal the reach of Chavín interests and influence, for both jaguars and caymans are rainforest animals.

Chavín's sculptural style provides the main signs of the spread of the cult, as shown by portable objects produced by its temple craftsmen and copied locally. It is fundamentally representational, employing conventions that were intentionally mystified. The principal image of the deities was reduced to a series of straight and curved lines and scrolls, and animals were portrayed in formal poses with only essential details – a process termed 'idealization'.

Above: The ritual, sunken enclosure of the Kalasasaya Temple at Tiwanaku provided a large, confined area where worshippers gathered for religious ceremonies.

The intricacy of Chavín temple architecture provided a sense of convention, unity and mystery. There was ritual use of water, an upper platform in the Lanzón idol's chamber that enabled priests to hide and act as the voice of the oracle, and a secret interior passage that permitted priests to emerge suddenly from 'nowhere' on the terrace above the Black and White Portal façade to address the crowds in the plaza.

This combination of idealized imagery and intricate construction presents a series of religious metaphors whose deep meanings were understood only by the initiated. The archaeologist John Rowe likens Chavín's visual metaphors to the literary metaphors used in Old Norse poetry. In both, 'kennings' are direct substitutes whose meaning must be learned. In use they provide mystery and unintelligibility, the understanding of which only priests can provide.

PACHACAMAC

The cult of Pachacamac was so important and powerful that its influence has survived even the colonial conversion to Christianity. Native Andeans to this day travel to the ancient site to make offerings to Pachacamac (the creator) and to Pacha Mama (earth mother). No other Andean site played such a significant role for such a long time.

The widespread influence of the Pachacamac Cult probably dates back to about 1000AD, although the site was founded some time in the 1st century AD and soon became locally influential. Inca and early colonial sources describe it in detail, revealing its longevity and acknowledging its importance and power.

The principal monuments from this period were constructed by the Ichma, who united the Lurín and Rimac valleys of the central coast. Fifteen terraced adobe platforms were raised, with great ramps leading to their summits, along the city's two main streets, running north–south and east–west.

Walls and cell-like rooms surrounded each platform compound, which provided the settings for pilgrim accommodation, public feasting and public ritual preceding consultations of the Pachacamac oracle.

UNIFYING POWERS

We know that Pachacamac was feared because the god was believed to control earthquakes. It is reasoned that Chavín deities' powers lay in control of the weather: rainfall, thunder, lightning, hail, frost and drought.

Both Chavín's and Pachacamc's influence was primarily religious. It was the power of their cults that united people throughout the Andes. The political spin was provided by the Wari and later by the Incas, who each conquered Pachacamac and used its religious prestige to enhance their imperial powers.

Below: The New Temple at Chavín de Huántar hid a labyrinth of inner rooms, and a secret stair used by priests so they could suddenly 'appear' on top of the temple.

SOCIAL AND POLITICAL EVOLUTION

Ancient Andean civilization increased in social and political complexity through time. Bands of hunter-gatherers undoubtedly had leaders, and tasks must have been divided among band members, probably partly along gender lines.

SOCIAL HIERARCHY

From the Preceramic and Initial periods, religious architecture, differential burial treatment and the importation of exotic items reveal important differences in social hierarchy. Possession of special items enhanced social prestige, increasing an individual's power and influence. Two early examples occurred at La Galgada: a single salt crystal was placed beneath the head of the female in an early burial; and a bed of large salt crystals beneath a layer of charcoal formed the base of two later Galgada burials.

Special treatment after death continued throughout Andean prehistory as ancestor worship increased in elaborateness. By the Late Horizon, mummies were regularly included in social occasions and every community had its ancestor mummies.

Below: Burial practices of the Qullasuyus as depicted in Poma de Ayala's Nueva Corónica, *c.1615.*

Above: Establishment of colonies and provincial capitals was an essential part of empire building and control, as exemplified by the regimented streets of the Wari provincial capital at Pikillacta.

CONSTRUCTIVE LEADERSHIP

Monumental architecture requires co-operation among large numbers of people, and directors. The association of differential burial and increasingly complex religious symbolism with ceremonial centres implies the emergence of rulers.

The spread of religious influence throughout large areas, especially from the Early Horizon Chavín Cult, shows the importance of inclusion, though inevitably the power of decision-making became the prerogative of some individuals over others.

In the Early Intermediate Period, coastal state organization was manifested in the Moche state and in the Nazca confederation of city-states. Individual highland city-states flourished, with shifting alliances, until greater unification came in the Middle Horizon with the rise of the Wari and Tiwanaku empires.

RELIGION AND POLITICS

Long-distance trade increased in volume and range through time, bringing tension as well as co-operation and reciprocity.

Tracking the spread of architectural, ceramic and other artefact styles helps us to trace cultural influences. The growth of the Wari and Tiwanaku empires is revealed by the presence of their distinctive ceramics and architecture as they conquered other peoples and built colonizing settlements. Wari outposts included Pikillacta, Viracochapampa, Jincamocco and Azángaros, and Wari pottery appeared at Pachacamac on the coast; a Tiwanaku lowland colony was established at Omo.

Politics and religion were never fully separate. Elaborate Paracas and Nazca burial bundles of important individuals included the cult trappings of trophy heads, while the Moche Sipán Lord burials included the costume of religious ceremonial leaders. The Inca emperor was the representative, perhaps even the incarnation, of Inti, the sun god.

INCLUSION

Organizational structures combined Andean economy, religion, society and politics alongside the unifying cultural and artistic concepts of collectivity, reciprocity, transformation and essence. The goals of Andean social and political arrangements were to secure basic stability and relative prosperity for all, guided by religious belief.

Andean civilization became grounded in state-like institutions (organized groups from across the social divisions working with understood rules of conduct); common beliefs – with powers of interpretation vested in a formal priesthood; state regulation of output; trade and the redistribution of wealth according to accepted social divisions; and state sponsorship of crafts and artistic production.

Inca inclusion of the gods of their subjects reveals the strength of Andean desire for continuity, as does their admiration for and imitation of earlier imperial structures, especially Tiwanaku and Wari. Admiring the ruins of Tiwanaku, they recognized the city and islands of the lake as sacred. They incorporated the ancient city and its beliefs into the imperial state religion, making Tiwanaku and Titicaca the womb of the universe. The official storyline became that the ancestral Inca founders came from there, sanctioned by Viracocha.

Below: The ostentatious regalia of the Moche Lord Sipán burial demonstrates the wealth accumulated by Moche rulers and the skill of their state-controlled craftsmen.

Similarly, Inca inclusiveness adopted Pachacamac, both the deity and the sacred city. Typical of Inca mastery, they acknowledged Pachacamac's antiquity, but took over the shrine, making their supremacy clear by building a temple to Inti next to the ancient temple. To them, it was important to maintain continuity, but also to demonstrate who was in charge.

INCA EXPANSION AND DECLINE

The nature of Inca expansion shows these elements in action. As one tribal state among several in the Cuzco Valley, early Inca expansion required warfare.

As their power grew, however, they employed a variety of strategies. Military conquest continued – for example, the growth of alliances in the Lucre Basin powerful enough to rival their confederation resulted in Inca conquest. In other cases, subjugation was achieved through marriage alliance, or long-established cultural affiliation with the Inca led to gradual political incorporation by the more powerful Inca. Inca interest was in control, not destruction.

An interesting twist is that at the arrival of Spaniards equally resolved on control, sibling rivalry over the imperial succession threatened its continuity internally alongside external threat.

Above: The Spaniards built their Church of Santo Domingo on the shrine of the Inca Temple of the Sun in Cuzco.

A final contributing factor in the demise of the Incas and Andean civilization was biological – the unintentional biological warfare of smallpox. From a population of about nine million in 1533, the native Andean population had been reduced to 500,000 by the early 17th century.

EVERYDAY SURVIVALS

Many fundamental Andean patterns survived the Spanish Conquest. Dietary staples remain maize, potatoes and tubers, as do ways of growing, processing and storing them. Rural markets remain essential. Weaving remains important in Andean economy, both for local consumption and, now, for tourism. Patterns persist, including designs and garments that identify regions. Pottery is still made with coils and moulds, although the art is being slowly eroded by use of plastic containers.

Finally, rural 'vernacular' architecture itself has changed little: cane thatching and adobe mud bricks are still in use, retaining ancient practical solutions to local environments.

STRUCTURE OF EMPIRE

The nature of the Inca Empire was grounded in the slowly evolving principles of earlier imperial states, especially those of Wari, Tiwanaku and Chimú. But although many Inca achievements were based on existing institutions and technologies, it was the scale of their empire that distinguished it.

INCREASE AND ELABORATION

Not only was the Inca Empire the largest in area of any empire in the New World, covering even more territory than the contemporary imperial Aztec state of Mesoamerica, but large size and scale also characterized everything the Incas did. Urban organization, buildings of large, dressed stone blocks without mortar, extensive road building, terracing and landscaping, and their complex administration and organization of textile and ceramic production and metallurgy were all sized and scaled to impress. Inca enterprises often utilized what other states had established or achieved, but they always elaborated, expanded or increased it.

Right: An Inca provincial administrator with his staff of office, depicted in Poma de Ayala's Nueva Corónica, *c.1615.*

The Incas defined their empire through physical structures imposed on the lands of their conquered provinces. The great emperors Pachacuti, Tupac Yupanqui and Huayna Capac – who expanded the empire beyond the confines of the Cuzco Valley – negotiated settlements with their subjects for the right to build roads, way stations and cities. Before embarking on military conquest, they professed friendship along with veiled threats, offering rich gifts to local rulers and the prospect of economic benefits through Inca administration. If such negotiations failed, however, Inca armies could be raised quickly and their well-organized supply systems enabled them to maintain standing armies at great distances from the capital. Inca repute was cumulative – the power and strength of organization in subject territories made the threat of conquest if non-coercive agreements failed all the more persuasive.

DIVERSITY ACCEPTED

While imposing their social regimentation, taxation system, laws and overall rule on conquered peoples, the Incas accepted the diversity of local customs. They incorporated local religious cults and deities into the state pantheon, while insisting on the overarching superiority of Inti and Viracocha. They imposed no dress codes, but allowed regional costumes to distinguish subjects and give them a sense of identity. Although Quechua was the language of administration, and became prestigious to use, they made no attempts to suppress local languages.

EFFECT ON ORDINARY SUBJECTS

The effects of the Inca Empire on ordinary lives were undoubtedly substantial, yet daily routines must have changed little.

Left: Forming the head of the crouching puma in the plan of Inca imperial Cuzco, the Sacsahuaman Temple to Inti, the sun, and fortress-weapons store emphasizes the power of Inca religion and state.

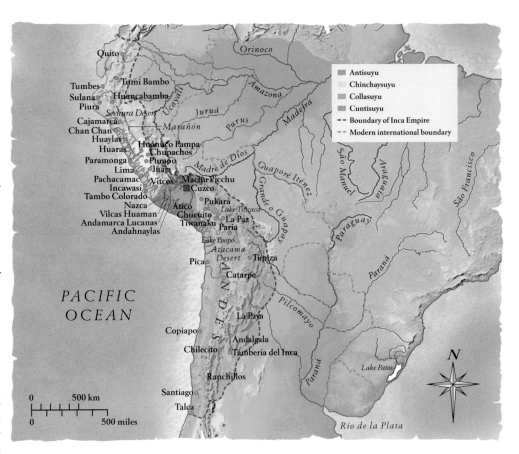

The changes were in emphasis and organization. To an ordinary subject, loyalty must have remained primarily to one's local officials. The systemization of work and the channelling of state quotas into its tripartite application (to the imperial household, the state religious establishment and the people) probably differed little in kind to the burdens of life that existed before incorporation into the empire.

Inca strength was in their brilliant and systematic organization of these matters, and in the powers of their ability to persuade populations to accept this organization, and to see the benefits it could have in times when environmental conditions and drought cycles adversely affected production, but when the state stores could then be drawn upon to redistribute goods.

Below: Inca architecture advertised Inca power, as here at the imperial palace and estate of Huayna Capac at Quispihuanca in the Urubamba Valley near Cuzco.

CITIES FOR STABILITY

The Late Intermediate Period was a time of political fragmentation in the highlands, although as Inca expansion began, Chimú continued the Moche and Lambayeque-Sicán succession on the north-west coast. Highland conflict punctuated the centuries from 1100 into the 15th century as El Niño weather events and consequent adverse environmental conditions led to competition for resources. The rise of the Inca Empire and its infrastructure offered resolution to this situation. Inca cities were established in response both to unsettled conditions and to the diversity of landscapes and cultures. The Incas established cities where they did not exist, to lay the foundations for rule, or altered and imposed their cultural stamp on existing cities to achieve the same result.

Their cities established a stage for pageant, spectacle and the display of wealth and power designed to win over their subjects. As ever in Andean civilization, reciprocity underlay this process, for it was a bargain. Not only was it necessary (to avoid military conquest) to gain the hearts and minds of the people, in other words their consent, but it was also

Above: Map of the Inca Empire (Tahuantinsuyu), showing the four quarters (suyus) of the empire and major Inca towns and cities.

an offer to fill their stomachs through an 'equitable' redistribution of life's necessities. People were accustomed to supporting the religious establishment, for it was an integral part of their worldview. They were also used to elite members of society – royal households and local rulers – having more. The Incas, however, offered to add stability and protection to what had been a more unstable arrangement, in return for loyalty and submission to an institutionalized labour tax (the *mit'a*).

The very name of the Inca Empire incorporates a subtlety that reveals the Andean concept of essence. Tahuantinsuyu means 'the four parts'. It was made up of a confederation of alliances, with varying degrees of loyalty, achieved through persuasion, military conquest and kinship ties through arranged marriages. The empire itself was relatively short-lived and, after decades of continuous expansion, had reached a state of civil war when the Spaniards arrived.

CHAPTER FOUR

THE WORLD OF WORK

Work in general in the ancient Andean world was primarily a continuous routine. Tasks were repetitive and linked to the succession of the seasons.

Much of our information about the economy of the Andean world comes from the ethnohistorical record of the Incas. For pre-Inca times, including the civilizations of the Nazca, Moche, Chimú, Wari, Tiwanaku and Sicán peoples, there is an increasing body of archaeological evidence, which gives us a great amount of detail, particularly about ancient technology. The nature of monumental architecture, and even of domestic architecture, helps to project much of what we know about Inca culture into the past, particularly concerning matters of religious worship. This evidence shows us where pre-Inca cultures differed as well as enabling us to deduce that many practices were similar in pre-Inca societies.

For example, the nature of trade and agriculture in Andean civilization as early as the Initial Period indicates that forms of social organization involving kinship relationships and the divisions of society were developed very early. Similarly, religious concepts and the roles of priests and shamans endured through the centuries.

Inca culture, although distinct, inherited a long legacy of ancient developments. Inca emperors and their administrators adopted and often adapted to local conditions within the confines of their own regimented organization of administration, taxation and social regimentation.

Left: State-supported craftspeople produced exquisite textiles, such as this Chimú nobleman's tunic with its long-billed birds.

CIVIL ADMINISTRATION

We know almost no detail about exactly how pre-Inca states organized society. There were buildings clearly for religious and administrative functions, including the storage and redistribution of goods. Usually the two 'institutions' were inseparable or closely linked, and there were specialists who governed or advised the ruler and others who were priests.

BEFORE THE INCAS
From at least the Early Intermediate Period on there were states, such as the Moche Kingdom of the north-west coastal valleys. The legendary Naymlap, the conquering king following the southern Moche collapse, had a court retinue listing numerous officials: 'Preparer of the Way', 'Blower of the Shell Trumpet', 'Master of the Litter and Throne', 'Royal Cook', 'Royal Cellarer', 'Maker of Feather Garments', 'Steward of Facepaint' and 'Master of the Bath'.

Not until the Chimú Kingdom (Later Intermediate Period) and the Inca Empire (Late Horizon) do we have any records of how states were organized.

SUYUS AND PROVINCES
The Inca Empire was divided into four quarters, called *suyus*, around Cuzco. These were divided into more than 80 provinces, each with a governor. If a conquered population was large,

such as the Chimú, it was designated as a single province, while smaller groups were amalgamated to form provinces. Groups of people were also moved from one province to another to induce loyalty to the empire or as punishment for rebellion.

In theory, each province had about 20,000 households, the basic unit of Andean society (comprising several nuclear families and several generations of related kin). The state bureaucracy was organized from the province downwards, to designate the proportions of land for imperial/state, religious and common use, to collect and distribute tribute, to regulate the *mit'a* tax system, to apply the law and administer justice, and to keep the peace.

THE ADMINISTRATIVE PYRAMID
The Inca emperor was the pinnacle of the administrative pyramid. Immediately below him were four *apos* (officials) in charge of the four *suyus*. Apos were close advisers to the emperor, and usually relatives. A governor of each province reported to the *apo* of its *suyu*. Provincial governors were usually Incas, but local chiefs were also used, especially in lower ranks of the administration.

Each province of 20,000 households was divided into administrative units on a decimal system. Two government officials

Above: A richly painted wooden Inca kero drinking cup showing a house and farmers with foot-ploughs and large storage jars.

called *curacas*, each in charge of 10,000 households, reported to the governor. Each *curaca* directed five lower-ranking *curacas*, each in charge of 1,000 households; each 1,000-household *curaca* directed two *curacas* of 500 households; and, finally, each 500-household *curaca* governed five 100-household *curacas*.

The *curacas'* main responsibility was to administer the *mit'a* labour tax – to make sure that the correct number of men turned up to work Inca lands, on building projects, serve in the army, work as a craftsman or various other Inca jobs. They also needed to make sure the burden

Left: Luxurious ornaments, such as these Moche gold earrings with lapis lazuli and shell inlay depicting Moche warriors, would have been worn only by rulers and nobles.

was equitably distributed among the household *ayllus* so that none was left with too few male workers. *Curacas* also collected the state tribute and saw to its delivery into state storehouses. They allocated lands to the households (on an annual basis as household constituencies changed). Lastly, *curacas* administered Inca law. Rewards came if all was done well; punishment if not.

SOCIAL CONTROL

Mitimaes (Quechua for 'foreigners') were people brought into a newly conquered territory to replace part of the indigenous population, and conquered subjects moved to the original homeland of the new settlers. They were groups of people forcibly resettled apart from their homelands.

The practice was used in order to exercise demographic and social control, and for economic reorganization. By resettling groups of people within the empire, the Incas could redistribute

Below: A native provincial administrator confiscates a llama as tribute, depicted in Poma de Ayala's Nueva Corónica, *c.1615 – the elderly owner claims that he is not subject to tribute.*

Right: The legendary northern coastal conqueror and ruler Naymlap, who maintained a large entourage of court officials, was depicted on numerous tumi *ceremonial knives, as in this gold Chimú example.*

labour and the commodities grown and produced by different groups, while also mixing together peoples' notions of geographic identity and religious/mythological concepts.

It served two purposes. By shifting people from their place of birth, the Incas exercised control over their destiny. It provided access to new geographical zones and enabled increased production in others. For example, moving a conquered group from a herding zone to a maize-growing zone increased the land available for imperial llama herds and simultaneously provided the workers to enable increased production in the maize-growing zone.

Such a move also helped to maintain control. Rebellious people removed from their homeland weakened both the group moved and their own or neighbouring populations left behind. Equally, moved now to live among loyal subjects, they were less likely to cause trouble. In practice, *mitimaes* moves often involved both purposes, as a loyal group was exchanged for a troublesome one, thus securing the province and continuing its production.

Given Andean reverence for the landscape, removal to an alien place must have had a huge psychological impact. The transplanted group probably had a part of its *ayllu* kinship relations severed from those left behind and was forced to live among strangers whom they could not trust, away from their local deities and sacred *huacas*.

The practice also combined details in the creation myth, such that a pan-Andean/pan-Inca version was propagated.

The result bolstered and legitimized Inca claims of a right to rule – as a 'chosen' people whose divine ruler had sanction by descent from the sun god Inti or from the creator god Viracocha. The term was even used in the creation myth, when Con Tici Viracocha ordered the two survivors of the great flood, thrown up on land at Tiwanaku, to remain there as *mitimaes*.

KINSHIP TIES

The foundation of Inca society rested in kinship relations. The rules and ties of kinship were so well established by Inca times that they appear to represent the result of a long development of social and cultural relationships that began in the earliest Andean cultures. The integration of highland–lowland relationships, and the exchange of products locally and regionally, required that several economic tasks be done simultaneously.

The minimum unit that could accomplish such a balance is, theoretically, a married couple. Yet even with children old enough to help, the requirements of farming, housing, water-collecting, herding, hunting and domestic chores cannot be as efficiently accomplished by a nuclear family as they can be by a larger group. It is arguable that this led to the development of strong kinship ties within larger groups of people to distribute labour better, and to established obligations that each member of the group understood.

Above: A structure of multi-generational kinship obligations developed from early times in ancient Andean culture – Manabí terracotta models of women and children, Ecuador.

AYLLU AND MOIETY

When the Spaniards arrived, Inca society was highly structured and involved a hierarchical arrangement of kinship relationships and obligations called *ayllu*. *Ayllu* comprised both community-bound kinship and territorial 'ownership'. As a social unit, it was defined in terms of economic, political and religious cohesion. As a kinship structure, *ayllu* was based on blood and marital relationships. Each *ayllu* was related back to an accepted common ancestor, a 'founder'. A single *ayllu* could comprise a band, a faction, an ethnic group or even a state.

An idealized extended kinship chart would begin at the *ayllu* level, starting with its founder or founding ancestors. Members of the *ayllu* were grouped into two halves, known by the anthropological

living descendants   living descendants

LINEAGES

SUYUS

hurin   hanan   hurin   hanan

MOIETIES

AYLLUS

founding ancestor   founding ancestor

Left: Diagram of the Inca (and earlier) ayllu kinship structure, showing relationships from the founding ancestors through moiety divisions to living descendants of two ayllu collectives. There is a founding ancestor for each of many thousands of ayllus; each lineage group descends from the two moieties of that same ayllu.

term 'moiety'. In the Late Horizon, the Incas called the two moieties *hanan* (upper group) and *hurin* (lower group), and the peoples of each town and province were thus paired.

AN ORGANIZATIONAL CHARTER

The next grouping (or 'tie') was the *suyu*. The *suyu* was the land division assigned to a man and his family (a household), and in Inca times was also used as the fourfold division of the Inca Empire. The lineage of the *suyu* and their descendants comprised the immediate living members of the *ayllu*. In Andean belief, however, physical death was regarded as only one stage or state of being. The dead were equal participants in 'life' through

Below: The family unit was the basis of Andean society – ceramic models of a man, woman and child from the Negativo Carchi people of Ecuador.

ancestor worship, so the mummified remains of ancestors continued to be included in the social structure through ritual.

Ayllu was, therefore, not simply the organization of a group of people, property, and goods and possessions, but rather an organizational charter of relationships and obligations that enabled the tasks and problems of daily work and existence to be shared. Individually it provided a sense of belonging for *each* member and collectively it provided for the security of *all* members.

Ayllu members were not all equal, however. There were individual leaders, although their authority was limited within the obligations of the kinship arrangement. Leadership and greater authority, and indeed nobility, were hereditary. At birth an individual became ranked by his or her genealogical proximity to their *ayllu*, moiety, *suyu* and lineage founders. He or she inherited reciprocal relationships: obligations to and claims upon other members of their *ayllu* for rights, farm and pasture land, water, labour and other collective assets.

EVOLUTION OF *AYLLU*

The argument for the development of *ayllu* at an early date is twofold, based on evidence for social and economic evolution. For economic reasons, the first hunter-gatherer bands entering the Andean Area would have been small groups. Many individuals in a group would be blood-related, but there is no reason to suppose that bands did not meet and intermarry, so establishing kinship relations between groups.

In maritime Andean society, rich marine resources enabled large groups

Above: Both men and women worked in the fields – the Cocha Runa, or First Age peoples, ancestors of the Incas depicted in Poma de Ayala's Nueva Corónica, c.1615.

of people to live sedentary lives in seaside villages. Likewise, as plant domestication developed from the selection and tending of, first, wild plants then semi-wild plants and finally domesticated crops, people led more sedentary lives and gathered in large village settlements. Increases in food yield, aided by developments in irrigation, terraces and raised-field agriculture, enabled larger settlements, social specialization and increasingly complex social interactions. Co-operation between individuals and groups involved mutual obligations and, eventually, 'rules' to govern those obligations.

The second part of the argument is that the exchange of products and ideas across geographical zones, as shown in archaeological findings, inevitably included the movement of people from valley to valley and between highlands and lowlands. It seems equally inevitable, therefore, that there would have been intermarriage among people of different zones. These associations were presumably freely entered into in times of peace. Competition for resources, bringing warfare and conquest, would no doubt have resulted in forced unions as well, either by capture and rape or as a result of peace negotiations. Either way, blood relations and kinship ties would be established.

TAXATION AND LABOUR

The fundamental Andean 'capital' was labour. Kinship obligations were enshrined in reciprocity: acceptance that something rendered required a return of equal kind or value, called *mit'a* (Quechua) and *ayni* (Aymara). The concept applied both to *ayllu* relationships and the relationship between the Inca state and its subjects. Like *ayllu*, the concept was of pre-Inca origin; Chimú society was similarly arranged.

Mit'a and *ayni* gave each household access to more labour than it could muster from its own members. *Ayllu* obligations from brothers, sisters, their children, in-laws, nieces and nephews were available for labour exchange under reciprocal obligations, enabling everything from house building to canal construction and maintenance, farming and herding to be achieved. For example, farming tasks were done by *ayllu* teams, plot by household plot. Sometimes repayment was in equal value rather than in kind, such as food for labour. The Incas formalized the *ayllu* social structure into a state institution.

LAND DIVISIONS

Land was divided into three parts: to support the gods, to support the emperor and his household and to support the local community. As the emperor was considered divine, the first two categories were both under his control. Their yields supported

priests, shrine attendants and other religious functionaries, and were stored for use in religious ritual and ancestor veneration on appropriate holy days; produce from imperial land was conspicuously stored against future needs in warehouses at provincial capitals.

Left: Terracing and numerous storehouses represent Inca control, and state produce and redistribution – imperial largesse – at the royal estate of Machu Picchu.

Above: The higher one ranked in Inca society the richer one could afford to dress – an Inca elite tunic depicting intricately woven geometric patterns, felines and plants.

Community land was divided into plots and assigned to *ayllus* and households by local *curacas*. Assignment was done annually, so that the proportions allotted could be changed to meet households' changing needs. A similar threefold division was also applied to Altiplano pastureland.

INCA AND PRE-INCA TAXES

The Incas exploited their subjects' sense of reciprocal obligation for state tax purposes. Tax in labour was extracted from both men and women, but labour tax on the two state-owned land divisions applied only to men. This was an annual draft of labour gangs from the *ayllus* and involved work on divine and imperial lands: agriculture and herding, imperial construction projects, military service, transporting goods from state storehouses, or being a runner in the imperial postal service.

We have no pre-Inca records of *mit'a* labour, but archaeologically recognized responses to periodic drought throughout Andean history indicate that *ayllu* and *mit'a* organization was practised and applied across geographical zones. For example, through centuries of lowland drought, *c.*AD1100–1450, the focus of intensive cultivation was gradually shifted from lower, warmer elevations to higher, cooler ones with sufficient rainfall, and to the better-watered eastern Andean slopes. Similarly, on a site scale, the marked adobe bricks of the Huaca del Sol

Below: An imperial Inca accountant with his quipu *record of produce and goods for redistribution, from Poma de Ayala (c.1615).*

pyramid at Middle Horizon Moche show that individual community labour gangs completed different sections.

Another form of state taxation involved textiles. Like reciprocation in textiles within *ayllu* exchange, the value of textiles, calculated in labour, was in effect also a labour tax. Both men and women rendered tribute in cloth production to local governors and to the imperial state. Specified quantities of fibre, wool and cotton were distributed annually, from which men made cordage and rope, and women made cloth. The former was stored and used for all sorts of containers (for example for llama sacks for imperial trade caravans), and for bridge making. Cloth, also stored, was used for the priesthood and the imperial household, as gifts to conquered rulers turned imperial governors, for army kit and for redistribution among communities according to need.

IMPERIAL OBLIGATIONS

Imperial Inca taxation brought vast revenues into state storehouses. The elite proportion of the population that was permanently subsidized by the system was perhaps 10 per cent. There were the higher-ranking decision makers and the lower-ranking implementers of state institutions and projects. The contribution of the first group was, of course, to govern and to preside over religious ritual. They ranged from local to state priests and other religious persons, to local and higher

Above: A symbol of Inca power – a kancha *storehouse (reconstructed) at the imperial provincial estate and administrative centre of Ollantaytambo in the Urubamba Valley.*

governors and administrators, to conquered royal households, and finally to the imperial household itself.

The second rank comprised individuals who were subsidized because their occupations and technical expertise employed them in non-subsistence jobs. These were the state accountants and historians (the *quipucamayoqs* and *amautas*), agronomists, hydrologists, architects, engineers, surveyors and all the specialist craftspeople employed by the state to produce metalwork, ceramics, masonry, gemstones and woodwork required for the imperial and other ruling households. Some of this production was purely and solely for the cults of the dead.

The distribution of goods from imperial storehouses was not one-directional. The entrenched concept of reciprocity meant that the state also realized and accepted its obligations. The use of state stores was critical to a mutually beneficial relationship between ruler and ruled. Holy days and special days were liberally supplied from the state storehouses with food and drink. Crop failures and other hard times brought by natural disaster could be alleviated through redistribution, according to rank and need, by the state of the goods produced by common labour.

TRADE AND ECONOMY

Neither the Incas nor any pre-Inca culture practised a monetary economy. There was no standard value system with a currency of fixed denominations. There was undoubtedly a sense of value in terms of prized metals, and derived from the efforts to procure commodities, but otherwise value was based on the relative worth of one object or commodity against another, on scarcity, environmental conditions and their effects on annual production, on distance and on the recognized labour involved in production.

ANDEAN VALUES

Even regarding precious metals, it is difficult to understand completely the Inca sense of their value as a contemporary European would have valued them. Metals were mixed, and sometimes the precious metal, say gold, was only a veneer over base metal, making the object appear gold even though it was not pure. This Andean concept of essence – the

Below: These Chimú kero drinking cups are of gold inlaid with turquoise.

appearance of an object (what it represented) being more important than the actual substance – is alien to Western ideas of value. Sometimes the precious metal itself was covered in paint.

Moche-Sipán and Lambayeque-Sicán elite burials show that precious objects were lavished on individuals in tombs, showing some sense of the intrinsic worth of precious metal objects on their own merit and as special pieces. Exquisite textiles and ceramics were made by the Nazca and other cultures, not as valued items in this life but as provision, as valued offerings, in the next. Their use was for the deceased in the next phase of their existence. The objects were made specifically for the tomb, and thus not for use until after death. Similarly, the real value of precious metal objects was as offerings to the gods. Their exchange rate was measured in rain to water crops, against a good sea harvest and for protection through appeasement against natural disasters such as earthquakes, flooding or drought, and for the general wellbeing of the people.

Above: Inca state control of textile production and trade can be traced back in Andean history to the earliest times – a Wari tunic of wool and cotton, whose fibres were exchanged between highland and coastal producers.

Textiles were especially valued, and the value of different qualities of textiles was well understood in terms of the labour involved to produce them. In Inca times textiles were the nearest Andean concept to 'coinage', and because their value was understood in terms of labour they were, in effect, reciprocal labour for labour. Because cloth was so highly valued in Andean cultures, it was used by the Incas in a similar way to currency. Regular allocations of cloth were given to army units and it was 'paid' as a reward for government services. Whether textiles were used in this way by any pre-Inca cultures is not known.

STATE-CONTROLLED TRADE

Many commodities were under state control, in terms of control of their production, for example coca growing, or in terms of state redistribution of commodities among the populace. There was also much production under state-commissioned enterprise or industry to provide ceramics, textiles, metal objects and even wooden drinking cups for the extended royal household and government officials and their

households. There were also mass-produced everyday goods, such as eating platters, for feeding *mit'a* labourers.

There was undoubtedly a sense of more highly and less highly regarded objects. No commoner in the Inca Empire used the highly carved and painted *kero* cups that were used by members of the royal household, or wore the sort of precious jewellery worn by elite members of society.

Trade between regions in the Late Horizon was state controlled. How far back into pre-Inca times such state control of trade was practised is hard to ascertain. Yet it seems logical that Inca practices were not late inventions. Rather, the institutionalization of regional trade must have been developed in earlier empires and their societies, such as Tiwanaku and Wari in the Middle Horizon, and by the Early Intermediate Period Moche states and the Kingdom of Chimú in the Late Intermediate Period, in the same area. A major reason for the rise of regional kingdoms was competition for control over resources.

In the Inca state no individual, apart from the emperor, owned land. By imperial decree, all land in the empire

Below: Transport in ancient Andean cultures was done on the backs of llamas – useless as draught animals, in mountain terrain, carrying side pouches, they were the ideal caravan animals for Andean trade.

Left: The image of a rainforest monkey in a Moche court represents trade across the Andes to the coastal kingdom – an intricate gold funerary bead, inlaid with turquoise, from a noble tomb.

belonged to the reigning Sapa Inca. The early development of agriculture throughout the Andean Area shows communal effort for survival.

Irrigation structures had to serve everyone and could not be built piecemeal by individuals. Water, whether it came from rivers whose ultimate source was in the distant mountains or from local rainfall, had to be redistributed from a common source across the landscape to fields, or had to be pooled and moved about among extended terracing and raised fields.

Individuals had rights to work the land but not to sell it. Land was owned by, or its use granted to, the *ayllu* kinship groups.

Individual ownership was limited to personal tools and objects – household tools, ceramics, personal clothing and jewellery – procured through barter or acquired as gifts.

BARTER

Local economies were based on local produce from the communal third land division. Goods were exchanged by barter, redistributed according to need and *ayllu* kinship obligation among households, and exchanged in local markets within and between communities. In bartering between individuals, worth was relative and open to negotiation at the time of exchange.

The ancient use of llama caravans confirms the pre-Inca existence of merchants to move goods between regions. Perhaps the Andean development of such strong *ayllu* kinship reciprocity made the need for a monetary system unnecessary. Where goods from one region to another were available under obligatory exchanges between extended relations, there would have been no need to 'buy' things in the Western sense. Local markets continue to be an endemic part of the Andean economy today.

ANDEAN AND INCA ROADS

Roads and trade routes were part of Andean civilization from early times. The spread of religious ideas and the exchange of highland and lowland commodities obviate the use of established routes. Until the Late Intermediate Period and Late Horizon, however, there is less archaeological evidence.

Water transport was also important. While steep mountain streams were un-navigable, the lower reaches of western coastal rivers were. The sea provided the fastest transport, along the coast between Pacific valleys, and boats criss-crossed Lake Titicaca between cities around its shores. Pizarro's second expedition to South America encountered Inca trading vessels from Tumbes off the north-west coast when he approached the northern border of the empire.

Roads and streets defined city and town plans. Roads from outlying residential areas focused on ceremonial precincts. For example, Nazca settlements were linked by straight routes across intervening desert (for example, from the

Below: The Inca road network was expanded from earlier Middle Horizon roads of the Wari and Tiwanaku empires – spanning seemingly impassable gorges with rope bridges.

ceremonial 'city' of Cahuachi to the 'capital' of Ventilla), and Wari settlements featured regular street grids. Anthony Aveni has described many similarities between the Inca road system and the Nazca lines across long distances.

LIFELINE OF THE EMPIRE

The Inca road system was the lifeline of the empire. Its core was based on earlier established routes. Inca roads connected many former Wari and Tiwanaku Middle Horizon cities and former Wari way stations. The Wari Empire was the first to use its road system for state control. Likewise, the Chimú road system was taken over and improved by the Incas.

Inca roads varied between extremes, from formally constructed, paved roads to narrow paths. John Hyslop has identified and traced more than 23,000km (14,300 miles) of Inca roads, and estimates that the entire Inca system totalled as many as 40,000km (25,000 miles). A main highland route ran along the Andean spine from Cuzco to Quito in northernmost Chinchaysuyu; later, an extension ran into modern Colombia. A second 'trunk' road went south, through north-west Argentina and Chile, from

Above: The Rumicolca route was the entrance to imperial Inca Cuzco, through which royal and noble parties and trader goods entered the city.

Cuzco beyond modern Santiago. Two branches circumnavigated Lake Titicaca and rejoined south of it.

A parallel route ran along the coast, tracing a route from Santiago, across the southern deserts, north-west to the pilgrimage city of Pachacamac, then hugged the mouths of north-west coastal valleys before turning inland to skirt the Sechura Desert. After returning to the coast, it looped back inland to Tumibamba to join the highland route to Quito.

Between trunk routes, roads connected major Inca towns and cities, with as many as 1,000 *tambos* (way stations) along them between cities. Several roads also linked the two major roads at intervals, facilitating highland–lowland trade along ancient routes.

CONSTRUCTION

Difficult terrain was avoided whenever possible. Roads followed the lie of the land, staying below high altitudes by traversing mountain passes and skirting swamps and deserts. The wheel was unknown in Andean civilization, and the llama is intractable as a draught animal, so apart from litters to carry Inca and other elites, there were no vehicles. Thus road shapes could be adapted to the terrain. Travel was on foot and transport was by load-bearing llama caravans.

Widths of Inca roads varied between *c*.1m and 25m (*c*.3ft and 82ft), sometimes even wider. Mountain roads were narrow, while coastal roads were normally wider and straighter. Although natural contours were followed, the Incas were remarkable for coping when the shorter route was desired or when they encountered what might seem insurmountable obstacles or chasms. Some roads took direct routes, ascending steep slopes, while others used zigzags to lessen the angle of ascent.

Mountain roads often followed cliff faces, and Inca rope suspension bridges spanned deep chasms, anchored at either end with wood or stone superstructures on stone footings. Constant use required frequent repair, yet some Inca bridges were still in use in the 19th century. In a

Below: The Chaka Suyuyuq, *Governor of Bridges, was an important Inca state official, shown here inspecting a rope bridge in Poma de Ayala's* Nueva Corónica, *c.1615.*

Above: The Puyupatamarca way station ruins are one of many along the 'Inca Trail' to Machu Picchu.

few cases, natural stone bridges were used. In other cases, for example at Lake Titicaca, there were reed pontoons across rivers, sections of lake and wet ground, and sometimes travellers were carried across rivers in baskets on cables. There were also river ferries of balsa wood, reed and gourd-float rafts.

Coastal roads were frequently defined by low stone or mud-brick walls, especially to keep desert sands from encroaching, or by rows of wooden posts or stone markers. Side walls lined routes across agricultural lands, and stone pavements formed causeways and canals across wetlands.

TRAVEL

Settlements and *tambos* along the roads served for lodgings and storage. They varied in size according to need, and also often served as seats of local administration. Large *tambos* were located in towns, while smaller ones were sited, theoretically, at intervals of a day's journey apart (in reality they were anywhere from a few hours' walk to a long day's march).

Traders drove llama caravans to transport exotic items between highlands and lowlands and along the coast, but day-today necessities were obtained in local barter and by imperial redistribution from provincial stores. General touring was infrequent, except for religious pilgrimage (most likely undertaken by designated representatives, i.e. religious leaders).

Religious processions travelled along the *ceque* system, feeding into the roads to and from the provincial capitals for hostage-holding and sacrificial victims.

IMPERIAL COMMUNICATIONS

Inca roads were a means of control, meant to impress subject peoples with Inca power. They were used to move the army from province to province, to move groups of people (*mitimaes*) among the provinces and for royal pilgrimage. Imperial permission was required to travel on official roads.

Imperial communications between the capital and administrative cities was conducted by a system of runners. Roughly every 1.6km (1 mile) along the major roads, huts were built on either side of the route to shelter a *chasqui* messenger. As a runner approached a hut, he called out and the waiting messenger joined him as he ran. The message was relayed orally and perhaps a *quipu* was passed, after which the fresh messenger ran as fast as possible to the next hut. Messages could be relayed *c*.240km (150 miles) a day in this way; a message could reach Lima on the coast from Cuzco in three days. Each runner served a 15-day rotation and the service was part of the *mit'a* labour obligation.

FARMING, HERDING AND HUNTING

The Andean Area is one of several prime areas in the world where peoples observed and learned to control the cycles of natural plant and animal reproduction, thus domesticating a selection of plants and animals and basing their subsistence on them. Throughout ancient times, subsistence agriculture was supplemented by hunting, fishing and collecting wild animals and plants.

From the Early Horizon the bulk of ancient Andean economy was based on agriculture and llama herding. Hunting, fishing and collecting formed important parts of the economy and were more important in earlier times than later.

Hunting became less important because the staple diet was fixed on the principal food crops, and gradually became the sport of the elite. Fishing on Lake Titicaca remained important for the cultures of the Titicaca Basin and on Lake Poopó to the south. The annual sardine and anchovy runs in the Humboldt Current and the migrations of sea mammals provided important protein sources in the diets of coastal cultures throughout Andean history (and still do).

Below: The other protein and vitamin plant food of ancient Andeans was maize. It was first domesticated in Mesoamerica and its cultivation eventually diffused through to South American ancient cultures.

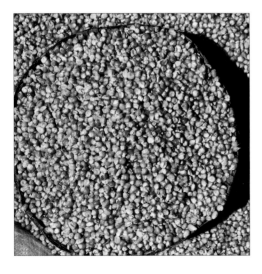

Above: Potatoes were an essential source of carbohydrates and vitamins for Andean peoples, from the collection of wild potato tubers through to their domestication in the Preceramic Period. In winter they were freeze-dried and stored.

Alongside agriculture were the state-organized industries such as textile, ceramic and metal production.

EDIBLE PLANTS

By Inca times a considerable variety of plants and animals was grown, herded and hunted. Principal as a subsistence crop was maize. It was grown both as the staple proportion of dietary intake and for the production of *chicha* beer, used both as a general drink in its weaker form and as an important libation in religious ritual in stronger form.

Other plants were more regional and included potatoes and other tubers (oca and ullucu) in more highland zones, low-altitude tubers such as manioc and yuca, mashwa (a higher-altitude tuber), the high-protein grain quinoa, a variety of beans and also squashes, sweet potatoes, tomatoes, chilli peppers, avocados and peanuts.

Non-edible plants cultivated and/or harvested included coca, cotton, gourds for containers and reeds and fibres for construction and basketry and containers. Tobacco was also grown for medicinal and ritual use. After the earliest phases of domestication, the distribution of these crop plants was primarily altitudinal.

Many plants could be grown in a range roughly from a few metres or yards above sea level to about 1,000m (3,300ft). Others – one variety of chilli pepper, a variety of squash, coca, cotton, gourds, oca, the avocado – were grown in a mid-range zone of about 300–400m (985–1,310ft) above sea level to 1,000–1,500m (3,300–4,920ft). Still others had a much wider range, such as quinoa (28–3,878m/92–12,720ft), the common bean (2–3,700m/6½–12,140ft), potatoes (2–3,830m/6½–12,565ft) and maize (2–3,350m/6½–10,990ft); or a more restricted high-altitude extreme, such as ulluco (an edible tuber, 3,700–3,830m/12,180–12,560ft) and mashwa (850–3,700m /2,788–12,140ft).

Collected plants included wild fruits and many herbs for medicinal and ritual purposes. Eastern forest and tropical hallucinogenic mushrooms were, like

Below: Chilli peppers, first domesticated in the coastal lowlands, added flavour to the staple Andean diet of maize and potatoes.

tropical feathers, traded into the Andean Area. The San Pedro cactus was harvested for its buttons, which are a rich source of hallucinogenic mescaline.

DOMESTICATED ANIMALS

Ancient Andeans domesticated only a few species of animals. The principal herded animals were the llama and the alpaca, both New World camelids. In addition to these, guinea pigs and ducks were bred

in captivity or semi-captivity for meat. Dogs were pets and hunting companions, though were also bred for meat.

Herds of llamas and alpacas were kept throughout the highlands, but formed an especially important part of the Altiplano economy of the Titicaca Basin and to the south of it. Here, vast herds were kept and their needs controlled the rhythm of life. The llama and alpaca were kept principally for their wool and as pack animals, but they also provided meat and sacrificial animals, and their bones were used to make into tools.

HUNTING AND FISHING

Hunted land animals were principally deer and the guanaco (the wild camelid from which the llama was domesticated). The fourth New World camelid, the vicuña, was semi-domesticated – herds were trapped, sheared for their extremely soft wool, and released back into the mountains. Wild birds, both coastal and mountain, were also taken, especially eastern tropical rainforest birds for their colourful feathers, although these were mostly bartered for rather than collected directly.

Fishing and shellfish collection supplemented most coastal people's diets, and surpassed agriculture as the main dietary sources in rich coastal areas in earlier periods. Anchovies and sardines were staples in coastal cultures. Sea mammals, especially seals and sea lions, were also hunted. In addition, there were crabs and a wide variety of shellfish. Shellfish were traded to high altitudes in small amounts, and in Inca times fresh seafood was brought to the emperor in a matter of a day or two by *chasqui* runners. Peoples of the Titicaca Basin made extensive use of freshwater fishing.

Left: So important was maize that it was even rendered in silver by imperial craftsmen. It was both secular, as essential food, and sacred, used to make chicha *beer for consumption in religious festivals.*

Above: Maize planting in September, Quya Raymi Killa *or month of the feast of the moon, depicted in Poma de Ayala's* Nueva Corónica, *c.1615.*

COMMUNAL FARMING

In Inca times, agricultural work was separated into repetitive, modular tasks that could be undertaken in succession in the various plots held by individual households. It seems logical to assume that such practices were pre-Inca, although in the various earliest cultures it is uncertain how communal agricultural practices were.

The evidence for communal activities, revealed in monumental architecture, increases at sites in the later Preceramic Period and especially in the Initial Period. It can be argued, therefore, that if labour forces were marshalled for work on building projects, this must have resulted in a division of labour between farmers and builders by which the latter were fed by the former. Alternatively, building projects might have been undertaken during slacker periods of the agricultural year. Even so, communal efforts in architecture may indicate the same for agriculture.

In Preceramic and Initial Period coastal societies, farming in the valleys was separate from the rich fishing and foreshore shellfish collection. However, the two communities obviously needed to co-operate on a communal basis, especially for the cotton fibre that was essential for fishing nets and other tools.

85

irrigation systems. The communal labour foundations of farming, of labour division in societies practising mixed farming and herding economies and of monument building were utilized in building and maintaining canals and required the development of strict rules of access, probably including designated 'officials' to regulate quantities and timing of access to water.

Competition for water and land frequently caused conflict, sometimes leading to open warfare, of which there is ample evidence during some periods of ancient Andean history. Prolonged periods of drought were especially stressful, and caused conflict and population movements.

TERRACING AND RAISED FIELDS

Increasing the amount of land available for crops was achieved in two ways: terracing and raised fields. The steep sides of mountain valleys and the slopes of lower river valleys were modified to create elaborate systems of terracing, often to the point where some terrace 'fields' were only about 1m (3ft) wide. The Inca are famous for their extensive

terracing, which was necessary to feed a growing population and to provide food for the storehouses as insurance against drought years. The co-operative effort required to build and maintain terraces, and to collect and channel rainwater to them, shows high levels of communal organization, which, as with most such practices, were intensified and formalized by the Inca in their *mit'a* labour tax structure.

The same co-operative efforts were required in draining marshlands by digging canals using wooden digging sticks and spades between plots of raised fields – raised with the soil from the channels. Extensive systems of raised-field agriculture surrounded cities in the Titicaca Basin especially. In drought times, when the water level fell, raised fields had to be abandoned, causing population shifts and even the abandonment of cities in the basin.

Ancient Andean fields were fertilized from two principal sources, depending on location: llama dung was the main source of rejuvenating soil nutrients in the sierra and Altiplano, while coastal peoples collected huge amounts of seabird guano from offshore islands to bring to their valley fields. Fish fertilizer was also used by coastal and lake peoples.

Above: Fishing, both in lakes and off the western coast provided essential protein in the Andean diet from the earliest times – Moche pot of a man fishing with a line and bait.

IRRIGATION AGRICULTURE

As populations increased, the richest lands for run-off water agriculture in coastal valleys and rainfall agriculture in the sierra were brought into cultivation. The need for more land surface for growing became acute in coastal plains, mountain valleys and in the Titicaca Basin. To bring water to land farther and farther from rivers, or to channel it from hillsides to mountain valley fields, prompted the invention of

Right: A Moche pot showing two men fishing from a reed raft with a chicha beer jar placed between them.

The tools of agriculture were primarily wood, stone and base metal implements. Andean peoples possessed no draught animals, but the llama was used as a pack animal as well as for its wool and meat. Agricultural fields were prepared and sown using three simple tools: a foot-plough, a wooden club and a slicing-hoe. The foot-plough was used to break the soil's surface and turn the ploughed chunks of earth. The wooden club was used to break up the clods into finer soil. Further soil breaking, weeding and tending the crops after planting was done using the slicing-hoe, which had a blade parallel to the wooden handle.

Planting was by hand, as was harvesting. Both men and women worked the fields, especially in non-Inca cultures.

Above: Hunting remained a 'sport', particularly for nobility, through ancient Andean cultures even after it ceased to be a major source of food – Moche ceramic bottle with fine-line depiction of a deer hunt.

INCA FARMING

In Inca agriculture, ploughing, planting and harvesting were done by the assembled workforce plot by plot, but each couple in the force worked designated segments or rows in the plot. This practice of segmentation of labour kept the service rendered and thus the obligational returned service clearly defined. Similarly, if several *ayllu* kinship groups worked on a canal-building project, although each built and maintained a designated section, the entire canal gave benefit to the whole community of fields for which it was built.

HUNTING AND FISHING

Ancient Andean hunting was done with spears and the *atl-atl* – a stick with a notched end into which the butt of the spear was rested while the other end was held along with the spear shaft. Use of the *atl-atl* greatly extended the distance and power of the weapon when thrown. The bolas (leather strips with stones tied at the ends) was also used; it was thrown so that it wrapped itself around the prey's legs and brought it down for dispatching with spear, club or knife. Birds were also taken with the bolas, and with slings and snares. The bow and arrow was not an Inca weapon, but was used by semi-tropical and tropical peoples.

Fishing was done primarily with nets thrown from small boats, including single-man reed craft on which a fisherman sat astride. Sea mammals were hunted with spears and harpoons 'riding' such craft. Many Moche ceramic pieces depict seal hunts and sea fishing with nets.

Below: The coast at Quebrada la Vaca, near Chala, where the Incas caught fish.

CRAFT AND CRAFT WORKERS

Specialized craftsmen and women were among the subsidized people of the Inca Empire. Archaeological evidence that some of the best, finest and most elaborate metalwork, textiles and ceramics were produced especially for burials shows that specialists had been employed by pre-Inca states as well, such as the Moche, Nazca, Wari and Tiwanaku, Lambayeque-Sicán and Chimú. Weaving, ceramic and metalworking compounds have been excavated at sites of these cultures and of the Inca.

Other specialized craftspeople included workers in stone (both masons and gemstone artists), feather workers, and carvers of shell, bone and wood (who made, especially, the decorated *kero* cups for *chicha* beer drinking).

VALUED SPECIALISTS
There was a variety of crafts and a high degree of distinction and expertise within crafts. The fact that craftspeople were

Below: This decorated Moche dish rim depicts a scene of two weavers, possibly a mother teaching her daughter to weave, as well as Moche potters' skill in fine-line decoration.

subsidized highlights their valued places in Inca and pre-Inca societies. Cloth and other crafted goods could be given in exchange within *ayllu* kinship *mit'a* and *ayni* exchange obligations.

WEAVING AND WEAVERS
Weaving was a premier specialized craft from very early times. Textiles preserved in Paracas and Nazca graves reveal the use of intricate patterns, depictions of deities and narrative scenes, and numerous colours, showing the care with which they were made. The numerous layers of mummy bundles demonstrate their importance. Many pieces were included in the mummy wrap before being finished – a clear indication that the pieces were planned specifically for burial and were begun well in advance, most likely when the person was in good health.

Weaving was specifically a female craft, although men worked rougher fibres into cord and rope for more utilitarian uses. In Inca times all women wove, from the common women subjects of the empire, through women of elite households, to the wives of the emperor. For commoners,

Above: From its invention, weaving remained an essential task throughout life – an old woman weaving on a backstrap loom, depicted in Poma de Ayala's Nueva Corónica, *c.1615.*

weaving was a craft and hallmark of femininity in which a woman took pride in clothing her family; to the elite, weaving was a symbolic demonstration of femininity, rather than a necessity. Textile production occupied more people and labour than any other Inca craft, and in intensity of labour was probably surpassed only by agriculture.

CERAMICS AND POTTERS
Pottery, once established and spread among ancient Andean cultures, replaced much of the early roles of rough fibres and gourds for containers, although never completely. Beyond its basic role for practical purposes of storage and cooking (the pots for which were homemade, unspecialized and often plain), ceramics soon became more and more elaborate. Pottery began to serve more than just as containers and took on roles within ritual and burial and as an indication of social rank. Some pots must also have had no purpose other than ornament. At the same time, some pottery simultaneously served, consciously or otherwise, as a record of culture by depicting mythological scenes and scenes of daily life as well as holding liquids and food.

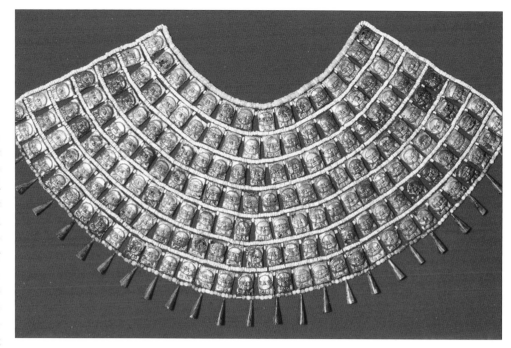

Such increased complexity of design, decoration and use fostered the existence of dedicated potters who could be supplied with food, accommodation and clothing by other members of society. The Incas, and perhaps earlier empires such as Wari and Chimú, established communities of potters specifically to supply uniform vessels. The plates and large, pointed-based, long-necked storage jars used by the Incas in their storehouses to distribute food and drink to *mit'a* workers were uniformly decorated so that there could be no doubt as to the source of the hospitality.

The exquisite craftsmanship of Moche pottery has always stood out among Andean wares. Not only are Moche ceramics a source of narrative information through scene painting on red-on-cream vessels, but also many Moche ceramic

Below: Finely woven Paracas wool textiles in southern coastal Peru reveal trade for Altiplano wool and depict ritual decapitation for the cult of trophy heads. Their complexity and use as mummy wraps involved their preparation through one's lifetime.

pieces are clearly portraiture and depictions of specific rituals, including shamanism, animalistic transformation, healing, combat and sexual acts.

METALLURGY AND METALLURGISTS

A third premier craft in ancient Andean society was metalworking. Exquisite, elite gold, silver, copper and alloy pieces were made from Paracas and Nazca times. Metalworkers flourished in Moche culture and later in the Lambayeque-Sicán and Chimú states – all three successive cultures in the north-west coastal valleys.

Above: A silver pectoral from a Late Intermediate Period rich lord's tomb in the Lambayeque Valley is one of thousands of examples of the superb minute craftsmanship of ancient Andean metalsmiths.

This is perhaps not surprising, as they are geographically the closest to the areas in modern-day Colombia and Ecuador where the earliest, and most elaborate, metallurgy in the Americas developed.

Gold and silver were used extensively, both by the Incas and pre-Inca peoples. These metals were used exclusively for luxury jewellery and ritual objects. They were used both pure and as gilding and plate, and in some cases were even covered with paint. Many specialist pieces, for example gold and silver llama figurines, were made especially for burial with a sacrificial victim. Among the Incas, gold and silver were restricted to use by the nobility. Commoners could use only copper or bronze (a copper and tin, or arsenic, alloy), but the craftsmanship involved in the manufacture of such base-metal objects was no less skilled.

Copper was made into items of personal adornment, such as pins to fasten clothing, pendants, earrings, bracelets and armlets; also for sheet-copper burial masks and for *tumi*, crescent-shaped sacrificial knives. Copper is too soft for tools, so in addition to jewellery, bronze was used to make axes, knives, chisels, pins and tweezers, and the heads for war clubs.

MILITARY SERVICE AND WARFARE

We know little of the pre-Inca armies, except that they were successful in conquering and controlling large areas. The Moche were particularly warlike; the Naymlap legend may be an Early Intermediate folk memory of the invasion of the Lambayeque Valley, establishing the late Moche dynasty by conquest.

EARLY CONFLICT

Early warfare is depicted in stone and ceramics. The more than 300 carved slabs at Initial Period Cerro Sechín have been interpreted as a war memorial. The large slabs, which constitute about 7 per cent of the total slabs, portray a procession of triumphant warriors wearing pillbox hats and loincloths, and carrying staffs and darts. Other slabs show the disembodied remains of the vanquished, and at least one warrior has a decapitated head dangling from his waist. Two slabs carved with banners flank the compound's central gateway.

Are these sculptures evidence of small-scale, seasonal raiding between towns? Or are they commemorating a great historical victory, or a symbolic battle, rather than a specific event? Another view argues that the scene is an elaborate hallucinogenic ritual. One slab depicts toad eggs (representing toads known to carry hallucinogens?). Disembodiment is typical of Andean hallucinogenic transformation.

Cerro Sechín dates to the beginnings of Andean civilized society, when towns were becoming cities, and their locations and spacing across the landscape imply conflict and equidistant positioning in competition for resources, especially water. Early Intermediate Period Nazca pots show battle scenes – complex depictions of intertwined warriors in chaotic mêlées.

RITUAL COMBAT

Moche battle scenes usually depict pairs of warriors, both Moche. They are thought to depict ritual combat rather than scenes of conquest. The Huaca de la Luna walls at Moche, however, and at Huaca Cao Viejo near by, are painted with ranks of armed warriors, leaving little

Above: As well as building an empire through conquest, the Moche had a cult of celebrated 'gladiatorial' or ritual combat, as depicted here on a moulded spouted bottle.

doubt that Moche Sipán Lords, buried with war clubs and other war regalia, were military leaders as well as statesmen. Accompanying tombs include warrior burials, and Moche metalwork frequently depicts individual warriors.

Moche city-states saw frequent conflict. Individual combat scenes may represent minimal battles between rival Moche city-states, much as Black Figure paintings did in ancient Greece. This interpretation is in keeping with the ancient Andean concept of 'essence'.

Left: One of the best-known portrayals of ancient Andean warfare is the Cerro Sechín highland temple of sculpted slabs that forms the wall around the temple complex, including both victorious warriors and the severed heads of the defeated.

The Middle Horizon Tiwanaku and Wari empires were built by conquest. Each expanded within its territory, and maintained frontiers with fortresses. Wari expansion was marked by stone forts with regimented barrack-like planning – for example at Cerro Baúl in the Moquegua Valley and Pikillacta, strategically located in the Cuzco Valley roughly halfway between the two imperial capitals of Huari and Tiwanaku.

ARMS, ARMOUR, TACTICS

Andean warfare was conducted in pitched battles of hand-to-hand fighting, until one side broke. A pair of hammered gold and silver Wari figures portrays imposing warriors holding shields and spear-throwers, wearing four-cornered helmets and geometrically patterned rectangular tunics. Their whole composition

Left: A spouted, polished, moulded effigy bottle of a warrior with his spear and feathered war bonnet – Moche, showing earlier Chavín-style influence.

resembles the rectangular, compartment-like nature of Wari military architecture and is not dissimilar to Inca soldiers in their chequered tunics. A Wari vessel depicts heavily armed warriors kneeling in a flotilla of reed boats, apparently on a raid heading towards Tiwanaku across Lake Titicaca.

Late Intermediate and Late Horizon conflict is demonstrated in Inca legendary history. Typical is the tale of the turning point in Inca history – the defeat of the Chanca and the establishment of Pachacuti's reign. The provincial garrisoned town of Huánuca Pampa near Quito includes both identifiable barracks in the north of the city and 700 storage houses for tribute, army rations and civilian stores.

Weapons were similar to those for hunting: clubs, knives, spears and spear-throwers, slings and the bolas. The bow and arrow was known, but was not an Andean weapon – the Incas employed bowmen from the rainforest. The bolas was thrown at an enemy's legs to bring him down, after which he could be speared or clubbed to death. Warriors carried shields (Inca shields were rectangular or trapezoidal) and wore quilted cotton armour. Inca soldiers depicted in Guaman Poma de Ayala's *Nueva Corónica y Buen Gobierno*, c.1615, wear black-and-white chequered tunic uniforms and are shown in ranked squadrons in battle and storming city walls.

INCA CONQUEST

The success of Inca imperial expansion is undoubtedly the result of superior military leadership and organization. As territories were conquered and assimilated into Inca society, the army increasingly comprised recruits

Above: An Inca warrior presenting a severed head, from Poma de Ayala's Nueva Corónica, *c.1615.*

from conquered peoples. Service in the army was part of the *mita'a* labour tax. Another factor in Inca military success was their catering organization: Inca roads and storehouses for military supplies made deployment in far-flung provinces rapid and efficient.

Some provinces were subdued without battle, the people being persuaded that submission to the Incas was preferable to resistance. Confrontation always ended in defeat, immediately or eventually. Battle against an Inca army resulted in many killed. Inca terms of conquest, either after submission or defeat, were the same – 'fair' but severe. If a city or people submitted without a fight, no one was killed. All land was transferred to state ownership and the Incas gave the conquered people permission to use it. Produce was divided into three parts: for the state (meaning the royal household), for the state religion and for the people. Local leaders were usually retained and incorporated into Inca state structure. Sons of local leaders were taken to Cuzco to be trained in Inca statecraft and policy, and were then made leaders when their fathers died. Similarly, local shrines were left, but idols were often removed to Cuzco as hostages, and could be damaged or destroyed as punishment for rebellion.

CIVIL SERVANTS AND JUSTICE

The division between a royal or imperial household and members of a state civil service is not an easy one. The entourage of the legendary King Naymlap included a number of special court posts whose holders accompanied the king and performed specific duties exclusively for him.

CIVIL SERVICES

Without records, we have no knowledge of pre-Inca civil duties, but can surmise that there must have been some informal or formal organization for urban planning and maintenance. An annual round of religious ceremony must have been in the hands of the priests. Daily secular administration must have been in the hands of citizens appointed by rulers or chosen by the mutual agreement of some members of society (e.g. the 'elders'). As always, these functions in pre-Inca society were obviously fulfilled but until the Incas we have little evidence of how they were organized or performed.

The Incas copied much from those who came before them, as a continuum in Andean civlization's evolution. We can therefore only assume that what little we know of civil administration from the Inca records might also apply in pre-Inca

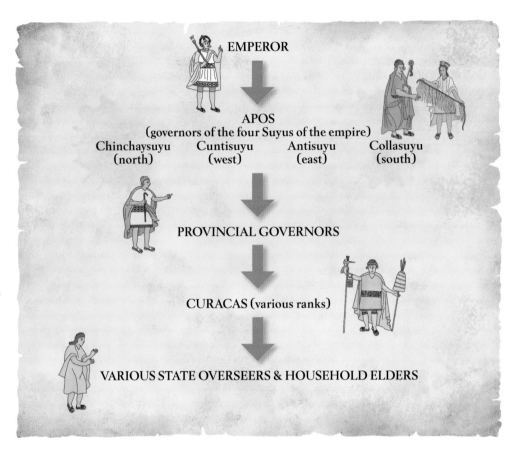

urban society, such as the kingdoms of the Chimú and the Moche, or the empires of the Wari and Tiwanaku.

Many workers in the Inca state economy and social organization, who would be called civil servants in modern Western society, were either appointees of the emperor or draftees of the *mit'a* labour system such as record-keepers, storehouse administrators, road engineers or messenger runners.

GOVERNMENT APPOINTEES

Government posts comprised appointed individuals in a hierarchy based on heredity and/or ability. The highest ranks, the *apo* appointees of the emperor, governed each of the four *suyu* divisions of the empire. Those below them were also

Above: Diagram of the Inca imperial government administrative hierarchy, showing delegation of power from the Sapa Inca *through* apo suyu *and provincial governors, curacas and household elders.*

appointees, as governors of provinces and *curacas* of decreasing numbers of households. The day-to-day regulation of labour was in the hands of household elders.

Other administrative roles included the court historians and record-keepers, overseers in state workshops for the production of pottery, metalwork and textiles, clerks to oversee the collection and redistribution of goods in the state storehouses, and engineers and military commanders. Owners of imperial and noble estates chose their own administrators, which were thus private appointments, but the functions they performed were similar to those of civil servants on state lands.

Left: An imperial Inca prison with prisoner depicted in Poma de Ayala's Nueva Corónica, *c.1615.*

Amautas (historians) and *quipucamayoqs* (record-keepers) were selected from the nobility and their posts became heredi-tary; army commanders likewise. There was formal training for these jobs. Other civil servants were no doubt selected for their skills and aptitudes for the tasks, having been trained on the job. Many were no doubt also hereditary in practice.

RULES
Performing these jobs in Inca society was according to established 'rules', allegedly established by the ninth emperor, Pachacuti, who also decreed the punishments applic-able to each type of crime. There were quotas of agricultural produce, numbers of pots, tools, weapons and jewellery, lengths of cloth, and sections of road, irrigation canals, terracing or buildings set by imperial decree to be fulfilled.

Below: Vilcashuamán was an Inca administrative centre with a large plaza flanked by the Temple of the Sun and with an ushnu *platform.*

Successful fulfilment of quotas, keeping the peace, and efficiency in administering the *mit'a* labour tax was rewarded. Failure was treated by a regime increasing punishment from public humiliation to beatings to execution. There were also prisons for holding suspects and criminals.

ADMINISTRATION OF JUSTICE
Application of Inca law was part of the administrative system and presided over by the *curacas* (officials below Inca provincial governors, in charge of a cer-tain number of households) of the places in which the crimes were committed. Cases involving parties within the same division of 100 households, for example, were ruled on by the appropriate *curaca* of those 100 households; a case that involved individuals from different units of 100 households was presided over by the *curaca* of the 500 households in which the two smaller divisions resided. Trials were normally within five days of being caught; punishment was immedi-ate upon conviction.

Above: Capital punishment by stoning was the ultimate fate of convicted adulterers in Inca society, here depicted in Poma de Ayala's Nueva Corónica, c.1615.

Inca *curacas* were given rewards for doing a good job, but if the opposite were the case, they too were punished. Punishment for laziness might be a public and humiliating rebuke by the provincial governor. Gross misconduct and dishonesty, such as abusing the *mit'a* system or embezzling state property, was punishable by execution.

Punishments for violating the laws were strict and could be severe. They included capital punishment. When the crime was one punishable by death, the case was overseen by the provincial governor rather than by a *curaca*. For if a *curaca* executed a person without the permission of his governor, he would have a heavy stone dropped on his back from a height of about 1m (3ft); if he committed the transgres-sion a second time, he was put to death.

There were no formal courthouses as such, although the open, high-walled courtyards called *kanchas* must have included buildings among those surround-ing their plazas specifically for hearing criminal cases. The *ushnu* platforms in such courtyards might have been used for this purpose.

The Spanish Colonial administration naturally placed Spaniards in the highest ranks of their new government. But at more local levels, like the Incas before them, they continued to use native leaders.

PRIESTS AND SHAMANS

Throughout Andean civilization, priests existed, residing at temples and pilgrimage sites. The oracle above the Lanzón monolith in the Old Temple at Early Horizon Chavín de Huántar must have had priests to act in giving answers to supplicants. Later, the oracle at Pachacamac had similar specialists. From the Initial Period, temple buildings and precincts must have served as places to instruct acolytes into the priesthood by in-service training.

The rich Early Intermediate Period Moche burials, and those of the Late Intermediate Period Sicán-Lambayeque,

Below: A Moche pottery jar representing a shaman holding a wooden stick used to prepare coca balls.

appear to be of priests or lords. Moche ceramics and murals depict several scenes of priests and priestesses administering at ritual ceremonies.

GODS OR PRIESTS?

It is often difficult to tell, however, if the stone sculpture and other depictions in many Andean cultures are of priests or of the gods themselves. For example, the Early Horizon Pukará Decapitator figure depicts a seated male figure, holding an axe and a severed head. His cap is decorated with supernatural faces. He is either a supernatural composite being, or a man wearing a representative mask with a fanged mouth. Similarly, buried at the base of the western staircase of the Akapana temple at Middle Horizon Tiwanaku was a black basalt image of a seated, puma-headed person (a *chachapuma*), also holding a severed head. Another Tiwanaku *chachapuma* sculpture is of a standing figure holding a severed head. Are these representations of the gods or of priests impersonating them?

In early civilizations it seems likely that rulers and priests were the same, or were of the same family. Separate roles were evident in some cultures, however, as shown in the story of Fempellec. This twelfth ruler of the Naymlap Dynasty, sometime in the late Middle Horizon or early Late Intermediate Period, came into conflict with the priests of Chot when he attempted to remove the idol of Yampallec to another city. The story also demonstrates the considerable power of priests in at least this Andean society, for the priests, acting for the gods and in behalf of the people, expelled Fempellec.

RELIGIOUS POWER

The power of religious cults, and thus the influence of priests, is amply shown by the Early Horizon spread of the Chavín Cult. Earlier, the Kotosh Tradition may have been the earliest such regional Andean cult. The cult and priests of

Above: A terracotta model of a shaman with an elaborate headdress from the Jamacoaque culture, Ecuador.

Pachacamac, an oracle and pilgrimage centre that endured more than a millennium on the central Peruvian coast, certainly exercised great power, for they were even recognized and honoured by the Inca emperors. Such was the power of the cult that priests of distant communities solicited the Pachacamac priests for permission to establish branch shrines in their home towns to the creator god Pachacamac. If deemed to have the ability to support cult activities, a priest from Pachacamac was assigned to the new shrine and the community supplied labour and produce from assigned lands to support him and the shrine. Part of the produce was kept for the shrine and

Above: This elaborate hand-painted French wallpaper dates from 1826 and shows the European fascination with Inca sun worship.

the rest sent back to Pachacamac. Such branches were thought of as the wives, children or brothers and sisters of the main cult city.

SHAMANS AND HEALERS

Temple priests were supplemented in local communities by shamans and healers. The careful preparation and mummification of bodies before burial at Chinchorros as early as 5000BC, and at the Paracas and Nazca cemeteries demonstrate their early existence. Many Moche pots portray men and women healers at work, laying on hands and administering herbs and drugs.

Transformation, in which a priest or shaman changed into another being (part-human, part-beast), is a common Andean religious theme. From the Initial Period onwards, wall sculptures, murals and depictions on pottery and textiles show figures in various states of transformation. Some of the earliest are the Initial Period wall paintings of insects with human heads at Garagay, the wall sculptures of shamanic trance at Moxeke and the staged stone sculpture of jaguar transformation in the Early

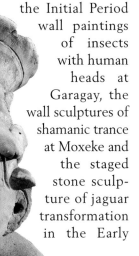

Horizon sunken circular court at Chavín de Huántar. Spiders with human heads were frequently depicted in the Moche and later cultures.

Drug paraphernalia has frequently been found among grave goods, but a unique late 5th-century AD cave burial near Wari is that of a local medicine man, herbalist or shaman. He was accompanied by his tools: a wooden snuff tablet decorated with a Tiwanaku 'attendant angel' figure, a basket with multicoloured, front-facing deity figures and various herbal plants.

PRIESTS AND PRIESTESSES

Inca priests and priestesses were full-time specialists, supported by the state. A third of conquered lands were designated for their upkeep. Such a large portion indicates that there was a correspondent sector in Inca society devoted to state religion.

Inca priests were organized into a hierarchy resembling that of the Inca civil service. Priestly ranking went according to the importance, and thus rank, of the shrine he served. The top priest was a close relative of the emperor, and the high priest of the state cult of Inti (the sun). Each of the chief priests or priestesses of the other five principal Inca deities came next in rank, each housed in a separate *wasi* (chamber) in the Coricancha: Viracocha (creator), Quilla (Moon), Chaska-Qoylor (Venus), Illapa (thunder, lightning) and Cuichu (rainbow). A similar hierarchy existed in each shrine or temple, from the chief shrine priest or priestess down to his or her attendants and trainees.

Left: A lively terracotta figurine of a shaman wearing a headdress decorated with snake heads and dancing during a ceremony of the Bahía culture, Manabí, Ecuador.

CHAPTER FIVE

DAILY LIFE

Most of what we know about the daily lives of ordinary people in Inca and pre-Inca times comes from archaeological evidence. The private lives and education of Inca subjects is hardly commented on in the early Spanish sources, whose authors were more interested in the lives of the Inca emperors and in the workings of the *mit'a* labour tax system and collection of wealth. Native writers, such as Garcilasco de la Vega and Felipe Guaman Poma de Ayala, give some information on daily life, and the 398 drawings in the latter's book show many aspects of Inca life and culture.

Archaeological work has concentrated on the more monumental and central areas of sites, or on wide aerial studies of sites in their settings. Much work also focuses on the art of Andean civilization and on the most spectacular objects. As a result, we know less about the ordinary ancient Andean. We know little of the daily routines followed by most subjects of the empire, except that they must have been taken up by a regular annual cycle required by an agricultural way of life for most people.

For the ordinary citizen, life in Inca times would have been a repetitive round of routine tasks and mutual obligations within one's *ayllu* kinship group, punctuated or relieved by *mit'a* labour tax duties for the state, and by a regular schedule of religious ceremony and festivity. In earlier times, as civilized state societies increased in territorial control, population and administrative complexity, divisions within societies of different tasks created more varied roles for different groups of citizens.

Left: Inca kero *cup showing a man hunting llamas with bolas, a weapon using cords weighted at the ends.*

COMMUNITY, HOUSEHOLD AND ADULTHOOD

Andean society was based around the family household, and family structure and ritual bound society together.

COMMUNITY

From the early farming villages of the Initial Period and Early Horizon, much larger towns, and eventually cities, developed near or around increasingly large and elaborate ritual centres. The building of such sites required some form of civil control and organization of labour on a formal basis, most likely utilizing the forms of kinship obligations that developed in agricultural communities.

Andean cultures did not formally divide state and religion, although as civilization developed there were specialist leaders, rulers, administrators and priests. In everyday life, civil duties and religion appear always to have been mixed in the daily tasks of making a living, seasonal work routines and an annual cycle of ritual and supplication to the gods for prosperity and wellbeing.

Nevertheless, certain sites were devoted to religious and ritual activities, while other sites were the thriving towns and cities of residents engaged in

Below: Silver Inca figurines of an alpaca, whose long, fine wool was used in the finest textiles, a llama and a female votive figure.

day-to-day agricultural tasks, community and state administration and regulation of the economy.

HOUSEHOLD

The household was the basic unit of most Andean societies. Agricultural families were nuclear, but indications are that the formal kinship ties (*ayllu*) described in the sources for the Incas and their subjects in the Late Horizon were developments from much earlier times. Their formulation and development probably began and operated on some scale to regulate labour and economy from the beginnings of village and town life. In Inca society, both men and women lived in their parent's household until marriage.

Daily tasks were planting, tending and harvesting crops, herding llamas, hunting and fishing, making household items, building and repairing houses, irrigation structures and terracing, and making cloth, clothing, jewellery, and weapons and tools.

While men worked in the fields or were away on

Above: Originally spreading to South America from Mesoamerica via the Central American cultures, maize remained a daily staple of the Andean diet.

mit'a labour service for the emperor, the daily domestic chores of cooking, cleaning and washing were done by women. Before the Inca conquest, gender roles were less differentiated: women helped in agriculture, men span, wove and made pottery as well as women.

As inheritance in Inca society was through both the father's and mother's sides of the family, a noblewoman could own land and llama herds in her own right. Women thus controlled a certain proportion of Inca economic resources, but it is unknown how much.

PUBERTY AND ADULTHOOD

A girl's puberty began with her first menstruation, shortly after which a ceremony was held to recognize this life transition. The girl remained in the house for three days, during which she could eat nothing until the third day, when she was allowed some raw maize. On the fourth day, her mother bathed her and plaited her hair. Relatives assembled at the house. The girl dressed in new clothes made for the occasion, came out

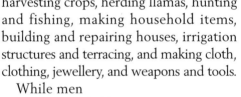

of confinement and served food and drink to the assembly. Her most important uncle pronounced her permanent name and, as at the first-naming ceremony, she received gifts.

Inca boys' puberty was marked by a common ritual, held at age 14 (considered to coincide roughly with the onset of puberty). For commoners, the ceremonies were less elaborate than they were for boys from the Inca royal, noble and elite provincial classes. The principal purpose was to initiate boys as men and warriors, and as proper members of Inca society. The rituals took place over three weeks, requiring preparation during the preceding several months. Mothers made their sons fine garments specifically for the ceremonies.

Below: The popularity of 're-recreating' Inca ceremony and ritual incorporates modern elements (laced shoes and balloons) as well as 'traditional' textiles.

In November, the boys went on pilgrimage to the Inca sacred mountain of Huanacauri, near Cuzco (or a local sacred mountain in the province). Each boy led a llama. He asked the spirit of the mountain for permission to perform the ceremonies of puberty. The llamas were sacrificed by having their throats slit and a priest smeared the blood across each boy's face. Each boy received a sling to signify his warrior status. The boys danced, then performed certain ritual 'chores': collecting

Above: A typical Inca house was open plan with a central hearth and a trapezoidal doorway. Most household activities were performed outdoors.

straw for their relatives to sit on at the final ceremony and chewing maize to ferment *chicha* beer for the ceremonies.

The formal puberty rites took place in December, within the Capac Raymi summer solstice festival. The initiates made a second pilgrimage to Huanacauri, where they sacrificed more llamas. When they returned home, waiting relatives whipped them on their legs to make them strong and brave. The boys performed a sacred dance and drank *chicha*.

After a week's rest, they sacrificed more llamas, were whipped again, and performed a dance atop the hill of Anahuarque near Huanacauri (or other local sacred *huaca*). The boys then raced down the hill's rugged terrain; at the bottom, girls from the same class gave them more *chicha*.

The next task was to walk to several other hills around Cuzco, then receive a loincloth in formal recognition of manhood. The final visit was to the sacred spring of Callispuquio, where initiates were met by relatives who gave them their warrior's weapons: a boy's principal uncle gave him a shield, sling and war mace; other relatives lectured him on the proper male and Inca noble conduct. His ears were pierced for earplugs that marked his status as an Inca noble (or provincial elite) and warrior.

FOOD AND DRINK

The wide variety of early domesticated plants exploited by ancient Andeans provided the basic diet, which was supplemented by hunting and fishing, depending on local availability. Sea fishing and shellfish, for example, were more important at coastal sites, as was fishing at Lake Titicaca and other Altiplano lakes. In the sierra, hunting was mostly for a small number of mammals and rodents after the large game animals of the late Ice Age had become extinct.

FROM HUNTER-GATHERING TO GROWING

In the Archaic Period, hunting and gathering prevailed and at rock shelters and cave sites such as Pachamachay and Guitarrero almost all faunal and floral remains are of wild varieties hunted and collected. Even in the Preceramic Period the wild components of bone and plant remains at sites such as Kotosh, La Galgada, Huaricoto, Salinas de Chao and

Below: The elaborate channelling and distribution of water was essential for Andean daily household use as well as for agriculture. Fountains at Inca Yupanqui's imperial lodge at Tambo Machay.

others, including caves still occupied in the Ayacucho and Calejón de Huaylas, are high.

Coastal sites were able to rely on hunting and collecting of shellfish well into the late Preceramic Period because the coastal food sources were so abundant. Only from the Initial Period onwards, when the domestic flora and fauna remains at sites predominate, can we see the full range of domesticated plants and animals from the physical changes brought through domestication.

DAILY DIET

We cannot know the daily meal routines of pre-Inca cultures. It may or may not be legitimate to project what we know from Inca records back into pre-Inca times.

The principal foods of Andean peoples were maize, potatoes, oca and ulluca (both tubers), quinoa and tarwi (high-protein grains), and kidney, lima and string beans and squashes. More regional staples included peanuts, manioc and mashwa (a higher-altitude tuber). These were supplemented with a variety of herbs as seasoning, especially chilli peppers and mint, and with fruits and nuts (both

Above: An elaborately decorated Inca kero cup depicts a puma or jaguar, an ever-present religious image woven into daily use.

domesticated and wild), including peanuts and cashews, tomatoes, pumpkins, palmettos, pineapples, sour cherries, custard apples, cactus fruits, elderberries, guavas, avocados and an ancient variety of banana. Animal protein, including fish, was available, but the main sources of meat in the highlands were guinea pigs and ducks. Llama and deer meat was also eaten.

Locally, day-to-day meals were fairly staple and monotonous, though redistribution of foodstuffs between highlands and lowlands made it less so. Local markets supplied by traders provided the opportunity to barter for highland and lowland produce. Nevertheless, commerce in the Inca Empire was virtually non-existent because all aspects of the economy were so regulated by the state. Within provinces, people were allowed to have local markets, where they could exchange everyday foods and other items such as tools and common jewellery. Luxury

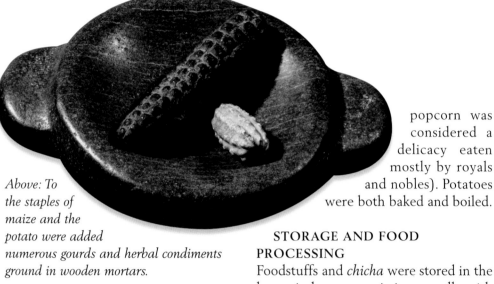

Above: To the staples of maize and the potato were added numerous gourds and herbal condiments ground in wooden mortars.

items and exotic foods, however, were held in the state's monopoly and were produced, collected and stored by the state.

Apart from water, the main drink was *chicha* – weakly fermented beer made from maize and several other plants. Although it was drunk daily, it also played a significant role in religious ritual and in life-stage ceremonies. Bernabé Cobo claims that water was only drunk when no *chicha* was available!

COOKING AND EATING

The Incas ate only two meals a day: a morning meal (8–9 o'clock) and early evening meal (4–5 o'clock). Meals were taken seated on the ground outdoors, with the women facing the cooking pots and sitting back-to-back with the men.

It is not known whether different foods or combinations of foods were consumed for the different meals. Ordinary people ate off flat pottery plates and drank from wooden or ceramic beakers (*kero* cups). Royals and nobles ate and drank from copper, gold and silver plates and cups.

Cooking was done in ceramic pots set on tripods or pedestals placed directly over the fire. Food was both boiled and roasted in the flames. Mixed foods in soups and stews were common as the main dishes. Maize was prepared in several ways, including roasting on the cob, in stews, as a kind of baked or boiled cornbread, and popped (although popcorn was considered a delicacy eaten mostly by royals and nobles). Potatoes were both baked and boiled.

STORAGE AND FOOD PROCESSING

Foodstuffs and *chicha* were stored in the house in large ceramic jars, usually with pointed bases to stabilize them in the ground. Uncooked household storage was kept in attics and rafter space, or in mud-plastered cornstalk bins, or in mud-lined floor-pits. General harvest and main stores were kept in outdoor adobe brick buildings until needed in the house. Maize, peanuts and other grains and nuts were stored dry.

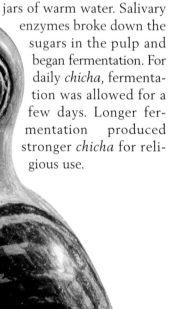

Right: Inca ceramic figurine of a parrot eating a rather plump maize cob or gourd links western coastal food with a tropical import.

Meat, fish and potatoes were freeze-dried for preservation and storage. Freeze-drying was done in the cold, dry winter. Meat (*charqui*) and fish were cut into thin strips, pounded, then left to dry in the sun during the day and freeze at night. Potatoes were soaked in water to soften them, then left to freeze at night; during the day, thawing evaporated the water. Repeated freezing and thawing eventually left the dried pulp (*chuño*). Freeze-drying enabled the Incas to store large quantities of staples in state storehouses (*collcas*) for imperial use and for redistribution, and made food much easier to transport.

Chicha was made by chewing the maize kernels (or other seeds) to split the pulp, then spitting the mash into jars of warm water. Salivary enzymes broke down the sugars in the pulp and began fermentation. For daily *chicha*, fermentation was allowed for a few days. Longer fermentation produced stronger *chicha* for religious use.

BIRTH, CHILDHOOD AND EDUCATION

Birth in Inca society, like all events through life, was considered part of a great cycle. Death was not an end, rather the continuation of the cycle in a different state of being. Other significant Inca childhood events were the first haircut and recognition of the onset of puberty; later rituals were marriage, then death and burial.

BIRTH

There were no special places for birth to take place, and it was not an especially marked event. Women relatives might assist at the time of birth, in the house. A woman simply delivered the child, then took it to the nearest stream to bathe herself and the baby. The newborn child was carried in a cloth sling for the first four days of its life and was then laid in a cradle. It then spent most of its life in either a sling or a cradle until it could walk. Garcilasco de la Vega

Below: As most daily activities took place outdoors, Inca babies were kept warm and close-by swaddled in layers of textiles (month-old baby from Poma de Ayala's Nueva Corónica, *c.1615).*

claims that Inca women never picked up their babies to suckle or play with them, lest they became 'cry babies', but it can hardly be the case that women did not regularly suckle their babies until they could take solid food.

More or less immediately after birth, a woman returned to her daily duties in the household. It is likely that elite women had an easier experience, and there were *yanaconas* (servants or personal attendants) to help at birth and in nursing and raising the child.

CHILD-NAMING

In Inca society, the naming of a child was delayed until it was weaned, at about 1 year old. This was known as the 'first-naming' and was associated with the child's first haircut. To mark the event, the parents gave a party to honour the child, to which they invited relatives and friends. The party included much drinking, music-making and dancing, and must have provided welcome relief from daily routines. The party came to an end when the eldest male relative cut a piece of the child's hair and trimmed his/her nails. Then he gave the chosen name. Other relatives cut locks of the child's hair and presented gifts to it.

The name given at this ceremony was used throughout childhood, but was not considered permanent, for a lifelong name was not given until the child reached maturity, marked by puberty ceremonies. The onset of puberty was considered the

Left: Moche potters depicted every scene imaginable, including this scene of a woman giving birth, helped by two 'midwives', on a stirrup-spout bottle.

end of childhood and beginning of adulthood, and the event was marked by special, different, initiation rituals for boys and girls.

PLAY

There is little evidence of toys, but play must have been part of a child's life, perhaps learning to play a flute or drum, making miniature pots and clothing for figurines, and dancing.

Much of childhood was occupied in learning household activities appropriate and achievable as the child grew up. When strong enough, boys began to help with farming tasks and with herding animals. They also began to learn skills with weapons, both for hunting and for eventually serving in the army, and perhaps accompanied adult men when they went hunting and fishing. Girls helped with the numerous household

Above: Andean boys and girls took on daily chores and daily responsibilities at an early age. This Inca boy depicted in Poma de Ayala's Nueva Corónica, *c.1615, hones his hunting and warrior skills with a sling.*

chores of preparing meals, cleaning, spinning and weaving, and minding younger sisters and brothers.

EDUCATION

There was no formal state education in Inca society, or, as far as we know, in any pre-Inca culture, at least not for all boys and girls. No archaeological evidence can be clearly identified as a place of learning or instruction, although from the Initial Period onwards temple buildings and precincts must have served as places to instruct acolytes into the priesthood by in-service training.

Likewise, the skills needed for farming, fishing, hunting, spinning, weaving, potting, metalworking, construction and any other daily tasks and crafts were basically taught in the home by parents or by practising professionals to novices in workshops or on-site in informal apprenticeships. With no writing system in any Andean civilization, all knowledge was obviously passed on verbally and by demonstration.

There are only four exceptions to this picture. The first two are the Inca state accountants and historians (*quipucamay-oqs* and *amautas*), whose positions were nevertheless hereditary and therefore taught to sons by their fathers. The only

boys and girls who were taught in a 'school' were the sons of Inca and provincial nobles, and the girls chosen to become *acllas* (or *acllyaconas*), 'chosen women' to serve in the state cult of Inti (the sun), and some as imperial concubines or to become 'gifts' in imperial political alliances.

The sons of the nobility (including provincial *curacas*) received four years of education at a school in Cuzco. Their teachers were the *amautas*, who taught them Quechua (the Inca language) in the first year, Inca religion in the second, *quipu* 'reading' in the third and Inca history in the fourth. Learning was by rote through memorization and repetition, and through practice. Discipline was strict and included beatings, although these were restricted to a single beating per day – striking the soles of the feet 10 times with a cane. The principal purpose of this education of the sons of nobles and provincial *curacas* was to indoctrinate them as loyal subjects for when they took up leadership in local administration.

Girls were chosen to become *acllyaconas* at about 10; they were selected from the daughters of conquered peoples. They were first taken to a provincial capital, where they were taught in the *acllahuasi* (house of the *acllya-conas*) cloisters for four years: learning to spin, weave, cook, make *chicha* (beer), and the elements of Inca religion, especially how to serve Inti (the sun). Then they were taken to Cuzco and presented to the emperor, who decided whether they were to enter the Cuzco *acllahuasi*, become

Right: Face markings, an elaborate hat and earrings, and a poised kero *cup in this Chancay anthropomorphic ceramic vessel possibly indicate that the girl is participating in a libation ritual.*

part of the emperor's court (perhaps one of his concubines) or be given in marriage or concubinage to a provincial governor or nobleman.

The daughters of the imperial court and of provincial nobles were also 'educated', although not so formally in a school, rather in the houses of Cuzco noblewomen.

MARRIAGE AND INHERITANCE

Inca marriage was normally monogamous. Such an arrangement was not, however, a legal or social obligation, rather an economical one. A man could have more than one wife but only if he had sufficient wealth to support them and their children. Nobles often took several wives, and the Inca emperor could have as many wives as he wanted. In a glimpse of pre-Inca practice, the tale of Naymlap, founder of the northern coastal dynasty of the Lambayeque culture, mentions among his 'noble company' his wife, Ceterni, and a harem. The wives of some of his sons are also named.

CHOOSING PARTNERS

Inca emperors had the pick of the *aclla* (or *acllyaconas*) 'chosen women' from the cult of the 'Virgins of the Sun', and could also use the chosen women as favours and in marriage alliances with other rulers.

If a man had more than one wife, there was always a distinction between a principal wife and any secondary wives. The distinction was established in the formal

Below: Terracotta figurines of a couple wearing headdresses and with pectorals and earplugs, holding cups, Chancay culture.

Right: Exemplifying the ancient union of marriage on a brightly painted spouted bottle (known as a huaco*) from a Nazca tomb.*

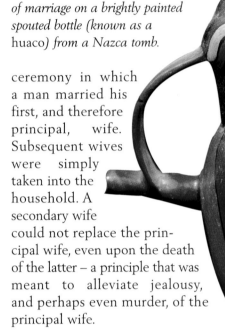

ceremony in which a man married his first, and therefore principal, wife. Subsequent wives were simply taken into the household. A secondary wife could not replace the principal wife, even upon the death of the latter – a principle that was meant to alleviate jealousy, and perhaps even murder, of the principal wife.

IMPERIAL BLOODLINES

In the imperial line, because the Incas believed the imperial *ayllu* had ultimately been founded by, and was therefore descended from, Inti (the sun god), the emperor was considered to be divine. To keep the imperial bloodline pure for purposes of ascent to the throne, therefore, the emperor was also required to have one official wife, the *coya*, who was supposed to be his full sister. The heir to the throne, chosen by the reigning emperor, was selected from the children of their union. The children of the emperor's secondary wives formed the *panacas* (royal *ayllus*). Marriages within non-royal *ayllus* were not obliged to be to sisters because no question of divinity or pureness of descent was involved.

Despite these theoretical 'rules' or laws of imperial descent, by the 12th–13th generations of

Inca rulers, the succession of the death of Huayna Capac (twelfth emperor) was disputed by two half-brothers, Huáscar and Atahualpa, from different imperial wives.

One other curious Inca elite marriage custom was the pairing of noble couples. One Inca source claimed that marriageable young men and women of the highest nobility lined up annually in the main plaza in Cuzco, whereupon the emperor selected pairs and formally married them. It would seem safe to conjecture that pairs lined up such that pre-arranged or hoped-for matches could be achieved.

WIFELY DUTIES

One of the main duties of the secondary wives in a large household was to act as child-carers for the legitimate sons of their husband, both their own sons and the sons of the principal wife. When these sons reached puberty, one duty of the secondary wife was to teach him about sex, including having intercourse with him, although presumably not with her own sons.

And when such a son married, the secondary wife remained in his household and continued with the duties of a secondary wife.

Such complicated arrangements were not the norm among the bulk of Andean society. Inca marriage was usually within one's *ayllu*, as this practice maintained the existing rights, property and obligations of the collective. Related families usually lived near each other in their *suyu* quarters, divided into their two moieties. A woman normally moved into her husband's *suyu* and moiety, but remained a member of her ancestral moiety and lineage. Inheritance was both through the male and female lines. This 'gender parallelism' represents an aspect of the fundamental Andean concept of duality. Men traced their ancestry and birthrights through their fathers, while women traced theirs through their mothers.

MARRIAGE RITES

The marriage ceremony incorporated and ritualized this gender equality between husband and wife. Marriage agreements and arrangements were made either by a

couple's parents or by the couple themselves. The ancestral *mallquis* mummies were often consulted on the suitability of the match, although how their opinion was determined is uncertain. The usual age for marriage was about 25 years for men and between 16 and 20 for women.

The marriage ceremony was simple, if formal. The groom, accompanied by his family, went to the bride's house, where he was greeted and his bride formally presented to him. The groom's family signalled their acceptance of the girl by placing a sandal on her foot – a wool sandal if she was a virgin and a grass sandal if she was not. (Virginity was not a requirement of marriage, although the Spanish sources give no information about how virginity, or otherwise, was determined.)

Left: Chimú polished black bridge-spout bottle showing a domestic scene of a woman with braided hair holding her baby.

Above: Moche potters were not shy of depicting old age, as on this stirrup-spouted bottle of an elderly couple embracing.

Next, both families travelled to the groom's home. His bride presented him with gifts, and the elders of the two families expounded to the couple on the many duties and responsibilities of family life. Once these sober rituals were completed, the wedding was celebrated with a feast and the presentation of gifts to the newlyweds by family members. As a formal acknowledgement of the reciprocal relationship being established in this first stage of marriage, between both the marrying couple and their respective lineages, the bride's parents often signified their agreement by accepting a gift of coca from the groom's parents.

Divorce was not recognized in Inca law, and a man who cast aside his wife was punished and required to take her back.

GENDER ROLES

In the earliest times, we can only surmise and use the example of hunter-gatherer societies of today to reconstruct gender roles. Game-hunting must have been predominantly a male pursuit; gathering while tending children a female role. Coastal cultures, for example, probably combined these occupations seamlessly as men fished and hunted sea mammals from small boats offshore while woman and children gathered shellfish along the foreshore.

However, it is too easy to slip into this apparent 'obvious' division of labour. If children participated in gathering, they would have included both boys and girls, at least up to a certain age. The necessary collection and preparation of materials for building shelters must have been a combined effort by both men and women.

Below: Spinning and weaving were a continuous task for Inca women. As well as the more mobile backstrap loom, large textiles were made on horizontal single-heddle looms.

Similarly, there is no reason to think that spiritual matters – shamanism, divining and soliciting the gods, and medicinal and herbal practices – were the exclusive realm of one gender or the other. In early times of basic survival, roles must have been more mixed, and the group effort as a whole was the most important factor.

Before Inca conquest and their institutionalization of life, gender roles were less fixed. In Inca society, male and female roles became more defined, especially in the primary conception that men were soldiers and women were cloth makers. The elite classes had servants and personal attendants to make life easier, but elite men still served as soldiers in the imperial army and elite women still spun and wove to demonstrate their respective masculinity and femininity.

Spanish sources say more about men's roles than women's, especially about men's obligations under *mit'a* labour, as craftsmen and in the imperial court.

Above: Both men and women performed tasks in the fields. Here men turn the soil with foot-ploughs while women crush the sods into finer soil (depicted in Poma de Ayala's Nueva Corónica, *c.1615).*

MEN'S ROLES

The principal role fulfilled by men in the Inca Empire was their obligation of tax. All taxpaying individuals, that is heads of households, were required to provide someone to work for a certain period of time each year in the state *mit'a* labour system. Inca practice was formalized, but there is every reason to believe that the system was not wholly invented by the Incas.

Evidence from pre-Inca coastal and highland cultures indicates that labour levies were employed for major communal constructions. The makers' marks on the adobe bricks of the Moche Huaca del Sol show that the monument was built by organized gangs of workers using some system of state regimentation of the workforce. Similarly, the regimented nature of Wari architecture indicates that the labour forces that built them were marshalled on a regular basis as and when additions were built at the capital city, provincial cities and fortresses.

The Inca *mit'a* required men to discharge various roles, depending on their individual skills. A man could be drafted into the army, or he could be employed in road and bridge building, or other state constructions. He could serve as an administrator in the state redistribution system, or be a transporter of food and goods to and from them. If he was a skilled craftsman, his services might be employed in the production of metalwork or ceramics for the state. A large proportion of *mit'a* labour was used to work the lands or to tend the llama flocks designated for the support of the imperial and elite households, and of religious cults.

WOMEN'S ROLES

Women were typically in charge of the household. In common households, women performed the principal tasks of child rearing, especially when children were young, and were responsible for preparing meals, cleaning, washing and making cloth and clothing for the family. When old enough, children contributed to household activities. At this time, boys' and girls' roles differentiated and they began to take on traditional gender roles.

A particular role fulfilled by women in Inca and pre-Inca society was spinning and weaving. Cotton was the predominant fibre in the lowlands and wool in the highlands. Spinning was done with a drop spindle and therefore enabled women to spin thread almost anywhere and while otherwise preoccupied. For example, when simply walking between tasks it was possible to keep the spindle whorl in motion while feeding cotton or wool to it from a ball in the hand.

The importance of cloth and the persistent demand for it by the Inca state bureaucracy meant that all women span and wove, from the humblest citizen to the women of the imperial household. Women also played a significant role in religion, one special role being life in the imperial cult of 'chosen women', the *acllas* (or *acllyaconas*). Women also played the principal role tending the temple and in the cult of the Moon.

Left: Service in battle was a principal obligation of Inca men and also in much earlier empires – as shown by this Moche warrior with shield and war club as a stirrup-spouted pot.

Above: Small gardens for growing gourds and herbs and other condiments were tended near the household. The man is offering coca leaves to the woman (note the early adoption of European chickens); depicted in Poma de Ayala's Nueva Corónica, *c.1615.*

COMMUNAL TASKS

On lands designated for the support of commoners, both men and women performed the planting, care and harvest of crops. Hunting and fishing remained men's work, although shellfish collection probably remained a task for women and children.

The nature of *ayllu* kinship ties and obligations shows that much of farm labour and local building activities such as irrigation canals and house-building was accomplished by the combined efforts of men and women, each having roles in the preparation and use of the various materials and tasks involved.

Members of the imperial Inca court and other elite society had an easier life. They could draw upon the resources of private estates and *mit'a* tribute. (They were themselves, of course, exempt from *mit'a* obligations.) Noblemen could also fill command positions in the Inca army or serve as officials in state administrative positions. Priestly positions were also open to them.

CLOTHING AND HAIRSTYLES

People's clothing and hairstyles established their ethnic identity. Among a tribe or nation, differences in style and quality of clothing and jewellery indicated social rank and status. In Andean creation, Viracocha made figurines and painted them with the costumes and hairstyles of different nations. In his wanderings, he assigned distinctive clothing, hairstyles and languages as he called forth peoples and nations from the Earth.

INCA DAILY WEAR
Ordinary Incas wore simple clothing. Women wrapped a large cloth around the body, pinned at the shoulders and tied with a belt at the waist. A mantle was draped over the shoulders and fastened at the front with a large copper pin (*tupu*). Thickened thighs and ankles, considered by Incas a special attribute of feminine beauty, were enhanced by tying string above and below the knees.

Men wore a loincloth wrapped around the waist and groin and a cloth tunic over the body. The tunic comprised a

Above: Elaborate ceremonial hats brought together elements of design and materials from throughout the Inca Empire, as in this wool hat with volutes and stepped-fret designs, and tropical feather adornment.

Below: This tunic of fine alpaca wool, with its elaborate interlocking geometric designs and stylistic feline and crab motifs, would have been worn by a nobleman, and perhaps accompanied him to his tomb.

large cloth folded double and sewn together, leaving slits for the head and arms. Men covered their legs from knee to ankle with wraps of cotton or wool fringes. In the cold, they wore long capes over their shoulders.

Despite its simple design, clothing was usually decorated with symbolic, brightly coloured patterns. Ordinary daywear was decorated with a single band of square designs around the waist and along the lower edge, plus an inverted triangle at the neck. Designs on men's clothing were standardized to signify membership of a particular group – distinct for his *ayllu* or as a member of one of the royal *panacas*.

Footwear for both men and women was sandals, secured with woollen straps tied across the foot. Commoners wore sandals woven from wild plant fibres, or of cotton, llama or alpaca wool. Soles were leather (deer or other animal hide).

HATS
Both men and women wore headdresses, the shapes of which were, in addition to cloth decoration, indicators of ethnic

identity. Inca men wore cloth headbands. Hats were conical or flared cloth pieces, with elite versions being decorated with cloth and metalwork tassels and feathers. Nazca burials include elite individuals with tall, feathered headpieces, revealing wealth and long-distance contacts with sources of brightly coloured tropical bird feathers. Nazca figures on pottery and figurines wear tight, rectangular 'hats', perhaps representing the cloth turbans (wrapped around and over the head with the ends tied in front) found on Nazca mummies.

Moche people wore a variety of helmet-like headpieces. Examples of Wari and Tiwanaku hats are blocky, often cube-shaped, and sometimes have cloth horns at the corners. But such headgear is probably the elaborate wear of ritual, for priests and nobles, rather than common wear.

STYLES AND DISTINCTIONS
There was little difference in style between commoner and elite; quality and quantity were the main distinctions – the cut of the cloth and its fineness, the amount of jewellery and other accoutrements, and the decorative elaboration and materials used. Whereas common *tupus* were copper, nobles used silver and gold ones. Inca and other nobles wore feather headdresses and crowns of silver and gold. Nobles

attached gold and silver ornaments to their sandals, and Inca emperors wore non-functional silver or gold sandals; copper and gold sandals were also found in earlier elite Moche and Lambayeque-Sicán burials.

The Inca emperor's headband was long enough to wrap several times around his head and only he could wear a headband decorated with a fringe of tassels that hung over his forehead, and carry a stick with a dangling pompom.

Inca imperial and other heads of state, and priests, wore clothes cut from the finest textiles, dyed with the richest colours. Only they had access to exotic fibres, such as alpaca and vicuña wool, tropical bird feathers and embellishments of gold and silver thread. Inca elites were especially fond of tropical feather decorations: mantles were sometimes covered entirely in feathers, or in gold, silver or copper discs, to emphasize high social status.

Above: Distinctive ceremonial costumes are also known from decorations on objects, as on this painted kero *cup showing priests or priestesses in ritual dress and headgear.*

PRE-INCA CLOTHING

Inca clothing and jewellery reflects what was worn in earlier cultures. The fine clothes and featherwork of the Lords of Chimór (Chimú) are especially notable. The elaborate wraps of Paracas and Nazca burials and the costumes worn by figures on pottery, murals, metalwork and stone sculpture must be viewed with caution regarding everyday wear. Much of the special cloth and headgear in burials is costume for special occasions – burials, ritual ceremony or battle gear – or is worn by representations of deities. Interestingly, Viracocha (Creator) is described as wearing a simple, rough cloak or even rags!

SPECIAL COSTUME

More elaborate, special costumes, styled on the themes described above, were made for special ritual occasions.

Left: As well as garments, llama wool and elaborate patterns were applied to utilitarian accessories, such as this Inca coca leaf bag with opposing rows of llama figures.

Jewellery was worn mostly by nobles. Inca women wore *tupus* and necklaces. Men wore little or no jewellery, but the insignia of Inca nobility was the large earplugs given at puberty. These were round, about 5cm (2in) in diameter and held by a shaft through the earlobe. They were made of copper, silver, gold or metal alloy, or stone. Men also wore metal bracelets.

Men who showed particular bravery in battle were awarded metal discs to wear around the neck. They often donned necklaces of the teeth of their human victims. The Incas also painted their faces in mourning, and Inca warriors wore warpaint into battle.

HAIRSTYLES

Inca hairstyles were simple: men cut their hair short and bound it by a cloth headband, whereas women grew it long with a central parting. A woman cut her hair only in mourning or as a sign of disgrace. An Inca girl grew her hair throughout childhood, for at the onset of puberty it was braided by her mother on the fourth day after her first menstruation, as one of the signs of her transition to adulthood.

CRIME AND PUNISHMENT

Inca life was highly regimented, both because the general necessity to make a living took up most of people's time, and because the state regulated most activity in some way or other. Such must have been the case in pre-Inca cultures as well. There would consequently *seem* to have been little crime as we know it.

THE LAW

There was, however, Inca law, and pre-Inca societies undoubtedly had social rules, the transgression of which, if discovered, entailed punishment of some sort by the state or by one's peers. No archaeological evidence can be definitively ascribed to a crime or punishment. Even the gruesome treatment of the individuals in some Nazca graves seems to be religiously motivated rather than owing to criminal punishment. (At Cahuachi some men, women or children had their mouth pinned by cactus spines or tongue removed and placed in a pouch, or had their eyes blocked, their skull perforated for threading on a cord, or even excrement inserted into the mouth.)

There is a hint of such control, inevitably involving religion, however, in the famous tale of Fempellec, the

Above: Incarceration was one option for crime: the so-called prison buildings at Machu Picchu, possibly also used to hold noble captives for ransom.

ambitious twelfth descendant of the conquering king Naymlap of the northern coastal valleys. Fempellec attempted to remove the greenstone idol of the state dynastic god Yampallec from the capital Chot to another city. The cult priests, however, heartily disapproved of this sacrilegious act. A demon appeared (conjured up by the priests?) in the form of a beautiful woman, who seduced Fempellec – an act that caused 30 days of rain followed by a year of drought and the inevitable crop failures and famine. In retribution the priests seized and bound Fempellec, then threw him into the sea and left him to drown. Such rough justice probably represents a moral tale about what respect is owed to the gods and the consequences

Left: Punishment for crime was scaled not only according to the crime, but also according to social rank – the higher your rank the more severe your punishment. Plucking out an eye was one punishment for treason (from Poma de Ayala's Nueva Corónica, *c.1615).*

that can be expected if they are not honoured. The gods wreaked punishment on the people, and the priests exercised their punishment on the person responsible for the 'crime'.

APPLICATION OF LAW

Inca civil law applied to various social and state activities. Pachacuti Inca Yupanqui (tenth emperor, 1438–71) is credited by Garcilasco de la Vega with having set down basic Inca law, including punishments for blasphemy, patricide, fratricide, homicide, treason, adultery, child-stealing, seduction, theft and arson. Inca law governed tribal rights and obligations to the empire, the division of land and other property, the system of work rotation and the *mit'a* tax system. (The basic laws were few: laziness, lying, stealing, murder and adultery were crimes.) It also applied to

Above: Pachacuti Yupanqui, tenth Sapa Inca, is credited with setting out the basic Inca laws in the 15th century after his successful defence of Cuzco and defeat of the Chancas (oil on canvas, 18th-century 'Peruvian School').

proper conduct as an adult and as a married man or woman and the treatment of others, including the support of the elderly and disabled.

PUNISHMENT

There was a different punishment for every crime; but the punishment meted out to the perpetrator was scaled according to his or her social rank: the higher the status of the individual, the more severe the punishment. For example, although virginity was not a requirement of marriage, adultery by a commoner was punished by torture. But if a noblewoman committed adultery, both parties of the

crime were put to death. A common punishment was beating with a stone club, sometimes to death. Other methods of execution were to be thrown off a cliff, or to be hung over a ravine by the hair until the roots gave way. A slovenly housewife was made to eat the household dirt; a husband who did not keep a tidy house had to eat dirt or drink his family's dirty bath water. Laziness was punished by whipping; chronic laziness by death.

CAPITAL PUNISHMENT

In a state that so highly regulated the collection and redistribution of property (the foodstuffs and materials produced under state organization), it was inevitable that a crime against the government was dealt with especially severely. Stealing from fields, whether they were state, religious or commoners' lands, was punishable by death. The same applied to theft from llama herds or from state storehouses.

It was rare for an Inca citizen or subject to be without the basic necessities of life. Therefore maltreatment of the elderly or disabled, to whom one would owe obligations in the *ayllu* kinship system, would be harshly dealt with.

Divorce was not recognized. A husband who cast aside his wife was forced to take her back; doing so again brought public whipping; a third time meant execution by clubbing or being thrown off a cliff.

Treason was punished by imprisonment, which almost always resulted in death. The traitor was thrown into an underground cell filled with venomous snakes and dangerous animals in Cuzco.

In addition to the basic laws of the land, the Inca emperor was entitled to enact new laws to suit his needs and new occasions. For example, Pachacuti is credited with decreeing that only princes and their sons could wear gold, silver and precious stone ornaments, multicoloured feather plumes or vicuña wool.

Below: Adultery was a serious crime: commoners were tortured, as depicted here by Poma de Ayala, c.1615; nobles who committed adultery were put to death.

MUSIC, DANCE AND RECREATION

We do not know what ancient Inca or pre-Inca music sounded like. The Peruvian or Andean panpipe music that became popular in the latter half of the 20th century cannot be taken as representative of pre-Hispanic Andean music for two reasons. First, accompanying guitars, and probably the harp, are post-Spanish Conquest introductions; second, new rhythms, melodies and musical concepts from European and other cultures have inevitably influenced it in the 500 years since the Spanish Conquest.

There is undoubtedly some continuity, however. The so-called Peruvian panpipes have an ancient Andean history and thus at least physical continuity. Andean rhythms are also distinctly different from Western European cadences, and might also reflect continuity. But we have no written examples of Andean music, so cannot be certain.

THE INSTRUMENTS

Archaeologists have found examples of instruments dating from at least the Early Horizon. There are Paracas and Nazca flutes, resembling modern recorders. Flutes were the only instrument in general use throughout the Andes. Panpipes comprise joined pottery or cane flutes of different lengths to produce different notes and tones. Ancient pottery examples differ from modern panpipes in that they have closed ends; thus sound is produced by blowing across the tops rather than through them.

Seashell trumpets were also used, different sizes and shapes producing haunting single tones. Moche pots, for example, depict figures blowing conch trumpets. Among the entourage of the legendary Naymlap is one Fonga Sigde, 'Blower of the Shell Trumpet'. Finally, there was a variety of percussion instruments: drums, tambourines, bells, rattles, and clackers of animal bone and wood.

THE ROLE OF MUSIC

Ancient Andean music and dance appears to have been predominantly for ceremony, played at special occasions for specific purposes, rather than as pure entertainment, although they undoubtedly gave participants and onlookers pleasure. Music formed a central role in Nazca ritual, as depicted on wall paintings at Cahuachi. Ritual processions along Nazca line figures were probably accompanied by flutes, drums, bells and trumpets.

Moche music appears to have been primarily associated with religion, sacrifice and war. Moche pots frequently

Above: Music and dance were frequently portrayed by the Moche in pottery, as here in this flute player effigy stirrup-spout bottle.

depict groups of musicians – principally flute, trumpet and drum players – as part of ritual combat and sacrifice scenes, and shamanism. Copper, gold and silver bells were attached to the metal plates covering the body of the Sipán Lord burial, and the accompanying burial of one of his ritual assistants was evidently a panpipe musician. The Moche associated the peanut with flute-playing.

Moche flutes and rattles in the handles of ritual vessels were for trance-inducement. Drums were used in religious ritual, and may also have been used to set a pace for weaving – a drum was found in the Pampa Grande textile workshop.

Left: A Chimú bottle with a group of musicians around the spout, showing a panpipe player flanked by two percussionists with gourd drums.

Inca music accompanied dance at festivals and initiation rites. It was also important in 'entertaining' labourers who worked on Inca engineering and agricultural projects. Gifted individuals were also trained as royal court musicians, and it is recorded that some players played several flutes together to extend the sound range. Flutes were also used for love songs, and drums, trumpets and flutes accompanied Inca armies on the march.

STRANGE MUSIC

Curiously, some Late Horizon Chimú double-chambered vessels, the two parts connected by a bridge, produced a whistle. The liquid level in the chambers changes tone, which escapes from a hole at the top of one chamber.

The tonal qualities of water for religious inspiration were also appreciated at Chavín de Huantár. Running gushing water around the interior conduits of the chambers of its labyrinthine temple produced an awesome roar from the door (mouth) of the temple that was heard by the assembled worshippers in the courtyard outside.

THE DANCE

Inca dancing was restricted to ritual occasions: seasonal festivals in the agricultural year, to accompany religious ceremony,

and at life-stage recognition. The idea of social dancing did not exist. Such was undoubtedly the purpose of dance in pre-Inca cultures as well.

Inca dance was formal, with participants performing a series of specific movements in unison. Special dances were performed by men (for example at puberty rites), and women (for example at harvesting rituals); other dances involved both sexes. When *mallquis* mummies were brought out to participate in the ceremony, songs and dances were performed before them, and stories of their exploits recited.

RECREATION

Almost nothing is known about ancient Andean 'leisure' activities, probably because there was little time for anything other than the necessary daily tasks. Even ritual dancing, singing and music were considered essential for life and wellbeing rather than recreation or entertainment. Children began to fulfil daily tasks as soon as they were capable.

Chicha beer drinking on ritual and ceremonial occasions could obviously *de facto* become 'recreational'.

Left: Drums made of wood, pottery, gourds and stretched hide were also common instruments for ritual and dance ceremonies. This Moche stirrup-spout bottle is in the shape of a drummer with his bone or wooden beater, his hat held with a chin strap.

Above: Various pipes and flutes were the most common instruments. Sets of pitched panpipes were made of both pottery and reeds bound with twine or decorated textiles, such as these Nazca examples.

Inca children played with balls and tops and at games using rounded pottery pieces for markers and counters. Adults played a dice game with five, rather than six, numbers. There were also board games that used bean counters. The Incas also gambled, often for high stakes. Inca nobles played a game called *aylloscas*, in which entire estates were wagered. We do not know the rules for any of these games.

Warfare being so important in Inca society, boys were 'trained' in games of skill intended to test them and make them brave and tough. There were races and mock battles that were taken with such seriousness that severe injuries are recorded.

Nothing is known of recreation in pre-Inca cultures, except perhaps the ritual combat of the Moche, in which individuals had lifetime careers. This was a deadly profession, however, for religious purposes and sacrifice.

By Inca times, hunting was mostly recreational. It broke the monotonous routine of agriculture, and also had the outcome of providing meat. Hunting by Inca and provincial noblemen was surely recreation for them.

DEATH AND BURIAL

Death in the Andean world was not considered the end of existence: it was the next stage or state of being after life on Earth. Archaeological evidence of elite and common burials shows that elaborate preparations were made, almost throughout life, for this next state of being. Moreover, the Andean worldview applied this belief to all living things – humans, animals and plants – and to the Earth itself as a 'living' entity.

LIKE A PLANT
Anthropologist Frank Salomon describes the Andean outlook on life's cycle as a "pervasive vegetative metaphor". Plants provide a metaphor for human and animal life as they progress from tender shoots through firmer, resilient stems and plants, then mature, rigid, but drier plants, and finally to a desiccated state – just as humans progress from newborns, through infanthood, puberty, young adulthood, old age, and death, though enduring as mummies. The mummified body was likened to a dried pod from which seeds of new life dropped.

ELITE AND COMMON
Burial and afterlife, however, varied throughout Andean civilization. The greatest contrast is in the treatment of elite members of society and common people. The rich burials of nobles and priests in Moche-Sipán and Lambayeque-Sicán tombs and the elaborate burials of some Nazca dead, for example, contrast with simpler interments in common graves with a few tools and pots.

PRESERVING THE BODY
The Initial Period Chinchorros and La Paloma peoples of the Chilean

Above: A Nazca mummy bundle, the final wrapping being a plain woven shroud bound with cord.

coast show attempts to preserve the actual flesh in addition to the soul or essence of 'life'.

In the Early Horizon and Early Intermediate Period, the unfinished states of some Paracas and Nazca mummy textile wraps show that they were being prepared long before, and in anticipation of, physical death. Paracas and Nazca elaborate burial procedures show that considerable care and planning were involved. Nevertheless, burial in tombs removed the bodies from the living. Ancestor worship or honour was evident in these cultures, as demonstrated by the care of burial and by the fact that most tombs were reopened periodically to place other kin members inside

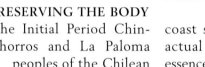

Left: A bulky Paracas mummy bundle with effigy face and feathered cap – the higher your rank, the more elaborate the bundle and textile patterns.

Above: On the southern Peruvian coast, the Nazca are noted for deep, mud-brick-lined tombs, ancestral vaults, which they reopened for successive burials through generations.

them. Late Intermediate Period people in the Titicaca Basin placed their mummies in special burial towers – *chullpas* – as sepulchres meant to be reopened periodically for the deposit of other mummies.

Other cultures, however, treated their mummies differently. Chimú mummies of deceased rulers were housed in their own compounds, within a virtual city of the dead, within a city of the living. Each compound housed a living retinue to look after the dead ruler's remains, perform rituals respecting it, and collect food and other goods for daily life.

Inca mummies were kept very much as a part of the lives of the living. They were visited regularly and brought out on ritual occasions. They were consulted for advice, honoured with recitals of poetry and stories, and even 'fed' on ritual occasions.

PACARINA

Andean cultures believed that the essence of a dead person ultimately went to a final resting. The physical body was only a vessel for this life – the person's 'vital force', or soul, found its way to *pacarina*. *Pacarina* was the place of origin of one's ancestors and the ultimate source of rebirth. It could be a tree, rock, cave, spring or lake – a magical shelter from the world's ravages.

There were different names for *pacarina*. The people of Collasuyu and Cuntisuyu called it Puquina Pampa and Coropuna. Documents from Cajatambo call it Uma Pacha; and the peoples of the Lima region called it Upaymarca. Coastal peoples named the 'Island of Guano' as the final resting place.

Of common belief was a final resting place of farms, where the dead sowed their seeds. The spirit continued to tend the fields and crops, and to experience thirst and hunger as the body does on Earth, and so was fed by the living with offerings of food and drink. Those still living nevertheless also considered the spirits

of the dead to be dangerous. It was thus necessary to help the dead person's soul reach the end of its journey, lest the spirit wander among the living causing violence, sickness and accidents.

SACRIFICE

Death by ritual sacrifice was a special form of death and burial that was practised throughout Andean civilization. Human and animal sacrifices were performed to honour and supplicate the gods, commemorate the building of temples to them and appease the forces of nature. Decapitation, bludgeoning and strangulation were common.

Moche ritual combat was a special form of sacrificial death, as was the Inca practice of sacrifice and burial on remote high mountaintops. Another Inca practice was deliberate exposure to lightning, and if killed by it, burial of the *qhaqha* (lightning victim) at the place of death.

Below: Ancestral sepulchres were common in Andean cultures from early times. The Collao are famous for their stone chullpa towers, one group of which is at Sillustani near Puno, Lake Titicaca.

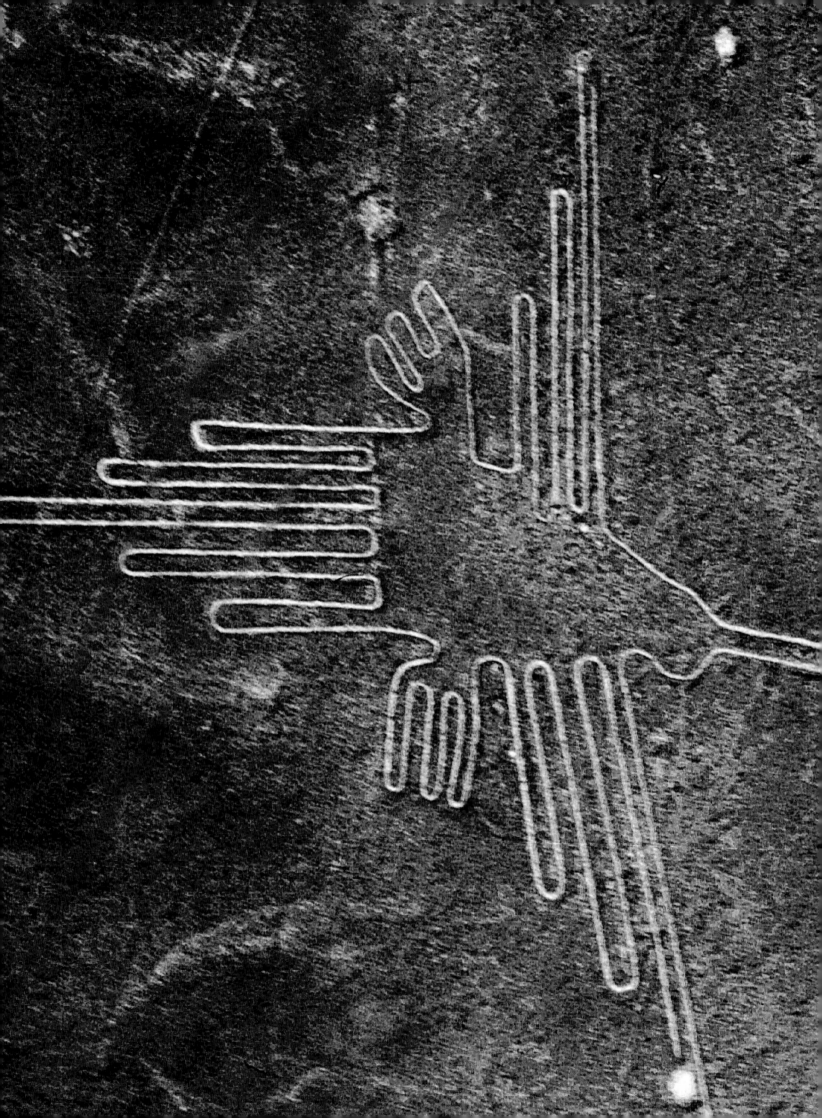

CHAPTER SIX

RELIGIOUS BELIEFS

Ancient Andeans' cosmogony and cosmology – their stories of how the world came into being and how it worked – helped them cope with the events of everyday life and with the periodic stress they faced in what was to them a sometimes unpredictable environment. The ancient Greek word *cosmeo* means 'to order or arrange', and incorporates the idea of 'good order'. Not surprisingly, then, ancient Andean mythical explanations of their cosmos and its origins put them in good order.

Astronomical observations, especially of the sun, moon and Milky Way, revealed to ancient Andeans a regular relationship between solar and lunar cycles and the seasons. Their observations enabled them to create a calendar, regulate their religious ceremonies and plan their work. Irregularities, such as natural disasters, were less understood because they appeared to be unpredictable. They were regarded as punishment by the gods for wrongdoing.

The gods created the world and divided it into its parts: the world of the living (the Inca *Kai Pacha*), the world above (*Hanan Pacha*) and the world below (*Uku Pacha*). Overseeing all was a supreme god or being (with various names, the two most common being Viracocha and Pachacamac), and a large pantheon of other deities. This world worked and was in good order because the gods made it so. The reciprocal part to be played by humans, in order to keep the world in good order, was proper deference to and worship of the gods.

Left: Symbolism and ritual pathways were a hallmark of ancient Andean religion, as in this Nazca hummingbird geoglyph.

BELIEF SYSTEMS AND LITERATURE

Without the favour of the gods, life could be difficult. At a daily level, religion permeated every aspect of Andean life. Thought about how the world was created and humans' place within it is evident in early burials, within which everyday items were included, presumably in the belief that the buried person would need them in some sort of afterlife. The careful treatment of bodies, attempting to preserve them, or to clothe and prepare them for burial in other special ways, shows that a belief in an afterlife had developed in Chinchorros, La Paloma, Paracas and other early cultures, and continued into Inca times.

RISE AND INCREASING COMPLEXITY

Religious beliefs became formalized alongside an increasing complexity in social and political organization. Imagery of deities representing the forces of nature and creation increased as religion developed its own organizational status within the state. A separate hierarchy of

Below: The Chincha in coastal Peru, one of many Inca conquests, had a shrine at La Centinella, a characteristic adobe brick temple mound forming the focus of an urban ceremonial centre.

individuals became dedicated to looking after the appeasement of the gods as intermediaries between the deities and the common people. Elaborate histories, now called mythology, developed as accepted explanations of how the world came into being, how humans were created, and what constituted proper conduct towards the gods.

The gods controlled the forces of nature and were believed to be responsible for events that brought benefit and wellbeing to humans, as well as disaster and hardship. It was therefore believed necessary to plead with them and make special efforts to solicit their approval. Specialists with powers and status that enabled them to negotiate with the gods on behalf of humans had to be provided for. Their needs (or demands) became substantial. In the Inca Empire the produce from a third of all lands was given for the upkeep of the state religion.

PRIESTS AS INTERMEDIARIES

Priestly communication with the gods was through trance-like states, even shape shifting (it was believed), to solicit guidance and sacred favour; conducting ritual and sacrificial offerings (animal and human) to the gods; and making images of them in stone, pottery, wood and

Above: Many Andean beliefs in natural deities endure. A 20th-century Aymara couple here prepare offerings at the Huaca of Mount Illimani.

metal, which were housed as idols in special temples. Priests also gave instruction and guidance to individuals and groups at mass ceremonies through omens and oracles.

Ceremonies to honour the gods became increasingly elaborate as Andean civilization evolved. The course of the seasons, regulating daily and seasonal patterns of life and work, together with observations of the heavens and the regular movements of celestial bodies, fostered the development of a cycle of rituals performed on specific dates. These included the solstices and equinoxes, and were co-ordinated with human lifecycles through the stages of birth, childhood, initiation into adulthood and death.

SACRED PLACES AND SPACES

Natural and man-made sacred places were numerous and varied. Mountains, bodies of water, springs and the sky were all sacred in their own right. In them and on them the gods were thought to dwell or be embodied. The term *huaca* (Quechua) was applied to any sacred location – natural, man-made or a

modified natural place – embodying the spirit of a deity, and where offerings were made: caves, islands, springs, outcrops of rock, mountains, a boulder or pile of stones, even a field in which a significant event took place. The term *apu* (literally 'lord' in Quechua) was used for sacred peaks in a land dominated by prominent volcanic cones.

Designating space and building special structures for ceremonial performances began early. A Y-shaped structure was built on one side of the village at Monte Verde some 14,800 years ago. It had a raised, sand and gravel floor and associated artefacts differentiating it from the ordinary houses. These included clay-lined braziers at the rear of the hut,

Below: Diagram of Yana Phuyu *(the 'Dark Cloud' constellations): animal shapes seen by Andean peoples in* Ch'aska Mayu, *the 'celestial river' of the Milky Way.*

medicinal plants and chewed leaves, seeds, hides, animal bones and apparent burnt offerings.

In time, all Andean cultures built large, elaborate structures and enclosures for ceremony and worship. Different forms were combined in ceremonial complexes within cities, or in the landscapes around them. There were raised mounds, pyramid-platforms for supporting temples; sunken courts (round, square or rectangular); labyrinthine buildings or complexes housing images of the gods; walled sacred compounds; and geoglyphs or designated routes laid out on the ground, such as the Nazca lines and figures, and Inca sacred *ceque* site lines and routes.

SACRED LITERATURE

The only ancient Andean literature known is Inca. However, the recurrence in Chimú and Inca culture of the story of the 'Revolt of the Objects' (graphically

Above: The Ponce Monolith at Tiwanaku, believed to be a petrified member of a former race of giants, is representative of Andean belief systems featuring successive ages of creation.

depicted in Moche murals at the Huaca de la Luna) reveals that this tale had been told for at least a millennium!

Inca literature was oral, and mostly dealt with religion and history. There were stories, legends, songs, poems and doctrines. Being passed down verbally, they were subject to variation and personal interpretation. Few examples survive because so little was recorded or translated by Spanish officials. On the contrary, they resolutely destroyed it as idolatrous.

There were four categories: religious prayers and hymns, dramatic histories or legends, narrative poems, and songs. Prayers and hymns praise the gods and goddesses. Only two dramatic pieces survive, as poor translations. Narrative poems, memorized for recital at public ceremonies, almost all concern religion and histories of the emperors. Dramatic pieces, also emphasizing religious themes, were performed at dances, recited by one or two 'actors' and a chorus. Poetry and song (the former set to music) were mostly love songs.

YUTU
(tinamou-partridge)
SOUTHERN CROSS
HANP'ÁTU
(toad)
YACANA
(adult llama)
MACH'ÁCUAY
(serpent)
ATOQ
(fox)
UÑALLAMACHA
(umbilicus of llama)
YACANA
(baby llama)
SOUTH POLE
CH'ASKA MAYU
(celestial river –
Milky Way)
YUTU
(tinamou-partridge)
(13° 30' SOUTH)
DECEMBER
SOLSTICE SUNRISE
DECEMBER
SOLSTICE SUNSET
MISMINAY
(13° 30' SOUTH LATITUDE)

YANA PHUYU
(DARK CLOUD CONSTELLATIONS)

COMMON THEMES AND CONTINUITY

Religious beliefs about how the world worked were the enduring matrix that bound Andean civilization. Concepts that developed in Preceramic times continued, with cultural distinctiveness and elaboration, through to Inca times.

NATURAL AND RELIGIOUS CONTROLS

Ancient Andeans believed that natural forces were created and controlled by the gods. With so much of daily life and survival bound by the landscape, the ancient Andean worldview reflected the landscape by adhesion to it and through a sympathetic harmony with it.

Andean cities and, before true urbanization, the earliest ceremonial complexes of the Preceramic and Initial periods, maintained their relationship with the natural world not only through their physical configurations and economic viability but also through their religious institutions. Priests and shamans mediated society's ties to nature and relationships with the gods.

URBAN FOCUS

Ceremonial complexes and, later, religious precincts in cities were the focus for religious activities. Cities and buildings

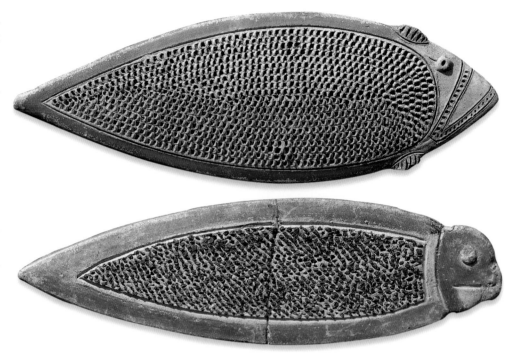

Above: Aquatic themes were common in Andean art, here exemplified by two fish carved from manioc (cassava) husks, La Tolita culture of Ecuador.

were oriented according to sacred concepts. Astronomical orientations sometimes guided routes and alignments. Temples and pyramid-platforms frequently faced sacred mountains, and sometimes even mimicked their contours

or profiles. Canals brought water to cities from holy springs. Even the plan of Cuzco, a crouching puma, honoured a revered animal.

Common architectural forms endured throughout ancient Andean history. The raising of tiered platform mounds began as early as 6000BC at Nanchoc in the Zana Valley. The combination of platforms and sunken courtyards, and the U-shaped configuration of temple complexes begun in Preceramic Period cultures, continued to the Late Horizon. Open plazas hosted large ritual gatherings, while enclosed courts were for more intimate worship. Sacred lines, predetermined pathways in the deserts and walled complexes, including sunken courts, controlled people's movements and directed them into ritual patterns. Windowless chambers and hidden passageways accommodated exclusive ritual and promoted mystery and power.

Left: Mount Parinacota, Chile: the permanence of the landscape was revered in the animism of mountains especially, each of which had its own huaca or spiritual essence, or was dwelt in or on by a deity.

Open ceremonial space was juxtaposed by elements of hiddenness and obscurity: temple interiors and ceremonial compounds could be labyrinthine; oracles were housed in dark inner chambers; some ceremonies were performed by and for specialists only; sunken courtyards restricted numbers and obscured or regulated ritual.

These structures and activities were designed to ensure a proper relationship with the gods and nature. Offerings were made of the most precious objects, including the lives of animals and humans offered in dedication, honour and placation.

SUPREME BEINGS

A distinctive principal deity or creator being is recognizable in most cultures or regions. Mountain deities naturally predominated in highland cultures and sea gods in coastal valleys, yet early widespread contact between highlands, coasts and tropical forests spread more universal themes, even if imagery was culturally distinctive.

Below: Crustaceans were a common symbolic theme on Andean pottery and textiles. Here prawns are featured on a Nazca bridge-spout bottle.

The supreme deity at Chavín de Huántar, represented in the Staff Deity, was widespread in the Early Horizon, and could be male or female. The evolution of this supreme deity through several hundred years of the Chávin Cult incorporates combinations of feline, tropical cayman, serpentine and avian imagery.

Sky deities or attributes are common, and in addition to deities embodied in terrestrial features such as mountains or springs, the sun and the moon were commonly worshipped. The Moche supreme deity, often known as the Decapitator, features a rayed head, like the sun, and feline fangs. The Paracas–Nazca Oculate Being is distinctly celestial, depicted most frequently horizontally and with streaming appendages as if flying. Pachacamac, from his centre of worship in the city of Pachacamac, represented a supreme being with whom lesser deities throughout the Andean Area sought alliance through their priests. Official Inca religion simultaneously worshipped the supreme being Viracocha, the Creator, and promoted a state cult of the Sun (Inti), as well as worshipping other deities.

Above: The great Inti temple of Sacsahuaman was the ultimate sun temple and ceremonial precinct of Inca worship.

RELIGIOUS CEREMONY

People came to ancient Andean cities not for markets, as in other ancient civilizations, but for ritual. Special quarters housed craft workers who produced only luxury items and purpose-made ritual vessels destined for the elite, for offerings to the gods, and for burial. Annual cycles of ceremonies brought people into the cities in huge crowds during certain seasons. Elite goods, stored by the priestly and noble classes, were bestowed upon the celebrants on these occasions.

Regular ceremonies throughout the year were portrayed in art. Common animals and themes were depicted in all media and there was colour everywhere: in murals on temples and compound walls; on stone and wood sculptures; in polychrome ceramics and textiles for daily, ceremonial and funerary use; and in shimmering metalwork. Such imagery was a perpetual reminder to people of their religious obligations and need to solicit the favour of the gods.

Above: The great mud-brick temple mound at Moche, the Huaca de la Luna, forms a pair with the Huaca del Sol to honour two ancient fundamental Andean deities.

COMMON IMAGERY AND DUALITY

Ceremonial centre planning and common imagery developed in the Preceramic and Initial periods and became entrenched in the Early Horizon.

Widespread connections between coastal, highland and tropical forest cultures for exotic materials spread ideas and knowledge of plants and animals. Thus feline, serpentine and avian imagery became universal in the earliest textiles and later on in pottery and architectural sculptures. Insects, spiders, fish, and crustaceans and shellfish were also common themes. Composite beings, part-human/part-beast, were frequently portrayed as manifestations of deities, humans taking divine parts in ritual or humans in transformation under the influence of hallucinogenic substances.

Duality, with juxtaposed imagery and two-headed creatures, was commonly used in all media. From the Huaca Prieta twined double-headed crab and serpent cloth of *c.*2500BC, via the hawk and eagle images on the Black and White Portal columns at Chavín de Huántar's New Temple *c.*500BC, the male-female Yaya-Mama sculptures of the Titicaca Basin, the paired Tiwanaku, Wari and Inca gold figurines, and the two-faced Pachacamac idol to the twinned facing birds on a Chimú spondylus shell ornament, duality was a vital artery in Andean belief.

The use of hallucinogenic substances – another common religious practice – was believed to induce transformation, and is frequently depicted. Priests or shamans under the influence were believed to be able to gain insight regarding the cosmos and divine intentions, to take on the characteristics of revered animals such as a jaguar or raptor, and to heal the sick. Hallucinogenic trance was a means of temporarily departing this world and entering the 'other side' – yet another manifestation of duality.

Even economic and social structure reflect this concept, in the reciprocal trade relationships between highlands and lowlands and the division of kinship groups into two moiety groups: *hanan* (upper) and *hurin* (lower).

Right: The majestic condor, symbolic of the Andes, was sacred. Here a condor soars with extended talons on a Nazca bridge-spout bottle.

SACRIFICE

Sacrificial offerings to the gods solicited good weather and productive harvests, herding and fishing. They were also atonement to angry gods who caused natural disasters and El Niño weather cycles.

Human sacrifice frequently accompanied temple dedications and elite burials. From the sacrificed adult buried near the infant at Huaca de los Sacrificios at Preceramic Aspero, through the blood groove in the Lanzón Stela at Chavín de Huántar, the Moche and Tiwanaku decapitator deities, the mass grave behind the Huaca de la Luna at Moche and the 17 sacrificial victims in a Sicán tomb at Batán Grande, to Inca *capacocha* sacrifices, the taking of human (and animal) life pervaded Andean religion.

There was also a special cult of severed heads. At Preceramic Asia on the Peruvian central coast, eight severed heads were wrapped in a mat and ritually interred, while Nazca collectors perforated trophy head skulls and strung them on cords. Chavín de Huántar and Tiwanaku temple builders mounted stone-carved severed heads on plaza walls, and Inca warriors drank victory toasts from the skulls of slain opponents.

Above: A Moche portrait vessel, one of hundreds of individual portrait stirrup-spout bottle, shows a 'chief' – possibly a successful 'gladiator' – wearing a winged bird helmet.

ANCESTOR WORSHIP

Ancient Andean religious beliefs regarded 'being' as a perpetual cycle or revolution (*pachacuti* in Quechua). Death was considered a different state of being, in which the dead person entered another world and in some respects carried on in a life not dissimilar to the one departed on Earth.

Thus it was important to maintain links with the 'other side' through ancestor worship. Special preparation before burial is evident in the Chinchorros and La Palma cultures in southern Peru and northern Chile from *c*.5000BC. Efforts were made to preserve the body, and make it look alive with a wig and painted face.

Nazca tombs were periodically opened to deposit the bodies of generations of deceased, and the Cahuachi mound complex is thought to be a religious complex expressly for the mausoleums of kin groups from surrounding Nazca residential towns.

The ultimate in ancestor worship is exemplified in Chimú and Inca *mallquis* mummies. The preserved mummies of Chimú kings and Inca emperors and nobility, the founding members of kinship groups, were housed in elaborate settings. The core of the Chimú capital, Chan Chan, comprised vast walled compounds to house the dead rulers' mummies and their living retainers. Inca imperial *mallquis* were kept in special rooms in the sacred Coricancha temple. Virtually every Andean community in the Late Horizon had its *ayllu* ancestor mummies, stored in temples or in nearby sacred caves, to be brought out at religious rituals and consulted on communal and personal matters.

RELIGIOUS TRADITIONS, PILGRIMAGE AND ORACLES

Religious continuity was secured in ancient Andean civilization through the early development of recognizable 'traditions'. The earliest of these are perhaps the Kotosh Religious Tradition, exemplified by the successive Temple of the Crossed Hands and Temple of the Niches at Kotosh, and the Plazas Hundidas Tradition (hidden courts), both prevailing in the Preceramic and Initial periods.

Continuity and coherence in the Early Horizon was through religious belief rather than political unification. Two spheres, although not exclusive, focused on the Chavín Cult and Staff Deity in the northern and central Andes, and in the Pukará Yaya-Mama Cult of the Titicaca Basin.

Many early U-shaped ceremonial centres and Kotosh Tradition sites were centres for local communities. Whether their religious influence was more widespread because they were cult centres is open to debate. Later sites, such as Chavín de Huántar, Moche, Tiwanaku and Pachacamac, and imperial Inca Cuzco itself, were certainly cult and pilgrimage centres, recognized as such through analogy with the pilgrimage and oracle city of Pachacamac, which endured despite Wari, Inca and Spanish conquest and is thus described in chronicles.

Below: A whistle-spout/bridge-spout bottle of the Early Intermediate Period Vicus culture features crayfish on gourd bases and a feeding bird.

123

CREATION AND COSMOLOGY

Andean cosmological belief was 'organic'. The universe was regarded as an animate being, a living entity, rather than as a mechanical object. Celestial motions, the seasons and the ways the natural world functioned were ordered, and could be relied on. They believed that the universe was ordered, and thus showed design. But at the same time, it was believed to have been created by the gods and so was controlled by them.

CREATION AND CREATORS

Beliefs stemming from the forces of nature provided a common base from which later Andean cultures constructed elaborate stories of creation. Most included a great flood and the survival of

Left: One of the many stone stelae at Tiwanaku, believed to be the petrified bodies of a former race of giants.

a single man and woman. Variations explain several stages of creation, in which the gods made the universe, the sun and moon, and perfected their design of humankind to make beings capable of worshipping them properly.

The two most important creator gods were Viracocha and Pachacamac. They were almost interchangeable as all-powerful gods, somewhat aloof and removed from day-to-day affairs, although Pachacamac was predominantly a coastal and lowland deity, while Viracocha predominated in the highlands.

VIRACOCHA AND THE BASIC STORY

The creation of the universe was thought to have taken place in the Titicaca Basin. Viracocha emerged from Lake Titicaca and made a dark world, without sun, moon or stars, and a race of giants. This race was to live peacefully and worship Viracocha, but instead it defied him. He turned some of the giants into stone; others were swallowed by the earth and sea. A great flood (*unu pachacuti*) swamped the land, drowning everything but one man and one woman, who landed at Tiwanaku.

Above: To many Andean cultures Tiwanaku and Lake Titicaca were the place of the origin of the world and of humans. Tiwanaku's Akapana temple mound and stellae, depicted here in 1845 by Alcides D'Obigny, was long a site of religious pilgrimage.

Next Viracocha created the sun, moon and stars, and set them in motion from the Island of the Sun and Island of the Moon in the lake. He made a second, normal-sized human race from stone and clay, named them and painted them with their national costumes and hairstyles, then dispersed them underground in their future homelands. With two or three helpers he then travelled through the land, calling forth the nations to re-emerge through caves, and also from hills and lakes, as he went, until he reached the north-west coast and disappeared across the sea – in one version on a cloak raft, in another walking on the water.

THE FIVE AGES

An Inca version of creation, retold by Guaman Poma de Ayala, was of five ages of creation.

The first age was darkness. Its inhabitants, the *Wari Wiracocharuna*, were primitive, wore leaf clothing and ate 'unprocessed vegetal matter'. They

worshipped Viracocha and Pachacamac, but they were later destroyed in an unspecified manner.

The second age had the more advanced race of the *Wari Runa* as its inhabitants. They wore animal skins, practised primitive agriculture and lived in peace, believing Viracocha to be their creator. Nevertheless, a great flood ended their existence.

The third age, inhabited by the *Purun Runa*, was civilized. People practised irrigation agriculture, span and dyed wool and cotton, made pottery and mined for metal to make jewellery. Each town had a ruler, but there was increased warfare as the population increased. Pachacamac was worshipped as the creator.

The *Auca Runa* inhabited the fourth age. Civilization and technology were more sophisticated in every regard. Conflict had increased to the point where people lived in fortified towns on hilltops. The social arrangements of *ayllu* kinship divisions and decimal administration came into being. It is not specified how this age ended.

The fifth age was that of the Incas and all they brought and created: imperial rule, *ayllus* and bipartite 'moiety' divisions of *hanan* (upper) and *hurin* (lower), and decimal bureaucracy. There were six principal gods, the most important being Viracocha, the Creator, and Inti, the Sun.

These creation stories, and many permutations of them, were meant to explain how the world came to be, why the gods were important and should be honoured, and how the technology and craftsmanship came into being. Guaman Poma de Ayala's version amounts to a potted history. The Incas became a repository for religious developments going back to the Preceramic Period. They embraced the multitudes of local deities and creation stories.

COSMOLOGY AND CALENDARS

The regularities of the seasons, the cycles of the sun, the phases of the moon and the progression of the Milky Way across the night sky were evidence of a plan, of a supreme intelligence who had created them and set them in motion – a being

Above The Wari Runa *were the second race of people in the Inca creation myth of successive 'ages', depicted in Poma de Ayala's* Nueva Corónica, *c.1615.*

or deity who afterwards took an overarching position but left daily issues to lesser, local deities.

The Incas tracked the movements of the sun and moon and created two calendars: a solar ('day-time'), 365-day year and a lunar ('night-time'), 328-day year. They do not seem to have been overly concerned with the 37-day discrepancy, possibly due to the fact that Inca calendrical observations were not essentially for the purpose of timekeeping. More important was to determine the correct times for religious rituals and festivals, to mark the beginning of important agricultural tasks, and to worship the sun and moon as deities.

The rotation of the Milky Way was important, but only the Pleiades, possibly the Southern Cross, and the summer and winter solstices were especially noted. More importantly, the voids between the stars, called 'dark cloud constellations', were envisaged as beasts known on Earth, and named after adult and baby llamas, the fox, the partridge, the toad and the snake and other animals.

Left: Believing Lake Titicaca to be the origin of the world, including the sun and the moon, the Incas built a temple to Inti on the Island of the Sun in the lake, to which Inca emperors made annual pilgrimages.

PILGRIMAGE, ORACLES AND SHRINES

Religious power and the ascendancy of priests in Andean civilization is evident in the monumentality of religious architecture. Ceremonial centres of terraced platforms, temples and ritual courtyards were focuses for communities of the surrounding regions. With true urbanism, from *c*.500BC, cities were dominated by their central ceremonial precincts.

RELIGIOUS TRADITIONS

Construction of common elements in ceremonial centres suggests widespread similarities in belief. Archaeologists recognize several early 'religious traditions', two of which flourished in the late Preceramic and Initial periods: the Kotosh Religious Tradition and the Plazas Hundidas Tradition. Significant in each is the division of space into forms that reflected religious belief, and that classified space horizontally and vertically, and as open and closed.

No ceremonial centre, however, appears to be dominant, although U-shaped ceremonial centres did serve local regions. The association of platform mounds and sunken courts nevertheless suggests the early link between a celestial deity and an earth mother.

Below: The fanged jaguar deity was one of several major themes in Chavín religious ritual, featured here in bas-relief on stone at Chavín de Huántar.

CHAVÍN DE HUÁNTAR

This settlement, which appears to have been deliberately located between the highlands and the coast, with access to exotic materials from deserts and tropical forests as well as locally, emerged in the Early Horizon as a unifying centre.

It was not a residential city. Rather it perpetuated the U-shaped temple tradition. A restricted residential complex was sufficient only for priests and attendants, and a limited number of craftspeople to produce portable objects with Chavín Cult imagery.

Celestial and earth deity association is evident in the embracing of a sunken court between the arms of U-shaped platform mounds. The Old Temple enclosed a circular sunken court and the New Temple a rectangular one. Projecting back the known importance of earth and sky association in Inca creation mythology, the Lanzón Stela in the central chamber of the Old Temple provides a metaphor of transition from earth to sky in its perforation of the upper gallery floor. So, too, the pairing, skyward gaze and invertibility of the Tello Stone caymans, the eagle and hawk of the Black and White Portal columns, and the Raimondi Stela in the New Temple.

Above: As well as animal figures, Nazca geoglyphs depicted sacred plants, here a cactus, on the desert floor. It forms a continuous line that never crosses itself, to form a ritual pathway.

The widespread distribution of Chavín symbolism in the north and central Andes, even as far as Paracas in the southern coastal desert, strengthens the argument that it was the earliest Andean 'international' pilgrimage site. The enlargement of the temple to a size that could accommodate 1,500 people in its courtyards and plazas reveals a growing importance over several hundred years of existence.

PACHACAMAC

The idea of a truly international pilgrimage site, a 'cathedral' for Andean religious worship, is well attested archaeologically and in Spanish documents for Pachacamac on the central Peruvian coast. Established in the early first millennium AD, its platform mound and windowless temple housing a wooden Pachacamac idol soon became a destination for pilgrims throughout the Andes.

Right: The pilgrimage temple and cult at Pachacamac endured for more than a millennium, a longevity and sacredness that the Incas could not ignore, but rather honoured and joined by building additional temples, including the so-called Temple of the Virgins.

Spanish eyewitness accounts in 1534 record that the city thronged with pilgrims, whose dress showed them to have come from throughout the Inca Empire. Priests, nobles and pilgrims were admitted and given accommodation in the vast complex of courts and rooms surrounding the temple. To enter the lower plaza of the temple, the supplicant had to 'fast' for 20 days. To enter the upper plaza meant a year-long 'fast'. ('Fasting' in this context required abstinence from salt, chilli peppers and sexual intercourse.)

ORACLE AT PACHACAMAC

The Pachacamac idol was veiled and only priests were allowed into the temple room itself. Questions put to the Pachacamac oracle concerned the weather, harvests, health matters and warfare. A priest relayed the god's answers to the supplicant, followed by hefty demands for tribute and donations. So powerful was the oracle that failure to comply with his mandates was believed to bring earthquakes and other natural disasters. Tupac Yupanqui, eleventh Inca Emperor and conqueror of the region, was made to fast for 40 days before he was allowed to consult the god; and, like other pilgrims, he was allowed to do so only through a cult priest. Even the mighty Inca had to recognize the importance of Pachacamac!

Lesser cults and their priests from all over the Andes sought alliance with the cult. Branch shrines were established only if they could assign lands and produce sufficient food to support a Pachacamac priest on site. Allied shrines were considered the 'wives', 'children' or 'brothers and sisters' of the Pachacamac Cult.

TIWANAKU

The power and well-documented status and longevity of Pachacamac provides archaeologists with powerful arguments for interpreting other sites as pilgrimage cities and oracles. As well as Chavín de Huántar, the Titicaca Basin appears to have been the focus of an early cult called the Yaya-Mama (male-female) Tradition, one of whose ceremonial centres was Early Horizon Pukará, north of the lake.

The region was soon dominated by Tiwanaku, however, whose empire flourished in the Middle Horizon. The size and complexity of Tiwanaku's platforms, sacrificial burials, sunken courtyards and symbolic statuary clearly reveal it to have been another pilgrimage and cathedral city. Recent research shows that in addition to its Akapana, Kalasasaya and Semi-Subterranean Court complex in the city centre, the Pumapunku complex almost 1 km (½ mile) to the south-west served as both a ritual gateway into the sacred city and a ceremonial theatre for worshipping pilgrims.

Left: Tiwanaku, pilgrimage centre and religious capital of an empire, had several large, stone-built temples and sacred compounds, including the Pumapunku – ritual gateway to the sacred city.

SACRIFICE, SLAUGHTER AND RITUAL

Human and animal sacrifices played an important role in ancient Andean civilization. They were widespread and very ancient. Sacrificial rituals accompanied religious worship and were often an aftermath of warfare, presumably also with religious motives.

The earliest example of human sacrifice is from late Preceramic Period Aspero. At the summit of the Huaca de los Sacrificios platform there were two burials, apparently dedicatory offerings to the gods to inaugurate the temple. One was an infant, specially adorned in a cap of 500 shell, plant and clay beads,

Below: On a Moche effigy stirrup-spouted red-line painted bottle, a transformed skeletal priest sacrifices a deer.

accompanied by a gourd vessel, wrapped in layers of cotton cloth and a cane mat and placed in a basket, then covered by a sculptured four-legged stone basin. The second was a sacrificed adult, whose body was so tightly flexed that that limbs had had to be cut to force the body into a small pit.

HUMAN SLAUGHTER

The great wall of carved stone slabs at Cerro Sechín is an early example of war-related sacrifice. Stacks of smaller slabs between tall slabs depicting triumphant warriors are carved with mutilated, contorted victims. The wall appears to be a war memorial. Agonized victims are shown nude, their torsos sliced with incised slashes, their eyes bulging with pain. Some bodies are headless, others limbless, some upside down. Blood and entrails spill out. There are disembodied legs, arms, rows of eyes, stacked vertebrae and heads with closed eyes. One victorious warrior carries a severed head dangling from his waistband.

Parallel themes occur on north coastal Cupisnique stone vessels and pottery. Carved steatite (soapstone) bowls depict spiders with exaggerated pincers, surrounded by severed heads. Ceramic effigy vessels show captives with bound hands, and stirrup-spout bottles are incised with severed heads, linked by cords or in net bags.

Farther north, at the late Valdivian Real Alto site, a stone-lined tomb on the summit of the low platform called the Charnal Mound contained a female burial. Next to the tomb was a dismembered male sacrificial victim surrounded by seven chert knives. Seven other male skeletons were in a common grave near by.

Two of the three high-relief adobe sculptures at Moxeke are of headless torsos, probably deliberately

Above: A principal Moche deity, and ritual sacrificer, imitated by priests was the Fanged God, depicted here in polychrome murals at the Huaca de la Luna at the Moche capital. He holds a sacrificial copper blade in his left hand.

decapitated, and the third is a colossal head, also probably a decapitation. The latest temple at Kotosh, towards the end of the Initial Period, included three headless bodies beneath the floor, presumably ritually decapitated to dedicate the temple.

SEVERED HEADS AND SACRIFICES

The tradition of severed heads was widespread and long-lived. Following these Initial Period examples, Early Horizon examples include more than 40 stone heads with tenons for mounting on the wall of the New Temple façade at highland Chavín de Huántar.

Within the central chamber of the Old Temple, the top of the Lanzón Stela comprises a spike from the deity's head, leaving a flat surface on top of the head. A groove carved from the tip of the spike down to the flat surface becomes shaped like a cross with a central depression, mirroring the plan of the Lanzón Gallery and the circular plaza. It is thought that blood from sacrificial victims was poured down the groove into the cross, eventually spilling over the stone itself. An engraved human finger bone was found in the gallery above the Lanzón.

Above: Ritual decapitation, probably combined in warfare and religious belief, began in the pre-Chavín Initial Period, as shown here by a warrior and decapitated victim on one of the temple wall slabs at Cerro Sechín.

In Paracas and Nazca on the south Peruvian coast, many burials include decapitated skulls and mutilated bodies, often with a cord around the neck or perforations in the skull meant for stringing them on a cord as a collection of trophy heads. Severed heads also adorn many Paracas and Nazca ceramics and textiles, especially in association with the Oculate Being – a flying deity figure shown trailing severed heads on streamers. Many Paracas and Nazca textiles are bordered with miniature woven severed heads.

THE MOCHE DECAPITATOR
Decapitator deities and imagery are known throughout Andean civilization.

Some of the most dramatic evidence of human sacrifice is that from the Moche. From the walls of Platform 1 of the Great Plaza of the Huaca de la Luna stares the grim face of the Decapitator God, with glaring white eyes, black hair and beard, and snarling mouth containing both human teeth and feline fangs. On Moche artefacts throughout the northern kingdom – ceramics, metalwork and textiles as well as architectural decoration – the Decapitator reminded Moche citizens daily of his grim presence.

As well as his face, he was depicted full-figured, holding a crescent-shaped *tumi* (ceremonial knife) and a severed human head. Intricate metalwork also shows spiders brandishing *tumi* knives and severed heads.

At Cao Viejo–El Brujo, the top terrace of a platform mound shows the segmented legs of a spider or crab Decapitator God brandishing a *tumi* sacrificial knife. (Before its destruction by looters, its fanged mouth was also visible.) Such imagery harks back to Cupisnique depictions in the same region.

SACRIFICE RITUAL
The Sacrifice Ritual depicted in Moche murals and in fine-line drawings on pottery involves four principal protagonists: the Warrior Priest, the Bird Priest, a Priestess and a feline-masked figure wearing a headdress with long, jagged-ended streamers. The ritual scene includes figures slitting the throats of naked sacrificial victims, then presenting the priests with goblets filled with the victims' blood. The now-destroyed Moche murals at Pañamarca showed the Priestess leading such a presentation procession: she carries a goblet and is followed by smaller figures presenting goblets and by a crawling, fanged serpent.

Moche sacrifice was intimately related to ritual combat. Warriors in Moche armour are depicted on pottery and as effigy vessels, pitted in single combat. The scenery appears to be the

Right: Sacred mountains were scenes of ritual sacrifice right up to Inca times. Here a Moche potter has depicted a ritual sacrifice on a mountain-shaped spouted bottle.

margins of fields. Successive scenes show the losing warrior stripped naked and with a rope around his neck, to be led away for sacrifice.

THE DECAPITATOR
Equally prominent among southern cultures was the Decapitator. Nazca portrayal of the Oculate Being with streaming severed heads has been mentioned. In the Pukará culture of the Titicaca Basin and its successor, Tiwanaku, the Decapitator and severed heads feature incessantly in stone sculpture, on pottery and textiles, in metalwork, and in wood and bone carving.

Scores of carved stone severed heads are mounted on

At San José Moro were found two graves with women buried in them. Both women wore and were accompanied by items identifying them as representatives of the Priestess in the mural at Pañamarca.

MASS GRAVES

Discoveries behind Moche's Huaca de la Luna platform, at Tiwanaku's Akapana platform and at Late Intermediate Period Batán Grande exemplify scenes of mass sacrifice that are reminiscent of the victory mutilations at Cerro Sechín.

At Moche an enclosure contained a mass grave of 40 men, aged 15 to 30. They appear to have been pushed into the grave from a stone outcrop after having been mutilated, then killed. Skulls,

Below: A Moche effigy jug in the form of a priest, partly transformed with feline fanged mouth and drug-glazed eyes, sacrificing two animals symbolic of Andean religious belief – a bird and a snake.

the walls of the Semi-Subterranean Courtyard. A special group of Tiwanaku stone sculptures known as *chachapumas* are puma-headed warriors holding a severed head and *tumi* knife.

Cut and polished human skulls found at Tiwanaku are evidence of the taking of trophy heads in battle – an Inca practice documented by Spanish chroniclers. (Inca warriors celebrated victory using drinking cups made from the skulls of important vanquished leaders.)

UNLOOTED TOMBS

Direct evidence of the reality of Moche sacrificial scenes was found in unlooted tombs discovered at Sipán in the Lambayeque Valley (dated *c.*AD300) and at San José Moro in the Jequetepeque Valley (*c.*AD600), showing that the practice was both widespread and of long duration. One Sipán tomb contained the burial of a figure that was dressed and

Above: The so-called prison quarter at Machu Picchu features a tomb-like cavern and sacrificial stone block carved as a condor (foreground).

accompanied by regalia identical to that of the Warrior Priest: back-flap, crescent-shaped rattles, ear-spools, a gold, crescent-shaped headdress, two *tumi* knives and a gold sceptre.

Not far from his tomb, a second tomb contained a body wearing an owl-adorned headdress, with grave goods, including a copper goblet and other items identifying him as the Bird Priest. Approximately 10m (33ft) west of the Bird Priest's tomb were sealed chambers filled with hundreds of pots, miniature copper war clubs, shields, headdresses and goblets. Scattered among these offerings were the skeletal remains of severed human hands and feet – presumably collected from sacrificial victims and stored.

Above: The Early Intermediate Period Nazca continued a long-practised tradition of ritual beheading, shown on this brightly painted bridge-spout bottle of a warrior holding his trophy head.

ribs and finger, arm and leg bones show cut marks. Some skeletons were splayed out as if tied to stakes; some had their femurs torn from the pelvis; and several skulls had their jaws torn away. The thick layer of rain-deposited sediment that covered the grave suggests that the sacrifice was performed in response to an El Niño weather event that disrupted the kingdom's economic stability, and that the offering was made to supplicate the wrath of the gods.

On the north-west corner of the first terrace of the Tiwanaku Akapana platform, excavators found 21 human burials mingled with llama bones and elegant pottery (dated *c.*AD600–800). Cut marks and compression fractures on the human bones reveal hacking with knives and heavy blows from clubs. Some skeletons had selected bones removed; other burials were only of skulls or torsos. Many belonged to adult males aged 17–30; others were children.

Another Akapana 'burial' (dated *c.*AD600) was a destroyed chamber containing deliberately smashed pots, over which were splayed the skeleton of an adult male and the skull fragments of a juvenile. It has been suggested that these Akapana burials were sacrifices associated with a single momentous event, such as the dedication of the temple.

At the Sicán-Lambayeque city of Batán Grande, another mass grave contained 17 sacrificial victims accompanied by Ecuadorian conch shells, lapis lazuli, precious metal artefacts and 500kg (1,200lb) of copper artefacts.

CAPACOCHAS

Almost all Inca rituals included sacrifice, usually of llamas or guinea pigs. Brown llamas were sacrificed to Viracocha (the Creator), white to Inti (the Sun God) and dappled to Illapa (the Thunder). Animal sacrifices were performed by throat-slitting.

Coronations, war and natural catastrophes involved human sacrifice to solicit or supplicate the gods. The victims were provincial (non-Inca) children aged 10–15 years old. They needed to be physically perfect. After the victim had

Right: The ritual sacrifice of a black llama, depicted in Poma de Ayala's Nueva Corónica, *c.1615.*

been feasted, so as to offer him or her to Viracocha well satisfied, he/she was clubbed or strangled, and had the throat slit or the heart cut out and offered to Viracocha still beating.

A special child sacrifice – the *capacocha* – was preceded by a ritual procession along a straight sacred *ceque* line in Cuzco. The child's parents participated and considered the choice of their child to be an honour. *Capacocha* victims were sanctified in the Coricancha temple in Cuzco before walking back to be sacrificed in their province.

All of the ancient Andean cultures worshipped mountain gods. Only the Incas, however, ventured onto high peaks to kill and bury sacrificial victims there. Special sacrifices were made of children, who were marched barefoot to the mountain-top, where they were clubbed or strangled – or even buried alive – and interred with miniature dressed human figurines, miniature gold or silver llama figurines, and pouches containing their baby teeth and nail parings. Such sacrifices have been discovered on Cerro el Pomo and Mount Acongagua in northern Chile, and on Ampato in Peru and Llullaillaco in northern Argentina.

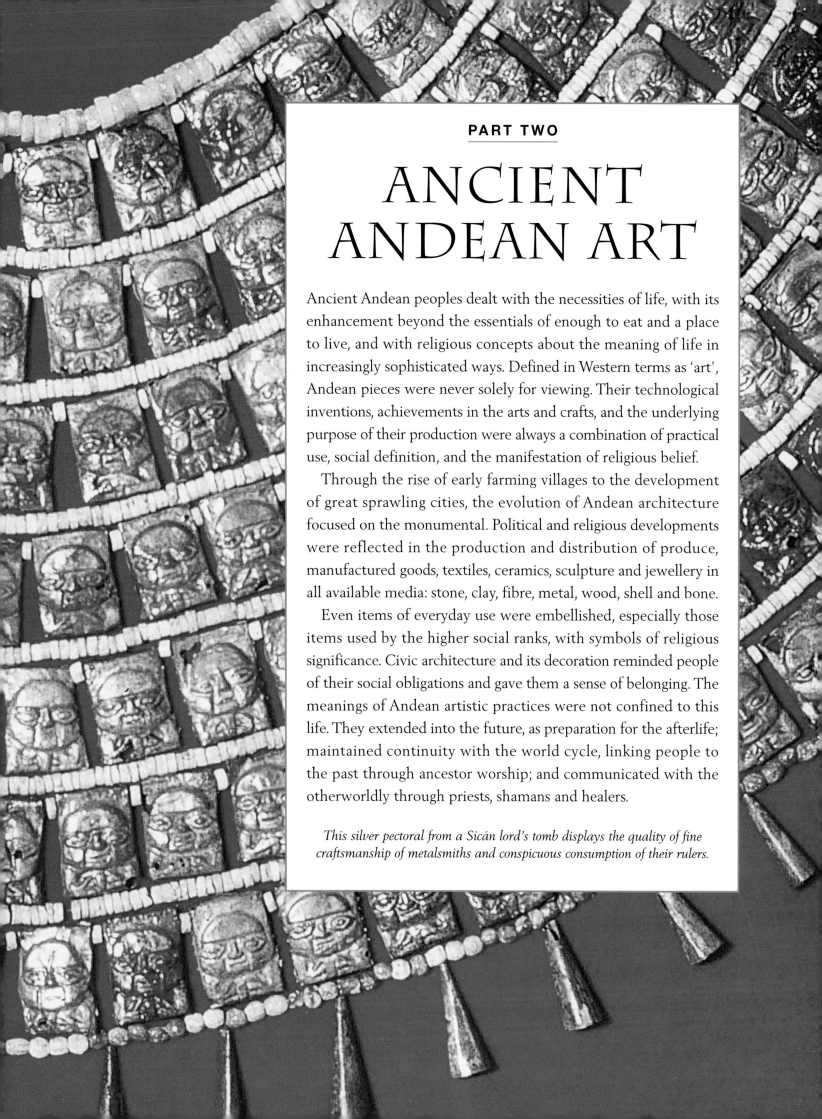

PART TWO

ANCIENT ANDEAN ART

Ancient Andean peoples dealt with the necessities of life, with its enhancement beyond the essentials of enough to eat and a place to live, and with religious concepts about the meaning of life in increasingly sophisticated ways. Defined in Western terms as 'art', Andean pieces were never solely for viewing. Their technological inventions, achievements in the arts and crafts, and the underlying purpose of their production were always a combination of practical use, social definition, and the manifestation of religious belief.

Through the rise of early farming villages to the development of great sprawling cities, the evolution of Andean architecture focused on the monumental. Political and religious developments were reflected in the production and distribution of produce, manufactured goods, textiles, ceramics, sculpture and jewellery in all available media: stone, clay, fibre, metal, wood, shell and bone.

Even items of everyday use were embellished, especially those items used by the higher social ranks, with symbols of religious significance. Civic architecture and its decoration reminded people of their social obligations and gave them a sense of belonging. The meanings of Andean artistic practices were not confined to this life. They extended into the future, as preparation for the afterlife; maintained continuity with the world cycle, linking people to the past through ancestor worship; and communicated with the otherworldly through priests, shamans and healers.

This silver pectoral from a Sicán lord's tomb displays the quality of fine craftsmanship of metalsmiths and conspicuous consumption of their rulers.

CHAPTER SEVEN

ARCHITECTURE

Ancient Andean builders tended to use materials as close to hand as possible. Thus, coastal peoples regularly built with mud – or adobe – bricks, while highland peoples favoured stone. Cobbles and rough field stones were also used, often plastered with mud or clay. Little is known of quarrying techniques until Inca sources, but quarrying consisted mostly of collecting from convenient sources rather than actually cutting the stone from outcrops.

Monumental architecture emphasized power and authority. The use of materials that had to be imported also enhanced prestige and indicated superior social standing. So, too, did elaborate decoration on buildings and walls. Monumental architecture, both in size and complexity of form, appeared at around 2700BC in the Andean Area and developed early traditions that lasted through to Inca times. Each successive culture copied and borrowed from predecessors, but also developed its own distinctive innovations.

From the beginning, much Andean architecture was devoted to religious purposes and themes. It was used to worship the gods, reflect the sacred landscape and impress human populations. There were cults, annual religious rituals, pilgrimage and oracle sites. Open and restricted spaces controlled participation in ritual, creating uniformity and mystery, through form and layout.

The architecture involved a variety of decorative techniques and styles: plastering, stone facing, stone carving, plaster carving, mud moulding and mural painting, as well as the combination of several techniques together.

Left: The stone architecture of the circular Temple to Inti, sun god of the Incas, forms the head in Cuzco's crouching puma.

STONE QUARRYING AND WORKING

One of the most recognizable Inca skills was their mastery of stoneworking. Their use of large, dressed stone blocks follows a 4,000-year history of the use of stone architecture, beginning with the first stone-clad platform mounds of the Preceramic Period.

QUARRIES

The Inca, and presumably pre-Inca, builders did not quarry building stone in the modern sense: they did not cut blocks from rock faces or detach sections of bedrock by undercutting. Instead, quarries were established at scree faces or prised loose from fragmented rock faces.

Blocks weighing 5 tons (tonnes) or more were roughly dressed at quarries by being hammered with river cobbles (hammerstones) before being transported to construction sites. Smaller blocks were dressed on five of their six faces, then transported for refined dressing and fitting at building sites. Quarry sites are littered with whole and shattered hammerstones, which were brought from riverbeds and were selected for their shape and hardness.

Most stone for building construction was obtained locally, or from as near as possible. By contrast, stone for sculpture was imported from greater distances when special stone was wanted, because it was precious, or because it was a desired colour or texture, or exotic or valuable in some other way. For example, as early as the Preceramic Period, coastal peoples imported small amounts of obsidian (a natural volcanic glass) from highland sources hundreds of kilometres (miles) away for superior or more prestigious knives and other tools. The Late Horizon Inca central plaza of Haucaypata–Cusipata in Cuzco was covered with a layer of sand imported from the coast.

Several Inca quarries are known, for example at Kachiqhata near Ollantaytambo, for that site and perhaps earlier constructions, and at outcrops just north of Sacsahuaman.

TRANSPORT

Ancient Andean transport was on human and animal backs. There were no transport vehicles, as the wheel was unknown and llamas are notoriously adverse to pulling. Transporting goods through mountains in vehicles would also have required an extensive road system – not just trunk roads connecting major cities, but more than just pathways within and between local communities.

Above: Inca stonemasons fitting blocks on a wall, depicted in Poma de Ayala's Nueva Corónica, c.1615.

These methods were unsuitable for transporting stone blocks. Instead, gangs of men dragged the blocks with ropes, on the ground or possibly on log rollers or sledges. Earth and cobble ramps were built at quarries to drag stone blocks down; other ramps at construction sites enabled blocks to be hauled into position. Ramps at Sacsahuaman were levelled after construction, but some ramps were left at Sillustani near Lake Titicaca.

STONEWORKING

Inca stonework is remarkable for its huge stone building blocks, which were carefully and painstakingly fitted together by matching angle for angle at the points of contact between blocks, so that no mortar was needed to hold them together. The oft-repeated phrase that not even a knife blade can be slid between blocks

Left: Closely fitted block stonework at Tambo Machay hunting lodge. Multiple trapezoidal niches and steep staircased passages form solid blocks that 'sympathize' with the landscape.

describes their precision. Withstanding 500 years of earthquakes also shows the strength of their construction. Earthquakes often destroy most modern houses, leaving only Inca buildings and foundations standing.

Precise fitting was used only on the most important buildings: temples, administrative offices and palaces. For other buildings techniques were less recognizably Inca, but continued methods developed for millennia and used local, undressed stone or adobe blocks (mud bricks).

Such strength is also true of Inca terracing and irrigation systems. Despite being in an active volcanic region, Inca terraced fields and irrigation conduits continue to be used.

As with almost everything else in Andean civilization, construction was related to and intimate with the landscape.

SHAPING TECHNIQUES

The careful fitting of Inca fine masonry walls was achieved by laboriously pecking the surfaces with harder stone 'hammers' and chiselling with bronze tools. The rock surface was more shattered and ground away than cut, but

unwanted stone could also be sheared away by hitting the face with glancing blows. Grinding with smooth stones and perhaps wet sand (although there is no evidence of smooth polishing) achieved final fitting. Inca blocks retain the small pitting left by these methods.

Blocks were usually of various shapes, but for the most important buildings uniform rectangular prism or cube blocks were fitted in courses like bricks. Varyingly shaped blocks were dressed along their edges to fit snugly, and used especially when very large blocks were fitted, such as on massive walls for terracing or stabilizing riverbanks. The final grinding and fitting of stone blocks on refined buildings were done *in situ*, and therefore blocks must have had to be lifted and taken down repeatedly to

Above: A typical trapezoidal Inca doorway, with main and inset jambs, in the palace of the Inca emperor Huayna Capac at Quispihuanca.

achieve their exact fit. Corners were made strong by interlocking header and stretcher construction.

Inca engineers used plumb-bobs and two-stick slide rules for positioning and possibly for transcribing the shape of one face to another as a template. Bronze and wooden levers and crowbars were used to manoeuvre blocks.

LABOUR

These tedious and time-consuming methods suggest the massive labour forces needed to complete masonry work. Specialist engineers and skilled stonemasons did the fine work, but the tasks of quarrying or collecting, hauling and rough shaping involved large gangs, as did the making of earthen ramps for raising stones up to higher courses. Construction was one of the tasks that could be assigned to workers in the *mit'a* tax draft. The chronicler Pedro de Ondegardo recorded that as many as 20 men could work for an entire year on dressing and fitting some of the largest stone blocks.

Left: The most famous Inca stone – the 12-cornered, carefully fitted block in a monolithic wall on Hatun Rumiyoc Street, Cuzco. The base is a single side, the right and left sides have three angles each, and the top no fewer than five.

MONUMENTAL ARCHITECTURE

The size and monumental nature of ancient Andean architecture is undoubtedly impressive, and this is true even when most of the features are flattened and only the foundations survive.

FIRST MONUMENTAL STRUCTURES

Large-scale monumental architecture began as early as 2700BC, in the Preceramic Period. In the Initial Period, from c.2000BC, at a time when the use of ceramics and other technological innovations (including irrigation canals) was beginning, ceremonial centres were built throughout coastal and highland river valleys. It was the beginning of large-scale public architecture, including huge individual monuments, and extensive and complex ceremonial compounds. These were some of the largest structures ever built in the Americas.

These centres were monuments to the gods and their purpose was for religious gatherings. They were not cities, for there were few associated dwellings and they lacked the density of buildings and area coverage characteristic of cities, but as focuses of public labour and worship they provided the core idea that later became

Below: Machu Picchu. Inca architecture followed a long tradition of 'fitting' the landscape. In mountainous terrain, ridges were levelled for enclosures and buildings, while steep slopes were terraced with stone bulwarks.

a feature of Andean cities. The few dwellings were those of resident attendants of the cults. Each ceremonial centre served groups of scattered towns and villages.

ASPERO

The earliest such ceremonial centre was Aspero (c.2700BC), on the northern Peruvian coast. Covering more than 12ha (30 acres) along the north bluff of the Supe River, Aspero comprised six or seven large platform mounds (4m/13ft or more high), eleven smaller mounds (1–2m/3¼–6½ft high), plus interspersed plazas and terraces. The outer walls of the mounds were faced with locally quarried stone set in mud mortar. The bulks of the mounds were built up using loose mesh bags of sedge fibre filled with rubble, cobbles and quarried stone.

EL PARAÍSO

Construction at El Paraíso, near the central Peruvian coast on the south bank and plain of the Chillón River, began c.2000BC. El Paraíso initiated two significant trends: settlements were established inland, a short distance from the coast, and their general plans took the shape of a U. El Paraíso covered 50ha (125 acres) or more and its builders used about

Above: Huaca de la Luna, Moche. Whatever the building materials – adobe bricks or colossal stone blocks – Andean architects aspired to imposing, monumental structures for their ceremonial centres.

100,000 tons (tonnes) of quarried stone to make platform mounds and other buildings. The two largest mounds are each about 50m (165ft) wide and run parallel for 400m (¼ mile) to form the sides of the U-plan, enclosing a 7ha (17 acre) plaza. The base of the U was formed by a building of 50sq m (540sq ft), 8m (25ft) high, with two stairways.

KOTOSH AND LA GALGADA

In the highlands, at about the same time, monumental architecture was not so grand in scale, but provided the same function of public focus. At Kotosh, the Temple of the Crossed Hands was a square chamber on a raised platform, one of two mounds at the site. At La Galgada there were also two temple mounds, flanking a circular court.

THE BIG ONES

The heyday of U-shaped ceremonial structures began c.1500BC, and it is estimated that these centres had about 1,000

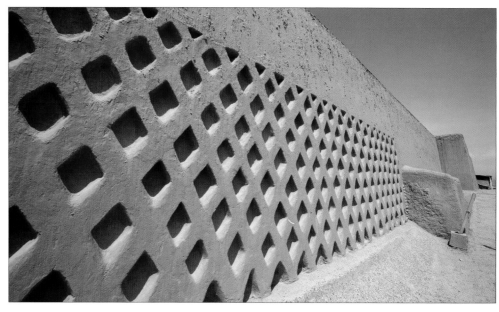

residents each. Up to the beginning of the Early Horizon and the ascendancy of Chavín de Huántar, three monumental architectural traditions developed at coastal sites, representing culturally related regions of independent ceremonial centres and their communities. These were the U-shaped ceremonial centres of the south-central Peruvian coast, the rectangular mound and circular forecourt complexes of the north-central coast, and the low-platform complexes of the northern coast.

Sites include La Florída, Cardál, Sechín Alto, Pampa de las Llamas–Moxeke, Las Haldas, Cerro Sechín, Caballo Muerto, Cupisnique and many others. Sechín Alto and Moxeke were the largest U-shaped complexes ever built in the Andean Area: nearly 1.5km (just under 1 mile) and 1km (just over ½ mile) long, respectively. By comparison, the Las Haldas U-shaped complex was c.440m (less than ½ mile) long.

MONUMENTALITY WITHIN CITIES

The monumental tradition started in the late Preceramic and Initial periods continued through the remainder of Andean prehistory. Early Horizon people continued to build ceremonial centres of platforms and plazas, exemplified by Chavín de Huántar and the Nazca centre of Cahuachi.

From about the middle of the Early Horizon (c.500BC), the complexity of sites began to include the variation in structures, craft specialization, social hierarchy and population densities characteristic of cities. Early Intermediate Period architecture included the huge platforms of the Moche, which were seemingly attempts to build miniature mountains on the coast in honour of the gods of the distant inland peaks.

Monumental architecture in the Middle Horizon, exemplified by Tiwanaku and Huari, show this continuity in large, high platforms in combination with rectangular ceremonial plazas. Tiwanaku featured huge monolithic gateways, and introduced the innovations of standard units of measurements, blocks prepared ready to fit, and grooves for using ropes to manoeuvre them into

Above: Wall of the Tschudi ciudadela, Chan Chan of the Chimú. Fine river-laid silts in the western coastal valleys provided abundant material for poured-mud walls to create huge compounds, elaborately moulded and carved.

position and hold them with T- or I-shaped metal clamps. Wari architecture developed a military-like precision of grid planning, built with huge cut-stone blocks.

Late Intermediate Period cities, such as Pachacamac, Chan Chan, Batán Grande and La Centinela, to name but a few, were huge complexes of compounds, plazas and administrative buildings surrounded by dense populations in suburban housing.

Late Horizon Inca monumental architecture is self-evident. From the city of Cuzco and its temple-fortress of Sacsahuaman through the mountain retreat of Machu Picchu to the numerous Inca provincial capitals, monumental and ceremonial architecture was built to impose and advertise Inca power. Huge blocks of stone were shaped to fit together without mortar and to build massive walls for temples and other public buildings, and for agricultural terracing and the encasement of rivers in Cuzco.

Left: Sacsahuaman, Cuzco. Inca architects frequently used the base rock itself to shape monumental structures, almost seamlessly integrating such stonework into the parts constructed from colossal cut and shaped stones.

RITUAL FOCUS

The organized nature of Inca cities and their focus on religious ritual did not develop suddenly, but began with the first Preceramic monumental architecture. Organization of space as a perception of the universe and as a reflection of the landscape was endemic in Andean architectural form.

The development of U-shaped ceremonial centres, pyramidal platforms, sunken courtyards and clustered temple chambers around courts were fundamental Andean architectural forms. People in different regions developed different forms, singly or in combinations. Such forms reflected the essence of religious belief and how religious ritual was conducted, and the shape of the landscape in which the beliefs developed. The forms endured throughout Andean ancient history.

THE U-SHAPED PLAN

During the Initial Period, the U-shaped plan developed in in the northern coastal cultures, spread into the adjacent mountainous regions, and might be regarded as reaching its fullest expression at Chavín de Huántar, where the holy city seems to have been located deliberately between

Below: Worshippers' attention in Moche's ritual enclosures was directed to lurid murals. Here the Decapitator God stares menacingly from a wall of the Huaca de la Luna, Moche.

Above: The Nazca lines of Peru's southern coastal deserts reveal the early development of ancient Andean ritual focus in architecture.

coast and high sierra. Combined with sunken courtyards and labyrinthine interiors, the temple fulfilled a third religious function: that of a pilgrimage centre.

The U-shaped form endured into the Late Horizon. It was used in miniature at Chan Chan, within the *ciudadela* compounds of the Chimú rulers.

CONTROL

The focus on ritual in ceremonial centres and urban ceremonial precincts included public and private architectural elements. The key was an emphasis on control.

Religious ritual became highly structured. The nature and layout of structures at ceremonial centres and city precincts suggest that they guided public processions along designated routes. Inca Cuzco had a radiating set of sacred pathways, called *ceque* lines, for religious observation. They were the routes followed by priests in leading religious processions, by initiates in coming-of-age rituals, and by sacrificial victims on their way out of the city.

Similarly, of more ancient date, the Nazca lines in the deserts of southern coastal Peru were pathways for religious procession. It has been suggested that they were even sometimes purpose-built

for a single event, and that the pathways along individual figures and geometric shapes belonged to specific kinship groups.

VARIOUS STRUCTURES

Elements of ceremonial complexes reveal different aspects of religious ceremony. There were specific areas for large gatherings, in which the general public was clearly meant to congregate and in which their level of participation was accommodated. Other areas were equally clearly built to restrict participation in religious worship to a privileged few.

PLAZAS

Huge areas, plazas and courts, enclosed by large platforms or walls, characterized Initial Period U-shaped ceremonial centres and platform mound complexes in the Early Horizon and Early Intermediate Period. Chavín de Huántar's two succeeding temples each wrapped themselves around an open-ended courtyard for crowds. The ceremonial cores of Moche cities and the pilgrimage city

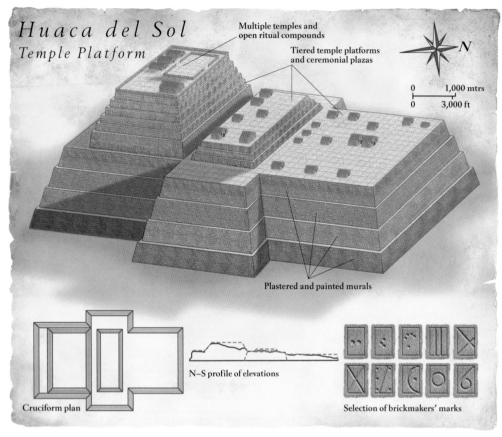

Huaca del Sol
Temple Platform

Multiple temples and open ritual compounds

Tiered temple platforms and ceremonial plazas

N

Plastered and painted murals

Cruciform plan

N–S profile of elevations

Selection of brickmakers' marks

of Pachacamac on the central Peruvian coast were formed of intricate collections of large and small courtyards for large and small gatherings.

The Middle Horizon Moche successors at Pampa Grande surrounded the dominant platform mound of Huaca Fortaleza with a complex of large walled courts and more open plazas beyond them. The singular walled enclosure at Galindo comprised a large court with a sunken rectangular court within it. In Wari cities large public plazas were enclosed within grid-planned walls and streets. At Tiwanaku the Akapana temple platform fronted a large, open plaza.

Late Intermediate Period cities continued the tradition. Sicán Batán Grande's ceremonial precinct comprised large open plazas defined by clusters of platform mounds and other buildings, reminiscent of Pampa Grande. Each *ciudadela* compound at the Chimú capital Chan Chan included a large courtyard within high walls, separated from the highly subdivided area beyond. There were similar courts at Tucume Viejo, where the compounds were anchored around the Huaca Larga platform and the huge, artificially stepped peak

Below: The Kalasasaya and Semi-Subterranean Court at Tiwanaku, where rulers and priests performed their rituals.

of La Raya. The ceremonial precinct at Chincha La Centinela comprised walled courts and low platforms clustered around a dominant higher platform mound.

Inca cities included large plazas with *ushnu* platforms for observing and addressing gathered crowds.

RESTRICTIONS

The counterparts to public areas were smaller courts, sunken courts and enclosed rooms. These were an equally long-lived tradition. They began in the subdivided buildings atop platforms at

Above: Reconstruction of Huaca del Sol temple, Moche, showing ground plan, north–south elevations and brickmakers' marks.

sites such as Kotosh, La Galgada, Huaca de los Reyes, Cerro Sechín and many others in northern and central Peru. Farther south, Chiripa in the Titicaca Basin exemplifies a tradition of single-roomed buildings surrounding a courtyard atop a low platform.

In later periods the intricately subdivided temples of Chavín de Huántar and Pachacamac, through to the complexes of rooms at Chan Chan and the Coricancha temple of Inca Cuzco, were meant to restrict the performance and observance of religious ritual to a select few.

Between these two extremes, combinations of plazas containing sunken courtyards, fronted by platform mounds supporting temples, reveal the controlled nature of ancient Andean religious ceremony. Participants were gathered, then led in managed processions along prescribed routes into and through sunken courts or other restricted areas, before priests and selected individuals mounted the platforms to perform special rites within private temples.

LABYRINTHINE SECRETS

Restriction of intimate religious ritual to selected individuals formed the counterpart to great public extravaganzas. The Incas impressed their subjects with glittering spectacles and public addresses to advertise and emphasize their power. As in other spheres, they were following Wari and Tiwanaku practice in a long-lived tradition of public ceremony.

PUBLIC AND PRIVATE RITUAL

From the Initial Period onwards the importance of religion as a driving force in the development of cities nurtured the growing power of the priesthood. Religious influence in everyday life was exemplified in the development and spread of cults, three of the most famous being those of Chavín, Pachacamac and Inca Inti.

Priestly power and control were revealed in the secretive nature of some elements of worship and the restriction of some rituals to selected individuals or as private events.

PRIVATE ROOMS

Constructions of platforms supporting subdivided temples began towards the end of the Preceramic Period and flourished in the Initial Period. The Temple of the Crossed Hands at Kotosh, the round-cornered chambers at La Galgada, the

Above: New Temple gateway, Chavín de Huántar. Not all ritual was witnessed by crowds of worshippers, as much took place within inner chambers whose passages were known only to the priests.

chambered compounds atop the Huaca de los Idolos and Huaca de los Sacrificios at Aspero, and the complex of interconnected rooms at El Paraíso all typify the development of intricate temple interiors.

The importance of religious figures, whether priest-kings or separate from the rulers, developed early and grew in strength through Andean civilization. The extent of cults was relatively localized until the Chavín Cult spread an unprecedented religious unity in the Early Horizon. Chavín de Huántar became a pilgrimage centre to which people came from great distances to consult the oracle of its chief deity.

Intimate religious practice is suggested by the labyrinthine nature of Chavín de Huántar's temples, Old and New. While the platform arms of each temple embrace a circular (Old Temple) and square (New Temple) sunken court, the

Left: The Lanzón carved stone monolith, Chavín de Huántar. Hidden deep within the multi-storeyed chambers at the back of the Old Temple, it served as an oracle chamber and place of ritual bloodletting, channelled and pooled by grooves and a dish carved in the notched stone.

Right: Entrance to the Semi-Subterranean Court, Tiwanaku. The central ceremonial core formed a complex of temple mounds and enclosed courts for more intimate rituals.

temple interiors comprise mysterious dark corridors connecting inner rooms and chambers, water conduits and niches. Its courts and plazas could hold 1,500 worshippers, while its inner chambers had room for a mere fraction as many.

ORACLES AND ROARING TEMPLES

A staircase rises from the Old Temple plaza in alignment with steps into and out of the sunken circular court. Crowds could participate in ritual and processions in the plaza and circular court, but could hardly do so inside the temple's constricted spaces. A corridor leads to an inner two-storey chamber within which stood the Lanzón Stela, the chief idol. The floor of the chamber above its base is holed to accommodate the notched upper portion of the stela, and it is suggested that a priest could conceal himself in the upper chamber to act as the voice of the deity to pronounce oracles.

The increasing status of the Chavín Cult was shown by more than doubling the temple's size with the addition of the New Temple *c.*500BC. Further secrecy was

incorporated because no staircase leads to the top of the New Temple terraces. Stairs led only to a platform and square court before the Black and White Portal on the first terrace. Instead, priests could appear mysteriously on the top terrace, or at two rectangular 'reverse balconies' above the Black and White Portal via interior stairs.

The Old and New temples were used together, maintaining the continuity of the deities and cult, and the elaborate interior chambers were multipurpose. Ritual paraphernalia and stores of manufactured and exotic goods were probably kept in niches and smaller chambers. It has also been suggested that some chambers were hermit-like cells for priests and temple attendants. It is also thought that the winding conduits and shafts served the dual purpose both of ventilation and as conduits through which to flush water and cause a roaring noise to echo through the empty corridors – a noise that could have its pitch modulated by the opening and closing of ventilation ducts.

Such measures, together with oracular status, certainly would have enhanced and perpetuated Chavín as a centre of supernatural power and authority.

Left: Temple of the Moon. For more than a millennium Pachacamac was a centre of pilgrimage and worship, focused on its oracle temple, and replete with additions of new temples, courts and accommodations for pilgrims.

PATIOS AND COMPOUNDS

The tradition of controlled worship was obvious at Tiwanaku as well. At Tiwanaku, instead of enclosed chambers, worship was regulated by a complex of open-air plazas, platforms with sunken courts and semi-subterranean courtyards. The elements were linked by monumental gateways marking the boundaries of sacred spaces and isolation atop the Akapana temple platform, thus restricting who entered and how many could participate.

At the sacred oracle site of Pachacamac (from the 1st century AD) the Pachacamac idol and oracle was housed in a small temple atop a platform mound. Its isolation and size restricted it to worship by a few people at a time. North and west of the oracle temple were ramped platforms and an elaborate complex of room suites, passages and small patios around larger courtyards. These were quarters, halls and sacred spaces in which pilgrims could worship in small groups.

Finally, in the imperial compounds of Chimú kings at Chan Chan, walled off from large courtyards, were the intricate complexes of miniature U-shaped ceremonial precincts and seeming mazes of large and small rooms, niches, store blocks and palaces of the dead rulers, each an inner city within greater Chan Chan.

ARCHITECTURAL DECORATION

Ancient Andean stone and mud-brick constructions were often highly embellished. Decorations included stone facing, mud plaster, adobe-brick friezes, sculpting in poured mud and mural-painting on walls.

Traces of paint on walls have been found at some of the earliest coastal and highland sites. Common Inca practice was to plaster cobble- and fieldstone walls with mud and then paint them. Tambo Colorado, a typical example, has traces of red and yellow ochre paint surviving on its adobe walls.

According to Spanish chroniclers, the Incas covered the interior walls of the Coricancha temple with sheets of gold!

PAINTED WALLS
The earliest evidence of wall painting and sculpting was discovered at Aspero, on the central Peruvian coast. The platform mound of Huaca de los Idolos supported a series of room complexes, one replacing the other through continuous use. The rough stone walls were mud-plastered and some were painted red or yellow. Passageways lead from a main court to more private chambers behind it, one of which is decorated with a white clay frieze of five parallel horizontal bands, clapboard-like. There are also plastered benches and cubical niches around some walls.

Below: Huaca de la Luna, Moche. Worshippers were constantly reminded of the gods in vivid murals of the Decapitator God.

Above: Huaca de la Luna, Moche. Colourful murals on the courtyard walls included rows of figures holding hands.

Paint was also found on the walls of the Temple of the Crossed Hands at highland Kotosh. A stylized white serpent was painted on the stairway leading to the temple, and the entryway was painted red. Inside, two sets of crossed hands were sculpted into the yellow-brown mud-plaster below cubical niches. It is thought that they represent a male and female pair, characteristically exemplifying Andean duality.

EARLY MURALS
The Initial Period U-shaped ceremonial complex of Garagay, on the central Peruvian coast, has one of the most remarkable early wall friezes in its Middle Temple. Running the length and height of the walls, low-relief mud-brick sculpturing shows a fanged face with a whorl (an arachnid pedipalp or mucus secretion?) within spider web-like cross-hatching; a long-bodied insect with a human head; and two facing fanged faces. Stylized geometric motifs separate each figure, and traces of bright red, blue, yellow and white paint were found on the various elements. The insect probably represents shamanistic transformation.

Early murals were also found on the walls of the earliest (*c.*1800BC) building phases at Cerro Sechín. Exterior walls were painted pink, interior walls blue, and the entryway to the main chamber had a mural of large black felines with red-orange

paws and white claws on a yellow background. The main façade of the second-phase temple had clay friezes and multicoloured incised line figures, including an upside-down human with closed eyes and blood streaming from the head.

MOCHE MURALS
Early Intermediate Period Moche sites are famous for their murals. A mural on Huaca de la Luna's Platform III walls

Below: The massive poured-mud walls at Chan Chan of the Chimú were elaborately moulded and carved with repetitive motifs.

Right: Cerro Sechín commemorated a military victory or a ritual battle in low-relief on slabs forming a wall around the temple complex.

shows the story of the 'Revolt of the Objects', in which inanimate objects counter depictions of ordinary humans: a warrior with a fox's head, a boat with legs, a ceremonial staff with legs and arms chasing a fallen warrior. It appears to be a mythological portrayal of chaos, a story that was told to Spanish chroniclers at the time of the conquest.

Walls in the Great Patio of Platform I feature a grimacing, fanged face with bulging red-and-black-rimmed eyes and curling black hair and beard. The face is of a sea god or the Decapitator, set within a diamond frame and surrounded by stepped-motif figures with red-and-white-circle eyes. Another wall depicts a line of Moche warriors.

Now-destroyed murals at Pañamarca (Mural E), south of Moche, showed part of 'The Sacrifice Ceremony', led by a priestess holding a goblet and followed by a procession of smaller figures presenting goblets, plus a crawling, fanged and forked-tongued serpent. It represents the conclusion of Moche ritual combat by sacrifice of the loser and 'The Presentation Ceremony'.

PACHACAMAC AND CHANCAY

Mud-plastered walls at coastal sites were the ideal medium for mural-painting. The Middle Horizon and Late Intermediate Period temple mound terrace walls of Pachacamac were once covered in bright murals, repainted up to 16 times. Plants and animals were depicted in bright reds, blues, greens, yellows and whites, emphasizing the natural abundance of the long-lived pilgrimage city in its fertile river valley. Reed and human-hair brushes were found near one of the terraces.

At Cerro Trinidad, one long adobe wall was painted in four colours with interlaced fish – a design used on Chancay pottery.

STONE WARRIORS

The carving of stone friezes along walls was another characteristic form of Andean architectural decoration. One of the earliest and most famous is the great wall surrounding the temple complex at Initial Period Cerro Sechín. A wall of more than 300 upright slabs comprises alternating tall single slabs and shorter stacks of small slabs. Each is carved in low relief with incised lines. The tall slabs show triumphant warriors wearing pillbox hats and brandishing war clubs or staffs of authority. Stacks of smaller slabs between them display their mutilated victims. Some lack legs, or are twisted in painful contortions; others are mere decapitated heads with streaming hair; one shows his intestines spilling out. The figures appear to be in procession, marching around the temple to converge at the front staircase, where two tall flanking slabs depict banners. Flanking the rear stairway are two warriors holding a club and staff.

Below: Artist's reconstruction of Huaca de la Luna, Moche, and plan of the ceremonial precinct showing the relationship between the Huaca del Sol and de la Luna.

Not far away, and of similar date, at Moxeke a single, rectangular stone slab was found, carved on two adjacent sides. One side has a naturalistic human hand carved inside a hand-shaped depression, and the other face has a central, forked-tongue snake head with two bodies curling back on themselves in incised lines on either side of the head.

CHAVÍN TRANSFORMATIONS
The highland, Initial Period cult site of Chavín de Huántar features rows of carved stone friezes at its Old and New Temples. Portraying religious themes of shamanistic transformation, a procession of figures marches around the walls of the Old Temple's circular sunken court. An upper register of slabs has a low-relief procession of side-facing humanoid figures with fanged mouths and streaming, snake-headed hair. They wear serpentine belts, tunics and trousers. Their finger- and toenails curl in harpy eagle-like claws. One carries a San Pedro cactus branch and another a conch-shell trumpet. The register below them, separated by two rows of plain slabs, is a row of prowling jaguars on rectangular slabs.

The seven or more paired humanoid and jaguar sets depict a scene of shamans displaying the hallucinogenic cactus used for mystic ritual, and to induce transformation from human to jaguar.

Similar themes and imagery were continued in the New Temple, which more than doubled the size of the complex.

Above: Murals at Garagay depict a human-feline-serpentine face within a cross-hatched spider's web on the Middle Temple wall.

The façade forming the lowest tier of the New Temple's main platform was decorated with fully sculpted heads, mounted on the wall with tenons. Although only one was found in place, more than 40 were found during excavations.

The heads display a succession of 'states' in human transformation into beast. The mouths show successive alteration of the lips and teeth from human to feline fangs and curling sides; snouts become projected; noses become progressively flatter, with frontal nostrils; almond-shaped human eyes change to bulging round ones, weeping mucus (a characteristic reaction to drug-taking); cheeks become scarified to represent whiskers.

The heads flanked the Black and White Portal, the columns of its entrance themselves carved in low-relief with two avian figures, heads tilted back to peer straight up, and wings outspread in typical raptor hunting flight. The pair represents Andean religious duality in two ways: the north column, supporting the white (female) granite half-lintel, depicts an eagle – identifiable by an eagle's pronounced cere (nostril hole in the beak), and as female by the 'vagina dentata' between its legs; the south column, supporting the black (male) limestone half-lintel, is a hawk – identifiable as a

hawk by the band running through the eye and as male by his central frontal fang 'penis metaphor'.

TIWANAKU STONE FRIEZES
Highland Tiwanaku, whose citizens built their stone temples, platform mounds and sunken courts through the late Early Intermediate Period and Middle Horizon, also features sculptured stone decorations. Around the walls of the Semi-Subterranean Court were mounted scores of severed heads, tenoned into the walls at various heights.

Tiwanaku's builders also carved the monumental Gateway of the Sun. Made from a single huge slab measuring 3.8m (12½ft) wide and 2.8m (9ft) high, with a 1.4m (4½ft) opening, above its rebate jambs is a frieze in low- and high-relief depicting the Staff Being flanked by running 'angels'. The high-relief, central, front-facing, staff-bearing figure is the ray-headed Sun God/Staff Deity, standing on a stepped platform. Running (or flying?) towards him are three flanking rows of 48 bird-like figures, with feathered heads and wings, each holding a single staff. Beneath the whole runs a strip of geometric shapes, and flanking the entryway are two rectangular niches.

Below: Faint traces of rich temple murals at Cerro Sechín – crabs flanking the entrance to a chamber – are some of the earliest Andean murals.

Above: Moche El Brujo includes courtyard murals with a 'dancing' figure linking hands with others.

Many other Tiwanaku monolithic wall slabs are decorated with rows of inset stepped-diamond shapes – sometimes called the 'Andean Cross' – a shape first used in the Middle Horizon and also used on textiles and by the Incas.

FORMS IN MUD AND PLASTER

The characteristic coastal use of mud-bricks and thick plastering lent itself to carving and moulding. The mud-brick painted friezes at Garagay are described above, and atop Mound A two clay sculptures of humans with circular shields were set into the terrace wall.

To announce elite power and authority, huge carved adobe sculptures adorned the faces of terraces and sunken courtyards. At Moxeke, three sculptures depicted a caped figure, a central shaman with snakes, and a grinning face. At the Huaca de los Reyes mound of Caballo Muerto, four huge adobe heads decorate the summit. Almost 2m (6ft) high, they portray human-like faces with clenched teeth, but also feline fangs, flared nostrils and gaping eyes. They were probably once painted.

Middle Horizon Moche Cao Viejo–El Brujo, in the Chicama Valley, has, on a base terrace, a frieze of 10 life-size naked prisoners, ropes around their necks, led by a warrior. The top terrace shows the legs of a spider or crab Decapitator God brandishing a *tumi* sacrificial knife. (Before its destruction by looters, its fanged mouth and double ear spools were also visible.)

POURED-MUD MOULDING

The ultimate expression in decorated mud walls are those at Chan Chan and other Chimú and Chincha cities, such as Huaca del Dragón and La Centinela.

In a riot of variations, in disciplined and regularly uniform applied forms, Chimú poured-mud walls depict all manner of creatures and geometric shapes. There are rows of identical fish, birds and other creatures, and stacked staff-bearing humanoids with animal heads. There are diamond-lattice patterns and parallel horizontal lines of moulding creating a shutter-effect. Stylized, stepped-fret fish, birds and other animals add an abstract dimension.

Huaca del Dragón features walls with rainbow-like arcs topped with curled solar flares (or waves?) framed by moulded rectangular borders. Mythical creatures support the ends of the arcs, together flanking and framing twinned, facing mythical creatures with sinuous bodies and web-like tails. Long-tailed mythical figures holding axe-bladed staffs march in a frieze above them.

Contemporary Chincha La Centinela's builders painted most of its walls brilliant white and carved them with similar high-relief friezes of birds, fish and geometric patterns.

Below: The great 'Gateway of the Sun' at Tiwanaku is perhaps the most famous single shaped and carved stone in ancient Andean civilization. It depicts a central Staff Deity flanked by numerous 'running' attendants.

INCA STRUCTURES

Inca buildings, with rare exceptions, were rectangular in plan, regardless of size, purpose or quality. Most were a single room, with one door in a long wall, or several if the building was exceptionally long. Most were single-storey, although often had a second level when built against a hillside, but in Cuzco there were two-storey and occasionally three-storey buildings. More rarely, U-shaped and round structures were built.

The standardization of form simultaneously fulfilled the goals of practicality, aesthetics, a perverse sense of 'equality' among official Inca citizens, and political power. Fineness of stonework, décor and size reinforced social hierarchy. Even the sacred Coricancha temple was a standard form – although one elevated to a higher status with sheet-gold-plated walls.

MATERIALS

Fine, fitted masonry was used only for the most important structures. Most walls were of unshaped stone set in mud mortar, using materials collected from nearby fields. Coastal buildings were of adobe blocks (mud bricks), though in the rainier highlands adobe was less practical. Both fieldstone and adobe walls were smoothed with poured mud or clay plaster, then painted.

Below: Careful interlocking precluded the need for mortar in Inca stonework; and the use of huge blocks and inclining the walls of structures made them resistant to earthquakes.

Above: Sacsahuaman. The close-fitting shaped stone blocks of the Inca Sun Temple integrate with the shape of the hill of which they form a 'natural' extension.

Roofs were of thatch, supported by wooden or cane poles, steeply sloped at an angle of about 60 degrees in highland regions to shed rain. Highland builders used *ichu* grass. Nails were unknown; the pole frames were lashed together with rope, and secured to the walls on stone pegs built into the walls. Some Inca walls also have stone rings at the gable crown.

The Incas are renowned for the fineness of their masonry dressing and for the precision of fitting. Huge blocks in the most important temples and administrative buildings were laboriously pecked, tested, removed and adjusted, then refitted until not even a knife blade could be slid into the joins. One famous block, on Hatun Rumiyoc Street, Cuzco, has 12 angled sides!

INCA FEATURES

Three notable Inca features are: battered (inclined) walls, a lack of interior room divisions (with rare exceptions) and the use of trapezoidal (narrower at top than at base) doorways, windows and wall niches.

Inca walls are inclined at an angle of 4–6 degrees from base to top, being thicker at the base. Reasons for this are uncertain. At a practical level, the incline counters the outward thrust of the roof structure, and so the walls may be more earthquake resistant. Undoubtedly, however, part of the reason was aesthetic. The visual effect, called entasis, is an appearance of greater height and refinement, making Inca walls look more imposing and so impressing and displaying power.

The significance of trapezoids is equally uncertain, but they were probably also chosen for earthquake stability and aesthetics. Many trapezoidal entrances, especially gateways to compounds, have double jambs; windows and niches are

Below: The most careful sizing, shaping and dressing was used on temples and imperial buildings, as here in the Temple of Inti at Ollantaytambo, north of Cuzco.

Right: At the country palace at Pisac, the contrast in the quality of stonework for the Intihuatana quarter (Place of the Sun) and a more ordinary building is evident.

often double-framed. Trapezoids are a central and northern feature; rectangular forms were used south of Lake Titicaca.

Dressed stone walls often have protruding stone pegs on gables and inside. Pegs are dressed stone cylinders imbedded into the masonry, or, in more important buildings, carved from single ashlar building blocks. Some are square in section. Exterior pegs were anchors for roof ties; interior pegs presumably for hanging things on them, as Inca buildings had little furniture except for wall niche repositories.

BUILDING TYPES

A *kancha* was a group of three or more rectangular buildings around an open courtyard, the whole enclosed by a wall. *Kanchas* varied in size and purpose: dwellings, temples, factories, administrative buildings, sometimes combined in the same compound. Residential *kanchas* probably housed extended families.

Kallankas were large, long buildings, often with several doorways opening into a plaza. Their size and public nature

Below: The temples of the Coricancha have some of the finest examples of dressed-stone walls and trapezoidal windows and doorways.

suggests that they were for ceremony and for housing Inca officials touring the imperial provinces.

The *ushnu* is a platform at the centre or one side of the main plaza of state settlements. It was used for state occasions as a viewing stand for rituals, reviewing troops and receiving subject leaders. Built only in Cuzco and imperial provincial cities, it was a symbol of Inca domination.

Inca public buildings – administrative *kanchas* and temples – are normally identified by their size and fine masonry, and by the use of trapezoidal doorways. These features are more readily identifiable in the Cuzco area and in the provincial capitals of the central and northern provinces, but are rare in the western and southern provinces. It seems that impressive buildings were felt important as symbols of power and dominance, either to demonstrate conquest in areas without imperial traditions or to emphasize Inca superiority in kingdoms with them.

INCA HOUSES

Houses were similar for all social ranks: a single-roomed rectangular building with one door, often no windows and a pitched thatch roof. Walls were mortar-fitted fieldstones, mud-plastered and painted for commoners, while of finer masonry and larger for royalty, nobles and high officials.

Outside the core area around Cuzco, provincial housing was often different, of local shapes and materials (for example adobe bricks in desert and coastal regions; or round in plan and with flat, woven reed roofs). Inca policy was to leave local customs in place so long as they did not conflict with the state system. Often the only way to tell if an area was under Inca control was the presence of an Inca official *kancha* or *kallanka* among local buildings and the presence of Inca pottery.

Below: A trapezoidal doorway at imperial Ollantaytambo has the remnants of projecting stone pegs flanking the entry.

CHAPTER EIGHT

ANCIENT ANDEAN CITIES

Ancient Andean urbanism developed from about 500BC. Before this time, huge ceremonial centres were built to serve the religious needs of collected communities. The sheer size of many early ceremonial centres reveals the rise of leadership and the power of religious beliefs. Co-operative labour had to be organized to gather huge amounts of stone, mud for adobe bricks and mortar, wood and other perishable materials for superstructures, and fibre baskets and ropes for containing rubble core material and for hauling stone blocks into place.

The monumental architectural traditions of ancient Andean civilization preceded true cities. Once class systems had developed and cities housed rulers, priests, craftspeople and commoners, structures reflected these developments in both the elaborate palaces built near urban ritual precincts and the smaller, more squalid and irregular clusters of suburban housing in urban sprawl. Domestic architecture mostly used local materials in rough-and-ready structures, while more elite architecture brought materials from farther afield.

As petty states, kingdoms and empires waxed and waned, administrative compounds and cities incorporated vast storage structures for the collection and redistribution of wealth. Times of conflict brought social movements and the construction of hilltop forts as competition increased over valuable lands and commodities, culminating in the vast Inca Empire briefly uniting the Andean peoples.

Left: Imperial Machu Picchu in its remote mountain fastness provides an enduring image of ancient Inca civilization.

URBAN CIVILIZATION

In the Andes, urban centres evolved around early monumental architecture built as focuses of religious devotion, from about the middle of the 3rd millennium BC. Urban civilizations evolved independently in Mesopotamia, Egypt, the Indus Valley, China, Mesoamerica and the Andes. General reasons for initial urban developments are similar, but in detail the shapes of their evolution are specific to the cultural and environmental circumstances in each area.

PRE-INDUSTRIAL CITIES
The first ceremonial complexes appeared in coastal and adjacent highland valleys in the central and southern Andes by 2500BC. The earliest pattern, not truly urban, comprised stone-faced platforms with ceremonial buildings on top,

Below: Imperial Inca Pisac. Urban compounds in mountain landscapes are a constant feature of Andean urbanism.

surrounded by scattered farming and fishing villages, whose inhabitants organized the communal labour to raise the monumental structures. Their construction obviates central political powers capable of organizing and regulating the work.

None of these early sites had dense, permanent populations. They were focuses for religious devotion by the people of the surrounding communities, and had only limited residential accommodation.

Above: Andean civilization began to appear more urban from the late Initial Period onwards, here exemplified by the walled remains of Cerro Sechín.

Structures were temples and ritual courtyards, lacking the variety in shapes and sizes that indicates the social hierarchy and occupational variety characteristic of a city.

Pre-industrial urbanism is difficult to define. Scholars agree, however, that, in addition to large populations in densely concentrated residential buildings (say, more than 5,000), there must be monumental architecture, and other buildings, large and small, that serve other purposes (administration, craft production and various civic functions).

From early ceremonial complexes and surrounding towns and villages, Andean cities became large, dense urban environments. They remained the focus of religious observance, but also regulated the economy, were the centres of state manufacture and housed the political rulers. After several thousand years of evolution, Andean cities had become urban networks linked by roads, and embodied state institutions to rule empires, the ultimate culmination of which was the Inca Empire.

Public architecture represents a huge communal commitment. Even in a non-monetary economy it demands considerable resources and powers in organization and redistribution. Builders of public architecture must be motivated and fed. At the end of 4,000 years of development, the Incas were masters at this process.

RELIGION AND ECONOMY

Two institutions governed Andean urban growth and purpose: religion and economy. These settlements were not market places (although there is some evidence of a market in Inca Cuzco); rather, they were repositories for produce, collected into storehouses by the state for communal redistribution. Supplying religious celebrants with food and drink at ceremonies linked religion and economy for a common purpose. At times of agricultural stress, stores were also used to help people through lean times.

Cities were also locations for state 'factories' – compounds in which craftspeople, supported by the state, produced elite ceramics, metalwork and textiles for royal and noble consumption.

In these ways, Andean cities fulfilled economic functions – exchange through redistribution and gift-giving – and were places of religious focus, hospitality and entertainment. Giving was reciprocal: cities were sources of gifts but also places to which to bring tax, tribute and religious offerings. Andean cities were sources of innovation and influence

Below: At royal Chan Chan, capital of Chimú, the vast city was made up of a grid plan of streets and compounds.

Above: Reconstruction of the temple tomb of the imperial Lords of Moche Sipán in the Lambayeque Valley.

through these combined roles, which in turn enhanced and perpetuated their importance and power.

A specific trait of ancient Andean cities was that much of the population lived in them only part-time: urban populations rose and fell in conjunction with the ceremonial calendar. From surrounding agricultural towns and villages, and suburbs around ceremonial centres, people flocked into the great plazas for religious observances. At other times, city centres may have been largely vacant except for rulers, priests, their service personnel and elite craftspeople, watching over hundreds of empty halls and plazas.

FITTING INTO THE LANDSCAPE

Cities were part of the landscape, both physically and metaphorically. Their plans often conformed to contours – built against hillsides, terraced, set in grid plans, or sprawled across the flat desert plain incorporating natural mounds in their constructions. Principal ceremonial centres were often oriented towards specific mountains, and their profiles sometimes mimicked distant horizons. Most famously, the plan of imperial Inca Cuzco formed the shape of a crouching puma, while 4,000 years earlier, U-shaped ceremonial complexes stretched their 'arms' out to the distant rainy mountains.

The Incas often combined a dual statement – carving rooms into rocky outcrops and thus embedding their architecture in

nature, modifying but following the landscape, at the same time emphasizing their domination of it. For example, rooms around a plaza at Chinchero mimic and complement the valley's terrace fields. At Machu Picchu, the profile of the Sacred Rock at the northern end follows that of a peak in the distance.

Tiwanaku also had a distinct imagery: it reflected Lake Titicaca, making the ceremonial core an artificial 'island' within a moat, and the Akapana platform mound simulated, in essence, the distant peak of Mount Illimani.

URBAN CONTROL

The layout of Andean cities, especially in the imperial cultures of the Wari, Tiwanaku, Chimú and Incas, controlled people's movements. Inca officials regulated access to and movement within and through public areas. Inca city plans dictated the areas and buildings to which people had access and the people with whom they interacted. Just as the land was regulated and controlled by designating different parts for the upkeep of the populace and state institutions, so cityscapes comprised buildings, streets and plazas that reflected both imperial political power and control, and also religious ideology.

CEREMONIAL CENTRES AND ENCLOSURES

Ancient Andean ceremonial architecture began with mound-building. Elevated architecture gave a structure special status, segregating it from ordinary construction: height gave spatial separation and conferred sacredness. Even the 'special' building at Archaic Period Monte Verde had a raised floor.

Mounds emulated mountains, and mound summits provided ritual spaces and platforms for sacred buildings. Ascending them was a ceremonial act, approaching the sky gods. In association with enclosed spaces, mounds were the characteristic duo of Andean ceremonial architecture.

MONTE VERDE AND NANCHOC

Andean ceremonial architecture began more than 14,000 years ago at Monte Verde in south-central Chile. Here, hunter-gatherers built a village with two groups of structures: dwellings and a special, Y-shaped building separated from them. In the latter's floor were clay-lined braziers and remains of medicinal plants, chewed leaves, seeds, hides, animal bones and apparent burnt offerings.

Truly monumental structures came several thousand years later at Nanchoc, a late Archaic Period village in the Zana Valley of north-western Peru. Between 6000 and 5500BC the inhabitants erected

Below: Interior of the Temple of Inti, Cuzco, whose niches held gold and silver figures and whose walls were allegedly lined with sheet gold.

Above: The Semi-Subterranean Court at Tiwanaku, a sunken enclosure adjacent to the Kalasasaya and Akapana temple mounds, is lined with carved stone trophy heads.

two long parallel mounds – lozenge-shaped, c.35m (114ft) long, c.1.5m (5ft) high and 15m (49ft) apart. Each had three tiers, built over a period of time, enlarged with layers of rubble between flat tops and faced with stones.

Nanchoc's mounds established several enduring Andean architectural and religious patterns: twinned terraced platforms indicate that mound-building and the concept of duality evolved simultaneously. There was periodic construction between periods of use. Each renewal involved 'temple interment', and enlargement as the old mound became the core of the new one.

Unique among nearly 50 Archaic sites in the valley, Nanchoc was probably built by and to serve these communities. It required organized community labour. Episodic construction reveals not only sacred continuity but also enduring leadership. It was a means of reaffirming corporate identity, and twin mounds suggest early social division of kinship groups into two 'moieties'.

SETTING THE STAGE

With the stage thus set, the Preceramic and Initial periods became the platform for Andean ceremonial architecture.

Ceremonial complexes became the focus of Andean architecture for the next 5,000 years throughout the western coastal valleys and Andean highlands. Some were huge; some were raised above the flat valley floors; others were terraced against hillsides. They embodied a wealth of styles and structural combinations, but always involved the formal organization of space in order to accommodate ritual and to control worshippers' access and movements.

Early ceremonial centres were nodes of religious focus among settlements, with little domestic settlement immediately around them. The same elements – platforms and enclosed spaces – became the religious precincts of later cities, surrounded by sprawling urban complexes.

Vast complexes of temple mounds and sunken court enclosures were built at Sechín Alto, Las Haldas, Huaca de los Reyes and dozens of other sites. Sechín Alto exemplifies a long, linear arrangement with a principal platform from the summit of which is a view down a succession of huge open plazas and circular sunken courts flanked by mounds. In contrast, Huaca de los Reyes comprises a large, but compact block of smaller U-shaped temple-mound groups, each embracing a rectangular sunken court, the whole itself forming a U-shaped complex with a large rectangular sunken court, beyond which is an even larger one.

THE EARLY HORIZON AND BEYOND

The multitude of U-shaped ceremonial centres that dominated the Initial Period gave way to urban centres in later periods, as political powers unified larger areas. A handful of cities began to dominate. They became the 'cathedral cities' of Andean religion and places of pilgrimage among a host of lesser sites and deities.

First Chavín de Huántar, Chiripa and Pukará introduced a new level of religious coherence in the spread of cults. Chavín feline, Staff Deity and reptilian imagery became widespread in portable and statuary art throughout the north and central Andes. The temples at Chavín de Huántar replicated the U-shaped temple formula, and introduced elements of complexity and secrecy in temple interiors previously unseen.

Below: The Pumapunku sunken court at imperial Tiwanaku, the gateway and first port of call for pilgrims to the sacred city.

Chiripa and Pukará, in the Titicaca Basin, developed a tradition of low mounds to support symmetrically arranged groups of single-room buildings around a sunken rectangular court. Pukará exemplifies a cult centre for double-sided Yaya-Mama (male-female) statuary that spread throughout the southern Andean Altiplano.

URBAN PRECINCTS

Cities incorporated the patterns established in these early periods. In the Early Intermediate Period, Moche and Tiwanaku brought the beginnings of state formation, with satellite administrative towns. In the southern coastal deserts, Cahuachi and Ventilla represent two aspects of administrative city and religious centre, among several forming a loose confederation.

Middle Horizon Huari and Tiwanaku were simultaneously imperial capitals and religious cities. Late Intermediate Period

Above: One of the monumental gateways into the Sun Temple and fortress of Sacsahuaman, on the promontory north-west of imperial Cuzco.

Chan Chan, capital of the Chimú Kingdom, was the ultimate combination of extensive urbanism surrounding a complex of ceremonial enclosures – the enclosed cities of the dead Chimú rulers.

By the 15th and 16th centuries, Andean cities had become the focus for ceremony that symbolized the nature and existence of the state in a close alliance of religion and imperial government. Cities hosted ceremonies that were deeply imbued with meaning, ostentatious mass gatherings for festivals and the redistribution of wealth through imperial gift-giving. Precinct plans and ceremonial enclosures became imperial tools for control of both ritual and people.

RITUAL AND FUNERARY COMPOUNDS

Two ancient Andean traditions were the association of burials with temples and the establishment of cemeteries separate from residential areas. For example, Early Horizon Paracas and Early Intermediate Period Nazca cemeteries were dedicated ceremonial sites and necropolises. By contrast, Late Intermediate Period Chan Chan had cemeteries interspersed within the vast urban complex among the residential districts.

Funeral monuments were seen as a way of maintaining contact between the living and the dead. A common practice in many cultures was the periodic re-opening of tombs for the deposit of more bodies.

CEMETERIES

The most famous cemeteries are those of the Paracas and Nazca in the deserts of the southern coast. Paracas tombs show not only the characteristic Andean tradition of preserving the interred person as a mummy bundle, but also the established

tradition of kinship mausoleums that became common in Andean civilization. Tombs were regularly entered to insert new burials through the generations, and the existing mummies often rearranged to honour the new occupant. There were two 'types': bottle-shaped 'Cavernas' shaft tombs, which formed a round burial chamber at the base of a shaft, with a stone-lined entrance at the top, and 'Necropolis' underground vaults of stone-walled, rectangular, upper-entry chambers, with steps leading down to stone-walled, rectangular crypts.

DEDICATORY BURIALS

Sacrifices often accompanied temple dedications. The Preceramic infant burial and sacrificed adult at Huaca de los Sacrificios at Aspero is perhaps the earliest example.

Many later temple platforms were also so honoured. Phase III at Moche Huaca del Sol, Cerro Blanco, included sacrificial burials within adobe-brick tombs, the

victims laid on fibre mats within the tombs. The Phase IV mound included the burial of a man, woman and llama in a grave atop the second tier.

At Tiwanaku, headless burials were found beneath the first terrace of the Akapana temple platform. Attendants were sacrificed and interred to accompany the royal Moche burials, and one Sicán tomb at Batán Grande was accompanied by 17 sacrificial victims.

PILGRIMAGE BURIALS

The powerful oracle shrine of Pachacamac near modern Lima operated for more than 1,000 years. Its pronouncements were so honoured that even the Incas recognized its authority and sought its advice. In the Late Intermediate Period Pachacamac Ichma Kingdom, the city witnessed the establishment of numerous foreign compounds, which expanded the city.

Terraced adobe-brick platforms with ramps were surrounded within walled compounds dedicated to foreign deities. Built as elite residential compounds and sanctuaries, they included forecourts, cell-like rooms and cemeteries for pilgrims.

LINKING LIVING AND DEAD

Anticipating later Chimú practice, one mound at late Moche Galindo lies within a large, walled enclosure. With platform, storage compartments and burial mound, it may have been the residence of the city's ruling elite.

At Middle Horizon Huari, the Vegachayoq Moqo sector was first a royal palace, then 'converted' into a mortuary monument and cemetery for the deceased ruler. Parts of the royal palace were ritually interred or 'retired' – an Andean treatment of buildings as alive and needing burial.

Left: A pre-Inca burial tower or chullpa *of the Lupaka people situated at Paucartambos, near Cuzco.*

In the Monjahayoq sector, a royal tomb comprised a complex of four superimposed stone-slab burial chambers, creating a subterranean funerary 'palace'. Four rooms in the top level overlay a 21-chamber second level, then the royal tomb – a shaft and chamber forming a llama profile in plan, the entrance through the mouth and the tail forming the fourth-level tomb.

CHULLPAS AND CIUDADELAS

These practices entrenched the tradition of continuous contact between living and dead. In the late periods, burial chambers became true funerary monuments or compounds.

The Late Intermediate Period and Late Horizon Collas in the Titicaca Basin built fitted-stone towers called *chullpas*. Of volcanic masonry, circular or square in plan, one to three storeys tall, they are dressed on the exterior but left rough on the interior to form a rubble wall with beaten earth. Their interior vaults have domed tops of corbel arching, with an exterior rim projection. Access is through a small, rectangular entry at the base, facing the sunrise. Burials within are flexed and placed in a series of superimposed niches in the walls.

Erected near towns or in separated groups, the *chullpas* were family mausoleums, containing generations of burials, the bodies wrapped in rich textiles. They were regularly entered to deposit new burials or alternatively to take the mummies out to be honoured at ceremonies.

Groups of *chullpas* were erected at Sillustani and several other sites around Lake Titicaca. They are associated with standing stone circles, whose entrances also face the sunrise.

The ultimate funerary monuments are the *ciudadelas* of Chan Chan, the Chimú capital. Each high-walled enclosure was a separate 'dead' city within greater Chan Chan, and, like the palace at Huari, had progressed from existence as an imperial palace enclosure housing the royal court, to a funerary compound to house the deceased king and his retainers. Each enclosed a large plaza for ceremony,

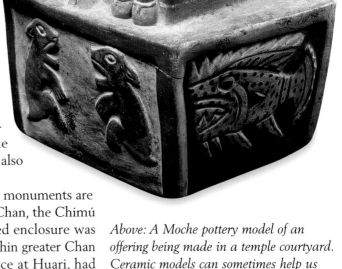

Above: A Moche pottery model of an offering being made in a temple courtyard. Ceramic models can sometimes help us visualize how temple structures were used.

smaller interior courts and patios, housing for the king's retainers, lines of storage niches to hold royal tribute and wealth, and the royal tomb within a platform mound forming a miniature U-shaped structure. Similar Chimú enclosures were built at Tucume Viejo and Chincha La Centinela.

The Chachapoyas in the northeastern Andes built numerous cylindrical tombs at Los Pinchudos containing multiple burials.

The Inca Coricancha temple in Cuzco included special chambers to house the deceased Inca *mallquis* mummies of deceased rulers.

Left: The chullpa *burial towers of Chusaqueri, Oruro on the Bolivian Altiplano form a funerary complex for ancestor burial through generations.*

ADMINISTRATIVE ARCHITECTURE

Administrative structures are difficult to identify, but the close relationship between rulers and religious leaders suggests that some structures at early ceremonial centres were administrative.

As social hierarchy developed, higher classes gained control over disproportionate amounts of wealth, and so administrative mechanisms were needed to redistribute it. In Inca times, religious festivals provided the venue for redistribution and we can conjecture that this practice was ancient.

MOXEKE AND STORAGE

Before they could be given away, or redistributed in elite burials, goods had to be collected and stored. Rows and groups of smaller buildings around the principal religious platforms, plazas and temples were probably storehouses.

For example, the Huaca A complex at Moxeke (Pampa de los Llamas, in the Casma Valley of northern coastal Peru)

Below: Within Chan Chan's compounds were vast complexes of administrative and storage buildings around inner courtyards.

was a well-planned, symmetrical arrangement. Long corridors connected large and small rooms with wall niches, the whole forming a large walled compound – the very image of a bureaucratic structure.

Two large halls occupied the centre of the low platform, each fronted by a court reached by steps. Between the halls was an inner courtyard. To either side there were smaller rooms along corridors. In groups and lining the outer compound sides there were even smaller rooms, some with intercommunicating doorways, opening onto long corridors running the length of the compound. The complex clearly accommodated storage and public ceremony, perhaps even banquets.

Huaca A sits on one side of a large rectangular public plaza. On the other side stood a tiered pyramidal structure, with round-cornered, tower-like mounds at the rear, backing an open terrace plaza reached by a monumental staircase. The tier faces were decorated with painted clay sculptures – clearly a temple.

Similarly, the massive complex at Huaca de los Reyes, also on the north coast, comprises a principal temple platform

Above: Fine stone shaping and fitting was reserved for imperial and state architecture, as here at one of Machu Picchu's many administrative kallankas.

and plaza, plus numerous smaller groups of platforms and rows of small, single-room buildings. The vast complexes of Sechín Alto and scores of other U-shaped ceremonial centres also include numerous smaller structures around them. At these and scores of other Initial Period and Early Horizon sites, the different groups of buildings are inseparably intertwined with bureaucratic and religious activities.

It is suggested that some of the small interior rooms at Chavín de Huántar were also for storage.

DIFFERENT APPROACHES

Moche and Nazca cities represent different administrative approaches. The Moche capital at Cerro Blanco provided a model at the apex of a hierarchy of administrative structures. The two great pyramid platforms of the Huaca del Sol and the Huaca de la Luna were religious

Above: The vast mud-walled enclosed ciudadela *compounds of Chan Chan of the Chimú formed imperial cities within the city. Their carved walls shielded complexes of administrative buildings.*

monuments surrounded by smaller complexes of administrative units. Like the capital, the Moche administrative centre at Pañamarca copied many of the capital's features. A principal adobe brick pyramid platform dominated the centre of a complex of spacious courts and buildings to administer the religious and economic affairs of the region.

The Nazca confederation of states in the southern coastal deserts separated religious centres and working cities. Ventilla, a sprawling residential city whose habitation terraces and walled compounds of mounds and administrative structures covered at least 2sq km (495 acres), was linked by a road to Cahuachi, a place of religious ritual and complex of family mausoleums.

IMPERIAL ADMINISTRATION

Middle Horizon Wari developed an administrative structure that became the hallmark of the Chimú and Incas.

The modular regimentation and additive nature of Wari architecture, with rows of walled precincts and multi-storey buildings at the capital, Huari, was repeated in several provincial centres. The well-preserved grid plan of Pikillacta on Wari's southern border is perhaps the best

known. Other Wari centres were at Jincamocco, Wari's 'gateway' to the south coast, Azángaro in the centre, and Viracochapampa and Marca Huamachuco on the northern frontier.

A fundamental factor in Wari administration was a compulsion to gather and control resources – to produce, collect and store them.

Tiwanaku, Wari's rival to the south, was primarily a ceremonial centre of ritual pyramids, sunken courts and plazas, surrounded by residential areas. Unlike at Wari cities, archaeologists have found no rows of storehouses or obvious bureaucratic structures. Tiwanaku has been described as a 'patrician city', in which residency near the centre may have been restricted to aristocracy and their retainers.

CHIMÚ AND INCA

At Chan Chan, the Chimú introduced an administrative twist. Its vast compounds housed row upon row of storage rooms and niches along corridors, within high-walled compounds called *ciudadelas*. These housed the accumulated wealth of successive dead emperors. Bureaucracies of retainers continued to collect, administrate and redistribute this wealth alongside the administration of the living emperor and population.

The Incas imposed distinct administrative architecture at their provincial cities – such as Huánuca Pampa and Tambo Colorado – built to impress conquered

subjects with Inca power and authority. Although not replicas of Cuzco, they contained similar elements: a main plaza for public ceremonies (and subsidiary plazas); an *ushnu* platform in the plaza for viewing, public hearings and the administration of justice; surrounding *kallanka* compounds of buildings for bureaucratic residency and official functions; and blocks of *collca* storehouses. In addition there were temples to Viracocha and/or Inti the sun god (and sometimes to other principal Inca gods) and an *acllahuasi* compound (for the chosen women weavers and *chicha* beer makers).

Below: Tambo Colorado, so-called for its red adobe mud-brick walls, was typical of Inca provincial administrative cities, with complexes of kanchas *and storehouses.*

ELITE AND ROYAL RESIDENCES

Building monumental architecture involved different layers of command. There had to be leaders to marshal the labour forces, and labourers and craftspeople to do the work.

EARLY DISTINCTIONS

There is evidence of differences in residential quality as early as the Initial Period. Moxeke dwellings include some with plastered and painted interior walls and storage niches, aligned with the ceremonial centre. Most Initial Period and Early Horizon commoners, however, lived in scattered villages and farmsteads.

In Early Horizon Chavín de Huántar, only priests and special craftspeople were allowed to live near the temple.

URBAN DISTINCTIONS

This pattern prevailed into the Early Intermediate Period. With the development of cities by c.500BC, the pattern became

Below: Machu Picchu, perched above the Urubamba River north-west of Cuzco, is the best-known imperial retreat of Inca Pachacuti.

one of elite residences sited near the monumental religious precincts, with common dwellings farther out, intermixed with lesser elite residences and workshops.

At the Moche capital, Cerro Blanco, finer houses were near the base of the Huaca del Sol and south-west of the Huaca de la Luna. They were built of shaped stone and mud-plastered walls and were often painted. They had larger rooms and storage structures than the jostled, simple housing farther from the religious precinct, and their owners used finer ceramics.

Moche Galindo elite residents lived in large, bench-lined rooms, and had separate kitchens and storage rooms. Their neighbourhood was segregated from common housing by a wall and ditch. Similarly, Pampa Grande (c.AD550 to the Late Intermediate Period) had elite residences with large rooms and plastered stone walls at Huaca Forteleza, the principal pyramid, and north of it. The rich burial of the Sicán Lord with hoards of specially crafted gold, silver and other jewellery and objects reveals the existence of an affluent social class.

Above: A recessed ('double-jam') doorway at the imperial Palace of Huayna Capac at Quispihuanca in the Urubamba Valley.

TIWANAKU PALACES

Unlike earlier cities, or contemporary Wari cities, there is no evidence of blocks of storehouses at Middle Horizon Tiwanaku, or any obvious 'administrative' structures. However, from c.AD400 there were elite residential *barrios* around the ceremonial precinct. High adobe walls on cobblestone foundations surrounded elite compounds. By c.AD750 these were razed to provide space for the Putuni ritual mound–palace complex.

The Putuni ritual mound occupied a raised platform 50m (165ft) each side, with a sunken court and an eastern entrance. Adjacent, on its north-west corner, the north and west palaces were two of four palace residences surrounding a central courtyard. Each had foundations of finely cut stone and adobe walls, smoothly plastered.

The 'Palace of Multicoloured Rooms' walls were painted with blue, green, red, orange and yellow mineral pigments. Up to 15 coats of the same colour on some wall fragments reveal numerous redecorations. It had a carved stone lintel (with strutting, ray-headed feline figures), stone-paved inner patios, canals supplying it with spring water, sewage drains into the city's main drains, and a large kitchen (suitable for preparing feasts). Rooms had their own hearths and storage niches.

Right: The imperial Inca provincial capital at Huánuco Pampa in Chinchaysuyu quarter included an imperial palace entered through a wide gateway leading to a complex of kancha *compounds.*

There were dedicatory human burials at its entrance and four corners, plus a llama foetus burial. All included rich burial offerings: gold, silver, copper and stone ornaments, including a turquoise-bead necklace, gold mask or pectoral with repoussé face and other jewellery, a silver tube filled with blue pigment, a carved marine shell and finely carved bone utensils, and fine ceramics.

Other residences near the Putuni complex were also made of fine, cut-stone buildings, making the whole area west of the Akapana–Kalasasaya ceremonial precinct an elite neighbourhood.

CHIMÚ AND INCA PALACES

The compounds known as *ciudadelas* at Chan Chan were the royal residences of Chimú kings and their courts. Each comprised an elaborate complex of hundreds of large and smaller rooms, rows of storerooms and miniature U-shaped temples.

Below: The Tschudi audiencia *compound: The centre of the Chimú capital Chan Chan comprised walled royal compounds (*ciudadelas*), one for the ruling king and one for each deceased king and an attendant court and administrative staff.*

When a king died, the compound became a 'dead' palace and his tomb was bureaucratically maintained. Their massive mud-brick walls and interior walls were embellished with moulded friezes of religious imagery and geometric patterns.

Cuzco and other Inca cities, following ancient precedent, had distinct districts: *hanan* (upper) and *hurin* (lower). Although described by Spanish chroniclers as having palaces and temples around spacious plazas, it is mostly impossible to identify individual Inca structures according to function, the Coricancha temple being an obvious exception.

Inca houses were similar for all social ranks: single-roomed rectangular buildings with one door, no windows and pitched thatch roofs. Those for royalty, nobles and high officials were larger and of fine masonry.

Spanish chroniclers describe a number of palaces around the Haucaypata and Cusipata plazas in *hanan* Cuzco. The Casana compound, north-west of the plazas, comprised several large halls encircled by a fine masonry wall. Garcilasco de la Vega says that its largest hall could hold 3,000 people. Two round towers flanked the compound's main entrance.

One palace of Huáscar (thirteenth Inca emperor) was east of Cusipata, but there are no details except that it was claimed by Diego de Almagro (Pizarro's second in command), and was therefore presumably an impressive residence.

Similarly, chroniclers name other palaces at Amarucancha (Serpent Enclosure), south-east of Haucaypata, facing the Casana, which was built by Huascar and awarded to Hernando de Soto. There was also the Hatuncancha compound at the eastern corner of Haucaypata and two compounds of fine masonry halls at Pucamarca and Cusicancha, south-east of Amarucancha.

All these compounds basically comprised large halls with single entrances, built of fine-dressed masonry. It is primarily their sizes, stonework and mention by Spanish chroniclers that identifies them as 'palaces'. (Even at Machu Picchu, clearly an imperial retreat, we do not know the actual use of most of the buildings.)

Below: Fine Inca masonry is preserved in many Peruvian buildings. At Andahuaylillas, the doorway of an elite residence has a lintel carved with two facing pumas.

DOMESTIC ARCHITECTURE

Evidence of ancient Andean housing is abundant but less explored then elite and royal residences. Materials varied through time and due to local resources.

EARLY HOUSES
Hunter-gatherers used rock shelters and caves, while coastal peoples, such as the La Paloma of Chile, built reed round-houses.

Materials and styles varied considerably among Preceramic coastal villages. Huaca Prieta houses were square, semi-subterranean buildings of river cobbles, with wooden and whalebone roof beams, while houses at Asia were of fieldstones and adobe set in clay mortar. Other coastal peoples used beach cobbles, basalt and granite fieldstones, adobe or coral blocks. Many had central hearths and most had storage pits.

Highland populations lived in small, scattered hamlets and farmsteads. La Galgada is one of the few sites where houses have been excavated. They were

Below: A black polished-ware Chimú bottle shows the steep roof pitch and rectangular form changed little in the Late Intermediate Period and Late Horizon.

oval, up to 14sq m (150sq ft), with unpainted walls of fieldstones in clay mortar, earthen floors and built-in firepits.

INITIAL PERIOD HOUSES
Residential hamlets occupied hillsides and the margins of cultivable land around U-shaped ceremonial centres. Houses at Ancón and Cardál formed quadrangular groups of dwellings measuring *c*.2.5m (8–9ft) on each side. They had stone footings, but the upper walls were of perishable materials: cobbles set in seaweed and marsh grass at coastal Ancón, and fieldstones and hemispherical adobe bricks in clay mortar at inland Cardál.

Storage pits were outside dwellings, sometimes as separate buildings. Cooking was done in separate buildings or outdoors. Associated artefacts suggest that there were separate buildings for 'industry', including stone and bone working, and fibre and cotton textiles making. Early pottery serving vessels remained the same sizes throughout the Initial Period, while cooking pots became larger, suggesting increasing prosperity.

Moxeke had two dwelling groups. One, behind and aligned with the ceremonial platforms and central plaza, had houses of quarried-stone walls covered with mud plaster (sometimes painted red inside), with interior wall niches and small storerooms behind them. The other group comprised irregularly aligned dwellings of cobblestone footings and perishable upper walls. Such differences, and associated artefacts, suggest distinct elite and common inhabitants.

At Montegrande, one of about 50 Initial Period sites in the Jequetepeque Valley, houses formed clusters around patios (inner courtyards), and were

Above: A bridge-spout bottle provides clues to ancient Inca house styles showing typical rectangular kallankas *with thatched roofs.*

built of cane and mud plaster. Alignment with the ceremonial platforms indicates agreed planning.

CHAVÍN AND MOCHE HOUSING
Although Chavín de Huántar was not a city, a residential section was built in flat areas around the temple (estimated population, 2–3,000). House groups comprised fieldstone dwellings, storage buildings and workshops. Associated artefacts show that different residential clusters produced different Chavín portable objects.

Contemporary Paracas housing continued coastal traditions of single-room residences of cobbles and adobe bricks set in mortar.

From *c*.500BC Andean cities comprised central ceremonial and administrative buildings surrounded by increasingly larger suburban residential areas. As at Moxeke, social differentiation was found at Moche Cerro Blanco. Dwellings at the base of Huaca del Sol and south-west of Huaca de la Luna range from simple dwellings of river-cobble foundations and walls of perishable materials, to finer houses of shaped-stone, mud-plastered walls. The latter had larger rooms and storage structures and their occupants used finer ceramics, which were made in dedicated workshops.

Moche Galindo had four zones of residential structures, exemplifying the nature of Andean urban suburbs. Anticipating the dedicated storage blocks of Inca times, stone-lined bins were built on hillside terraces. As at Cerro Blanco there were well-built elite residences, with large, bench-lined rooms, storage rooms and kitchens, while the common, smaller houses were crowded together on the hillside overlooking the ceremonial centre, and segregated by a wall and ditch.

A similar pattern – ceremonial mound and precinct, surrounded by residential *barrios* – evolved at Pampa Grande, established *c*.AD550 and occupied into the Late Intermediate Period. There were elite residences at and north of Huaca Forteleza; high-level citizens, who oversaw the workshops, in compounds; low-level administrators in smaller compounds; and craftsmen and farmers in irregular groups of single-room residences.

Below: Rows of domestic houses formed attached 'terraces' on a regular grid plan of streets at Middle Horizon Wari Pikillacta.

WARI, TIWANAKU

Great cities of the Wari and Tiwanaku included large, suburban residential populations around their ceremonial precincts, incorporating workshops for pottery, metalwork and textiles, and *chicha* beer breweries. Wari citizens lived in rows of houses along narrow streets within large rectangular compounds. Subdividing the compounds were groups of patios (inner courtyards) with low benches and stone-lined canals, and surrounded by one-, two- or even three-storey houses (probably housing extended families), and workshops, as found, for example, at Huari, Viracochapampa, Pikillacta and other sites.

Tiwanaku citizens lived in similar housing. Distinct elite residential *barrios* at Tiwanaku were near the ceremonial plaza, while common citizens lived farther out, in cobblestone- and adobe-walled houses with thatched roofs.

CHIMÚ AND INCA

These patterns continued into the Late Intermediate Period and Late Horizon. Chan Chan's vast urban population of

Above: The ruins of a kallanka *at Machu Picchu and the evidence from clay models enable accurate reconstruction, with a thatched roof – note the exterior stone 'pegs' on the gables, for securing the roof structure.*

commoners lived around and beyond the elite residences, in *barrio* complexes of small, irregular rooms with common walls, mostly in the south, west and south-west city. Walls were mud-plastered cane or *quincha* (wattle-and-daub).

These were self-contained neighbourhoods with winding streets, common wells and cemeteries. Patio areas comprised house, kitchen, storage areas and workshops.

The typical Inca house was a single-roomed, usually single-storey rectangular structure with stone walls and a pitched thatch roof. The house was the realm of women and children (until boys were old enough to help in the fields). Inca houses were primarily shelters; most activities were done outdoors. They had only open doorways and windows. Families slept huddled together on straw or twined fibre pallets.

FORTRESSES AND WARFARE

Most ancient Andean warfare involved pitched battles on open land. Early warfare is depicted in stone sculpture and on painted ceramics. However, as periods of political cohesion interchanged with periods of fragmentation, there was need for fortifications as places of safe refuge during times of competition between city-states and in times of imperial conquest.

EARLY WARFARE
Plant and animal domestication and development of irrigation agriculture in early times entailed co-operation within communities, but as the best lands were occupied, disputes arose between communities.

The 300 carved slabs at Initial Period Cerro Sechín are a procession of triumphant warriors and their victims. Whether a war memorial for a specific victory or representing a symbolic battle,

Below: Sacsahuaman, built by Inca Pachacuti atop the hill north-west of Cuzco, had both a sacred and military function – at its core was the Temple to Inti (the Sun), while its stout stone walls and terraces formed a defensive position and its rooms were used to store military equipment.

Above: The Chimú fortress at Paramonga guarded the kingdom's borders at a mountain pass and presented a formidable obstacle to Inca conquest.

they are evidence of conflict by c.1200BC, probably small-scale, seasonal raiding between towns.

Although the Early Horizon brought religious coherence and less conflict under the influence of the Chavín and Yaya-Mama cults, sacrifice and trophy-head collection continued.

The breakdown of these cults in the Early Intermediate Period brought social withdrawal, increased competition and the abandonment of many settlements. Populations moved to hilltop fortresses

both on coasts and in highlands. Periods of drought in the early centuries AD brought hard times.

HILLFORTS
The Santa Valley and its tributaries of northern coastal Peru has been intensively surveyed, locating 54 Early Horizon sites. Most were towns – groups of small 'polities' – but 21 were hilltop forts built in remote positions to enhance defensibility. They are best interpreted as citadels, as permanent occupation would have been difficult so far away from water and agriculture. Each features one or more massive 1–2m (3–6ft) high stone enclosure walls, from which slingers could repulse enemies, plus bastions, buttresses and narrow, baffled entrances. A few have dry trenches on vulnerable sides.

Similar forts were also built in the Casma and Nepeña valleys. Chanquillo (mid-4th–2nd centuries BC), in Casma, typifies these refuges: two outer sub-circular walls with steep entrances and bastions follow the contours, encircling a lozenge-shaped inner wall. Within this are two circular towers within circular walls and a multi-roomed rectangular structure for temporary occupation.

Citadels proliferated outside the north-central coast in post-Chavín times, for example in the Viru, Moche and Chicama valleys.

MOCHE AND WARI FORTS
A typical Moche fortified site was Galindo in the Moche Valley. It began as a fortress, strategically located at the valley neck, with stout rectangular walls and parapets with piles of slingstones. It changed to a hinterland site and elite burial enclosure in the early Middle Horizon as the Moche power base shifted from south to north – abandoning Cerro Blanco for a capital at Pampa Grande, in Lambayeque.

Cerro Chepén in the northern coastal mountains is perhaps one of a chain of Moche fortresses. It sprawls across a 450m

Left: A projecting tower at the Chimú
fortress of Paramonga provides a superb
view of the valley below, and of any
approaching enemies.

(1,500ft) high ridge and contained a central palace with hundreds of rooms and barracks for about 5,000.

Middle Horizon Wari and Tiwanaku imperial coherence put an end to regional conflict and fortifications. Tiwanaku cities were focused on ceremony and ritual, and although the Wari conquered the central and northern Andean states, there seems to have been a guarded peace between the two empires.

The only recorded Wari fortress, Cerro Baúl (*c*.AD600–700), represents a brief encounter and Wari retreat within Tiwanaku territory in the Moquegua Valley. It occupies a sheer-sided mountain top of 600m (1,970ft) with 10ha (25 acres) of circular, D-shaped and rectangular single- and multi-storey structures grouped around patios.

WARRING STATES

Political fragmentation and endemic regional conflict returned in the Late Intermediate Period. Inca records transcribed by Spanish chroniclers describe intense warfare between competing 'tribes' or ethnic groups broken up into numerous petty states. Strong, warlike leaders called *sinchis*

Right: Resembling the terraced monolithic stone 'walls' at Sacsahuaman, Cuzco, the imperial Inca city and fortress at Ollantaytambo, north-west of Cuzco, could be easily defended.

built hilltop fortifications that are called *pukarás*, as is shown in the archaeological record.

The Wanka of central Peru's Mantaro Valley, for example, were typical of the Inca Fourth Age. Regional warfare caused them to build their towns on high ridges and hilltops, fortified with stout walls.

The Chimú of the north-west coast carved out the largest state. Its southern limits were guarded by the mountaintop fortress of Paramonga in the Fortaleza Valley. Massive adobe brick walls rise in several tiers to a final, central citadel-palace, with characteristic trapezoidal doorways.

As the Inca Empire expanded, it incorporated existing cities, including the Chimú Kingdom. New Inca cities served

as anchors for regional stability, rallying points, and staging points for future campaigns. These Inca administrative centres were capable of defence, but were less fortresses than imperial provincial capitals, for Inca warfare involved large armies and pitched battles. The Incas conquered by force and negotiation. Once hilltop fortresses were taken and razed they ruled through intimidation and power rather than from garrisoned citadels.

Nevertheless, Ollantaytambo in the Urubamba Valley was a combined Inca imperial retreat, temple and fortress. Built on a mountain shoulder above a strategic pass on the Inca road north of Cuzco, it was one place where the Inca court made a last-ditch stand against the Spaniards.

The fortress-temple of Sacsahuaman formed the 'head' of puma-shaped imperial Cuzco. Its circular tower was a temple to the sun god Inti and its rooms were used to store weapons and armour for the imperial troops. Its massive stone walls would have presented a formidable citadel for the capital.

U-SHAPED CEREMONIAL COMPLEXES

Sechín Alto and Moxeke-Pampa de las Llamas are two fine examples of U-shaped ceremonial centres.

SECHÍN ALTO

One of the premier examples of a coastal valley U-shaped ceremonial centre, Sechín Alto is representative of early Andean coastal religious traditions. Built and occupied from about the middle of the second millennium BC, it represents a huge investment of labour and therefore demonstrates that tremendous political power must have been used to marshal and organize the workforces needed to complete it. Its sheer size is a mark of distinction, for it dwarfs almost all other U-shaped ceremonial centres built before it or contemporary to it. Its final form

Below: Artist's reconstruction of Sechín Alto, the largest U-shaped ceremonial centre ever built, comprising a succession of plazas and temple mounds stretching c.1.5km (1 mile).

covered more than 200ha (495 acres), making it 15 times larger than the later, highland ceremonial complex of Chavín de Huántar.

The site was located and excavated by the native Peruvian archaeologist Julio C. Tello in the 1930s, and its structures were further explored and analyzed by Sheila and Thomas Pozorski in the 1980s.

Sechín Alto was built in the Sechín branch of the Casma Valley of north-central coastal Peru, south-east of the Sechín River, and was one of many U-shaped ceremonial complexes of the Initial Period and Early Horizon. The huge complex is oriented roughly north-east–south-west. Forming the base of the U shape at its western end is a truncated mound measuring 300 x 250m (984 x 820ft), rising 44m (144ft) above the floor of the valley. Huge granite stone blocks were quarried and roughly dressed to face the platform, with the blocks set in a mortar of silty clay. Later, 20th-century looters

dug a pit 20m (66ft) into the platform, revealing an inner mound made of conical adobe 'bricks' – a preceding construction of 1500BC or earlier.

Running north-east of the core mound are four large plazas: three of them are roughly rectangular and the largest is square. The three rectangular plazas each has a round sunken courtyard, aligned along the axis of the ceremonial platform. The largest circular sunken court, in the farthest plaza north-east of the base platform, is c.80m (c.265ft) in diameter. From the base platform to the most easterly plaza it is some 1,100m (3,639ft); including the base monument, the entire central complex stretches nearly 1.5km (1 mile).

Subsidiary mounds and other constructions flank the plazas along their northern and southern edges. Some are long, narrow platforms, while others are groups of aligned small square and rectangular platforms, some of which are on the tops of the long platforms. Still others appear to be complexes of rooms on the small mounds.

Farther north-west and south-east of these main structures there are scattered remains of other square and rectangular mounds, but most of the evidence for any surrounding domestic structures has been destroyed by modern agricultural activities.

Sechín Alto functioned for some 800 years, from before 1500BC to c.800BC. Its size and complexity show that it must have represented a considerable political power in the valley, which probably extended to the surrounding region, although there were four similar contemporary ceremonial centres in the Casma Valley, and five others just before the rise of Chavín de Huántar in the north-central highlands, towards the end of the Initial Period. Adjacent coastal valleys also had dozens of contemporary U-shaped ceremonial complexes.

Architecturally and religiously, Sechín Alto is considered part of a tradition called El Paraíso. It stands at the height of the U-shaped ceremonial religious creed.

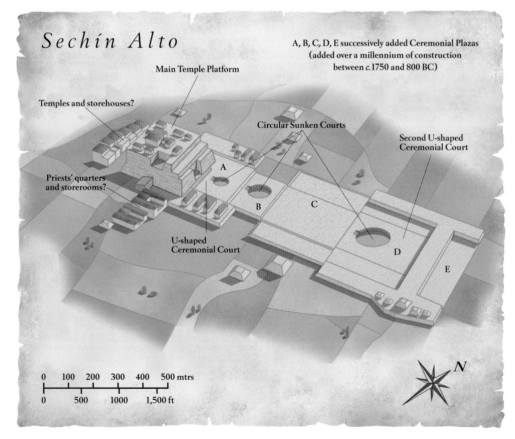

Sechín Alto

A, B, C, D, E successively added Ceremonial Plazas (added over a millennium of construction between c.1750 and 800 BC)

Main Temple Platform

Temples and storehouses?

Priests' quarters and storerooms?

Circular Sunken Courts

Second U-shaped Ceremonial Court

U-shaped Ceremonial Court

A

B

C

D

E

0   100   200   300   400   500 mtrs

0   500   1000   1,500 ft

N

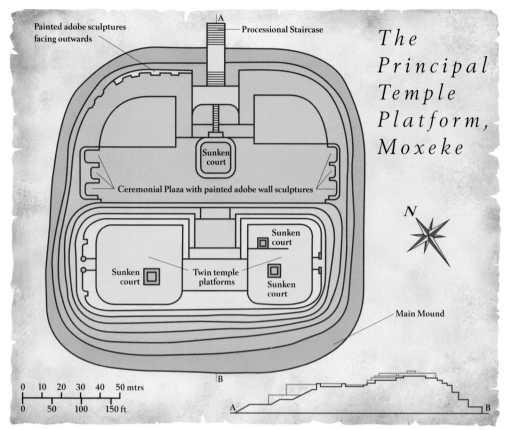

Painted adobe sculptures
facing outwards

Processional Staircase

*The
Principal
Temple
Platform,
Moxeke*

Sunken
court

Ceremonial Plaza with painted adobe wall sculptures

N

Sunken
court

Sunken
court

Twin temple
platforms

Sunken
court

Main Mound

| 0 | 10 | 20 | 30 | 40 | 50 mtrs |
| 0 | 50 | | 100 | | 150 ft |

A   B

Huaca A supports a central walled compound comprising scores of small chambers, possibly for the storage of religious paraphernalia and food. Along this central plaza more than 70 rectangular stone platforms, some never completed, were erected in lines flanking the north-west and south-east sides. In some cases domestic structures appear to have been destroyed to build them, but their function remains uncertain.

The Moxeke-Pampa de las Llamas complex was built and occupied for about 400 years. Like Sechín Alto, taking the Moxeke mound as the principal platform and base of the U-shape, the open arms of the U formed by the plazas and other platforms face the north-east, to the mountains and source of life-giving waters.

Above: Plan of the principal temple mound at Moxeke, a rival centre to Sechín Alto; it formed the base of a U-shaped ceremonial complex (profile in lower right shows platform elevations from north to south).

Below: View of Chanquillo in the Casma Valley, once an Early Horizon fortress and probable ceremonial centre, looking towards the mountains faced by many U-shaped ceremonial structures.

As well as the huge base platform and wings flanking the aligned plazas, there are five 'attendant' platforms – three behind (south-west) of the main platform and two south-east of it – each forming the base of a much smaller U-shaped structure. As in all complexes of the creed of the El Paraíso tradition, the arms of the U are open to the ultimate source of the waters that make the valley fertile: the distant mountains.

MOXEKE

The contemporary complex at Moxeke-Pampa de las Llamas, south of Sechín Alto, was undoubtedly a rival. It is the second largest such centre in the valley in the later Initial Period, also occupying about 200ha (495 acres). Moxeke was first excavated by Tello in 1937.

Like Sechín Alto, it was a linear complex. At Moxeke-Pampa de las Llamas, however, there were two monumental mounds – called Moxeke and Huaca A –

separated by a kilometre of aligned plazas, the largest of which is 350m (1,150ft) long. The Moxeke tiered platform was roughly square, but with rounded corners. Atop it were several chambers, and a central staircase ascends its north-east face.

PARACAS AND NAZCA CITIES

The abundance of exquisitely preserved Paracas mummy burials and their textiles has overshadowed the fact that the site was the residence of a living population as well. Archaeologists at first concentrated their efforts on what have been revealed as the dedicated cemeteries for the settlements of an entire region.

CENTRAL PARACAS

The central settlement of the Paracas people was on the Paracas Peninsula, on and around the hill of Cerro Colorado. An area of about 4,000sq m (1 acre) was occupied by habitations, known as the Cavernas phase. Square and rectangular structures of adobe walls with stone foundations were separated by narrower passageways, and compounds of such residences were scattered across the plain below Cerro Colorado. Later, the northern slope of Cerro Colorado became the new cemetery, known as the Necropolis (or Topará) phase.

Together with the deliberately separated cemeteries, the town was occupied c.300BC–c.AD200. From about 300BC

Below: The Paracas Peninsula, where three cemeteries contained generations of elite and common burials of mummified remains in multiple-layered textile bundles.

Paracas peoples were weaving not only with cotton but also with llama wool, revealing long-distance contacts with mountain herders and lending a metropolitan aspect to their culture.

TRIPARTITE 'URBANISM'

The area of the Pisco Valley and Paracas Bay is a rich environment for marine life, both on- and off-shore. Around the bay, numerous smaller, contemporary fishing hamlets were settled, whose inhabitants would have used the cemeteries as well. Similarly, in the adjacent Pisco Valley, other settlements were established for agriculture.

Altogether, domestic structures and refuse sprawl across some 54ha (133 acres). The central Paracas town was served by a spring for water, but the population relied on the settlements of the adjacent valleys for their agricultural produce.

Thus Paracas 'urban planning' appears to have comprised a tripartite pattern. Seacoast hamlets exploited the foreshore and sea, inland valley settlements irrigated and farmed the fertile lands for produce, and a central sacred town, perhaps regarded as the holiest shrine, maintained and administered sacred rites at dedicated cemeteries for the burial of the region's dead.

Above: An embroidered Paracas tunic showing a probable deity that seems to combine the Oculate Being and a Chavín-style Staff Deity, plus serpent and feline imagery.

NAZCA CONTINUITY

The partly contemporary and subsequent Nazca culture followed this pattern in the same areas of the Peruvian south coast. Nazca civilization, flourishing between c.100BC and c.AD700, was spread over a wider region of coastal valleys, making up the watersheds of the Ica and Río Grande de Nazca rivers and the Ayacucho highlands to the east.

However, in this coastal desert region many rivers never reach the sea, and in their narrow valleys support only limited irrigation networks. It has been estimated that the Nazca drainage, for example, would have been capable of supporting perhaps 15,000–22,000 people in scattered settlements.

A DELIBERATE SETTLEMENT

One of the best-known Nazca settlements is Cahuachi in the Nazca Valley, west of modern Nazca. Settlement began as a small village in the 1st century BC, and by about AD100 it had become the dominant regional centre.

Right: On the desert floor outside their cities the Nazca made and maintained hundreds of geoglyphs – ritual pathways of geometric shapes and ground images.

Its location was not accidental. For geological reasons the Nazca River flows on the surface up-valley from the site, then in mid-valley becomes subterranean, to re-surface down-valley. Cahuachi faces the Nazca Desert to the north-east, upon which the famous Nazca lines, or geoglyphs, are scattered – ritual pathways in the forms of animal and plant outlines and geometric patterns and lines.

In an area prone to drought, a need to exploit the nature of the water resource led the ancient Nazcans to develop an ingenious subterranean water-channelling system to tap the river and run-off water. Using river cobbles, they built underground aqueducts and filtering galleries, which led to reservoirs that minimized surface evaporation and fed irrigation canals. Thus the centre exploited an area of surrounding agricultural settlements and sacred landscape use.

Cahuachi comprised a core of about 40 low hills, enhanced with platforms of adobe bricks. The largest, called the Great Temple, rises *c*.30m (*c*.98ft) high in six or seven terraces. Surrounding the platforms are plazas and adobe-walled

Below: Some Nazca geoglyphs combine ritual pathways with aligned areas of large 'designated space', possibly for the gathering of crowds of worshippers.

compounds. There are no workshops or storage structures, or domestic refuse. These features support the interpretation of Cahuachi as a sacred centre, a religious city for worship and burial, which served the population in the settlements of the surrounding region. The entire settlement covers about 11.5sq km (2,841 acres).

In contrast, a nearly straight road leads north from Cahuachi to Ventilla. Here, covering at least 2sq km (495 acres; much of the site has been destroyed beneath modern agriculture), sprawled a residential city of habitation terraces, walled compounds and mounds. It is the largest Nazca settlement known, and believed to be the urban counterpart to Cahuachi.

Major construction at Cahuachi ceased *c*.AD550 as Nazca civilization began to wane.

Thus Nazca civilization, like Paracas, appears to have comprised a tripartite configuration. Dispersed settlements exploited the available coastal and valley environments, expanding on the Paracas pattern as regional population increased. Their inhabitants exchanged produce and marine resources among themselves (as well as trading with more distant cultures), and were served by specialized towns for civil administration and for sacred rites and burial. In addition, the adjacent desert floor became a canvas upon which ritual pathways supplemented the sacred purposes of the shrine and cemetery capital.

ROYAL MOCHE

The Moche people built several large man-made structures in their capital, including the alleged temples to the Sun and Moon.

SUN AND MOON PYRAMIDS

The Huacas del Sol and de la Luna formed the core of the most important ceremonial centre of the Early Intermediate Period Moche Kingdom. Construction of the two monumental platforms was begun *c.*AD100. By *c.*AD450 Moche was the capital of the southern Moche realm. Between *c.*AD300 and 550 several ceremonial centres were built to administer the southern Moche valleys: Huancaco in the Virú Valley, the misnamed Pampa de los Incas in the Santa, Pañamarca in the Nepeña, and Mocollope in the Chicama. Dominating them all was the capital at Moche in the Moche Valley.

The names 'Sol' and 'Luna' are modern. We are uncertain of the site's ancient name, but an early Spanish Colonial document refers to the site as 'Capuxaida'.

Below: Murals at Moche Huaca de la Luna include a rich array of creatures important to religious ritual and economic wellbeing – for a coastal civilization, sea fish were important.

The Moche complex follows planning traditions dating back to earlier periods in the northern and central coastal Peruvian valleys, with dominant ceremonial platforms within a working city. The two platforms stand 500m (1,650ft) apart across a now open area. The pyramids are constructed of millions of unbaked adobe bricks.

MAN-MADE MOUNTAINS

The Huaca del Sol, rising 40m (130ft) above the Moche Valley floor, is the largest single man-made structure ever built in the ancient Andes. In Andean religious tradition it appears that the Moche were attempting to create symbolic mountains on the river plain, perhaps to honour the sky gods, and in recognition that the ultimate source of the waters of their rivers came from the distant mountains to the east. Spanish treasure-seekers used those very waters in 1602 when they attempted to wash away Huaca del Sol by diverting the River Moche, obliterating about two-thirds of it. Enough of two wings remain to show the cross-shaped plan of the monumental platform.

Huaca del Sol formed a cross of thick arms on the long axis (345m/1,130ft) and stubby arms across the short axis (160m/525ft). Built in four tiers, the summit is reached by a monumental ramp up its north side.

Huaca de la Luna sits at the base of a small hill called Cerro Blanco. It was raised in three tiers against the western side of the hill to form a platform 290m (950ft) wide (north–south) and 210m

Above: San José de Moro, Jequetepeque Valley, Peru, where rich Moche tombs were found containing the remains of priestesses dressed like those in the Moche Pañamarca murals.

(690ft) deep (east–west) for the support of three smaller platform-mounds, four plazas and several roofed enclosures. It rises 32m (105ft) above the valley floor.

Below: A Moche ceramic effigy of a warrior with a war club from the Atacama Desert in northern Chile reveals Moche influence from northern coastal Peru.

Above: The huge Moche Huaca del Sol was built of an estimated 143 million adobe mud bricks. Its construction was apparently done by gangs of workmen.

Many exterior walls were whitewashed, or were painted with red or yellow ochre. The faces of many of the courtyard walls are decorated with a varied array of friezes in moulded mud-plaster and murals of religious themes. As with the Huaca del Sol, Spanish looters destroyed more than two-thirds of the uppermost tier when they dug a huge pit in the belief that the foundations contained treasure.

Archaeologists have identified eight stages in the construction of Huaca del Sol, as it was modified and enhanced over the centuries, most of them finished before AD450. At least six phases of construction are recognized for Huaca de la Luna.

NEARLY 200 MILLION BRICKS!
The millions of adobe bricks of the two pyramids themselves reveal something of the immense organizational effort necessary to build them, and the political power the monuments must represent. Archaeologists estimate that Huaca del Sol required some 143 million bricks and Huaca de la Luna 50 million. Many bricks were needed simply to bury earlier structures and make levelled platforms for new construction. The rectangular, moulded bricks are stacked in tall, column-like segments. Groups of bricks are impressed with distinct 'maker's marks', of which more than 100 marks and patterns have been found. Marks include single or multiple dots, placed at different positions on the brick faces, sometimes even in patterns resembling animal paw marks. Other marks are lines running across, down or diagonally on the brick faces. Still others are curved lines, or combinations of lines and dots. Some are miniature symbols: a dot and circle, or dot and curve; a crook-like line; an S-shape; a U-shape; a human footprint; a duck-like footprint; a dot with radiating arms; and a pottery jar profile.

A WORKING CITY
In its heyday, the ancient city covered about 3sq km (740 acres). Archaeological evidence shows that the expanse between the two platforms, and beyond them, was occupied by hundreds of workshops and houses, incorporating the religious structures within the city, much like a medieval European cathedral city. Most of the ancient city is buried beneath up to 2m (6½ft) of washed-in alluvium.

Excavations have revealed houses; pottery, metalworking and textile workshops of cobblestone foundations, with superstructures of perishable materials (presumably cane, thatch and wood); and more well-built housing of stone, with plastered adobe walls. The latter had larger rooms and finer ceramics associated with them.

Within workshops the excavators found large ceramic water-storage jars, stores of ground clay and finished vessels, and also the kilns and tools for pottery making, including scores of moulds. Finished products included containers, many of them painted with combat and deer-hunting scenes, and figurines, portrait heads, rattles, weavers' spindle whorls and crucibles for holding molten metal. Other shops had *tuyères* (ceramic tips of blow-tubes used in metalworking) and metal slag.

Excavators also discovered a winding canal especially dug to bring water into the workshops and residential areas.

Below: A mural at Moche Huaca de la Luna shows colourful ritual imagery of Andean creatures, including humans, fish, tropical birds and monkeys, and a jaguar.

IMPERIAL TIWANAKU

The capital of the Tiwanaku Empire was the world's highest ancient city, seated on the plain south of Lake Titicaca in modern Bolivia at 3,850m (12,600ft) above sea level.

EARLY BEGINNINGS
Tiwanaku was founded as early as *c.*250BC, one of several centres of the Yaya-Mama religious cult, based at the cities of Pukará and Taraco at the north end of the lake, and succeeding earlier architectural traditions at Chiripa, on the south lakeshore. Monumental construction had begun by *c.*AD200, in the middle of the Early Intermediate Period and by AD500 Tiwanaku was the capital of a substantial empire ruling the southern Andean region through the Middle Horizon until *c.*AD1000. In this period of political and religious unification, Tiwanku rivalled the central Andean Wari Empire. By the Late Horizon the city lay in ruins, but was recognized as a sacred city by the Incas.

Below: A carved stone alignment atop the Akapana ceremonial mound at Tiwanaku, showing slots, shelves and holes.

At its height, the capital covered some 6sq km (1,485 acres). Notice of the ancient ruins began with Cieza de León in the 16th century. Studies of the standing monuments were undertaken by Ephraim G. Squier, Alphons Stübel and Max Uhle in the 19th century and were continued by Adolph Bandelier, who excavated several parts of the site in 1911. Wendell C. Bennett did excavations in the 1940s, as did Alan Kolata in the 1980s along with surveys of the entire region.

Excavations concentrated on the main civic-ceremonial monuments, stone gateways, ceremonial platforms and stone sculptures of the city centre, and their art. Evidence of the surrounding residential city is substantial, but much lies beneath agricultural fields. The ancient city was surrounded by raised fields created by draining the wetlands of the southern lakeshore plain with canals – a technology lost during the Spanish Colonial period but revived in the late 20th century.

THE CIVIC-CEREMONIAL CORE
Among the high Andean peaks of the Titicaca Basin, Tiwanaku was believed to be the home of mountain deities and the

Above: The so-called Gateway of the Moon at Tiwanaku, like the Gateway of the Sun, is made from a single stone block. Its lintel is carved with typical Tiwanaku geometric patterns.

ultimate origin of the Supreme Being, Viracocha. The nearby Islands of the Sun and the Moon in the southern lake were believed to be the places of the origin of celestial bodies. The ceremonial core of the city appears to have been deliberately planned as an artificial 'island', surrounded by a moat, its monuments mimicking the surrounding landscape as symbolic 'mountains' and 'valleys'.

The shape of the carefully planned ceremonial centre was conceived by *c.*AD300. The principal monuments are aligned east–west, and are laid out in a grid pattern. A system of stone-lined and covered drains channelled rainwater from the monuments and plazas into the moat.

Assigning exact functions to the various structures is difficult. Undoubtedly some were sacred temples and others served more civic functions, including palaces for Tiwanaku's rulers. Several monumental stone gateways into open plazas, together with standing colossal statuary, show that the core area was public and provided large spaces for ceremonial gatherings – religious and civic.

Above: The Kalasasaya walled compound and Semi-Subterranean Court in Tiwanaku's ceremonial centre reveal a huge enclosure for large numbers of worshippers and a smaller sunken court for more intimate ritual.

TEMPLES AND SUNKEN COURTS

The most sacred structure was the Akapana Temple. Standing 17m (56ft) above the city plaza, it covered an area of 50sq m (540sq ft), in the shape of a 'stepped' cross. At its summit stood a sunken court, drained by covered water channels. Its core was built up of rough fill and clay when the moat was excavated. The top is reached by staircases up the east and west ends, continuing as staircases descending into the sunken court, itself in the plan of a quadrilateral stepped cross.

North of Akapana, the Semi-Subterranean Temple (a sunken court measuring 28.5 x 26m/94 x 85ft) is entered by a staircase on its south side. From the court walls protrude carved stone heads, and in the centre stand several carved stone stelae, originally including the 'Bennett Stela' (7.3m/24ft high) of a richly dressed human, possibly a monument to one of Tiwanaku's ancient rulers. North of Akapana and west of the Semi-Subterranean Temple, the Kalasasaya is a low-lying rectangular platform (130 x 120m/427 x 394ft), which forms a large precinct for public ritual. It is reached by a stairway between two gigantic stone pillars and its walls are made up of alternating sandstone pillars and ashlar blocks.

In the north-west corner of the Kalasasaya stands the Gateway of the Sun, comprising a single huge andesite block, carved with the 'Gateway God' – a deity reminiscent of the Chavín Staff Being, standing on a stepped platform and flanked by three rows of winged figures. Within the precinct stands the Ponce Stela (3.5m/11½ft), perhaps of another of the city's rulers.

Other nearby ceremonial precincts include the Putuni and Kheri Kala compounds, aligned west of Kalasasaya, and the Chunchukala off the north-west corner. South-east of Akapana the T-shaped Pumapunku temple mound comprised three sandstone slab-covered tiers (5m/16ft high and covering 150sq m/1,615sq ft). Its sunken summit courtyard might have been an earlier location of the Gateway of the Sun.

SUBURBS OF TIWANAKU

The surrounding residential city comprised dense concentrations of adobe-walled houses on cobblestone foundations. There were also distinct elite *barrios* of high, adobe-walled compounds on river-cobble platforms. Estimates of the ancient city's population range from 20,000 to 40,000 inhabitants.

Alan Kolata describes Tiwanaku as a 'patrician city', in which residence was restricted to those who served imperial functions – a precursor of Inca Cuzco.

Below: From within the Semi-Subterranean Court the Kalasasaya's entry gate frames the Ponce Stela, one of several monolithic 'gods' standing in Tiwanaku's ceremonial centre.

IMPERIAL HUARI

Huari, the ancient Middle Horizon capital of the Wari Empire, sits in a central Andean highland plateau about 2,800m (9,180ft) above sea level. The imperial rival of Tiwanaku, together the two empires ruled the central and southern Andes, sharing much in religious heritage but differing in artistic and architectural expression, and apparently in their imperial modes of expansion and operation.

NEGLECTED RUINS

Huari's ruins were neglected in comparison to those of Tiwanaku, for they lack the obvious monumentality of singular, outstanding structures and colossal statuary. Huari's principal 20th-century surveyors and excavators are Wendell C. Bennett and Luis Lumbreras in the 1940s and 1950s, and William Isbell through the 1970s and 1980s. The ruins were noticed

Below: Cacti and agave line ancient fields near the Wari city of Ayacucho.

by Cieza de León, who travelled through the area in the 1540s, though he commented only that there were 'some large and very old buildings' there 'in a state of ruin and decay'. The site has been much looted, its sculptures mostly found in nearby farmhouses and many of its walls robbed from Spanish Colonial times for building stone.

Huari did not have the ancient pedigree steeped in local cultural development that Tiwanaku did, and seems to have arisen rapidly in a region that earlier had only scattered small towns. It was a city planned according to what appear to be strict rules of modular units, incrementally expanded as need arose, but seemingly at random, without the deliberate and preconceived planning of Tiwanaku. Ancient Huari's heyday as an imperial capital was from c.AD600 to 800, when it covered as much as 5.5sq km (1,360 acres).

GRID PLAN

Huari is laid out across undulating terrain, disregarding local topography in favour of a uniformity of structural planning. Its architectural forms have no local or regional forerunners. It comprised a grid

Above: Ruins of the hillfort on top of Cerro Baúl in the Moquegua Valley, the only valley to house both early Wari and Tiwanaku colonies.

pattern of high-walled compounds made of roughly dressed megalithic ashlar blocks, a pattern that is the hallmark of Huari itself and of Wari provincial cities, which were built as the empire expanded.

From regional settlement, possibly as early as the 3rd century AD, the city began its rapid growth towards the end of the 5th century AD, and within 100 years had become the leading regional ceremonial and residential centre. The city grew quickly, from 1 to 2sq km (250–490 acres), until the core of ancient Huari covered up to 3sq km (740 acres), with suburban residential additions of up to another 2.5sq km (620 acres). Population estimates vary widely between 10,000 and 70,000 inhabitants.

The early city was built around several large ceremonial enclosures of dressed stone: the Cheqo Wasi enclosure, and temple complexes called Vegachayoq Moqo and Moraduchayoq. Moraduchayoq was semi-subterranean and made of finely dressed volcanic tuff blocks reminiscent

Above: This magnificent gold mask and mummy bundle from the Wari culture dates from c.AD800.

of the type of construction used at Tiwanaku, perhaps by design. Most other compound and structure walls at Huari are built of rougher, quarried stone blocks set in mud mortar.

The Moraduchayoq Temple was short-lived, however, for it was dismantled c.AD650, while more residential structures were built to fill the areas around the ceremonial enclosures. These urban and suburban dwellings were distinct rectangular and trapezoidal compounds separated by narrow streets forming a grid-like urban plan. In the northern sector of the city the compounds typically measured 150–300m (490–985ft) each side.

Within the high walls of the compounds were numerous square and rectangular courtyard groups surrounded by long, narrow, domestic rooms, some multi-storey, with narrow doorways into the courtyards and between rooms. Some compound and house walls still stand as high as 12m (40ft), indicating perhaps three storeys. Some compound walls are

massive, being several metres or yards wide. Projecting corbels supported the upper floors; roofs were probably thatched. Courtyards often had stone benches along their sides, numerous wall niches and stone-lined drains beneath their floors.

In addition to the domestic compounds, excavations revealed what must have been pottery workshops in the northern sector called Ushpa Qoto. These compounds had storage areas containing pottery moulds for producing multiple, uniform vessels and unformed lumps of clay and other pottery-making equipment.

INSTANT COLLAPSE

Much of this rapid civic expansion in Huari appears to have been unfinished. The long, massive walls, which appear to date from the city's final decades, surround compounds that were never filled in with domestic divisions, but rather reflect an ambitious urban renewal that

came to nothing. Political crisis appears to have caused the rapid collapse of the empire, for the city was abandoned shortly after the walls were erected.

Endemic of the rapid development of the capital, the Wari founded a provincial city, Pikillacta, near Cuzco, c.AD650. It comprised a huge, single rectangular enclosure 630 x 745m (2,067 x 2,444ft), enclosing nearly 0.5 sq km (124 acres). The compound was subdivided into four sectors, nearly all of which were further divided into regimented, cell-like rooms, and a few with long, peripheral galleries and halls lined with niches. There is only one larger and a few smaller open areas. Pikillacta was abandoned later than the capital, c.AD850–900. Some of the doorways were sealed and there is evidence of fire in the central sector of the city.

Below: Eroded hills tower over the stone ruins of Pikillacta, the provincial city founded by the Wari c.AD650.

CHAN CHAN OF THE CHIMÚ

The imperial capital of the Chimú Empire was founded between AD900 and 1000, and flourished until its conquest by the Incas in the 1470s. Chimú rulers were the inheritors of the north-west coast traditions of ancient Moche and Lambayeque-Sicán. Their capital, Chan Chan, was north of the river, not far from the ancient ruins of the Huacas del Sol and de la Luna in the Moche Valley.

LIVING AND DEAD CITIZENRY

Chan Chan was a city of both the living and the dead. Its centre covers 6sq km (1,480 acres), while greater ancient Chan Chan covered a total area of c.20sq km (4,940 acres). Not all of the city was occupied at the same time, and it is conjectured that city architects earmarked

Below: The central precinct of the vast city of Chan Chan, the Chimú capital, housed the compounds of the living and dead (former) rulers, and was a rich prize to the Incas.

areas of open land for future development. Nevertheless, Chan Chan at its height was the largest city ever known in the ancient Andes (and rivals the size of ancient Teotihuacán in Mesoamerica). A great wall marks the northern city limits, through which a long avenue runs north–south towards the imperial residential core of the city.

Chan Chan's most famous structures, and the ruins most examined, are its great rectangular walled compounds, called *ciudadelas* (a modern name meaning 'citadel'), enclosed within monumental mud-plastered walls. There are 10 named compounds and possibly several others recognizable in plans of the central city. Those named are: Chayhuac, Uhle, Tello, Laberinto (Labyrinth), Grán Chimú, Squier, Velarde, Bandelier, Tschudi and Rivero. All are oriented with their long axes north–south. North and east of them there are several larger structures, known as *huacas* (Huacas Obispo, las Conchas, Toledo,

Above: The Tschudi and other ciudadela *compounds at Chan Chan have hundreds of* audiencia *courtyards lined with sculpted poured-mud walls and storage niches.*

las Avispas and el Higo) – huge, presumably ceremonial, platforms, one of which (Obispo) is 20m (66ft) above the valley floor – that might have supported temples. (Treasure-seekers have so severely destroyed them with pits that we cannot be certain.)

The *ciudadela* walls are made of tapia (poured adobe or mud) on stone foundations. Most are well preserved, and stand as high as 9m (30ft). Each compound is believed to have housed the reigning Chimú emperor, along with his court retainers and civil servants to administer the affairs of state – perhaps much like the Forbidden City of imperial Chinese Beijing.

INTERIOR DIVISIONS

Most *ciudadelas* have a single entrance on the north side, through a doorway flanked by niches in which stand carved and painted wooden statues. Within, each compound is subdivided north to south, although internal organization varies in the earlier *ciudadelas*. There is first a large entry courtyard with walls decorated with mud-brick friezes, then miniature U-shaped temple structures called *audiencias* – reminiscent of the ancient U-shaped complexes of the Initial Period and Early Horizon more than 1,000 years earlier – and finally the burial platform

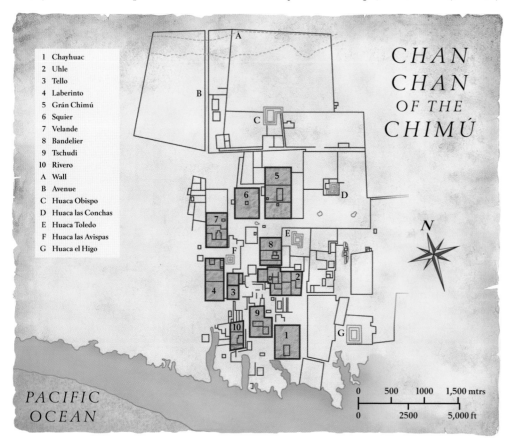

1 Chayhuac
2 Uhle
3 Tello
4 Laberinto
5 Grán Chimú
6 Squier
7 Velande
8 Bandelier
9 Tschudi
10 Rivero
A Wall
B Avenue
C Huaca Obispo
D Huaca las Conchas
E Huaca Toledo
F Huaca las Avispas
G Huaca el Higo

CHAN CHAN OF THE CHIMÚ

N

PACIFIC OCEAN

0   500   1000   1,500 mtrs

0   2500   5,000 ft

Right: The remains of a massive poured-mud wall at Chan Chan reveals the huge bulk of the royal compounds.

of the deceased ruler. Nine *ciudadelas* include a truncated pyramid in the southeast corner, concealing rooms entered from the top of the platform and a main room to house the mummified body of the deceased ruler.

Other inner courts, connected to the *audiencias*, are lined with rows of storerooms. Adjoining wings of patios and rooms contain walk-in wells and are thought to be the residences for retainers and servants to maintain the compounds.

A CONFUSING HISTORY

The named *ciudadelas* provide a tantalizing parallel with Chimú legend. Depending on how they are designated, scholars count between 9 and 12 palace compounds. An *Anonymous History of Trujillo* of 1604 records the legendary founder of the Chimú dynasty as Chimu

Below: The poured-mud walls of every royal compound at Chan Chan are covered with sculpted geometric patterns and imagery.

Capac or Taycanamu, followed by 11 more rulers. Inca sources, however, record only ten Chimú rulers.

The sequence of *ciudadela* history is uncertain. It is argued that *ciudadela* Chayhuac, the most southerly, is the earliest, and that the capital first expanded northwards, including Uhle. Gran Chimú and the great wall demarked the northern limit of the imperial centre. Further expansion filled in the western core, including Tello and Laberinto. After that the central city was filled in with *ciudadelas* Squier, Velarde, Bandelier, Tschudi and Rivero, with room being made for the last two by razing parts of the old southern core.

Some scholars reason that the rectangular plans and tripartite internal divisions of the *ciudadelas* were inspired by the walled compounds and cell-like divisions of Wari cities. Others argue that they reflect a pattern begun in the preceding civil government of the late Moche city of Galindo, a physically much closer model.

URBAN SPRAWL

The urban sprawl of Chan Chan comprised emulative compounds of elite citizens among and around the *ciudadelas*, and compact *barrios* of small-roomed residences of the ordinary citizenry, estimated at about 26,000, in the south and west of the city. Common citizens comprised a main group of farmers, and the personal retainers of elite households, skilled artisans and craftspeople such as potters, weavers, carvers and metalworkers, traders and labourers – about half in each group.

Whereas the *ciudadelas* contained as many as 200 storerooms, no elite residence had more than 10. Ordinary citizens lived in cane-walled and plastered (called *quincha* or wattle-and-daub) houses. These had common walls and were organized into distinct *barrios* (neighbourhoods) lining winding streets. Scattered among them were a few better houses of minor elites.

Among the southern suburbs were also several cemeteries and garden plots dug into the valley floor to tap the water table (some still in use today).

THE IMPERIAL INCA CAPITAL AND ITS CITIES

The Incas established provincial administrative cities at strategic locations throughout the empire. Sometimes Inca administrative buildings, temples and ceremonial plazas with *ushnu* platforms were built within existing cities, as in the Chimú Kingdom or at Pachacamac. In other cases they built new cities, colonizing unoccupied areas by moving whole populations of conquered subjects.

CUZCO

The imperial capital, the 'navel of the world', was mostly built by Pachacuti and his successors. It had a unique plan – that of a crouching puma. Other Inca cities followed more conventional grid plans. Wedged into the confluences of the Chunchullmayo, Tullumayo and Huatanay rivers, the river courses were channelled within conduits of stone walls.

The core of the city comprised two ceremonial plazas, around which were arranged numerous *kancha* compounds of large, thatch-roofed *kallanka* halls. Some were the residences of living Inca emperors; others housed the mummies (*mallquis*) of deceased rulers.

Cuzco's most sacred building, southeast of the plazas, was the Coricancha (the 'Golden Enclosure'), the temple of the principal Inca deities: Viracocha (Creator), Inti (Sun), Quilla (Moon), Chaska-Qoylor (Venus), Illapa (Thunder and the weather) and Cuichu (Rainbow). Its masonry exemplifies Inca stone fitting and now supports the Church of Santo Domingo. From the Coricancha radiated 41 sacred *ceque* routes and lines to shrines and holy sites.

North-west of the city, the sacred temple of Sacsahuaman sat on a hill looming over the plazas and formed the head of the puma. Made of closely fitted masonry blocks and planned with regular angles to mimic the peaks and valleys of the distant mountains, its revetments terraced the summit, on which stood a rare circular Inca Sun temple. Simultaneously sacred and military, Sacsahuaman was the venue for religious ritual and the storehouse for Inca army weapons and armour.

The four main imperial trunk roads emanated from the city, leading through planned agricultural settlements, terraced fields, canals and state storehouses.

HUÁNUCO PAMPA

This imperial administrative centre was built on the highland trunk road heading north from Cuzco to Quito via Cajamarca. It sat at an elevation of 3,800m (12,500ft) in Chinchaysuyu

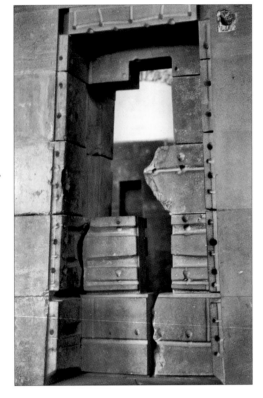

Above: Special niches were built into the Coricancha temple to Inti, the sun, at Cuzco, for mounting plate-gold sheets on the walls.

quarter. It was one of the largest Inca settlements, covering some 2sq km (495 acres). Construction began in the middle of the 15th century and was still underway when Pizarro invaded the empire. By then, it comprised some 4,000 structures.

Its two-tiered *ushnu* platform, symbol of Inca domination, was the largest in the empire. It measured 32 x 48m (105 x 157ft) at the base, and overlooked a ceremonial plaza of 550 x 350m (1,800 x 1,150ft).

The city contained elements similar to those at Cuzco, and fit for a major administrative capital. There was an *acllahuasi* (house of the virgins – devotees to Inti), a *kallanka* (administrative building for imperial officials) and several *kancha* compounds of administrative buildings.

Left: The rocky outcrops of Sacsahuaman to the north-west of the imperial capital were formed into the temple to the sun god Inti.

Right: Throughout their empire, along with the imperial roads system, the Incas established provincial administrative cities.

On the hillside south of the city the Incas built rows of hundreds of storehouses for goods collected by imperial tax officials.

OLLANTAYTAMBO

Like Machu Picchu, Ollantaytambo was an imperial estate and retreat north of the capital, at the confluence of the Urubamba and Patakancha rivers, in Antisuyu quarter.

The eastern part was residential, as distinct from the western side, which had a temple to Viracocha and Inti and its associated structures. Just north of Cuzco, on a spur road to Machu Picchu, it was a small city for about 1,000 permanent residents.

So close to the capital, Ollantaytambo was probably an imperial household residence, and an administrative and ceremonial centre for the empire. It was a late Inca foundation, and its Temple to Inti was still being built when the Spaniards invaded. Unused building stones, quarried from nearby Kachiqhata, litter the site.

Stone shrines at carved rock faces lie below and north of the temple hill, which is surrounded by elaborate waterworks.

Below: Huánuco Pampa, an Inca provincial administrative city, was built with mortarless, fitted stone blocks.

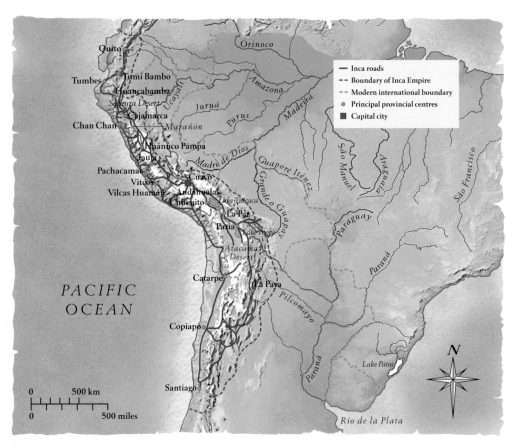

TAMBO COLORADO

At the end of a trunk road running west, this city linked Cuzco to the coast, near the Chinchaysuyu–Cuntisuyu border. It is the best-preserved Inca coastal foundation, deliberately planned and built in local style using adobe brick construction. Traces of red, yellow and white paint survive on the plastered walls of its *kallanka* and other administrative and residential buildings.

The city's trapezoidal-shaped ceremonial plaza has a low-lying *ushnu* at its western end.

TAMBO VIEJO

In Cuntisusyu quarter, south-west of Cuzco in the Acari Valley, Tambo Viejo was established on an ancient Nazca site. The coastal trunk road ran into its ceremonial plaza and led north to Tambo Colorado.

The rectangular plaza, built by a bluff of the river, has an *ushnu* platform of river cobbles, and overlooks the river as well as the plaza.

VILCAS HUAMÁN

As Inca imperial aspirations in the early 15th century expanded beyond the Cuzco Valley, Vilcas, 80km (50 miles) south-east of

Ayacucho in Cuntisusyu quarter, was one of the first regions conquered. The modern city covers most of the Inca buildings, but the Spanish Colonial plaza corresponds to the Inca ceremonial one. Its *ushnu* platform, on one side of the plaza, is constructed of classic Inca fine-fitted, block masonry, and is one of the most elaborate ever built. A stone staircase led to the summit through a double-jambed entryway.

Facing the plaza, the Temple to Inti sits on a triple-terraced platform with trapezoidal doorways and niches, and is approached by a dual stairway.

Below: Tambo Colorado utilized scarce local stone and the fine silts of the coastal plain to build its mud-brick walls.

179

MACHU PICCHU AND THE INCA TRAIL

Machu Picchu is probably the best-known and most-photographed Andean site. North of the Inca capital at Cuzco, it is perched dramatically in the high Andes above the Urubamba River, profiles of its structures framed by distant snow-capped peaks. Machu Picchu has been variously described as a remote Inca fortress, an imperial sanctuary, and a citadel – a last place of retreat and refuge of the Inca imperial household.

AN IMPERIAL ESTATE

In fact it was originally none of these things, but to some extent it effectively served in all of these capacities and more.

The site was chosen and established by the emperor Pachacuti Inca Yupanqui, the reigning Sapa Inca in the mid-15th century. Imperial and early Spanish Colonial records show that the site and area were an imperial estate of Pachacuti, subsequently inherited by his successors. Another imperial estate established by Pachacuti was at Ollantaytambo, farther upstream in the Urubamba Valley.

LOST AND FOUND

After the Spanish Conquest the site was effectively 'lost' because of its remote location. Although referred to in colonial records, its location remained a mystery and intrigued 19th-century explorers and archaeologists. It was re-discovered by

Hiram Bingham in 1911 on a general exploring expedition in which Bingham's own tale makes it seem as if he stumbled upon the ancient ruins by chance. In fact, locals had known of the site since colonial times, and a local farmer had described the site to Bingham when he and his team arrived in the valley.

Bingham brought the spectacular find to the attention of the Western world and claimed that he had discovered the last Inca capital. Subsequent systematic survey of the Urubamba Valley, however, has shown that the final Inca capital was established at Vilcabamba, much farther downstream.

Machu Picchu's inaccessible position, apparent defensive walls and surrounding dry moat led to its label as a fortress and retreat. However, its architecture is predominantly religious and these defensive

Left: The Torreón at Machu Picchu incorporates a stone outcrop with a rare Inca curved wall of fitted stones.

Above: Winding roads leading to Machu Picchu, probably the most evocative of all ancient Andean cities.

features appear to have been more for restricting access than for repelling attackers. A mountain road linked the site to a series of minor settlements strung up the Urubamba Valley along the forested slopes of high forest.

SACRED ARCHITECTURE

Its impressive architecture was certainly carefully built to special requirements. The granite building material was quarried locally on-site. The quality of the stone finishing and fitting is of the highest Inca standards, especially in the structures known as the Temple of the Three Windows and the Torreón (Tower; sometimes also referred to as the Observatorio). The latter was most likely actually a temple to Inti, the sun god, as indeed is perhaps the primary function of the entire site.

Map labels: Temple of the Moon *2,850m (9,350ft)*; Huayna Picchu; Aguas Calientes Hot Spring *Machupicchu Pueblo 2,000m (6,562ft) Train Station*; Inka bridge; Intipata; Inti Punko *2,700m (8,858ft)*; Machu Picchu *2,500m (8,202ft)*; Wiñay Wayna; New route; Old route; Inca tunnel; 3rd pass *3,650m (11,975ft)*; Phuyu Pata Marca *3,600m (11,811ft)*; Inca tunnel; 2nd pass *3,950m (12,959ft)*; Chaquicocha *Dry lake 3,660m (12,008ft)*; Concha Marca; Sayac Marca *3,600m (11,811ft)*; Runca Raccay *3,800m (12,467ft)*; 1st pass *4,200m (13,779ft)*; Urubamba River; Pacaymayu River; Machu Quente; Corihuayrachina *2,500m (8,202ft)*; Km 82 *2,500m (8,202ft) Road ends here & the train stops here*; Chilca; Patallacta & Pulpituyoc; Cusichaca River; Huillca Raccay; Miskay *2,650m (8,694ft)*; Hatunchaca; Huayllabamba *3,000m (9,842ft)*; Trail from Salkantay; *Inca Trail to* **MACHU PICCHU**

Elevation chart labels: Machu Picchu; Wiñayhuayna; Phuyupatamarca; Sayacmarca; Runcuraccay; Huarmi Wañusca; Lluluchapampa; Huayllabacta; Patallacta; KM 82; Chilca

Legend: Inca Trail; Railway; Archeological site; Campsite; Viewpoint; Pass; River

But we will probably never fully know the meaning of Machu Picchu. It is likely that the site's purpose altered through time, even though its rapid establishment and construction were planned. The Inca emperors developed a tradition of building commemorative monuments and establishing settlements to mark their conquests. Early in his reign, Pachacuti had subdued the area, in conquests that more than doubled the size of the empire ruled by his predecessor. Machu Picchu itself, together with the smaller sites and road to it (the 'Inca Trail'), are typical of such memorialization. Sixteenth-century Spanish Colonial documents of land-tenure suggest that the settlement was the headquarters of an estate founded by Pachacuti and managed through the later 15th and early 16th centuries by his lineage.

'CITY' OR MANOR?
Machu Picchu's architects integrated the structures and compounds into the lie of the land. The architecture is deliberately

Below: Machu Picchu, imperial city, estate and mountain retreat of the Incas built by Pachacuti Inca Yupanqui (1438–71).

sympathetic to Andean sacred regard for the landscape. Its dramatic structures appear 'draped' over a ridge overlooking the river. A chain of 16 spring-fed, stone-lined water channels lead into catchments to supply the site. Doorways and windows were positioned to frame views of nearby peaks of the Urubamba and Vilcabamba ranges, and natural outcrops were carved to imitate mountain shapes.

Above: The 'Inca Trail', a modern tourist contrivance, follows the route of the imperial Inca highway leading north-west of Cuzco up the Urubamba Valley to Machu Picchu.

The quality of the construction and the obvious religious purposes of many of its structures show that it was more than a remote outpost in the eastern Inca provinces, however. The residential remains at Machu Picchu indicate that about 1,000 people lived there. Together with administrative compounds and workshops it formed a functioning imperial source of income as well as a religious retreat – in fact, like many other estates, a sort of miniature city reflecting the capital at Cuzco.

BYPASSED
Machu Picchu was abandoned in the second decade of the 16th century, shortly before the Spanish invasion. It thus could never have been a last redoubt of the beleaguered Inca imperial household. The Spaniards, pursuing a rebel Inca force that had retreated to Vilcabamba, followed a route through the adjacent Amaybamba Valley to the north-east of Ollantaytambo, thus missing Machu Picchu entirely.

181

CHAPTER NINE

STONE AND CLAY SCULPTURE

Ancient Andeans sculptured in all materials – stone, clay, wood, metals and textiles. This chapter covers stone and clay sculpture.

Mountain peoples tended to sculpt in stone, while coastal peoples worked with mud and clay.

The range of styles and subjects is extraordinary. Much of the purpose of monumental stone sculpture, plaster wall carving and small clay figurines was connected with religious ritual. Whether they were made from adobe or stone, these colossal statues, sculpted walls, statuary and all kinds of imagery were carved to portray fearsome human-beast figures to awe ceremonial audiences and constantly remind them of their duties to the gods. Alternatively, statuary and imagery were buried as offerings in caches or human burials associated with temples.

Effigy vessels were especially popular from the Early Intermediate Period onwards. Almost every kind of animal and bird was sculpted. Bottles were made in the shapes of gourds. Humans are portrayed with almost every imaginable condition or doing everyday and ritual tasks.

And there are even models of buildings – curious, functional vessels in the shapes of houses and temples, which help archaeologists to understand aspects of ancient Andean life that are otherwise undocumented.

Left: Huaca del Dragón near the Chimú capital of Chan Chan – detail of rainbow and solar flare wall sculpture.

CARVING IN STONE

Stone sculpturing began in, or was brought to, the New World by the earliest hunter-gatherers. These were the carefully crafted stone tools used for hunting and food processing. Finely shaped projectile points demonstrate the developed skills of their makers as surely as do the artistic sculpted stone figures of deities, animals and plants of ancient Andean civilizations.

STONE WARRIORS

The earliest large stone sculptures of the Andean Area are the provocative incised figures on the flat stone stelae forming the wall of Cerro Sechín at the junction of the Sechín and Moxeke rivers in the Casma Valley. No other Peruvian Initial Period or Early Horizon site has more individual sculptures – nearly 400 in all.

Granite blocks quarried from the hill behind the site were carefully dressed by pecking and abrasion with sand and water to make flat-sided slabs of two sizes: c.3 x 1m (c.10 x 3ft) and c.85cm x 70cm (c.2½ft x 2⅓ft).

These were incised with fine lines c.7mm (⅓in) deep and c.11mm (½in) wide, depicting victorious warriors and their victims, plus two banners on tall stelae flanking the main platform's central staircase. Victims and their body parts – including numerous severed heads – have closed eyes and agonized mouths and are contorted in postures of torture and pain, some with spilled entrails. Marching victorious warriors carry war clubs, and severed heads dangle from their belts or hands. Two slabs with similar warriors flank the temple compound's back entrance.

The gruesome accuracy of these sculptures initiated an Andean tradition of realism in sculpture, as well as the glorification of beheading and collecting trophy heads. Similar stone slabs have also been found at Sechín Alto and Chupacoto.

Of similar date, a single, rectangular stone slab at Moxeke has two incised faces: a naturalistic human hand and a double-bodied snake.

Above: Some of the earliest Andean stone carving was monumental and commemorative, including this head from Cerro Sechín.

MORTARS, BOWLS AND A MOSAIC

In a completely different style, angular mythical humanoid figures, facing full frontal (anticipating Chavín staff-bearing figures), with one arm outstretched and a corresponding motif covering one eye, adorn the outsides of large stone mortars from Santa and Nepeña valley sites.

Initial Period Cupisnique steatite stone bowls continued the trophy head motif and anticipate the complex imagery of later sculpture. Their interiors have elaborate carved spiders – an imagery anticipating Moche spider art. With bulbous bodies, exaggerated pincer-jaws, pedipalps (male reproductive organs) or spinnerets (female silk-spinning organs), they bear human faces and frequently grasp trophy heads or net bags of severed heads. They are frequently surrounded by lush plant growth, from which sprout human heads, hands and other body parts.

Left: A wall of stone slabs at Cerro Sechín shows a procession of warriors and their defeated enemies, including many body parts.

A more bizarre form of stone sculpture is the geoglyph (65 x 23m/*c.*215 x 76ft) at Pampa de Caña Cruz in the Zaña Valley. Much earlier than the Nazca lines, thousands of small rock fragments (*c.*10cm/4in in diameter) make up a rectangular face framed with 'hair', with round eyes and nose, fanged mouth and squared jaw – resembling figures on Cupisnique pottery. Two long 'legs' form a simplified body. Contrasting with the surrounding soil, dark stones outline the white stone face and body and rose-coloured stone 'hair' piece.

This 'mosaic' has no known parallel in Peru. However, large-scale religious imagery became widespread in Early Intermediate Period and later geoglyphs formed by stone outlines, especially on the Nazca desert floor.

'LIVING' STONE
The Incas are known for their precisely fitted stone walls. They regarded stone as 'alive' – indeed the Quechua word for 'boulder' also means 'to begin'.

Whereas earlier cultures carved detached monolithic and smaller stone, the Incas literally carved and modelled the landscape itself. The Observatorio or Torreón at Machu Picchu, for example, begins with the huge boulder that forms

Below: Beneath the Torreón at Machu Picchu Inca masons enlarged a natural cleft in the stone outcrop into a temple room to Inti, the sun.

its foundation, and the cleft in the base of the boulder is itself carved into a semi-hidden temple room.

Also at Machu Picchu, the Intihuatana Stone (the 'Hitching Post of the Sun') is a stone outcrop carved into angles, recesses and a central square pillar. This and other *intihuatanas*, possibly used in astronomical observations, connect the sky to the Earth in characteristic Andean duality and cosmological wholeness and containment.

The Sacred Rock at the northern end of Machu Picchu has been carefully modified into a platform 'supporting' the natural outcrop shaped to mimic the outline of the distant mountain skyline – again linking earth and sky.

The rocky outcrop at Qenqo provides another example. A semicircular enclosure forms a ritual space around a natural outcrop left untouched, as its profile resembles a seated puma. A nearby outcrop is carved into steps and water channels, while a cleft beneath them, as at Machu Picchu, is carved into a room.

The very structure of the walls at Sacsahuaman forms a sculpture in stone and space as its angles change direction to 'sculpt' the sky into light and shadow, like the distant mountains and gorges that form its backdrop. And the vast outcrop of Rodadero opposite the walls has been carved into a huge stepped 'throne'.

Above: At Sayhuite, Peru, Inca sculptors modelled a huge glacial boulder sitting on the valley floor into a miniature urban model including houses, streets, temple platforms, platforms, channels and terraced garden plots.

THREE MODELS
Among the most remarkable Andean stone sculptures are three large-scale models of Andean architecture itself.

At Tiwanaku, the Kantatayita mound east of the Akapana includes a huge boulder carved into a maquette (roughly scaled 1 to 10) of a platform and ceremonial plaza. It is complete with staircases ascending to the flat-topped platform with sunken courts, just like those of the Tiwanaku central precinct itself.

The Incas, not content to carve stone outcrops into human-scale works, carved a large glacial boulder at Sayhuite into an entire town and landscape model. In cascading terraces there are miniature buildings, patios, platforms and water channels.

Finally, above the Chinchero Valley, Inca masons carved an entire outcrop into a miniature system of terraces and enclosures, echoing the actual terraces of the valley sides. The sculpture seems both to embed the work in nature and emphasize Inca domination of the land.

STONEWORK OF THE CHAVÍN

The body of stone sculpture at Chavín de Huántar dominated the religious imagery of the Early Horizon. It comprises three huge deity idols, carved stone slabs decorating the walls of the Old and New Temple courtyards, and many smaller pieces.

STONE IDOLS

The Old Temple housed the Lanzón Stela, or Great Image, a lance-shaped granite monolith (4.5m/15ft high) carved with human, feline and serpent attributes. Its monster visage is thick-lipped, drawn in a hideous snarl and punctuated by long, outward-curving canines. Its eyebrows and hair end in serpent heads. Its right hand is raised, its left lowered, towards sky and earth deities respectively, 'embracing' the universe; its feet and hands end in claws. Its tunic, waistband and headdress are decorated with feline heads, and snakes dangle from its waist. Its notched head has a carved, cross-shaped receptacle thought to be for channelling the blood of sacrifices.

Below: The Chavín Cult's Lanzón Stela had a notch for ritual blood sacrifice and was carved with the image of the jaguar-mouthed, taloned supreme deity and serpent imagery.

Above: Stone blocks at the entry stairway of the rectangular plaza at Chavín de Huántar embellished it with sacred cayman imagery, with rows of teeth and clawed feet, and serpents.

In the New Temple's courtyard, or perhaps in an inner gallery, stood the Tello Obelisk (2.5m/8ft high), also of granite. Its faces are carved with two jungle caymans. Notched like the Lanzón, additional carvings on and around the caymans depict plants and animals, including peanuts and manioc from the tropical lowlands, and *Strombus* and *Spondylus* shells of species native to the Ecuadorian coast, jaguars, serpents and raptors.

The Raimondi Stela, the third, and latest-dating, monolithic idol, is carved in extremely low relief on a highly polished granite slab (1.98m/6ft x 0.74m/2⅖ft x 0.17m/6½in). It depicts the supreme Chavín Cult god, the Staff Deity. Its stylistic similarity to the avian creatures on the columns of the Black and White Portal suggests that it once stood within one of the New Temple's chambers.

The Raimondi Staff Deity has clawed hands and feet, a mouth with huge curved fangs and ears bedecked with ornaments. Outstretched arms clutch elaborate plumed staffs. Unlike many other portrayals of the Staff Deity, its genitalia are non-specific, as if to embrace male and female duality and opposites at the same time, thereby balancing the Andean worldview. Further, when inverted, the image shows a new set of faces. The image appears to be rising and the eyes gaze skywards; the inverted figure's eyes look down and it appears to plunge from the sky – more duality.

In similar low relief, columns flanking the Black and White Portal depict two avian figures, heads tilted back to peer straight up, wings outspread in characteristic raptor hunting flight. The north column supports a white granite half-lintel and depicts a female eagle (identifiable by its beak cere – nostril hole – and 'vagina dentata'); the south column supports a black limestone half-lintel and depicts a hawk (identifiable by the band through its eye and a central frontal fang 'penis metaphor').

Above: The Raimondi monolith from Chavín de Huántar's New Temple was the final expression of the Chavín supreme Staff Deity.

SHAMANS AND JAGUARS

The stone walls of the sunken circular courtyard are carved with a scene of shamanic transformation. In low relief on an upper register marches a procession of profiled humanoid figures with fanged mouths and streaming, snake-headed hair. They wear serpentine belts, tunics and trousers. Their finger- and toenails are raptor claws. One carries a San Pedro cactus branch and another a conch-shell trumpet.

A lower register depicts a row of prowling jaguars on rectangular slabs. At least seven paired humanoid and jaguar sets depict a shaman in transformation from human to jaguar, using the hallucinogenic cactus in a mystic ritual.

A similar transformation is represented by fully sculpted heads on the New Temple façade. Of the 40 found, one was tenoned into the wall, revealing that the mounted set displayed a succession of 'states' in human transformation into beast. Faces alter as lips and teeth curl from human to feline fangs, snouts project, noses flatten, cheeks become scarified with whiskers and almond-shaped human eyes change to bulging round ones, weeping mucus – a reaction to drug-taking.

DUALITY IN STONE

In the Titicaca Basin, the Pukará–Yaya-Mama Cult style was contemporary with later Chavín. The hallmarks of its imagery were the depiction of yaya (male) and mama (female) figures or symbols on opposite sides of slab monoliths erected at Pukará Taraco, Tambo Cusi and other sites around the lake, and the Pukará Decapitator God. Other Pukará stone carving includes characteristic Andean feline, serpentine and fish imagery.

Writhing skyward- and earthward-facing snakes enhance the duality of the Yaya-Mama imagery. The Decapitator is a seated figure holding a sacrificial axe and severed head. With bulging eyes and feline snout and fangs, this sculpture represents the god himself or a priest wearing his mask. Many smaller Pukará figures bear female symbols of earth and water.

Portable Pukará stone sculpture included rectangular, twinned boxes, the sides depicting faces or masks surrounded with serpent and plant-like rays, anticipating the rayed heads of Tiwanaku sculpture and textiles.

Below: More than 40 jaguar-mouthed stone heads adorned the upper walls around the New Temple at Chavín de Huántar.

MONUMENTAL STONEWORK AT TIWANAKU

As an imperial capital and religious centre, everything about Tiwanaku was monumental and colossal. Titicaca was the birthplace of the world. Its city reflected the landscape; the city itself was a sculpture or model mimicking the mountains and valleys in its terraced platforms and plazas, and the rivers, lake and islands in its water channels, drains and moat.

Its statuary constantly reminded citizens and pilgrims who flocked to its temples and ceremonies of their duty to honour the gods. The Incas believed the great statues to be the ancient race of giants turned to stone by Viracocha as a flawed race.

Tiwanaku lacks Pukará occupation but inherited its sacred imagery. At least seven Yaya-Mama monoliths were found around the site, including Stela 15 (*c.*2m/*c.*7ft tall), which stood in the Semi-Subterranean Temple beside the much taller Bennett Stela. And the lower portion (the Thunderbolt) of the 2.5-tonne (ton), *c.*5.75m (*c.*19ft) Arapa Pukará monolith, which was removed 212km (132 miles) from Arapa at the north end of the lake to Tiwanaku Putuni palace.

Tiwanaku sculptors also inherited the Decapitator Cult. The black basalt image of a seated, puma-headed person (*chachapuma*) holding a severed head in his lap stood at the base of the western staircase of the Akapana platform. Another, standing, *chachapuma* also holds a severed head.

The walls of the Semi-Subterranean Temple are adorned with scores of tenoned severed heads. Unlike those at Chavín de Huántar, they do not depict shamanic transformation, but suggest that the courtyard was a place of sacrificial rituals.

SOUTHERN GIANTS

Tiwanaku sculptors carved colossal stone monoliths whose scale was unsurpassed until Inca times. The two most famous are the Bennett Stela (7.3m/24ft high) and the Ponce Stela (3.5m/11½ft high).

The Bennett Stela, the tallest Andean statue ever carved, represents a richly dressed human thought to be one of Tiahuanaco's rulers or a divine ruler. He/she holds a *kero* beaker and a staff-like object, perhaps a snuff tablet. Low-relief features portray large, sub-rectangular eyes, weeping, long, geometric-patterned streams

Above: One of several colossal monolithic stone statues in the Kalasasaya enclosed court at Tiwanaku, with hands motif.

down the cheeks, a pursed sub-rectangular mouth, and chunky fingers and toes. The massive, angular head, turban-like headpiece, belt band and short legs are reminiscent of Pukará sculpture.

Scores of small, incised figures and symbols adorn the giant's body. There are rayed faces, llamas, birds, and feline creatures and mythical beasts, snakes and panels of flowering plants – in all, some 30 figures facing frontally but with 'running' legs. The complex imagery is thought to encode Tiwanaku's state ideology and cosmology. The central rayed faces and front-facing, ray-headed figure with up-raised arms – resembling the central figure on the Gateway of the Sun – no doubt represent the creator deity Viracocha.

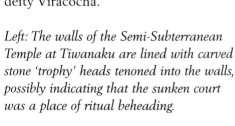

Left: The walls of the Semi-Subterranean Temple at Tiwanaku are lined with carved stone 'trophy' heads tenoned into the walls, possibly indicating that the sunken court was a place of ritual beheading.

Left: The Gateway of the Sun, standing at the north-west corner of the Kalasasaya enclosure at Tiwanaku has a central Staff Deity image thought by some to represent the supreme deity Viracocha.

Below: The Bennett Stela, the tallest Andean statue ever carved, is decorated with rich clothing and coca-snuff accoutrements.

Within the Kalasasaya precinct stands the Ponce Stela, perhaps another of the city's rulers, framed by the main gateway into the Semi-Subterranean Temple. Like the Bennett Stela, it portrays a richly clothed figure holding a *kero* beaker and staff or snuff tablet.

Numerous smaller stone sculptures, known as 'ancestor figures', mimic the Bennett Stela and Ponce Stela in their features and stance.

THE GREAT GATEWAY

At the north-west corner of the Kalasasaya stands the famous Gateway of the Sun. A large crack on its right side suggests that it was moved, and it is thought that it originally formed one of a series of gateways leading worshippers into the city. Several similar gateways found in the Pumapunku compound suggest that the Gateway of the Sun may once have stood there.

It is an extraordinary monolith. It appears to comprise two stone slabs supporting a carved lintel, but is in fact a single huge andesite block (3.8m/12½ft wide, 2.8m/9ft high, with a 1.4m/4½ft opening). The lintel is completely carved above its rebated jambs. The central figure portrays, in high-relief, the 'Gateway God', thought to be Viracocha the creator or Thunapa, god of thunder, a humanoid figure standing on a stepped platform that resembles the tiered mounds of the sacred precinct itself. Like other Tiwanaku imagery, he has 'weeping' eyes, an over-sized, rayed head and short legs below a serpentine belt band. Four head rays end in feline heads and the top, central ray is a front-facing feline. His outstretched arms hold staffs with raptor-headed ends. The resemblance to the Chavín Staff Deity is undeniable, but the style is definitely southern Andean. One interpretation is that the staffs are a spear-thrower and quiver of darts.

Flanking the god, in low relief, are 48 winged figures in profile (called the Tiwanaku 'angels'), in three rows of eight, running towards him. Some have human faces, others avian faces, and each holds a staff resembling one or the other of the god's staffs.

Flanking the entryway below are two rectangular niches. And the rear of the gateway has a band of three rebates to form a multiple jamb with false, blind doorways on either side and four upper niches.

Many Tiwanaku monolithic wall slabs are decorated with rows of inset stepped-diamond shapes – sometimes called the 'Andean Cross' – a shape first used in the Middle Horizon and also used on textiles and by the Incas. Numerous lintels are adorned with rows of ray-headed mythical beasts arrayed in facing lines.

PLASTER AND MUD WALL SCULPTURES

Sculptors in arid environments frequently worked in clay and mud, which did not perish as they would in the rainy highlands. This was especially true along the northern Peruvian coast in the Initial Period.

CROSSED HANDS

Kotosh, on the arid, rain-shadowed slopes of the eastern Andes, was occupied *c.*2500–*c.*2000BC. Two rubble-filled mounds supporting temples of field cobbles plastered with mud were enlarged several times. The Kotosh Tradition, probably the earliest Andean religious cult, not surprisingly also has the earliest plaster wall sculptures.

By *c.*2000BC the larger mound had reached a height of 13.7m (45ft), rising in three tiers and supporting groups of up to 100 successive, superimposed chambers, including seven successive temples on the lowest tier. On the middle platform, however, sat the most famous temple, the Temple of the Crossed Hands.

Below: One of the carved poured-mud walls at Huaca del Dragón near Chan Chan, showing creatures supporting a rainbow serpent and solar crescent.

Roughly square in plan (9.5 **x** 9.3m/31½ **x** 31ft), its upper walls were recessed to support a log-beam and clay-plaster roof. A painted white serpent adorns its stairway, and its entrance is red. The interior floor is split-level, with a stone-lined ritual fire pit in the centre.

The northern wall, facing the entrance, has five equal-spaced niches. The two flanking the larger central niche have low-relief sculpted clay friezes of crossed hands and forearms, one set smaller than the other. The symmetrical arrangement of niches and crossed hands are clearly early Andean expressions of duality. The different-sized hands are thought to be man and woman, signifying unity between otherwise opposing forces.

The sacredness of the temple is revealed by the fact that the friezes were carefully covered with sand before the temple was abandoned and filled with rubble.

SPIDER, INSECT AND MONSTER

Garagay, a coastal U-shaped ceremonial centre, was occupied from the mid-2nd to mid-1st millennium BC. Its Middle Temple had an entire wall carved and painted with a low-relief plaster frieze. Panels between stylized plant-like figures and geometric motifs there show three mythical creatures – humanized animals.

A face with thick-lipped, fanged mouth and languid, sinister-looking eye peers from a web-like ring. An arachnid pedipalp curls from its human nose. Farther along, a huge human-headed insect crawls along the wall, with detailed head, thorax and tail. On a third panel, an enormous split face has drooping, half-crescent eyes, thick lips and six long fangs. Traces of red, blue, yellow and white mineral paints were found on the friezes, and as many as 10 layers of clay and paint repairs.

Another wall, on the summit of Mound A, has two low-relief plaster sculptures of humans carrying round shields. The modelling of their hands and feet are especially realistic, including their nails.

Above: The Temple of the Crossed Hands at Kotosh is one of the earliest plaster wall sculptures in ancient Andean civilization. The smaller of the two pairs, crossed left over right, is thought to be female; the larger, crossed right over left, male; and together representing duality.

GODS, SHAMANS, RULERS?

The 30m (100ft), tiered rectangular platform at Moxeke was built of large conical adobe blocks and enlarged many times. The final rebuilding included massive stone revetment walls. On the third platform, large white and pink niches (3.9m/13ft wide; 1.7m/5¾ft deep), puncture the wall 10m (31½ft) above the plaza. Inside them stand colossal, high-relief unbaked clay sculptures.

Two are cloaked torsos, their heads destroyed – possibly in deliberate ritual beheadings. One holds the corners of its cape; the other wears a more elaborate cloak and twisted cord sash, and holds double-headed snakes in raised hands. Both wear short, pleated skirts. One is painted entirely black.

A third is an enormous, emerald green head with a grinning, thick-lipped mouth and rows of straight teeth. Pink vertical lines run from its squinting, half-crescent, black-pupil eyes, either side of flaring black nostrils, giving it a menacing appearance.

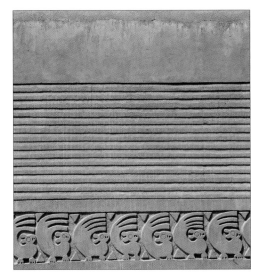

Above: Chan Chan surfaces were moulded like panelling and sculpted with rows of repeated animals and birds.

Another head has an expressionless face with closed mouth and eyes resembling the Cerro Sechín severed heads.

The scale, positions and appearance of these sculptures reveal a major role in ritual worship. Peering from their niches flanking the staircase, with several terraces rising behind them to a ritual platform summit, provides a dramatic, overpowering presence to worshippers crowded in the plaza below.

The Caballo Muerto mound at Huaca de los Reyes has four colossal adobe heads on its summit. Like the Moxeke sculptures, they dominate the ritual platform and the plaza below. Almost 2m (6ft) high, they portray humanoid faces with feline features: thick-lipped mouths in the same style as at Moxeke, clenched teeth, but also feline fangs, flaring, cat-like noses and huge staring, sub-rectangular eyes with deep round pupils. Like the Moxeke sculptures, they were probably once painted.

THE PUNKURÍ FRIEZES
Several successive tiers at coastal Punkurí have carved plaster friezes. The oldest one depicts a supernatural avian figure with fish and monkeys on its body.

The second platform is famous for its larger-than-life painted and carved frieze of a snarling feline on the middle of the staircase. With its green face, blue pupils, red gums, crossed white fangs and clawed

paws, it presented a startling, iconic image to priests ascending to the summit of the temple platform! Later tiers have stylized geometric forms.

A WARRIOR AND HIS CAPTIVES
The Middle Horizon Moche site Cao Viejo–El Brujo has a carved mud frieze showing continuity with the Initial Period themes described above.

Along one terrace trots a life-size warrior leading 10 naked prisoners by a rope around their necks. Like the figures of Mound A at Garagay, they show a studied realism in their movement and limb shaping. Sadly now destroyed, the top platform terrace showed the segmented

Below: The plastered walls of Moche sites, as here at the Huaca de la Luna temple, were brightly painted with geometric frames, symbols and sacred imagery.

Above: The tall, thick poured-mud walls and platforms of the Huaca del Dragón (Pyramid of the Dragon), Chan Chan.

legs of a spider or crab sculpture. One claw held a sacrificial *tumi* knife, an arachnid representation of the Moche Decapitator God.

The walls at Moche Huaca de la Luna depicting the Decapitator are also sculpted low-relief plaster, but are usually described as murals because of their vibrant colours.

191

The ultimate and most vibrant expression of mud-clay sculpting is that of the Chimú in the Late Intermediate Period. Continuing early traditions of wall decorations, the Chimú covered almost every bit of wall surface in their elite residences and temples with sculptured friezes. Like Inca carving of natural stone outcrops to modify the living landscape, Chimú mud structures themselves were sculptures in their totalities.

The Kingdom of the Chimú began in the 10th century AD with the founding of their capital at Chan Chan. They were the inheritors of the Moche and conquerors of the Sicán-Lambayeque, but both continued and broke earlier traditions.

ADOBE 'MOUNTAINS'
Chan Chan was built near the mouth of the Moche River, on the north banks. The vast bulks of the ancient Moche capital's pyramids of Huaca del Sol and Huaca de la Luna, by then having stood silent for several hundred years, were only a short distance away on the south banks. They must have been regarded by the Chimú with similar awe to that of the Incas for the ruins of Tiwanaku. Like their Moche ancestors, the Chimú raised huge platforms to create 'mountains' on the flat coastal plains. Forming a crescent north-east of the city centre are four great adobe mounds supporting the city's temples: Huaca del Obispo, Huaca de las Conchas, Tres Huacas and Huaca del Higo. A fifth temple, Huaca del Olvido, lies to the south.

The most celebrated structures at Chan Chan form the vast central civic and ceremonial city core. Tall, thick walls enclose between nine and twelve huge compounds, each a city within the city, housing first the living king and then his burial mound and morbid city. The Spaniards called these compounds *ciudadelas* (citadels) because of their formidable walls and the complexity of their interior arrangements.

Above: Chan Chan of the Chimú comprises a huge ceremonial urban centre in which every surface was sculpted in mud – walls, benches, niches and pilasters.

The *ciudadela* walls are made of *tapia* (poured adobe or mud) on stone foundations. Most are well preserved, and stand as high as 9m (28¼ft). The smooth, sheer wall surfaces were rarely left unadorned, especially the walls of the huge public plazas forming the first element in each *ciudadela*.

BUILT TO IMPRESS
Perhaps inspired by the ruins of the Moche, Chimú rulers sought to impress their subjects and foreign visitors with their power. They embellished their compounds with the labours of thousands of artisans, creating a city centre that rivals the exuberance, complexity and scale of the Alhambra of Moorish Granada and the mosques of western African cities such as Djenne.

Left: Long walls at Chan Chan were moulded into panels, with sculpted channels of swimming fish and rows of part bird, part four-legged creatures.

Right: The rainbow and solar flare theme sculpted in repetitious panels at Huaca del Dragón near Chan Chan cover the entire surface of the main platform.

The chronological sequence of the *ciudadelas* has several exponents, but it is generally undisputed that they were built as each ruler died and a new ruler ascended the throne. There is some evidence that they were built in pairs. As the kingdom grew, the compounds became larger and more elaborate.

The first was probably Chayhuac, possibly that of Chimú's legendary founder King Taycanamo; then Tello and Uhle together; next were Laberinto and Grán Chimú. The late-phase *ciudadelas* – Bandelier, Valarde, Rivero and Tschudi – were built in rapid succession, the last possibly being the palace compound of Minchançaman, the Chimú king conquered by the Incas. The Squier *ciudadela* appears to be unfinished.

Below: In detail the rainbow and solar flare arch scenes differ. The enclosed figures are always the twinned mythical creatures, but the supporting figures and serpent heads vary.

PATTERN MOULDING

Using wooden moulds, the *tapia* was poured onto the walls. The clay appears to have been applied in two layers, first the poured mud wall itself, then a 2cm (¾ in) or thicker layer, which was moulded or carved while drying. There was a limited range of motifs, the Chimú preference being for repetition on a vast scale.

Repetition and angularity are used to the extreme at Chan Chan in its late phases, but at other Chimú cities, such as Huaca del Dragón, there are more rounded forms. Although there are mythical animals, in contrast to earlier traditions there is less religious imagery in preference for secular themes.

At Huaca del Dragón, a platform mound north-west of Chan Chan sometimes called the 'Temple of the Rainbow', a repeated motif features rainbow-like arcs topped with curled solar flares or wave patterns framed within moulded rectangular borders. Mythical creatures support the arc ends, themselves flanking twinned, face-to-face mythical creatures with sinuous bodies and web-like tails. Long-tailed mythical figures holding axe-bladed staffs march in a frieze above.

At Chan Chan there are panels and bands forming row upon row of repetitious geometric patterns and marching animals, birds and fishes. Vast expanses of wall are covered with diamond lattices and stepped-fret patterning. Upon closer examination of some of the latter, they are seen to be curious flying seabirds or fish. Solid bands of moulding form lines upon which march long rows of curious half-bird, half-quadruped creatures.

Huge expanses of horizontal moulded bands resemble louvred panels, bordered by rows of creatures or rows of large circular 'buttons'. The walls of many of the vast storage compounds within *ciudadelas* are formed of deep, diamond-shaped niches, almost like stacked, square-sectioned cylinders, resembling giant wine racks.

At contemporary Chincha La Centinela, the walls are carved with similar friezes of birds, fish and geometric patterns, and painted brilliant white.

CERAMIC SCULPTURE

Andean figurines were made both as solid clay objects and as functional pottery.

LITTLE IDOLS

Late Preceramic Period Aspero produced some of the earliest unbaked clay figurines, dated earlier than 2500BC. Between two floors of a temple atop Huaca de Los Idolos archaeologists found a cache of fragments representing at least 13 figurines (5–15cm/2–6in).

Eleven are women, of which four appear to be pregnant. They are seated, legs crossed, arms against their sides and forearms across their chests. Eyes and mouths are mere slits. They wear thigh-length skirts, flat hats and necklaces. A male figurine was found near by.

Below: A Nazca effigy, spouted bottle of a panpipe player, whose wide eyes and odd costume with apparently exposed genitalia indicate a religious, drug-induced trance.

Like most such items, they were produced for the public domain rather than for individual use. Similar figurines have also been found at Bandurria, El Paraíso, Kotosh and Río Seco.

TEMPLE OFFERINGS

Baked and unbaked figurines were found at Kotosh. Two crude, baked human-animal figures were associated with the Temple of the Crossed Hands, and an unbaked figure wearing a conical hat, plus three other unbaked objects, were associated with the succeeding Templo Blanco.

At Initial Period Garagay, offerings of baked and painted figures were associated with the Middle Temple and its plaster friezes. Some are dressed in minute textiles and one has fangs. Again, the public nature of these offerings and the human-beast forms of some confirm their religious connotations.

HOUSEHOLD FIGURES

In contrast, Initial Period coastal villagers produced numerous small baked solid and hollow figures of nude women, always in domestic contexts. Particular attention was given to realistic modelling of hair, facial features, breasts and navels. A larger example from Curayacu has a headband, hair falling over the shoulders, delicately fingered hands on stomach, and disproportionately short legs. The strands of hair, eyebrows, lidded eyes with pupils, triangular nose, ears and full-lipped mouth are especially finely rendered. They are thought to be associated with household curing rituals, or perhaps childbirth.

Also in domestic contexts, solid clay figurines were found exclusively in the 'elite' residences at Moxeke, suggesting the development of social hierarchy.

Ceramic figurines were relatively rare in southern cultures. One example from a Paracas burial portrays a rotund

Above: A Paracas male figurine dressed in a short tunic and mantle resembling the patterns on Paracas textiles, and a headband that appears to hold a flute.

figure with puny arms and hands on hips. A thick-necked head has a stylized face with eyes, mouth and chin rendered merely as incised lines. He wears a curious headband with circles and a tube ornament. Incised lines and cream paint indicate clothing and a bib or collar similar to actual shell and stone ones. The slit eyes may possibly indicate death, and the piece might be an ancestor idol.

Above: A mould-made Moche spouted bottle depicting a man playing panpipes, apparently very much engrossed in his music.

SEALS, ANIMALS AND TUNICS

Cupisnique peoples of the northern coast made numerous baked clay figurines and seals, both rollers and stamps (presumably for decorating pottery vessels), found in houses and graves. Examples from late occupation at Huaca Prieta include a bird stamp with a long curved beak, and a seated figurine with curious over-sized hands and feet, big ears and a gnome-like hat.

Highland Pacopampa potters also made ceramic seals. One example shows a stylized feline of thick, angular, slab-like lines; there were also numerous crude animal figurines, including felines, dogs, bears and viscachas (a burrowing rodent).

In contrast, an ovoid structure, possibly a priest's residence, on El Mirador hill west of the Pacopampa temple, contained the broken remains of several fine hollow figurines. Originally c.48cm (19in) high, they portray tall, elegant male figures with shoulder-length hair, sideburns, unusually large ears, long, straight noses (with nostril holes) arching into eyebrows, pupil-less eyes, open, rectangular mouths, and ground-length, sleeveless tunics, but bare feet.

FUNCTIONAL FIGURINES

Later cultures made fewer clay figurines as such. The Moche and later cultures, however, excelled in making ceramic effigy vessels. Functional stirrup-spout and bridge-spout bottles, bowls and jars of all sizes and styles were made in the shapes of animals, birds and objects. There are human figurine vessels, monkey jars, jaguar bowls and deer bottles, bird vessels, vessels in the shapes of gourds, *kero* drinking cups with sculpted human faces on them, and ceramic panpipes.

A quite extraordinary Early Intermediate Period Recuay piece is of a warrior-priest in an elaborate disc and serpent headdress who is leading a sacrificial llama.

Highly polished, painted Nazca figurines of men and women are often naked except for a loin-cloth, and have tattoos or show full Nazca costume as effigy vessels.

The range of subjects depicted by Moche potters is legendary. Hundreds of Moche stirrup-spout bottles were shaped as animals and birds, and hundreds more portray human occupations and activities – everything from hunting with a

Right: A Chimú polished black-ware stirrup-spouted bottle of a dog nursing her four pups.

blowgun, warriors, flute-playing, shamans treating patients, childbirth and sexual acts of all kinds, as well as a huge range of human portrait vessels depicting all manner of human conditions and ages.

Tiwanaku and Wari, Chimú and Inca potters made jars and bowls with bird heads, humans holding oyster shells or catching lobsters, or drinking cups whose bases are shaped as human hands and feet, complete with nails.

CERAMIC MODELS

Finally, there are building models. Recuay and Moche potters, especially, made bottles shaped as houses: a Moche house with roof combs and a miniature human occupant; a Recuay court with small storehouses; a Recuay double-chambered pot with a house and man peering from beneath his gabled roof; a Lambayeque bridge-spout bottle replete with simulated stepped-fret plaster decorations and entryway flanked by two tiny human guards.

CERAMICS

Most ancient Andeans used no pottery for the first 10,000 years after humans entered South America. Once ceramics were invented, however, differences in style developed rapidly among coastal and highland peoples, dictated by available materials and by cultural preferences in expression.

Fired clay, being one of the most durable materials, survives in abundance in archaeological sites. It thus forms a large proportion of the finds from excavations both as whole vessels and in fragments. It provides archaeologists with the means to recognize differences in vessel forms and decorative styles over wide areas, and through time, and thus enables them to identify cultures through their characteristic ceramics, and to determine broad themes in economic and social change and contact through trade.

Andean potters were prolific and exuberant in their output, both in quantity and in the variety of what they portrayed in natural shapes and narrative scenes painted on their pottery. These features enable scholars to surmise meanings for the repeated themes and imagery they observe, as well as to deduce the power and influence of cultures spatially and through time.

Although ancient Andeans used flat, circular potting discs from early times, they never mechanized these in any way to create a potter's wheel. Instead, they continued to make pots by the coil method, building up the vessel walls and turning the potting disc by hand merely to position the part being worked on. Other pots were mould-made.

Left: A Nazca polychrome jar, possibly for chicha *beer, depicting a warrior or entranced shaman.*

THE FIRST CONTAINERS

From the time that humans entered the South American continent, about 15,000 years ago, for more than 10,000 years they used no pottery, neither for containers nor for figurines or other artefacts. Hunter-gatherer peoples travelled light.

EARLY BEGINNINGS

Even in areas where an abundance of food and other materials allowed denser concentrations of people, ceramics came into use only thousands of years later, in the Initial Period. In these places, where the inhabitants concentrated on marine hunting and gathering, pottery would have been less useful than cotton and other fibres from gathered, and eventually domesticated, plants. Cotton was essential for nets, lines and containers for fishing.

For millennia, until knowledge of potting spread geographically, fibres and gourds were used for containers of all kinds. No doubt animal hides and wood were also used.

Examples are very few, for preservation of organic materials requires special conditions (severe desiccation or oxygen-free environments such as waterlogging), and these occur rarely in archaeological sites. However, the regular twisting,

looping and knotting techniques used to make these early artefacts indicate that before the Preceramic Period (c.3500–1800BC) there had been a long development in techniques through the Lithic or Archaic Period. No early examples include patterning or other decoration.

BASKETS AND STONE MORTARS

For the Preceramic Period there is more evidence. Sites show the gradual evolution from relatively egalitarian societies living in small villages exploiting rich resources by the sea or in mountain valleys, to the beginnings of social status divisions and the marshalling of labour for the erection of monumental architecture in complex ceremonial centres.

Excavators found twined baskets and looped reed and sedge satchels at La Galgada, in the upper Tablachaca-Santa Valley, and at Huaca Prieta in the Chicama Valley near the northern Peruvian coast, and at other highland and coastal sites. Evidence of highland–lowland trade includes bivalve shells, used as small containers for pigments.

Above: Basketry from plant fibre was also used in early containers, decorated with vegetable dyes and sometimes preserved in dry sites such as the Atacama Desert.

Stone mortars were another late Preceramic non-ceramic container found at several sites. At Salinas de Chao excavators found a large number of stone mortars used to evaporate seawater into salt crystals, for trade with highland peoples.

GOURDS

Plain and carved gourd containers, including bottles, bowls and ladles, come from a few Preceramic sites. Plain gourds were also used as fishing-net floats, and appear to have been domesticated, along with cotton, at an early date, perhaps by 5000BC. A large twined cotton fishing net with attached gourd floats was found at Huaca Prieta.

After the inner vegetable matter was removed, gourds were decorated either by excising or scraping off the gourd's outer skin when it was still soft or by incising fine lines on the surface of the gourd once it had been left to dry and harden. In a few examples a technique

Left: The earliest containers were gourds – later pottery vessels sometimes mimicked gourd shapes, as in this Chavin Early Horizon spouted bottle in the shape of linked gourds with black plant-like motifs.

called pyro-engraving was used – incising fine lines by burning and cutting simultaneously. Of 10,770 gourd fragments found at Huaca Prieta, only 13 are carved.

IMAGERY AT HUACA PRIETA

Huaca Prieta is more remarkable, however, for the discovery of some of the earliest Andean art. In addition to thousands of fragments of twined and knotted cloth found in the midden layers, two small, carved gourds were found in a burial dated *c.*2000BC or earlier.

Each is cut around the top to create a separated lid, also carved. Although the gourds are spherical, each is carved on four 'sides' with identical, repetitious patterns, with small differences. One has the same pattern, a stylized face, repeated four times. A wide, sub-rectangular mouth is slightly less wide than the two

Below: The tradition of decorating gourds did not stop after ceramics were invented. Decorated gourds at a 20th-century market in Peru mix ancient and modern motifs.

rectangular-outlined eyes with rectangular pupils. Above the eyes are angular brows, or forehead outlines, extending halfway down the edges of the eyes. Separating the faces are geometric shapes and slashes. The lid is carved symmetrically with sets of four slashes and corner triangles, forming a square, undecorated void.

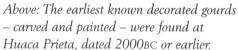

Above: The earliest known decorated gourds – carved and painted – were found at Huaca Prieta, dated 2000BC or earlier.

Decoration on the second gourd comprises two images on opposing 'sides'. One image is a small, angular face similar in essential features to the faces on the first gourd, but contained in a continuous outline formed by the outer lines of the mouth and eyes. The 'foreheads' above these include varying-sized incised and excised rectangles. The other set of images appears to be stylized serpents. Each is coiled clockwise from the base of the gourd, to a blocky, stylized snake head resting above and symmetrical to the coiled tail. Two Zs and other geometric shapes are carved on the base. Most remarkably, the lid has doubled serpent, or possibly raptor, heads forming a reversed S.

The fullness of the features can only be easily appreciated when rolled out flat in a drawing, making these some of the earliest examples of hidden or obscured meaning in Andean art. They also show the early Andean liking for serpents and double imagery. The imagery on Huaca Prieta gourds and textiles resembles that on contemporary pottery from Valdivia, where ceramics were already in use.

THE INVENTION OF CERAMICS

The first Andean potters were the early farmers of the Valdivian culture of southern coastal Ecuador, on the northern fringe of the Andean Area. The Valdivian cultural area is 400km (250 miles) north of the northern Peruvian coastal Preceramic cultures, and Valdivia itself is 600km (375 miles) from Huaca Prieta. Valdivian farmers began making pottery from about 3200BC. People at Puerto Hormiga, on the Caribbean coast of Colombia, also produced early ceramics, beginning a few hundred years later, c.3000BC.

THE EARLIEST ANDEAN POTTERY
Decorative similarities on late 3rd-millennium BC Valdivian pots and contemporary Peruvian coastal gourds reveal the strength of contacts between the two regions. Shells from bivalve

Below: Two Valdivian ceramic figurines of women from coastal Ecuador, possibly representing a fertility cult.

species native to Ecuadorian waters (in particular the thorny oyster) were traded south as exotic items. Coastal Peruvians, however, found no use for ceramics at the time and preferred their tradition of gourds and fibre containers, while they imitated Valdivian artistic motifs, and may have shared the religious ideas they represented. One hypothesis suggests that the heavily wooded coasts of southern Ecuador provided fuel for firing, while the desert coasts of northern Peru did not – making the use of fired clay uneconomic.

FIGURINES
The use of clay was not altogether absent in the Peruvian coastal Preceramic Period, however. At Huaca de Los Idolos, one of the larger mounds of the Aspero complex in the Supe River mouth of central coastal Peru, excavators found a cache of at least 13 small (each only a few centimetres/inches tall) fragmentary figurines made of unbaked clay. One is a female wearing a flat-topped hat. They were buried between two floors of a room and date to before 2500BC.

Other unbaked clay figurines were found at coastal Río Seco and El Paraíso, south of Aspero, and at highland Kotosh. A few late Preceramic figurines *were* fired, indicating that the idea of hardening clay by baking was not unfamiliar south of Valdivia. It seems that late Preceramic Period Andeans preferred to fire only a few items of special significance rather than waste fuel on everyday items.

POTTERY IN THE CENTRAL ANDES
Making pottery for ordinary wares in the northern Peruvian cultures was not adopted until about 1,000 years after Valdivians began making fired pots. By about 2000BC, towards the beginning of the Initial Period, coastal and highland Andeans began producing pottery for cooking and storage containers.

Above: Some of the earliest pottery was sculpture rather than container – a Valdivian bust of a woman from coastal Ecuador.

The pots produced by Peruvian coastal and highland peoples bear little resemblance to contemporary Valdivian ceramics. Thus, although imagery on contemporary Valdivian pottery was shared on late Preceramic gourds, when Peruvian cultures began potting, their vessels were simple and the shapes imitated those of spherical, open bowl-shaped and bottle-shaped gourds.

EARLY VARIETY
From the adoption of potting by peoples of the north and central Peruvian coasts and adjacent highlands, variety developed rapidly. Vessels from the coast were limited to gourd-like shapes and had walls only 2–3mm (⅛in) thick, for example from Erizo, Ancón, La Florida and Huaca Negra. Pots from La Florida were decorated with incising, while Ancón potters decorated their pots with black paint.

In contrast, early vessels from highland sites, such as at Shillacoto, show greater sophistication and variety in shape, and a resemblance to pots from the tropical

Above: This ceramic sculpture of a Valdivian mother and child is surely indicative of fertility.

However, the introduction of pottery at Peruvian coastal and highland sites was only one part of a wider range of cultural changes identifiable, for example at late Preceramic El Paraíso. Populations at coastal sites began to shift inland, abandoning some of the U-shaped ceremonial complexes of the Preceramic Period to build new complexes in the fertile lower river valleys. As well as making pots, economics had begun to shift from marine economies to agricultural crops. La Galgada, El Paraíso, Piedra Parada and other sites show the beginning of the use of small-scale irrigation works.

There seems to be a combination of reasons for these shifts, and for the increased importance of highland sites. Population

Below: An early Chavín stirrup-spouted bottle, one of the earliest container shapes, with highly stylized feline imagery.

Above: A bizarre two-headed Valdivian female ceramic figurine, possibly representing fertility, duality, or mythological transformation.

lowlands to their east, as well as imitating some coastal features. Surface decoration on highland pots is common, especially groups of incised parallel lines and hatching, filled with red, white and yellow mineral pigments after firing. Sherds of Kotosh- and Shillacoto-style ceramics have been found at the Cave of Owls in the eastern rainforest, while tropical forest trade sherds have been found at Kotosh and Shillacoto.

NOT JUST POTS

The beginning of ceramic production is one criterion used to define the Initial Period, particularly because pottery forms an important part of the archaeological records from that point onwards, is well preserved and provides archaeologists with varieties in styles that enable them to define different cultures.

increases may be one reason, although there is no convincing evidence that coastal agriculture or marine resources were being depleted. The coincident geographic coastal uplift and ocean shelf subduction did force fish shoals farther offshore into deeper waters, and also lowered coastal water tables. Non-environmental reasons may have included competition between groups for the richest, most easily worked farmlands and simply changes in dietary and work preferences. If production of crops could be increased by moving inland to fertile lower valleys rather than risking the open sea, people may have simply made that choice from one generation to the next. The coincidence of increasingly efficient farming and the use of ceramics in which to store and cook that produce cannot be by pure chance.

THE SHAPES OF POTS

The earliest Andean ceramics were limited to a few shapes and mostly imitated the familiar forms of gourd containers. From the simple shapes of the Initial Period, however, variety soon developed into regional styles. Distinctive forms were made that became hallmarks of pre-Hispanic Andean civilization.

MAKING POTS

Ancient Andeans never invented the wheel, either for transport or for pottery making. However, fired-clay discs were used as platforms to turn vessels as they were made, the earliest known being from Paracas c.500BC. Interestingly, although the use of drop spindles to spin fibres was an obvious example of horizontal rotary motion, it never occurred to ancient Andeans to apply this to a spinning disc on which pots could be formed.

Andean potting used three techniques: coiling, paddle and anvil, and moulding. Coiling and hand-modelling were the principal techniques until the Early Intermediate Period, when moulding became an added method, particularly on the north-west Peruvian coast.

Coiled ceramics were made by forming long coils of clay, building up the shape of the vessels by placing the rings one on top the other, then smoothing the ridges out to form smooth sides using maize cobs, bone or wooden paddles, pebbles or shells. Cloth or hide was used to achieve a final smoothness.

The paddle and anvil technique was begun by forming the base of the vessel from a lump of clay, using the hands, or by moulding it over an existing vessel or other shape, then adding more clay to build up the sides. The sides were formed and smoothed by patting the outside with a wooden paddle, against a smooth stone held inside the vessel wall as an anvil.

Moulding involved both forming the clay over an existing form and by pressing the clay into a prepared mould (a method used particularly by the Early Intermediate Period Moche, for example). The process for smoothing the clay pot was the same as for coiled vessels.

Different cultures preferred one or other of these methods, but all three methods were employed, depending on the style and purpose of the pottery. Simple wares for everyday use were

Above: A realistic ceramic hand pottery stamp from the Early Intermediate Period Jamacoaque culture of Ecuador.

most easily made quickly by coiling, or by paddle and anvil. Such wares needed little decoration and were primarily utilitarian.

PROFESSIONAL POTTERS

Apart from such utilitarian containers, made by the users, especially in earlier periods, potting soon became a specialist's art, particularly to produce complex forms and ceramics intended for special purposes. This development coincided with specializations within society and as agricultural production became efficient enough for fewer farmers to grow enough to support full-time specialists of many kinds.

Left: Despite their zoomorphic rodent shapes, these Early Horizon Chorrera culture 'whistle' spout bottles were utilitarian.

Left: This Nazca parrot-shaped bridge-spouted bottle reveals long-distance cultural contacts.

For the mass-production of vessels, an employment that became institutionalized in the great states of later periods (especially in the imperial states of the Moche, Wari, Tiwanaku, Sicán, Chimú and Inca), the use of moulds could speed up production. Nevertheless, professional potters, working full-time for the state, could also produce masses of coil-made vessels. Buildings and compounds that were pottery factories have been excavated at Wari, Chimú and Inca sites in particular. For example, Inca state potters produced uniform plates and pointed storage jars for feeding *mit'a* state workers.

TWO DISTINCT ANDEAN FORMS

Plates, shallow and spherical bowls, beakers or vases, bottle-necked jars (imitating gourds), globular jars and large storage jars were used across all Andean cultures from the later Initial Period and Early Horizon. Vessel sides and rims were straight, flared, incurved and rolled; bases were flat, rounded and in some cases had stout 'legs'.

Two distinct Andean forms were the stirrup-spout bottle and the double-spout-and-bridge bottle. The

Below: Another Nazca painted bridge-spouted bottle, of more 'conventional' container shape, depicts strange humanoid figures seemingly participating in drug-induced trances or transformation ceremonies.

first was a bottle with a single spout rising from a stirrup-shaped loop on the top of the vessel. The latter, as its name implies, had two spouts, between which was a handle-like bridge made from a flattened strap of plain or decorated clay. Both forms were made in a huge variety of shapes and decorations by different cultures in different periods.

Cultural styles were primarily the product of details in shape and in decoration using this range of forms.

USING POTS

The uses of pottery also quickly transcended mere utilitarian use, although that remained a principal function of form. Vessels were used for specific ceremonial roles as offerings and in the performance of ritual. Especially fine vessels were deposited in burials. And, both in life and in burial, the fineness and production quality of vessels reflected social status.

Within the range of utilitarian forms – bottles, plates, cups and jars, for pouring, eating, drinking and storage – shapes could be elaborate and even bizarre. Some pots were

undoubtedly purely ornamental – perhaps a household prized possession, or made specifically for burial.

EFFIGIES AND BIZARRE FORMS

Many ceramic pieces, especially stirrup-spout and double-spout-and-bridge bottles, and beakers/vases, were made as effigy vessels. They depicted either individuals as types within society (for example a shaman) or an actual individual (a practice possibly unique among the Moche). Bottles and other containers were made in the shapes of animals (for example for incense burning in a bowl forming the animal's body). Others imitated vegetable shapes, such as gourds, tubers and cactuses. Some bottle bodies were even rectangular-sided and stepped.

Still other vessels, perfectly functional, depicted whole scenes, such as a shaman healing a patient, priestly animalistic transformation, coca snuffing, combat and sexual acts. Moche ceramics are especially notable for such moulded imagery, while Nazca and other styles are especially notable for depicting such themes as painted decoration.

Fired ceramics were also used for other artefacts. Figurines were produced in abundance probably as votive offerings at temples and to represent deities. There were also ceramic masks depicting deities. Models of temples, houses and storehouses were made, and even fired clay panpipes.

CERAMIC DECORATION

Just as there was great variation in the details of shapes among the primary ceramic vessel forms in Andean civilization, so also were there a number of decorative techniques. Variation in the use of these produced distinctive styles among cultures and through time. The imagery and geometric or abstract decoration of Andean pots was done using all these methods, and by combinations of them.

POLISHING
Glazing was unknown in pre-Hispanic America, but a fine shine could be achieved by polishing the surface with a fine, hard stone, and by rubbing the partially dried pot with the hands or a cloth before firing. Moche potters polished the painted areas of their pots, while Nazca potters carefully polished the whole design area, sometimes smudging the paint colours. Early Horizon Chavín and Late Intermediate Period Chimú potters produced distinctive, highly polished, shiny black wares.

MODELLING, TWO-PART MOULDS AND CUT DECORATION
Modelling was accomplished by making the desired shape by hand moulding, building up the object, animal, plant or person in bits. Wooden and bone sticks and punches, and metal tools and knives were also used to achieve finer shaping. From the Early Intermediate Period onwards the use of fired-clay moulds in two halves became widespread, especially among north-west coast cultures.

If the vessel was not moulded, decorative techniques applied to the smoothed surface included punching, incising, excising, stamping and painting. Punched and incised decorations were some of the earliest techniques. Rows of punched dots, incised lines (cutting into the surface with a sharp tool) and shapes were used extensively on Initial Period ceramics among the coastal and inland cultures whose

peoples built U-shaped ceremonial centres. Excision (cutting out fine sections of clay from the pot's surface, leaving a recessed area) was also was used to make symbolic images and geometric designs.

SLIPS AND PAINTING
Pigments derived from vegetables and ground minerals were used to make paints and thick pastes to rub into incised and excised decorations. Runny 'paint' (a suspension of fine clay in water) was also used as slips to cover a vessel surface or chosen areas.

The earliest paints were used in the 2nd millennium BC in pottery from Kotosh, Shillacoto and other highland sites, whose potters applied red, white and yellow paint to rows of incised lines

Above: An Early Intermediate Period Tuncahuan bowl from Ecuador with geometric decoration.

and patterns. In the 1st millennium BC, potters in southern Peru began to apply mineral pigments mixed with plant resins into incised designs, after firing, to form a lacquer-like coating. Such post-firing painting and use of resin became a distinctive practice among Paracas potters.

Slips were usually applied by dipping the vessel in the paint. Areas that a potter wanted to remain free of colour were protected by the use of wax. After dipping, the wax was melted away to reveal the, usually lighter, clay colour, creating a negative painted effect. Paracas and Nazca potters were particularly fond of this method.

Paint colours included white, black, brown, red, yellow, purple and blue; variations in shades and intensity produced grey, orange, pink and violet. The Nazca used up to 15 distinct colours. Pigment sources probably included haematite (iron ore) for red, limonite (hydrated haematite) for yellow and possibly manganese and pyrolusite (magnesium dioxide) as sources of black.

In contrast, Moche potters used mainly red and white slips, both made from fine white and red clay, the latter being the same clay from which the Moche made their pots. Black and red were also used for fine-line drawing of narrative scenes, depicting everything from ceremonial sacrifice and ritual combat to hunting scenes. Often, both unpainted and painted areas were polished to create different shades of red and white to cream.

As well as rubbing paints and pastes into incised and excised areas, and negative painting techniques, paints were probably applied with fine animal-hair or vegetable-fibre brushes.

STAMPING
Another method of decoration was the use of stamps and pressing a negative moulded figure on to the vessel surface (as opposed to moulding the entire vessel using two half moulds). Combinations of lines and geometric patterns were made by pressing a wooden paddle stamp on to the wet pot to raise the design above the vessel's wall. Fired-clay stamps were also used to raise geometric, floral and animal designs and figures.

Left: A terracotta model of a house from the Cupisnique culture, c.700–300BC. Many such pieces were highly polished.

Above: A double-bodied, spouted Chancay bottle from the Late Intermediate Period possibly implies duality by its half-and-half painted body.

COMBINING TECHNIQUES
Nazca, Moche, Wari and Tiwanaku potters, in particular, excelled in combinations of all sorts of moulded and modelled, then painted, effigy vessels.

The potters made and depicted many kinds of people, deities, animals and plants. There are vessels showing single figures and groups of figures, young and old, performing all manner of daily tasks, from hunting, combat, sacrifice and ceremony, to washing one's hair, expressing the pain of a backache, giving birth or having sex.

Occasionally, shell and stone (e.g. turquoise) inlays were also applied to decorate pottery, for example as eyes.

CULTURAL STYLES

Cultural styles were mainly distinct in details of shape within a range of vessel forms, and in their methods and types of decorations applied to them.

INITIAL COASTAL AND HIGHLAND

After introduction *c*.2000BC, Andean ceramic styles began differentiating within coastal and highland cultures. North and central coastal potters used simple designs of incised lines and geometric shapes. Virú and Moche valley potters, by contrast, made thick-walled, dark red and black bowls and necked jars, mainly plain, but also with simple finger impressions, punched and incised patterns.

The central coastal Ancón style featured similar forms with incised and punched decoration, sometimes painted. Pottery making had reached south coastal sites by *c*.1300BC, where its most distinguishing characteristic

was the use of negative painting (masking areas before dipping the pot into slip paint).

The highland Wairajirca style – at Kotosh, Shillacoto and other sites – developed from *c*.1800BC. The most common forms were cups, bowls and vases, but the first stirrup-spout bottles were also made. Decoration comprised bands of incised lines and circles filled with red, white and yellow paints after firing. Raised patterns were created by excision. Highland styles show similarities to contemporary eastern tropical lowland Tutishcainyo ceramics.

EARLY HORIZON STYLES

Three distinctive Early Horizon styles were Chavín culture in the highlands, Cupisnique on the north-west coast and Paracas on the south coast. Chavín potters made distinctive polished grey-black ware – open bowls, globular and stirrup-spout bottles. Decoration was mostly incising, but also stamping and punching. Contrasting areas were defined by polishing and texturing with depressions by shells or combs and also by applying dark red and graphite grey paints. More complex geometric patterns and symbolic serpent, feline and bird imagery came later.

Cupisnique-style bottles and globular vessels are typically black or grey. Stirrup-spout bottles feature a trapezoidal-shaped stirrup, including effigy vessels of marine and terrestrial animals and people. Irregular incised lines were sometimes filled with red paint after firing.

Early Paracas potters produced Chavín-inspired stirrup-spout bottles and forms with fine-line incised feline imagery. In

Left: An Inca effigy jar portraying a man carrying a jug and kero *cups, probably for* chicha *beer for ritual drinking, and wearing a half-moon pendant.*

Above: An Early Intermediate Period Virú bridge-spouted, double-bodied bottle, possibly a whistle vessel, with a parrot head.

the later 1st millennium BC, the Paracas style developed distinctive, highly colourful ceramics using incised patterns and imagery filled with red, orange, yellow, blue, green and brown paints and resin after firing. Circle, dot and line patterns were used to create a negative painted effect in lighter slip-colour under a dark over-colour.

EARLY INTERMEDIATE PERIOD

Prominent styles in the Early Intermediate Period were dominated by north-west coastal Salinar, Gallinazo, Recuay and Moche wares and by south coastal Nazca and early Tiwanaku pottery. The quality and quantity of production indicates that potters had become full-time specialists, perhaps supported by the state. Mould-made ceramics became dominant in the north, while coil-made and highly colourful pottery characterized southern styles.

Salinar potters introduced the double-spout-and-bridge bottle. Use of Chavín-Cupisnique feline motifs waned, while human and animal effigy vessels proliferated, including erotic imagery. Gallinazo ceramics shared and continued these features with highly naturalistic modelling and introduced negative painting techniques on geometric and feline imagery.

Contemporary Moche coastal and adjacent highland Recuay styles introduced an exuberance of modelled and moulded effigy forms representing all manner of life scenes from the exotic to the mundane, including human portraiture. Utilitarian forms included bowls, bottles, jars, dippers and spoons. Moche pottery is distinctive for its highly polished, bright red colour, and for its depiction of narrative scenes in fine red or black line drawings. It has been intensely studied and is divided into five phases of development.

Recuay potters were the first to depict 'the common man'. Recuay ware is distinguished by its white paste, and by human and animal (most frequently feline) imagery, in white, black and red.

Nazca and early Tiwanku ceramics are highly polychrome styles. Nazca wares spread throughout the Nazca, Ica, Chincha, Pisco and Acari valleys. Modelling is infrequent (almost always of humans), while painting predominated, in up to 15 colours or shades of white, black, brown, red, yellow, purple and blue, as well as violet, orange, pink and grey. Complex scenes of intertwined

Below: A south-west coastal Peru Paracas drinking cup with typical geometric decoration reminiscent of textile patterns.

geometric patterns, deities, humans and animals cover whole pot surfaces, continuing the Paracas tradition.

Later Nazca potters changed from pre-firing painting to post-firing negative painting, using slips and wax to keep areas unpainted, paint resins delimited by incised lines to create a lacquer-like finish, and high polishing. Through several phases it evolved from more naturalistic to more abstract forms of decoration and imagery.

MIDDLE HORIZON MASS PRODUCTION

Growing political unity under the Tiwanaku and Wari empires spread their ceramics far and wide. Production was simplified and mass production in state-sponsored factories was introduced. Tiwanaku pottery is multicoloured on a distinctive orange base. Decoration is predominantly religious, depicting feline, serpentine and deity imagery (especially a figure holding staffs in outstretched hands), as on stone sculpture and textiles. Use of slips and colour range were similar to Nazca wares. A distinctive Tiwanakoid form is the tall *kero* drinking beaker; there were also huge, thick-walled, multicoloured storage urns set in pits.

In contrast, Wari pottery, also polychrome, is mostly secular. Geometric patterns and effigy vessels (both painted and moulded) predominate, and emphasis is on the world of humans. Towards the end of the Middle Horizon, decoration became more geometric and abstract, and quality declined.

CHIMÚ, CHANCAY AND INCA

The Chimú continued the Moche and Wari tradition of mass production using moulds, and decorating in several colours, but quality declined in favour of quantity. Plain polished black and red wares

Above: An Early Horizon north-west coastal Peru Cupisnique stirrup-spouted effigy bottle of a man carrying a llama, and presumably wearing regional headgear.

were also made. Plates and ring-based bowls were introduced for the first time, and tripod bowls also became common; stirrup-spout bottles declined.

Central-coastal Chancay ware was another main style. Using crude, gritty clay, forms include oblong, narrow-necked bottles and jars with handles. Human faces were painted in grey-black on white slip backgrounds; there were also nude female effigies with outstretched arms.

Inca ceramics are characterized by painted decoration in black and white on red. Designs are geometric, especially fern motifs, triangles and rhomboids. Bird and animal imagery is stylized to the point of being abstract. Characteristic shapes are flat, round plates, *kero* cups and pointed-base, globular bottles with flared necks and handles.

INTERPRETING THE POTS

Two categories of ceramics co-existed in Andean civilization: utilitarian and special. The groups were not exclusive – the same forms were used for both – but wares for daily use were not necessarily made by specialists. Special wares, although functional, were meant for ceremonial and ritual uses, and some forms, such as animal-shaped incense burners, were clearly purpose made. Despite changing decorative styles and predominant techniques of manufacture in different areas, there were several common symbolic motifs and imagery that reflected pan-Andean religious beliefs.

CULTURAL RECORDS
Even highly decorated utilitarian wares, produced for social elites, served simultaneously, consciously or otherwise, as a record of culture by depicting mythological scenes and scenes of daily life as well as holding liquids and food.

Below: An Early Intermediate Period Pashash lidded jar with geometric, textile-like decoration and the image of a double-headed serpent, probably representing duality.

Right: Vivid subjects and delicate images decorate many Nazca pots, such as this bridge-spouted bottle depicting hummingbirds sipping nectar from a flower.

Spanish documents make almost no mention of pottery, so it is only through archaeology and comparison of the imagery on ceramics with our knowledge of Inca and earlier religion that we can surmise what the decoration meant.

The effort taken, especially by potters up to the Late Intermediate Period, to decorate pottery obviates its importance to convey messages to those making and using it. As well as being purely aesthetic, the ritual use of pottery shows that it was made for specific purposes. Making pieces especially for burial with the dead emphasizes the importance of the afterlife and the need to prepare for it.

Pottery models of houses and temples give us a rare insight of how reconstructions of the archaeological excavations of their foundations might look.

RELIGIOUS MEANINGS
In the Early Horizon, Chavín religious influence became widespread through symbolism, especially of feline, serpentine and cayman imagery, on portable artefacts – pottery, textiles and metalwork. The snarling feline with bared teeth and long canines, and serpent heads and bodies are thought to symbolize the power of these

creatures and admiration of them. They were depicted through all the techniques – painted, incised in outline and moulded – showing their universal application across styles.

The snarling feline motif all but disappeared in the Early Intermediate Period, to reappear in Moche and later ceramics, again both as incised and painted imagery. The mouth is often wide open, and feline features are often combined with human features to represent transformation by shamans or priests. Bird and other animal transformation is also represented.

Imagery in different regions hints at predominant economic strengths, such as marine creatures on coastal wares. But the appearance of tropical animals (jaguars, caymans and tropical birds) on highland wares also shows the strength of highland–lowland contacts and the supernatural regard for those creatures by highland peoples.

Other deity imagery includes the Staff Deity, which characterizes Chavín, Tiwanaku and Chimú art, including on ceramics. Other local deities are also represented, such as the Oculate Being, which was so important in south coastal Paracas and Nazca culture.

THEMES

A ritual theme in Moche ceramics is the 'presentation scene', a simpler form of which also appears on Chancay pottery. In it, one figure, dressed in a shirt, short kilt and conical helmet, proffers a goblet to a seated or more prominent figure. There are also scenes showing cloth being offered.

A prominent theme in Paracas and Nazca pottery shows a deity or masked semi-human holding a severed head – trophy heads also being an important image in other media.

Below: Painted ceramic vessel with a snake-shaped handle from the Tiwanaku culture.

Above: A ceramic vessel from the Recuay culture (c.300–600AD) showing a snake with a feline head.

REMINDERS OF LIFE

The apparent exuberance of Nazca and Moche ceramics reveals the importance of the images and scenes as reminders to people of what was important. The portrayal of everyday narrative scenes, as well as more exotic events, from healing, to sex, to architectural models, and the care and time taken to mould and paint them, reveals the richness of life.

In Moche art, the ritual combat scene is often repeated, and Moche potters are the only ones known who definitely portrayed actual living people. One Moche man was portrayed 45 times, documenting much of his life. But whether depicting a living person or a type, Moche potters covered the range of human conditions from youth to old age and from health to sickness in effigy vessels showing backache, birth, healing and death.

The complex battle scenes on Nazca pottery contrast with ritual single-combat scenes on Moche pottery. Both, however, reveal an importance in conflict and in the ultimate outcome of sacrifice and death.

CONVENTIONS

Certain 'rules' of execution can also be detected in the uniformity and the stylization with Nazca and Moche pottery. Slip colours are only white or red. Background colours, on which detailed Nazca scenes were painted, are only painted in black, white or shades of red. Mythical beings on Paracas and Nazca pots are always shown frontal, and they are usually associated with severed heads.

Moche potters used conventions in the poses and actions of their animal, human and semi-human figures. The space between the feet indicated whether the figure was standing, walking, running or dancing. The angle of the torso and positions of the limbs showed speed, falling over or death. Despite such conventions, it is thought that the nuances of style in finishing and depicting facial features in the repetitious mould-made and painted forms sometimes reveals the hand of the same artist.

POWER AND CONTROL

The mass production of repetitious forms by the Wari, Tiwanaku, Chimú and Inca empires was a statement of power. It served to remind subjects of state control of production and provision of employment, alongside regulation of the economy.

SCENES AND PORTRAITS IN POTTERY

One of the most exuberant styles was the 'narrative' and 'portrait' pottery of the Moche. Like their revealing wall frescoes, tens of thousands of Moche pots depict scenes of everyday life: weavers, fishers, hunters, warriors, shamans, animals and plants. The scenes are painted in red lines on cream backgrounds (known as fine-line ware) on bowls, jars, cups and bottles. In addition, moulded effigy vessels were made in seemingly endless forms showing all manner of life scenes.

Moche mass production reveals state control of the industry and an imperial message that they were in control. As the Moche spread their empire by conquest, they stamped their style on other cultures through clay rather than textiles. Moche pottery has been found as far south as the Chincha Islands off the central coast of Peru, where Moche sailors in reed boats collected rich guano to fertilize agricultural fields back in the homeland.

Below: A red clay model of a house, probably Late Intermediate Period Chimú, shows us a domestic scene of seeming merry-making.

MOCHE VIRTUOSITY

There are lively and dexterous scenes in both media – fine-line and effigy. They are both aesthetically pleasing, even 'touching', and graphically revealing, for they show ritual as well as common life, individual portraiture as well as fantasy, and thus give us an astoundingly detailed picture of Moche culture, rich in the everyday and in the spiritual meaning of Moche beliefs. They depict both the ideal and the particular. On some they show, or are modelled as, individuals whose clothing and regalia announce their high rank and authority; others disclose their occupation or activity; others reveal a state of religious, drug-induced trance; and still others in everyday wear are occupied in ordinary tasks.

One animated scene painted around a globular vessel depicts a seal hunt. A line of presumably shallow shore waves underlines a violent scene of two hunters with clubs among a herd of seals, which flee in all directions from their pursuers. Shorebirds circle overhead and there is an island with spots, presumably meant

Above: Nazca religion featured a cult of trophy head collection. Here a bridge-spouted bottle has been painted as a trophy head, with stitched-up eyes and a pinned mouth.

to represent guano. The seals' arched bodies and outstretched, clawed limbs imply dynamic movement. Some are vertical, as if leaping into deeper waters and diving to avoid being clubbed. Two of them have been caught, their flippers flailing at right angles from their bodies and the hunters' clubs smacking against their heads. The seals are clearly frantic with fear as they attempt to elude the hunters. They have gaping mouths and dilated pupils within wide, white eyes.

Such dynamism is shown time after time. Battle scenes show warriors engaged in 'gladiatorial combat', in which the background, and the armour and weapons show both to be Moche, rather than captive warriors of other states. They fight in scrublands near the Moche cities. He who is defeated must undergo a gruesome ritual sacrifice, an act also depicted on pottery in exquisite detail with fully armoured warriors with helmets, shields and war clubs leading naked losers, their genitalia exposed as a sign of submission and with rope nooses around their necks.

SCENES OF DAILY LIFE

Effigy vessels show equally remarkable scenes. For example, a stirrup-spout bottle depicts a shaman or curer administering to a reclining, sick individual. The curer is a woman with a long shawl-like head-piece. She lays one hand on the body of the sick person, her other hand to her mouth. Perhaps she is chanting or attempting to suck the illness out. Next to her lies a severed head, perhaps to indicate that she will be executed if unsuccessful in curing her patient. There are fine-line drawings on pots showing curers' nude corpses being pecked by birds!

Other vessels show priests taking coca snuff. Another is the charming figure of a man bent over a flaring bowl, both hands stroking the water from his hair, which is curved over the bowl. Is he simply washing his hair, or engaged in some preparatory ritual before a religious ceremony? Another shows a hunter with a blow-dart tube shooting a bird in a tree.

Below: A Nazca bridge-spouted effigy bottle portraying a tattooed old, bearded man, who appears to be blind.

Right: One of hundreds of Moche red-ware portrait bottles. His distinct facial features, earrings and headpiece identify him as a living man whose face was copied in a mould.

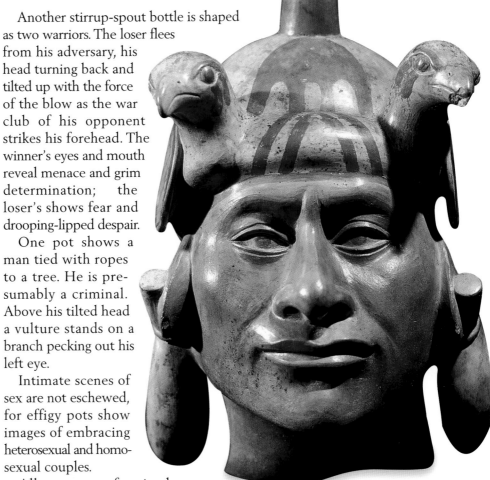

Another stirrup-spout bottle is shaped as two warriors. The loser flees from his adversary, his head turning back and tilted up with the force of the blow as the war club of his opponent strikes his forehead. The winner's eyes and mouth reveal menace and grim determination; the loser's shows fear and drooping-lipped despair.

One pot shows a man tied with ropes to a tree. He is presumably a criminal. Above his tilted head a vulture stands on a branch pecking out his left eye.

Intimate scenes of sex are not eschewed, for effigy pots show images of embracing heterosexual and homosexual couples.

All manner of animals are sculpted as pots. Three such stirrup-spout bottles are an enchanting llama complete with panniers holding miniature bottles; a captivating reclining doe licking the nose of her fawn; and a humorous monkey, sitting with wide-open mouth and a *pepino* fruit clutched in his hands, just about to enjoy his meal.

PORTRAITURE

Finally, and perhaps most remarkably, there are the hundreds of portrait vessels. Many are unique: they depict perhaps an individual or at least a type – young and old people, musicians, healers; people laughing, smiling, frowning, contemplative, worried and frightened, ailing, wide-eyed and narrow-eyed, scheming, chubby-faced and lean, some moustachioed and bearded. They wear all manner of dress and individual hats and jewellery.

Christopher Donnan has recognized more than 750 distinct individuals. Of most there is only one example; but several have three or four portraits. One remarkable individual, with a distinct scar on his left upper lip, was a chosen gladiator who survived many bouts, for he was depicted at least 40 times, and has been dubbed 'Cut Lip'.

CHAPTER ELEVEN

FIBREWORK, COSTUME AND FEATHERWORK

The importance of cloth and fibre arts in Andean civilization cannot be underestimated. Fibrous plants were among the earliest domesticated plants. Mostly utilitarian at first, in time cloth became the most important exchange commodity other than food, and in Inca times served, in value, as a sort of 'coinage' of the realm.

Preceramic peoples worked plant fibres by simple twisting, twining and looping, making twine and bindings for spear, arrow and drill points, bolas stones and for slings. Sleeping mats, sandals and simple clothing were made with simple looping, as were nets, bags and carriers. These were the first steps towards the sophisticated weaving that became a hallmark of Andean civilization.

All women wove. In pre-Inca times textile production may not have been so exclusive to women, but in Inca society spinning and weaving were symbolic demonstrations of womanhood and they were done by all women, from the most common subject, through the noblewomen of the imperial household to the Sapa Inca's principal wife.

The importance of textiles to the Inca is epitomized in a statement attributed to Atahualpa, last Inca emperor, upon meeting Pizarro in Cajamarca: "I know what you have done along this road. You have taken the cloth from the temples, and I shall not leave until it has been returned to me." This, despite the Inca wealth in gold and silver!

Left: A late Early Intermediate Period Nazca or early Middle Horizon Wari poncho with stylized bird and animal imagery.

TWINING, SPINNING AND WEAVING

The variety and quantity of Andean textiles that have survived are phenomenal. Whereas ancient Mesoamerican textile studies are greatly reliant on pictures in ancient manuscripts (*códices*), Andean preservation has provided thousands of examples to study directly.

USEFUL *AND* SYMBOLIC

Late Archaic and Preceramic peoples twisted and twined wild plant fibres primarily for utilitarian objects. Twine and cordage provided binding for spear, arrow and drill points, and for bolas stones and slings. Looped cordage enabled them to make a variety of basic 'textiles' such as simple clothing, and various nets, bags

Below: A Moche red-line ceramic dish showing an old woman (left, with wrinkles) allegedly instructing a younger woman in the art of weaving, and talking, or possibly chanting or singing.

and carriers. Containers were fibre sacks, as well as animal skins, dried gourds and wooden vessels, before the discovery or invention of fired ceramics.

Utilitarian uses never ceased, however (footwear, mats, tools and bags required constant quantities of twine and cordage, and ordinary daywear required plain woven cloth), and remained important right through to Inca times. For example, quotas of cordage were required of male Inca subjects for the many bridges and army weapons needed. Cords dyed and knotted into *quipus* provided a means of keeping imperial accounts.

Soon, however, alongside developments in irrigation agriculture, monumental architecture and sophisticated religious beliefs, cloth became more symbolically utilitarian, as a medium for conveying religious concepts, for social and regional differentiation in clothing styles, and for preserving the dead.

Above: Llama wool spinning and weaving in the Andes was developed simultaneously with coastal cotton fibre use from the 1st millennium BC.

TEXTILE PRODUCTION

Plant fibres were simply shredded, dried and twisted into twine and cord, then knotted and looped (weft twisted around weft) into bags, baskets, sandals and other items. The earliest items are of hemp-like brome and agave plant fibres from Guitarrero Cave, dated *c.*8000BC. Cotton was one of the first Andean domesticated plants. It was grown in the coastal valleys of Peru and Ecuador from *c.*3000BC, although its wild ancestor must have been collected and tended earlier, before it was actively cropped.

By the 3rd millennium BC (Initial Period), cotton textiles were being made from Ecuador, through Peru to northern Chile. The llama and alpaca were domesticated in the Altiplano around the Titicaca Basin during the Preceramic Period. Evidence is lacking, but it is assumed that llama and alpaca wool spinning and weaving developed during this period and through the Initial Period, for there is ample evidence in the Early Horizon of wool used in Paracas embroidery on the south coast. Some wool use was found at Preceramic Aspero, but it was not until the Early Intermediate Period that wool was used extensively by central and north coastal peoples.

Above: A Chancay Late Intermediate Period wool and cotton tapestry cloth demonstrates the constant contact and interchange between coastal plains and mountains.

Nearly three-quarters of the early cotton textiles from Huaca Prieta are twined; the remainder are woven, or looped as netting. Twining does not involve a loom. The vertical warp threads are diverted slightly right and left and held by twisted horizontal weft threads – thus the weft turn around the warp rather than interweaving with it. The process is manual. Using different coloured threads enables the maker to produce patterns and pictures by trading the warp threads from the front to the back of the cloth, creating zigzag designs and images.

Loom weaving began in the Initial Period, from *c*.2000BC, with the invention of heddles – flat sticks to raise groups of threads in order to weave between them quickly – and the backstrap loom. Twining died out, but looping and sprang (interlinking sets of cloth elements) continued to be used for bags and hats.

Cotton was spun by beating the fibres out, rolling them into a cylinder and attaching it to a post, then drawing out the thread while twisting the cylinder. Wool was spun with the drop spindle.

LOOMS

All the techniques used by ancient Andeans for textile production were known by the end of the Early Horizon (*c*.200BC). In addition to knotting, looping and twining, these were: the plying of several strands (of wool) together;

Below: The continuous need for wool and cotton thread and yarn for weaving required daily drop spinning by women of all ranks in the Inca Empire and earlier (depicted in Poma de Ayala's Nueva Corónica, *c.1615).*

braiding; the use of discontinuous warp and weft to create imagery and patterns, also of supplementary warp and weft threads and complementary sets of warp or weft; warp wrapping (creating the design on the warp by wrapping it in coloured yarn before weaving); embroidery and tapestry; textile painting; tie-dying; and the use of double and triple cloth (interconnected layering).

Most ancient Andean weaving was done on backstrap looms, although other types were known, especially the vertical (suspended) loom. Warp threads were wound in a figure of eight around two posts. The warp ends are tied to wooden bars, one of which is fixed to a post or wall peg and the other to a backstrap around the weaver's waist. Warp tension is adjustable by leaning back or easing up.

Warp sheds are created, first, by the figure of eight of the preparation, then by lifting alternate warps on loops of thread called leaches, attached to a heddle stick. Weft threads are passed through the sheds, as they are lifted and lowered, with thread on a bobbin, then beat down against the earlier wefts. By lifting different sets of warps in sheds less than the entire width of the cloth, and/or by passing the weft through less than the full-width shed, patterns and images can be created within the warp and weft.

EARLY COTTON TEXTILES

Wild cotton relatives grow in northern Peruvian coastal valleys. Evidence of fibre use at Archaic Guitarrero Cave, and widespread production of cotton textiles from Ecuador to northern Chile at late Initial Period coastal sites, indicates millennia of wild cotton collection and tending before planting and extension of its cultivable range. Truly domesticated cotton (*Gossypium barbadense*) grows at 320–1,000m (1,050–3,280ft) above sea level.

COTTON DESIGNS

Lowland textiles are dominated by cotton, although llama wool, as it became more available through highland–lowland trade from the late Initial Period, was increasingly combined with cotton, especially at Paracas. Cotton takes dyes less easily than wool, so use of wool increased

Below: A Middle Horizon Wari woven poncho of wool and cotton fibre, with characteristic geometric patterns (some are possibly highly stylized faces), reveals trade for fibre between coastal cotton growers and Altiplano llama herders.

the colour range through the Early Horizon. Textile painting was also developed on the coast, perhaps for this reason.

Preceramic coastal fishing peoples relied heavily on cotton for knotted nets and line, found at most sites, including nets up to 30m (98ft) long.

Preceramic Huaca Prieta produced some of the earliest cotton fabrics, of which more than 9,000 fragments were found. Their designs show the earliest Andean concerns with visual messages, including multiple meaning and composite imagery. Complex patterns and imagery were created using twining with spaced wefts and exposed warps of different colours (red, yellow, blue, black dyed, and natural white and brown cotton), plus looping and knotting, in characteristic zigzag contours.

Human, bird, serpent, crab, fish and other animal imagery was used singly and in repetitive interlocking patterns. Multiple meanings are conveyed in double-headed birds and snakes, crabs that transform into snakes, and other creatures with multiple attributes. One famous piece portrays

Above: A painted, cotton Paracas, southern coastal Peruvian burial wrap depicts Staff Deity figures within diamond panels, revealing the influence of the Chavín Cult from farther north.

a raptor with spread wings, and a snake inside its stomach. Similar imagery is found on textiles from Asia and La Galgada.

CHAVÍN TEXTILES

Early Horizon Chavín textiles include more than 200 pieces from Karwa and other southern coastal sites, where they have survived. They include the earliest painted Andean textiles. It is assumed that highland Chavín sites used similar textiles. Northern coastal Cupisnique weavers also painted cotton textiles.

Karwa textiles were a medium for the spread of the Chavín Staff Deity. Female Staff Deity imagery was painted in brown and rose on plain woven cotton cloth. Sometimes several pieces were sewn together, for example a circle of jaguars

reminiscent of the circular sunken court jaguar sculptures at Chavín de Huántar. Cloth belts resemble that on the Lanzón Stela and many painted figures carry staffs or San Pedro cacti.

Karwa textiles always portray supernatural beings as female. Eyes substitute for breasts; fanged mouths for vaginas; and they carry plant staffs, often intertwined, or as animated cotton plants and bolls. Profiled attendants are either male or genderless. Like the Raimondi Stela at Chavín de Huántar, the female images present a second image when inverted. It is thought that she portrays an Earth goddess, and that the pieces are hangings, canopies and altar covers. Other fragments are clothing or mummy wraps. Braiding around textile edges is thought to be a symbol of continuity.

PARACAS TEXTILES

Contemporary Paracas weavers developed embroidery, using imported alpaca wool from the Altiplano on cotton backing cloths, sometimes also incorporating tropical bird feathers. They also invented discontinuous warp and weft techniques. By not passing the whole lengths of weft or warp threads across or down the loom, they could make highly complex woven imagery and patterns.

Hundreds of mummy bundles in the Paracas Cerro Colorado, Arena Blanca and Wari Kayan cemeteries include rich textile wraps. Bundles range widely from rough cotton mantles to elaborate multiple-bundle wraps of plain and highly decorated textiles, holding gold, feather, animal-skin and imported shell offerings. (Incorporating grave goods was a means of maintaining an individual's integrity and possession.) The largest bundles are up to 2m (6½ft) tall, and the largest cloths are 3.4 x 26m (11ft x 85ft)!

Paracas embroidery covers the whole of the ground cloth in vibrant colours, patterns and images. Motifs and imagery are usually applied at borders, neck-slits and in columns in the centres of mantles

or wraps. The textiles include the work of masters and apprentices – many cloths have a central panel of perfectly formed figures flanked by panels less well executed, attempting to copy the master's panel. Some cloths appear to be practice pieces; some are unfinished before burial. Calculations of the hours taken to make these complex pieces and multiple mummy wraps indicate that they occupied lifetimes, suggesting that preparation was specifically for burial.

LINEAR AND BLOCK COLOUR

The linear style comprises stitches sewn in and out of the ground cloth, always moving forwards and leaving visible lines of thread. In contrast, Block Colour style covers the thread by stitching forwards, then half backwards, then forwards again with slightly overlapping diagonal stitches. Linear textiles are more restrictive than

Above: A complex Initial Period Paracas embroidered burial shroud, made of fine alpaca wool, with dual central figures. The figure with the golden diadem is probably the Oculate Being and the other a shaman in a drug-induced trance, plus serpent and trophy head imagery.

Block Colour ones, being limited to straight lines of thin colour in red, green, gold or blue, while more expansive Block Colour textiles have blocks of solid colours and outlined, curved figures and patterns, and a colour palette of 19 colours and shades. Linear designs accommodate the shape of the long, flying Oculate Being. Motifs and imagery are not restricted to borders but often occur in cloth centres and as symmetrical arrangements.

Moche and Nazca textiles continued Early Horizon techniques and themes into the Early Intermediate Period.

WOOL FROM THE HIGHLANDS

Camelid llamas and alpacas were fully domesticated by *c.*2500BC. The process lasted several thousand years in the grasslands of south-central Peru around Lake Junin and the Altiplano around the Lake Titicaca Basin. Their domestication is evident from the steady decline in deer remains and the increase in camelid bones at late Archaic and Preceramic Period sites.

THE IMPORTANCE OF WOOL
Llamas were bred for three reasons: their meat, their carrying capacity and their wool. Llama wool, heavier and greasier than alpaca wool, was woven primarily for coarse cloth used for heavy-duty articles such as mats, sacks, saddlebags and cordage. Softer, longer alpaca wool was spun and woven for clothing and other fabric. Still finer, softer, wild vicuña wool was highly prized, especially by the Incas, who captured vicuñas for shearing in special hunts.

Alpacas and llamas were shorn between December and March and their wool spun simply by pulling and arranging the fibres to lie parallel, then winding the resulting 'roving' around the forearm or on a wooden distaff, and spinning it with a wooden drop spindle.

Below: Llamas herded for wool also served as pack animals in caravans, carrying goods between the highlands and lowlands.

Above: A Late Intermediate Period Chancay woollen tunic with 'pink' flamingos, native to the Peruvian coast. Such finely woven cloth was worn by individuals of high rank.

Wool has two advantages over cotton: its staple is a longer fibre, which spins and adheres more readily, and it will take dyes more easily, thus increasing the range of colours and shades available for design. In Chimú weaving, cotton was almost always spun and used as single strands, whereas llama and alpaca wool threads were almost always plied: spun, then, two strands plied together. Spinning and plying were usually in the same direction.

WOOL EMBROIDERY AND DWW
Spun alpaca wool became prominent in Paracas embroidery, which provides some of the earliest combinations of cotton and wool (the wool embroidery being done on plain cotton cloth).

Paracas and Nazca weavers made huge quantities of wool and cotton cloth for everyday use and for burial clothing and wraps. With a wide colour palette, the hours required to produce large cloth wraps, both as wool embroidery on cotton backing and as discontinuous warp and weft (DWW) designs, shows that it was a major occupation.

Religious imagery was especially important. The principal Paracas and Nazca creator, the Oculate Being, was portrayed in many forms. A wide-eyed being, he is associated with water and the sky. Usually shown horizontal, as if flying, he faces front with large, circular, staring eyes and long, streaming appendages, an attribute easily achieved both with line stitching and DWW. Such streamers often end in trophy heads or small woven figures. In some cases he wears a headband like the gold headbands found on buried mummies.

Other themes are birds, serpents and shamans with streaming hair, frequently as scores of small, twinned and repeated figures. In the Linear embroidery style, Oculate Beings or serpentine figures are often interlocking in a continuous border around the cloth edge and in strips across its width.

usually in repetitive, interlocking patterns. The work was mostly in cotton, with wool worked in as superstructual patterns. Humans or deities wear large headdresses or have rayed heads. Some tapestries feature repeated small human figures with crescent-shaped headgear, surrounded by raptors holding trophy heads. Central coastal Chancay weavers began to make 'gauze' cloth – open weaving in which the image is almost invisible in the net-like fabric unless held against a dark background.

The Incas honoured local weaving traditions, but introduced standardization in cloth production. In organized textile workshops at provincial capitals and principal towns, specialist weavers produced regular quotas of cloth, mostly of interlocking tapestry with geometric patterns.

Below: A Nazca–Wari woollen bag with stylized animal motifs and fur fringes. Woollen bags served for personal possessions and as panniers for llama caravans transporting produce between regions.

TAPESTRY

Early Intermediate Period and Middle Horizon coastal weavers developed tapestry. As a convenient use of small lengths of wool of various colours, tapestry designs became extremely colourful and complex.

On the south coast, tapestry replaced embroidery in importance, depicting the same imagery as before, especially geometric designs. Painting on cotton cloth also became more important. On the central and northern coasts, cotton and wool tapestry continued side by side through the Early Intermediate Period. Imagery favoured double- and multi-headed snakes, fish and supernatural composite beings – humanoid snakes, birds and fish. Interlocking, stepped-fret geometric designs were also popular.

TIWANAKU-WARI TAPESTRY

New styles in wool weaving reached the coast in the Middle Horizon, originating in the highlands among Tiwanaku and Wari weavers. Environmental conditions in the highlands, however, preclude most preservation of fabrics from these sites, from which only poor examples survive.

Tunics and hangings depict the imagery seen on Tiwanaku pottery and stone sculpture. The central, staff-bearing, ray-headed deity on the Gateway of the Sun is frequently portrayed, sometimes as a central figurehead surrounded or flanked by smaller staff-bearing figures. Winged figures known as 'angels' copy the 'attendant messenger' figures on the same monument. Mountain pumas and condors also came into more prominence as images.

LATE INTERMEDIATE AND LATE HORIZON CLOTH

Coastal weavers continued split-woven and DWW tapestry, combining cotton and wool. Feline, serpentine, avian and fish imagery became extremely complex as interlocking patterns of figures, similar to imagery on ceramics and mud wall sculpture; there were also dignitaries, shamans or deities with elaborate headdresses. The use of brocade – using extra wefts – was introduced as well.

Chimú and other north coastal weavers specialized in complicated geometric motifs in endless repetitions, plus jaguars and pumas, raptors and condors, fish and snakes,

GRASSES AND FIBRES

Grasses were an early and essential part of Andean economy. From Archaic times they continued to play an important role throughout Andean prehistory. Grass fibres were made into the earliest basketry and net bag containers before ceramics were discovered. Alongside gourds and wooden containers, baskets were used for the collection, storage and transport of wild plant foods.

EARLY CORDS

Few examples survive, but the regular twisting, looping and knotting techniques used by hunter-gatherers to make these articles suggest that there was a long period of development in techniques throughout the Lithic Period. None of the earliest examples shows patterning or decoration.

Below: One of the principal uses for totora reed by coastal peoples was for one-man fishing boats (today called caballitos *– 'little horses'), combining a local product to catch locally abundant fish. Depicted on Moche pottery, such boats are still used today.*

The earliest Andean fibrework comes from Guitarrero Cave in the north-central Andes. The dry cave deposits contained the earliest evidence of domesticated plants in South America, plants collected, then tended and deliberately planted, not for their food value but for 'industrial' and medicinal use, including hemp-like plants of the *Fuscraea*, *Tillandsia* and *Puya* species. These plants and fragments of the containers and other articles made from them predominate over plant foods and wood.

Containers, rough clothing, sandals and sleeping mats were made of simply twisted cordage. An open-mesh net bag from the lower cave deposits was made with simple knotting and looping. Other fragments of fabric show twining, with each weft strand manually twisted around the warp threads. A chert stone scraper from Guitarerro Cave, dated *c.*5500BC, has its butt wrapped in deer hide secured with twisted cord binding.

Use of plant fibres at Lithic Period sites is the beginning of the long association of fibre wrapping and important objects.

Above: A Late Intermediate Period Chancay ceramic effigy bottle, showing a man holding a small dog on a fibre rope, perched on his shoulder.

BODY SUPPORTS AND STUFFING

Another early use of 'fibres' was of sacred significance. The world's earliest mummies, dated *c.*5000BC, at Chinchorros in northern Chile were supported and bound with cane sticks and cords. After allowing the body to decompose, the bones were reassembled and supported by thin cane bundles tied with twine. Then the 'body' was remade by stuffing its cavities with fibre and feathers before sewing the dried skin over the body and applying a clay coating or mask. It is assumed that these practices were attempts to honour the spirit of the dead in the beginnings of ancestor cults.

CONTAINERS, BOATS AND BURIAL

Twined cord satchels, and reed and sedge baskets formed prominent parts of the assemblages at Huaca Prieta, La Galgada and other coastal villages. Some of the earliest ancient Andean textiles are also of

rough fibre, mostly from the cactus *Furcraea occidentalis* (an agave-like plant). Its sharp, pointed leaves can be crushed and shredded to produce fibres up 50cm (20in) long, which can then be twisted together to make cordage. The bast from a milkweed plant (*Asclepias*) was also used to make fibre. The leaves needed to be soaked for a long time before they could be beaten to release their fibres, then crudely 'spun' by rolling them between the palms or with the palm on the thigh.

Fishing peoples often combined (plied) fibre bast with cotton, especially when stronger cordage or netting was required. The strongest nets and basketry were made from grasses alone.

Cotton, wild and later domestic, was essential for Preceramic coastal fishing villagers for lines and nets. In their fishing and foreshore shellfish-collecting economy, however, they also needed basketry for

Below: Rope making was a labour tax in the Inca Empire. Every man was required to produce a specified quota of cordage for rope, especially to make and repair bridges.

collection and storage, and reeds for their fishing boats. They grew totora bulrush reeds specifically for boat making, as did peoples around the lakeshores of Titicaca and other mountain lakes. Reeds were also used for sails by Late Intermediate Period coastal fishers and traders. These water-craft traditions continue today.

Preceramic burials usually included at least a mat and plain cloth wrapping, if not more elaborate clothing. For example, the infant burial bundle at Huaca de los Sacrificios at Aspero was placed in a reed basket before being wrapped in textiles. Women were often buried with their weaving baskets, which were reed or sedge containers for spindles, threads and loom tools.

ARCHITECTURAL SUPPORT

Plant materials and rough fibre cordage played important parts in early housing and even in the earliest monumental architecture. For example, La Paloma coastal peoples lived in cane and reed huts with grass roofs. Thatch roofing was used by coastal and highland peoples right through to Inca times.

Above: Traditional use of totora reeds for roofing endures in these houses on a totora-reed 'floating island' near the shoreline on Lake Titicaca.

Plant chaff was an important element in mud-plaster architecture, providing a binding both for smooth plaster coverings on stone walls and in adobe brick walls.

The earliest platform mounds were built up with rubble before being finished off with impressive adobe brick or stone facings. Open-mesh satchels, called *shicra* in Inca times, made of split reeds and capable of holding as much as 36kg (80lb), were used to haul stone rubble. The baskets were not emptied, but were deposited *en masse* on the mound. The *shicras* found intact at late Preceramic El Paraíso each held 17.6–36kg (40–80lb).

In Inca times, men's role in the imperial textile taxation was to produce required quotas of cordage. Without strong cordage, Inca quarrying (rope for haulage), house building (cordage for roof binding) and bridge building (for suspension bridge cables) would not have existed.

CLOTHING STYLES

In ancient Andean society, cloth was wealth: it was exchanged between rulers, given as rewards for good service, and used to fulfil reciprocal obligations between members of kinship *ayllus*. It was important in the relationship between state and subject, and was presented at public ceremonies as items in the redistribution of wealth. Special clothing marked changes in life cycles, both as costume for initiation ceremonies and as a mark of age, social status and distinction. Specific people wore specific clothes for specific occasions. Cloth was offered to the gods in burnt offerings, used to dress and preserve mummies, and offered in burials. Finally, cloth provided a medium for representing the gods and religious imagery reflecting cosmological concepts.

INCA CLOTH

The Incas defined two grades of cloth: fine cloth, called *qompi*, was divided into two sub-grades, for tribute fabrics and 'best' cloth for royal and religious use; and *awasca* cloth – a plain, coarser fabric – was for ordinary use.

Below: This llama wool hat with geometric designs from the Atacama Desert shows Tiwanaku influence.

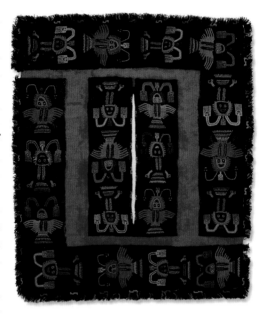

Above: Intricately woven textiles such as this Paracas poncho burial wrap with flying Oculate Beings were the preserve of the rich.

The Incas encouraged diversity among their subjects, not least in maintaining local textile traditions and clothing styles. Regional patterns and imagery, costumes and headdresses were badges of ethnic identity, for these were regarded as having been designated by Viracocha the Creator himself.

Ephraim G. Squier described the importance of clothing diversity in his 1877 book, *Peru: Incidents of Travel and Exploration in the Land of the Incas*: "If they were Yungas, they went muffled like gypsies; if Collas, they wore caps shaped like mortars, of wool; if Canas, they wore larger caps … The Cañari wore a kind of narrow wooden crown like the rim of a sieve; the Huancas, strands that fell below their chin, and their hair braided; the Canchis, broad black or red bands over their forehead."

STYLE

Andean clothing was mostly un-tailored. Tunics or shirts were made from two rectangular panels of cloth, woven at the maximum width of the loom, then sewn together along one edge, folded in half, and sewn down the sides, leaving openings for the head and arms. Capes or cloaks were made from two or more cloths stitched together.

Because clothing is often found in graves, it is sometimes difficult to determine what was daily wear, ritual costume or clothing specifically for burial. The mummy bundles of Paracas and Nazca vary in their richness and in the number of layers of cloth. Elaborate mummy bundles, presumably of rich, higher-status individuals, wore a loincloth, embroidered cloth belt, tunic or short poncho, shoulder mantle and turban.

Much Andean clothing is depicted on pottery and stone sculpture. For example, 13 late Preceramic figurines from Huaca de los Idolos at Aspero portray 11 women wearing thigh-length skirts, but no sandals. Some wear flat-topped hats and square-beaded red necklaces (two such beads were actually found). The capes worn by the Initial Period mud-sculptured figures at Moxeke are not dissimilar to those on the later

Below: Distinctive regional textile decoration and headgear is revealed on painted pottery, as on this Nazca jar.

Paracas mummies. And the elegant male figurines from Initial Period El Mirador wear full-length, sleeveless tunics, but also have bare feet.

Nazca effigy pots wear ponchos and tunics like those on mummies, with decorated neck and sleeve borders. A figurine vessel of a panpipe player wears a plain tunic with star-shaped neck decoration; other Nazca vessels depict a man's tunic and a woman's shawl-like mantle with circular designs; and a Nazca double-spout, stepped-fret bottle shows warriors wearing tunics with fringed borders and lampshade-shaped hats.

Another Nazca double-spout vessel portrays a stout fellow in a plain loincloth, brown and white chequered shirt and a matching, tightly wrapped turban around his head.

Below: This Middle Horizon Tiwanaku woollen unku *tunic shows a more unusual diagonal pattern of different coloured rows of flowers, requiring an extremely complex weaving technique.*

HEADGEAR

Moche ceramics are especially revealing, featuring an astonishing variety of geometric decorations on tight-fitting headdresses. Some are long strips of cloth wrapped twice around the head and tied at the back.

Others are bandanna-style cloths fitted over the head, with the front end wrapped around to the back and tied. Some Moche figures wear tight-fitting short-sleeved shirts.

Equally distinctive are Tiwanaku-Wari box-shaped wool hats. Made up of five tapestry woven panels sewn together to form sides and top, their vibrant colours, geometric patterns, and rows of winged beasts, birds and abstract human figures resemble the imagery on ceramics. Some sport little points or tassels at the top corners.

Tiwanaku-Wari hangings and clothing were made with interlocking DWW weaving rather than the slit-weaving tapestry of the earlier coastal traditions. Imagery and patterns are elongated and compressed. Faces are frequently split up into small rectangular elements.

Tiwanaku-style tunics were made so that the warp threads lie horizontally across the chest rather than vertically (as in earlier coastal tunics). They were made of two rectangular cloths sewn down the warp edges, leaving an unsewn mid-section for the head of the wearer. Some Tiwanaku tunics were made of a single

Above: This Middle Horizon Wari mummy bundle reveals the wealth of the buried person by the sheer number of wraps to create the bulky mummy, including an outer unku *tunic, woven wool and fibre scarf and 'hair'.*

cloth, the head slit being made by a long section of discontinuous warp from each side. Likewise, Tiwanaku and Wari effigy pots show figures wearing just such hats and bordered tunics.

Inca 'factory-produced' cloth was primarily of interlocking tapestry tunics, also with the warp running horizontally across the chest of the wearer and mostly decorated with geometric patterns. Vicuña wool, and cloth embellished with gold, silver or feathers, was restricted to imperial and noble use.

RITUAL COSTUME

Much of the cloth created in the Early Horizon was for ritual purposes. The complex imagery and geometric patterns on rectangular lengths of cloth bore religious significance, reflecting Andean cosmological concepts. They were hangings, canopies and altar covers for the temples, and burial wraps.

PRIESTLY GARB
The figurines from the highland Initial Period site of El Mirador were found in an unusual ovoid building separated from, but close to, the main temple site of Pacopampa. The sculptures were especially finely made and other finds included Pacific shells, foreign ceramics and exotic figurines of felines, dogs, bears and chinchilla-like rodents. The temple included an elaborate drainage system, anticipating that at Chavín de Huántar. This evidence and context suggest association with the temple. The figures are thought to represent priests and the ovoid building a priestly residence. If this is correct, then their long tunics are presumably ritual dress, for their length would make them impractical for daily work. Similarly, the mud sculptures at Moxeke, in niches atop the main public platform, were clearly

religious figures. Two cloaked torsos are either priests or gods, whose missing heads may represent ritual beheadings. Although the capes are 'typically' Andean, one figure also wears a twisted cord sash and holds double-headed snakes, which might be part of the costume. Both wear short, pleated skirts.

These Initial Period finds suggest both that some clothing was special to the priestly function, while other garb, although essentially the same as daily wear, was more elaborate in its decoration and of finer quality. An effigy bottle from a looted tomb in the Jequetepeque Valley is exemplary. The small spouted bottle (26.8cm/10½in) portrays an elegantly attired man playing an ocarina. His tunic, like those made throughout Andean history, drapes over his body, but is especially richly decorated with stylized feline and avian figures, whose details are picked out in many colours.

SNAKE MEN
The wall sculptures in Chavín de Huántar's circular sunken court also depict priests in ritual costumes. They are composite creatures, representing gods, shamanistic transformation or priests

Above: A Chimú wooden figure with a mud mask, carrying a kero *cup. The mask, earrings and headpiece are probably ritual costume.*

acting out these roles. They wear collared, long-sleeve shirts, trousers (or perhaps just anklets?), elaborate, braided-snake headdresses and snake belts. They have strange, stepped-fret 'wings' on their backs, decorated with feline mouths. Their own mouths have huge canines and their feet and hands are talons. The whole scene is one of ritual procession and transformation, and the elaborate costumes of the priests can only have been made especially for such occasions.

The richly adorned mummy bundles of Paracas and Nazca are also difficult to interpret. The care and time involved in making the textiles, and the labour of preparing the burials, can be attributed only to ritual beliefs. Despite variation in the quality and quantity of textiles,

Left: The Inti Raymi winter solstice, revived in 20th-century Peru, brings out latter-day Incas in 'ancient' ritual costume.

these burials reveal social hierarchy, although it is uncertain whether the clothing was specifically for burial or also represents daily wear, according to rank. The records of elaborate, rich clothing worn by certain classes in later periods by Chimú and Inca nobility, however, suggests that the standard loincloth, tunic, mantle and turban were 'normal' wear, although there were perhaps pieces specially made for burial. Perhaps Paracas and Nazca priests enacted ritual myth dressed in the mantles so richly decorated with mythical imagery.

PRIESTS AND PRIESTESSES AS GODS

There is no doubt that the elaborate costumes worn by the priests and priestesses depicted in Moche murals and on pottery are ritual costume. The Sacrifice and Presentation ceremonies show them dressed in colourful tunics with decorated neck borders, belts, a pleated skirt on the priestess, and various extraordinary head-dresses with tassels, crescent-knife shapes or bandanna styles.

There is little doubt, too, that the extremely rich burials at Sipán and San José de Moro represent individuals whose tasks were to impersonate these deities in the ritual. Their burial costumes are exactly those of the murals, showing the Warrior Priest, Owl Priest, and Priestess in feathered tunic. In addition to his gold and other jewellery, and gilded copper adorned capes, the Warrior Priest even wore ceremonial copper sandals.

Similarly, the gear worn by Moche warriors on pottery and murals, although undoubtedly the same as that used in battle, also represents ritual weapons and armour. It was a sort of gladiatorial combat, performed for religious purposes, the ultimate outcome of which was the sacrifice of the loser.

Equally revealing is the burial at Dos Cabezas of a tall Moche priest wearing a bat-motif hat. His tomb also included 18 other headdresses, assumed to be for the performance of his many ritual roles.

GOLDEN CAPES

Gold ornament was often applied to mantles, and it seems reasonable to assume that such clothing was not for everyday wear, with the exception of kings and emperors. Chimú weavers specialized in ritual garments incorporating

Above: From the earliest times Andean ritual costume required materials and dye colours from far-flung regions. This Nazca headdress from southern Peru has tropical bird feathers, traded in from the rainforest.

rich patterns of coloured tropical feathers, gold and silver spangles, beads and tasselled edges.

Inca dress was of standard type for all, the difference being in the richness of the wool, the elaboration of decoration and colour, and the embellishment with gold, silver and feathers.

New clothing was made for boys and girls for their initiation rites. The rather elaborate costumes donned today in re-enactments of Inca rituals bear resemblance to ancient costume, but inevitably have been elaborated in combinations of colonial influence and modern imagination. Nevertheless, such re-enactments represent a statement of independence and resistance.

Left: An Early Horizon Chavín effigy pot portrays a shaman or priest with facial scarification, wearing a jaguar headdress and playing a flute, probably using ritual music to induce hallucinations.

FEATHERS AND FEATHERWORK

Coastal and tropical rainforest bird feathers were important in Andean cultures from the Initial Period. Exotic tropical feathers were traded right across the Andes from the eastern lowlands and rainforests by coastal cultures.

Making feather costumes demanded great labour and conferred considerable importance to the wearer, advertising one's high status in society.

FEATHER OFFERINGS

In early periods, feathers were included in burials and caches as offerings. Ritual offerings on platform summits at late Preceramic Aspero included a buried offering of red and yellow feather arrangements. Loose green, pink, blue and yellow feathers and down were found beneath a floor at El Paraíso; a carved stick at Río Seco was covered with white feathers; and there were red and orange macaw feathers in burials at La Galgada.

Below: This Late Intermediate Period Chancay ceremonial headdress shows a characteristic chequered pattern and brilliant yellow tropical parrot feather decoration.

Below: Remarkable preservation in the Paracas Desert necropolis in southern Peru has left unspoiled a feather and rope-fibre fan and woven cotton bag decorated with tropical parrot feathers for holding personal burial items.

Among Initial Period burials at Ancón, one special individual was buried with a cebus monkey – covered with mica flakes and placed on his knees – and had strings of coloured feathers, iron pyrites and beads on his forehead. His head rested on a wooden bowl filled with coloured tropical feathers.

FEATHERED TEXTILES

Tropical feathers were also imported by Paracas and Nazca weavers. Feather decorations were inserted among embroidered patterns, and braided strips of cloth held long feathers to create a sort of tall bonnet. Feathers were also cached with gold, animal skins and exotic shells in burials.

By the Early Intermediate Period, elaborate ritual clothing included entire mantles of feathers. An unusual Nazca tunic is made of a cotton back-cloth covered in bright yellow tropical feathers, highlighting a turquoise 'running' monkey with yellow eyes, also of feathers. The monkey constitutes another connection between coastal peoples and rainforest tribes.

The Priestess in Mural E at Moche Pañamarca wears a distinctive feathered mantle in the Presentation Ceremony.

Middle Horizon cultures extended the use of feather garments as status items. A Wari mantle comprises intricately combined cream, orange, black and blue feathers to make two orange eight-pointed stars with faces, above an orange double-headed snake. The three elements are thought to represent duality and the four directions.

As well as actual feathers, Pukará, Tiwanaku, Wari and Lambayeque-Sicán Middle Horizon art features heads with rayed feathers. The most superb example is perhaps the gold mask from Huaca Loro Tomb 1 at Batán Grande: its human visage wears a tall headdress with a central vampire bat face and 90 delicate golden feathers.

CHIMÚ FEATHERWORK

Late Intermediate Period Chimú weavers were especially adept at incorporating feathers into costumes. On plain-weave white cotton back-cloths, they sewed rows of tiny, bright red, pink, orange, yellow, green and blue tropical bird feathers, creating garments as brilliant and shimmering as those covered in thousands of tiny gold squares.

Feathers were attached by bending their quill ends over a thread of the back-cloth and fixing it with a second thread, which was knotted around the bend of each quill. Each feather-holding thread was stitched down to the fabric so that the feathers overlapped, hiding the cloth.

Bird feathers included: tinamou, cormorant, great and snowy egret, Chilean flamingo, Muscovy duck, Salvin's curassow, macaws (blue-and-yellow, Scarlet, red and green), parakeet, trogon, purple honeycreeper, and various Amazonian parrots and tanagers.

One Chimú poncho bears images of light blue pelicans made up of feathers, with red feather eye circles and beaks. Two large pelicans are borne on litters of red and green feathers, carried by smaller, blue-feather pelicans along a blue-feather road. An exemplary Chimú piece, a ceremonial headdress, combines white, yellow, black, grey, turquoise and pink feathers from flamingos, macaws, razor-billed curassows and parrots. Its main body includes two human figures wearing axe-crescent hats, below a flared crown of long white macaw feathers and stepped-fret decoration in pink, yellow and black. Even the eyes, mouths, fingers and toes are intricately rendered in different coloured feathers.

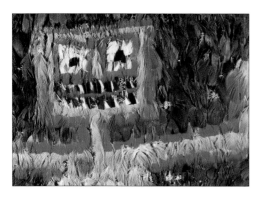

Left: Detail from a Late Intermediate Period tunic of brilliant tropical macaw feathers from the Amazon, probably depicting a shaman in ritual trance.

The expense of importing enough tropical bird feathers to cover entire tunics meant that only Chimú kings and nobles wore such clothing. They were ostentatious declarations of their power and wealth. The making of such garments required thousands of retained artists, supported by commoners through taxation.

INCA FEATHERWORK

Likewise, only Inca emperors and nobility wore feathered cloaks, and Atahualpa commissioned a mantle made from bat skins. The Chachapoyas of the north-eastern Andes, in Inca Chinchaysuyu, were specialist traders with Amazonian tribes for their tropical products, including feathers, to the Incas and the Chimú before them.

It is significant in this context that the roster of court officials in the legendary Naymlap's entourage includes one

Above: A Chimú ritual featherwork poncho, depicting a Staff Deity-like figure and different coastal birds and fish, reflecting the Chimú reliance on the sea.

Llapchillulli, 'Purveyor of Feathercloth Garments'. Clearly, valuable trade links for tropical feathers between the northern Peruvian coast and the eastern Andes and Amazonia were perpetuated for hundreds of years by Lambayeque-Sicán lords and their Chimú successors.

Inca featherwork was as important as, or even more valuable than, metalwork and cloth, because of its relative rarity. As well as being sewn on back-cloth for human garments, featherwork features in headdresses of great complexity, and also on miniature figurines. Some Inca ceremonial headdresses feature great crescents of long-tail raptor and condor feathers, as well as tropical bird feathers.

In addition to feather mantles and cloaks, Inca emperors, borne on litters, were shaded with macaw-feather parasols.

DRESSED FIGURINES

Andean peoples frequently used figurines as ritual offerings and in burials. Clay, metal and cloth figurines were 'dressed', mirroring their makers' clothing styles.

PAINTED AND ACTUAL CLOTHING

While some early figurines are naked, others wear clothing similar to cotton and woollen cloth found in excavations. There are, for example, late Preceramic figurines from Huaca de los Idolos of women wearing thigh-length skirts, flat-topped hats and square-beaded red necklaces; a rotund

Below: A Middle Horizon dated Chancay figurine of dyed cotton forming a face and body, plus garment wraps around cane and straw body and limbs.

Paracas burial figurine with a curious headband of circles and tube ornament, and incised-line and cream-painted clothing and 'shells' collar; tall Pacopampa figurines in long, sleeveless tunics; and numerous Nazca and Moche effigy vessels of people 'dressed' in typical garments.

At Initial Period Mina Perdida (2nd millennium BC), however, a fibre human effigy figure is made of a jointed, thread-wrapped gourd dressed in a cotton mantle. It was found face down on a platform terrace, and possibly represents a shaman in transformation, for it has condor markings on its face.

WOVEN FIGURE FRINGES

Many Paracas and Nazca cotton textiles feature fringes comprising rows of severed heads. Several, however, have rows of small woven human figures, *c*.30mm (1¼ in) tall. One such Nazca burial wrap shows a line of musicians, standing with arms in the air, or across their bodies, their hands holding tiny woven rattles or bells. Each wears a tunic with a decorated band at the hips.

MINUSCULE GOLD AND STONE CLOTHES

One of three earspools in Tomb I of the Moche Lord of Sipán depicts a tiny figure of Lord Sipán himself of astonishingly intricate workmanship. The tiny figure is dressed in a tunic made of polished turquoise chips, a gold mask (complete with miniature, movable, gold crescent-shaped nosepiece), a necklace of minuscule golden owl heads, minute gold belt bells, two minute circular gold and turquoise earspools, and a headdress of turquoise chips and gold *tumi*-knife crescent and stepped, golden 'horns'. He holds a round gold shield and a removable golden war club.

This figure is flanked by two even smaller warriors made of turquoise chips, each wearing a turquoise-chip tunic, necklace and multi-layered helmet with gold

Above: Two woollen textile figurines used as Late Intermediate Period Chancay funerary offerings, a female (left with longer tunic) and male (right), representing duality.

tumi-knife crescent. They also have gold and turquoise earspools and carry circular gold and turquoise shields.

At Wari Pikillacta, 40 tiny figurines, each about 25mm (1in) high, were made of tiny precious stones, and are 'dressed' in tunics, mantles and hats of gold foil, and belts of precious stone chips and shell.

THE WEAVING LESSON

An astonishing Late Intermediate Period cotton cloth 'sculpture', Chancay or Chimú, depicts a mother teaching her daughter to weave. The two tiny figures sit on a woven, stuffed 'pillow' with stripy white, black, red, orange and yellow decorations. The mother works a miniature backstrap loom fixed to a wooden 'post' stuck into the pillow. The loom is complete with warp and weft threads, wooden warp beam and shed sticks. She holds a heddle rod poised to insert into the miniature shed. She is inclined

towards her daughter as if explaining her work, and a head cloth of loose-weave, orange and yellow chequered pattern that resembles Chancay open-work weaving covers her long, dark brown hair.

Below: An Inca gold figurine, richly dressed in woollen clothing held with a miniature gold tupu *pin. Such figures represented* mamaconas *or* acllas, *the chosen women of the imperial court, and were sometimes deposited in child sacrifice burials.*

Her daughter sits beside the loom, her own long hair arranged in a minute topknot, spilling from a close-fitting hat with stripes and minute animal-heads decoration.

Both mother and daughter wear robes with stripy patterns and fringed bottoms. Details of their eyes, including pupils, noses and mouths are rendered in minute stitches.

Not only is this piece astonishing for its detail, but it is also one of the few actual images showing us ancient Andean weaving.

CLOTH 'DOLLS' AND DRESSED METAL

Many Late Intermediate Period Chancay burials contain offerings of cloth 'dolls'. Reminiscent of earlier Nazca fringe figures, they are of wrapped yarn and embroidered fabrics. Facial features and hair, stick-like arms and fingers, and decorated clothing are all of woven and stitched threads.

Inca gold and silver figurines of nude men and women have been looted from and found in undisturbed sacrificial child burials, often on remote mountaintops. Some are dressed, and miniature clothing has been found separately elsewhere, indicating that all such figurines were dressed. Their clothing was possibly removed for some sacred moment in the sacrifice ritual or burial ceremony.

The silver Cerro del Plomo figurine from Chile wears a brown and white mantle over a similar tunic. Both have strips and edges of red and yellow decoration. The mantle is tied

Above: A Late Intermediate Period Chancay reed figurine with cotton textile features, hair and clothing – probably a funerary offering.

with a tiny, decorated cord with rectangular shell toggles, and held with a miniature silver *tupu* pin. A magnificent, brilliant, red feather semicircular headdress crowns the head.

Two gold figurines from a burial of three sacrificed children on Mount Llullaillaco, Argentina, were equally magnificently dressed. Both wear white wool mantles, with red, yellow and black, and red and black borders. One is female, with gold and silver *tupus* pinning her mantle. Her long, tightly bound hair is moulded in gold, and a headdress of red and orange feathers frames her face.

The male figure has large, looped earpieces and a close-fitting cap, both moulded in gold. His mostly white mantel covers a red, yellow and black tunic, and he wears a grey turban with a sheet-gold ornament fixed to the front with a red and gold-headed pin, and an array of yellow feathers at the back.

229

CHAPTER TWELVE

METAL, WOOD, STONE, SHELL AND BONE

Apart from ceramics and stone sculpture, few ancient Andean items are of a single material. Most metal artefacts are alloys of gold and silver, gold and copper or silver and copper. Many stone, wood and metal objects are embellished with stone and shell inlay.

With these materials and media, Andean craftsmen created exquisite objects as well as utilitarian tools. Even some of the most common objects were highly carved, shaped or decorated. Most techniques were known from the earliest times. Shells and exotic stones were made into beads in the Preceramic Period if not earlier, and the first gold foil dates from *c*.1500BC.

Exotic materials were sought throughout the Andean Area and beyond, including turquoise, lapis lazuli and spondylus, or thorny oyster, shell. Working with gold and silver was highly controlled.

These materials advertised an individual's social status, and yet their value was primarily in the objects they were used to create and in the religious symbolism they represented. Ancient Andeans had no defined monetary values or currency. Only the copper *naipes* found in bundles in Sicán-Lambayeque tombs at Batán Grande (but rare elsewhere) possibly had an agreed exchange value. Spanish chronicles report that "6,000 seafaring Chincha merchants" used copper as a medium of exchange with Ecuadorian peoples.

Left: A Lambayeque sheet gold burial mask with Sicán 'comma-shaped' copper inlay eyes and nose beads.

MINING AND METAL TECHNOLOGY

We know little about Inca or pre-Inca mining. The Spaniards, primarily interested in gold and silver, quickly took over these areas and imposed their own techniques in the first century after the conquest.

Abundant sources of gold, silver and copper in Peru and Bolivia are found pure (gold and copper) and in ores (silver and copper). Most prehistoric Andean gold was retrieved from streams by washing the gravel in wooden trays. Sometimes streams were diverted to expose gold-bearing gravels. Lesser amounts were excavated from one-man trenches.

Mine shafts for silver and copper ores were 1m (1 yard) or so to perhaps 70m (230ft) long. Vertical shafts were only as deep as the dirt could be thrown up to the surface, then another hole was started near by. Wooden, bronze and antler tools were used to dig, and stone and deer antler hammers and picks were used to break up veins of ore, and to crush it. Excavated material was brought out in hide sacks and fibre baskets.

Spanish chroniclers record that Inca mines were worked only in the summer, from noon to sunset. Mining, like so many other tasks, was carried out as part of the Inca *mit'a* labour tax.

Crushed silver and copper ores were heated in clay crucibles to melt the metal and drain it from the ore. Relatively pure veins of copper yielded pieces that could be worked cold, as copper is relatively soft.

Above: Moche gold and turquoise necklace. Moche goldsmiths often combined gold beads with semi-precious imported stones.

Gold-bearing streams and ore deposits were considered sacred places. Ceremonies were held at them to honour their holy spirits and solicit ease of extraction. Gold and silver collection and mining were restricted under state control in the Inca Empire (and, as they were regarded as precious, probably under elite control in pre-Inca cultures as well). Copper extraction and use was widespread and less regulated.

METAL TECHNOLOGY

Andean metalsmiths were superbly skilled, and undertook extremely delicate work as well as large-scale pieces. They were specialized craftsmen, employed by the state or maintained as retainers of the elite to produce tools and exquisite items for elite consumption.

Left: Small figurines, such as this sheet-gold, sculpted llama, were made in abundance by the Incas, and often placed in the tombs of sacrificed children.

Objects were produced in small compounds, partly residential, partly workshop, where the metals were heated, hammered, bonded and formed into all manner of utilitarian and sumptuary objects.

Techniques included hammering into sheets to make the metal pliable, annealing, repoussé, incised and cut-out designs, joining and soldering, mould and lost-wax casting, gilding, burnishing and over-painting.

All of these methods were known in the Andean Area, although central Andean, Ecuadorian and southern Colombian metalsmiths preferred working with sheet metals and metal strands to create sculpture and jewellery, using sheet metal rolled, hammered and formed into objects and jewellery. Metalsmiths in northern Colombia and Central America favoured casting (including lost-wax casting, in which the figure is made of wax, then covered with clay, leaving a channel for molten metal to be poured in, which melts and drains away the wax; once the clay covering is broken, the object remains).

Utilitarian objects were made of copper and bronze, including knives, war club heads, agricultural hoes and digging implements, tweezers and beads. Gold and silver were used to make exquisite elite objects, including all sorts of jewellery, masks and figurines.

HAMMERING

Before being hammered, ingots of workable size were made from smaller pieces melted together. Hammering was done with hard, fine-grained stones (usually of magnetite, haematite or fine-grained basalt), formed into flat, round or cylindrical anvils and unshafted hammerstones, held in the hand. As hammering proceeded, the flattened sheet was annealed (reheated until it glowed red, then quenched with water) to prevent it from becoming brittle and cracking.

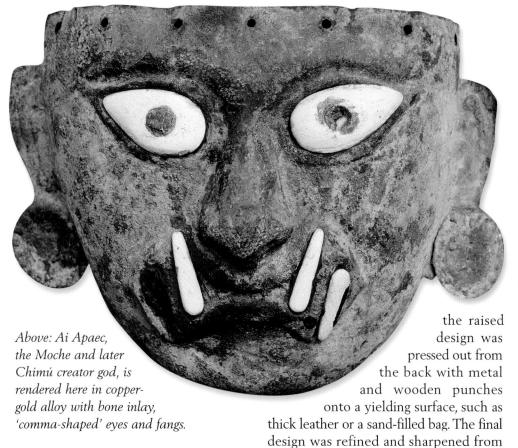

Above: Ai Apaec, the Moche and later Chimú creator god, is rendered here in copper-gold alloy with bone inlay, 'comma-shaped' eyes and fangs.

REPOUSSÉ AND INCISION

The process of repoussé – the creation of relief designs from behind – began with cutting out the shape with a thin-bladed chisel. The pattern was scribed onto the metal, sometimes using templates, then the raised design was pressed out from the back with metal and wooden punches onto a yielding surface, such as thick leather or a sand-filled bag. The final design was refined and sharpened from the front with fine tools.

Incised designs were also scored into metal figures, and areas of metal were sometimes cut out.

Below: Using the lost-wax technique, the Muisca people made exquisite gold necklaces of identical tiny figurine 'beads'.

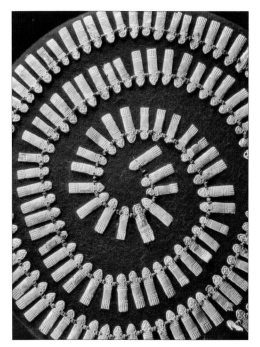

JOINING AND BONDING

Multi-piece objects, sometimes of different metals, were combined by several techniques. Edges were overlapped and hammer-welded, with annealing, sometimes including the clinching of the edges by folding them over on each other. Soldering and brazing were accomplished with melted bits of metal alloy. Moche spot-welding was second to none, with some pieces including hundreds of individual spot-solderings. Granulation, or diffusion bonding, was used for very fine work, such as tiny beads or fine wire. Copper compound and organic glue were applied at the joins of gold or silver parts, then heated to burn away the glue and form a copper-alloy brazed bonding.

Mechanical joins were formed in a variety of ways, including stapling, lacing with a metal strip, pinning and clinching.

Right: Inca metalsmiths made numerous solid silver (as here, with copper hairpiece) and gold male and female figurines.

MOULDING

Cast moulding was rare, as few pieces were solid. Chisels and axes were made in simple, open moulds of stone or clay, into which molten metal was poured.

FINISHING

Objects were highly polished, burnished with dried animal dung, wood, metal, leather and cloth. Sometimes the actual metal was over-painted. Many objects were gilded, using extremely thin gold foil.

PRECIOUS METALS AND EARLY METALWORK

All Andean metal that glittered was not gold, for Andeans were more interested in the essence of appearance. Most 'gold' objects were in fact alloys with a gilded surface. Alloys included tin and copper bronze, gold and silver, silver and copper or gold and copper (tumbaga). Different metals were also combined individually in pieces of work, as well as inlaid with stone, lapis lazuli from Chile and shell. Masks were often painted over, so hiding the metal!

VALUE AND SYMBOLISM

The production and exchange of sumptuary goods of all kinds was controlled by the elite in cities. Rather than a market economy, however, precious metal artefacts were used as items of prestige and as gifts and hospitality. Their value was in the political alliances they helped to seal and in the religious continuity and enforcement they secured. Most exchange was in the context of religious or political ceremony.

Below: The Chimú, successors of the Moche-Sipán and Lambayeque-Sicán north-west coast goldworking tradition, shod their buried kings with exquisitely fine leather sandals with sheet-gold clasp ornaments with turquoise inlays.

Above: Moche paired gold half-discs were embossed with solar flares or wave motifs – and may have been used as earrings or clothing ornaments.

Gold and silver objects were widely traded, yet neither had a market value. What was important was the symbolism of the objects. Apart from tools, metalwork was devoted to elite objects meant to be used and worn by upper classes and as funerary offerings. Thus, commoners ate from pottery plates while Inca nobles used identical plates but made from gold or silver. Decoration always involved religious symbolism, either as images of the gods, sacrifice and sacred animals, or the symbolic representation of life (for example in exquisitely modelled animals, birds and agricultural plants). Cuzco even had a zoo–garden of gold and silver replicas.

The ultimate symbolism is expressed in the Inca concept of gold as 'the sweat of the Sun' and silver as 'the tears of the Moon'.

EARLY METALWORK

The earliest known New World metalwork is gold. It comes from Waywaka, in the Andahuaylas Valley of the central Peruvian highlands. Here, a stone bowl contained a metalworker's tools, and a burial contained pieces of thin, beaten gold foil (nine pieces in the hand, with lapis lazuli beads, and one in the mouth), dated *c.*1500BC. The tools comprised a cylindrical, flared-top stone anvil and three stone hammers for beating the gold into foil.

Roughly contemporary, at Mina Perdida, on the central Peruvian coast, small pieces of hammered gold and copper foil

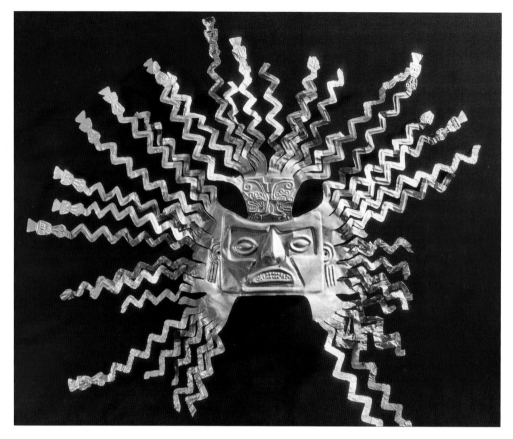

Right: La Tolita goldsmiths, in the far northern corner of Inca Chinchaysuyu quarter, were part of a northern tradition of smithing producing fine sheet-metal ritual objects, such as this Sun God mask with repoussé face and cut sheet-gold rays.

were found on its platform, dated *c.*1450–1150BC. Some pieces are gilded copper, and they appear to have been thrown from the ceremonial summit.

Slightly later, villagers of the Wankarani culture near Lake Poopó (south of Lake Titicaca) developed copper technology, as shown by pieces of smelted slag dated *c.*1200–800BC.

These mid- to late Initial Period finds are scant evidence of the prolific metallurgical technology subsequently practised in later periods throughout Andean civilization. Nevertheless, they demonstrate the early beginning of combining metals, 'essence' in representation through gilding, and the association of metal offerings both with burials and with religious ceremony.

EARLY HORIZON METALWORK
Metallurgy techniques in the Early Horizon period appear fully developed in comparison to the earliest finds, revealing that much intervening development must have taken place. Forged and annealed gold and silver figurines with Chavín motifs have been found at Chavín de Huántar and other Chavín sites. Soldering and repoussé were employed, as were alloys of gold, silver and copper. Chavín–Chongoyape goldsmiths used sheet metal to make objects to inter or store in caches. Gold sheets were decorated in repoussé and rolled into tall cylinders, thought to be crowns, face masks, pectorals and smaller pieces for application to clothing. Their imagery is typically Chavín and Cupisnique: the Staff Being and feline faces. Characteristic Chavín obscurity or illegibility is achieved in complex, busy designs bordering on the abstract. Whole images are obscured in the curvatures, and sometimes the work is so complex that symbols are revealed only in the play of light and shadow.

Gold, 'wholly other' and immutable, incorporates a sacred message, and is the reflection of the sun. Gold on the outside, as gilding or on clothing, reflected the inner quality of the elite wearer.

A gold alloy pectoral disc from Chavín de Huántar depicts a central feline fanged face, while around the edge an interlaced braid represents continuity and unity of the cult. A cylindrical crown from Chongoyape depicts in repoussé the full figure of the Staff Deity, with highly stylized staffs, snake-like swirls from its head and a flared-nostril feline face on the torso. Although it resembles the Staff Deity image on the Raimondi Stela at Chavín de Huántar, both pieces reflect the range of interpretation allowed within Chavín imagery as the cult spread north and south from the cult site.

PARACAS AND NAZCA METALWORK
Spanning the Early Horizon and Early Intermediate Period, Paracas, Nazca and Moche metalwork preserved many Chavín elements but also developed their own unique styles.

Gold objects placed in Paracas and Nazca graves of distinguished individuals reveal the growing differentiation in social hierarchy. Thin sheets of nearly pure gold were cut into elaborate silhouettes and decorated with sparse repoussé details, but highly polished to achieve maximum glitter. Mummy bundles include noserings, mouth and whole face masks, forehead ornaments, headdress plumes with sea animals, clothing discs and gold staffs.

Left: A Chavín gold jaguar figurine with embossed pelt markings.

MOCHE LORDS OF SIPÁN

The true glory of ancient Andean gold, silver and copper artistry comes to life in the rich tombs of the north-west Peruvian coast. Moche artisans were capable of the tiniest attention to detail, such as the kneecaps of a figure adorning an earring or a bead on the body of a spider. Moche metalsmiths also developed the use of shell and stone inlay, and combinations of gold and silver, to maximize colour contrasts between gold, silver, orange-red shell or turquoise lapis lazuli.

Moche gilding also merits special mention. Instead of applying gold to the surface, bathing gold-alloy objects in natural acids depleted the outermost layer of silver or copper to leave a thin layer of pure gold – thus gilding from within.

LORD OF SIPÁN

The greatest single collection of Moche gold, silver and copper objects comes from 12 elite, unlooted burials at Sipán in the Lambayeque Valley. Spanning roughly 200 years from AD100 to 300, and including the burials of several lords and retainers, the tombs contained hundreds of gold, silver, copper, turquoise and shell objects and textiles.

Tomb I, of the Lord of Sipán (identified as the Warrior Priest of the Moche Sacrifice and Presentation ceremonies depicted in murals and on pottery), contained some 451 objects. His solid gold head crescent spanned 60cm (2ft). Gold and silver back-flaps lay beneath him. Above and below the body were textiles

adorned with gilded-copper platelets forming full-on human figures with turquoise bracelets, also a gilded-copper headdress with the same figure. His face is covered with a sheet-gold mask, his forehead with a gold strip, and gold, silver and copper nose-crescents and other jewellery adorn his face. He wears three pairs of gold and turquoise earspools (one depicts the lord himself, with a miniature detachable war club, swinging nosepiece and necklace), a gold and silver necklace of peanuts, and turquoise

Above: The Sipán Lord 'royal' Moche tombs, among the few unlooted ancient Andean elite burials, produced prodigious amounts of gold and copper metalwork.

and gold bead bracelets. He holds gold and copper ingots and a gold rattle sceptre of war victims. Several gold and silver crescent-shaped bells depict the Decapitator.

OWL PRIEST

Tomb 2 contained the Owl Priest, wearing a gilded-copper headdress decorated with an owl with outspread wings, and a gilded-copper double necklace. Each strand comprised nine grimacing faces, the upper group with up-turned mouths, the lower group with down-turned mouths.

THE OLD LORD

Tomb 3 contained the body of the Old Lord of Sipán, buried 200 years earlier. He was buried with gold and silver sceptres and six necklaces (three gold and three silver). One of these was a necklace of 10 round gold beads depicting spiders perched on webs, a human face adorning each spider body. The delicate legs, webs, bodies and bead backing each required more than 100 solder points.

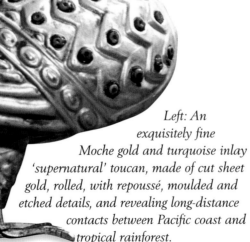

Left: An exquisitely fine Moche gold and turquoise inlay 'supernatural' toucan, made of cut sheet gold, rolled, with repoussé, moulded and etched details, and revealing long-distance contacts between Pacific coast and tropical rainforest.

The Old Lord wore a gold nosepiece, and four gold and silver earspools. A miniature gold warrior (only centimetres/inches tall) holds a war club and round shield. His tiny nose-crescent moves, his turquoise eyes have tiny black stone pupils, and he wears a square-beaded turquoise necklace, turquoise earspools and a proportionately enormous thin, sheet-gold headdress of flaring bands and gold discs that dangle, plus a central owl.

Beneath the funerary mask of the Old Lord excavators found the astounding 'Ulluchu Man', at nearly 60cm (2ft) tall the opposite of the miniature warrior masterpiece. The sheet-metal figure was originally fixed to a textile banner, itself covered with gilded metal platelets and on which were found samples of ulluchu (papaya-like) fruit.

He is a human crab of gilded copper, with inlaid shell ornaments as eyes and on his abdomen and crab legs. He has a human face and legs, plus large, upheld

Below: A Moche moulded sheet-gold and gold and turquoise bead necklace worthy of a princess, probably representing the creator god Viracocha, or the founder Lord Naymlap.

crab claws and six crab legs. His headdress has curled ends and an owl face, plus a crescent *tumi*-knife-bladed top. He wears a necklace of round-eyed owl heads. Such imagery is associated with war prisoners and sacrifice, and the fruit may have contributed anticoagulant properties to the goblets of blood drunk in the Sacrifice and Presentation ceremony.

LOOTED TREASURES

Many more Moche gold, silver and alloy objects have been recovered. Sadly, most are known only out of context and identified as Moche by their style. For example, from the looted tombs of Loma

Above: Delicate Moche rolled sheet-gold earrings representing hummingbirds with tiny turquoise inlay eyes, and minute suspended, dangling sheet-gold wings and feathers on gold wire.

Negra in the Piura Valley come 14 hammered gold and silver nosepieces, pectorals and textile adornments. One is a simple, plain crescent. Others depict a face wearing a flaring crown; rows of crawling spiders; a row of seabirds; a double-headed, braided snake; facing crayfish; facing iguanas; the Decapitator holding a *tumi* knife and a severed head by the hair; a row of snails; and a row of alternating snake heads and human skulls.

Such rich finds display the gamut of Moche imagery: human sacrifice and religious ceremony, closeness to the sea, and long-distant trade (for the inlaid stones).

A fine example of the continuing illegal trade in precious antiquities is the recovery in London in 2006 of a large sheet-gold mask of the Moche Decapitator, presumed to have been looted 20 years ago from a tomb. The god's grimacing, fanged face is surrounded by curling head rays, intricately cut out with triangular, denticulate edges and ending in stylized, round-eyed creatures – the very image of the Decapitator so vividly depicted on the walls of Moche Huaca de la Luna in the Lambayeque Valley.

SICÁN LORDS AND METALSMITHS

The succeeding Sicán culture of the late Middle Horizon and first half of the Late Intermediate Period in the Lambayeque Valley has produced equally rich burials at Batán Grande. One grave of a lesser individual had more than 100kg (220lb) of copper alloy objects; richer graves held hundreds of gold and silver ornaments and vessels. Analyses of more than 1,000 artefacts has shown them to be 12- to 18-carat gold-silver-copper alloy – about the same as much gold jewellery made today. Other pieces, and most of the waste scrap metal, are tumbaga – a gold-silver-copper alloy of less than 10 carats.

MORE LOOTED TREASURES

Sadly, between the 1930s and 1970s the Lambayeque and adjacent valleys of the now Poma National Historical Sanctuary were desecrated by looters. Generations of *huaqueros* excavated more than

Below: An elite Sicán burial skull adorned with a cloth headdress topped with feathers and rows of attached gold discs.

Above: An elite necklace of rolled and moulded sheet gold and moulded gold beads representing a Sicán Lord or possibly Viracocha the creator god.

100,000 pits, seeking ancient tombs and their precious artefacts to satisfy the demands of greedy collectors. Thousands of objects have been purchased and thus saved by museums for the enjoyment of all, but the evidence of their cultural contexts has been destroyed.

TREASURE IN THE TOMB

The Sicán Lord in Tomb I in the Huaca Loro temple mound, dated *c*.1000AD, contained a man about 40–50 years old, entombed seated, his body inverted, and his head turned 180 degrees to be right-side up. He wore a gold mask (46 x 29cm/*c*.18 x 12in) and his body was painted deep red with cinnabar (mercuric sulphide), possibly to represent blood. His burial was accompanied by the sacrifices of two women and two children.

His *c*.9sq m (96sq ft) grave at the bottom of an 11m (36ft) shaft contained 1.2 tons (tonnes) of gold, silver and alloy objects arranged around him and in caches and containers.

His cloth mantle (now decayed away), placed beneath his body, was sewn with nearly 2,000 gold foil squares. Objects immediately around or on him included a wooden staff with gold decoration, a gold *tumi* knife, a gold headdress, gold

shin covers, some tumbaga gloves measuring 2m (6½ft) long, (one grasping a gold *kero* cup with a silver rattle base), and gold earspools. He was covered in a thick layer of stone, amber, shell and metal beads. Near by were *c*.500kg (*c*.1,100lb) of tumbaga scraps and *c*.250kg (*c*.550lb) of copper-arsenic tools.

There were caches of objects in niches dug into the tomb walls. A box lined with woven mats contained 60 objects, including 5 gold and silver crowns, 4 headbands, 12 *tumi*-knife-shaped head pieces, 6 head ornaments set with delicate gold feathers, three 3 fans, 14 discs (staff attachments or headdress backings), and 4 parabolic headpiece attachments.

One niche contained 1,500 bundles of small, uniformly sized *naipes* (copper-arsenic I-shaped bars – each bundle containing 12 or 13 pieces), which were possibly a form of 'currency'. Also two silver-alloy *tumi* knives, thousands of gold foil squares and up to 24 tumbaga miniature masks identical to the one worn by the lord.

A LORDLY VISAGE

One tall head ornament comprised a gilded copper mask, painted red, and decorated with the face of the Sicán Lord, including inset precious stones. The forehead panel features a protruding vampire bat face and the tall crescent above it has etched geometric shapes, bulbous gold discs and an array of delicate golden feathers. There were several other similar pieces, the masks painted green or white.

The Sicán Lord image occurs on hundreds of objects, as a full figure or head only. He has a definitive half-circle face (the upper circle half being a crescent headdress) and eyes shaped like horizontal commas. His full figure often holds staffs. One Sicán grave contained more than 200 gold beakers with his image.

THE SICÁN METAL INDUSTRY

These objects come from the workshops of specialists. The placement even of the leftover scraps and inferior objects in tombs reveals their value, and emphasizes the prestige of the elite occupant.

Right: A Lambayeque-Sicán ceremonial bronze tumi *knife, topped with the delicate gold figure of a Sicán Lord or the Decapitator God, wearing a sun-flare or wave motif headdress.*

Batán Grande included mounds (the north platform of Huaca Loro and the north-east platform of Huaca Las Ventanas) supporting complexes of multi-roomed adobe buildings. They have split-level floors and integral adobe benches along their walls. In them excavators found copper slag and droplets of copper alloys from melting metal ore in bowl furnaces, no doubt using the locally abundant algarrobo (carob) trees as charcoal fuel.

Sicán-Lambayeque metalsmiths also ushered in the 'bronze age' of northern Peru. While gold-alloyed pieces advertise the social prestige of the owner, Sicán discovery and extensive use of arsenical-copper for making bronze enabled them to make sturdier blades and tools, the use of which was perpetuated by the Chimú and Incas after them.

Moreover, objects found in the Sicán Lord's caches reveal the existence of sophisticated metalworking training. Some of these pieces are of inferior quality and workmanship, as if made by lesser-skilled smiths or as practice pieces. The various stages of preparing the alloys, making the sheet metal, inscribing designs and cutting them out, and the artistry of forming and bonding the sheets, and producing

Left: Continuing the Moche tradition of fine sheet-gold work, Lambayeque-Sicán metalsmiths applied their skills to utilitarian objects such as this embossed copper-gold alloy kero *drinking cup, probably used for rituals.*

repoussé decorations and fine finishing, could be designated to apprentices and more skilled craftsmen as the work proceeded. For example, one gold cup with a Sicán Lord face has a raggedly chiselled chin, its silver base is pitted and traces of silver on the cup indicate that the silver was overheated and melted during bonding.

CHIMÚ AND INCA METALWORK

The spectacular Sipán and Batán Grande finds help to place ancient Andean metalwork into context and reveal details of metalworking techniques and 'industrial' output. Elite members of society, in control of the redistribution of wealth, dominated production and use. Spanish chronicles record thriving metallurgical industries in the Late Intermediate Kingdom of Chimú and among the Incas. The Incas forcibly resettled whole communities of metalsmiths in Cuzco to produce thousands of gold and silver objects in dedicated workshops.

MOCHE–SICÁN INHERITANCE
The Chimú subsumed and continued Sicán-Lambayeque smithing traditions, and much of their production is almost indistinguishable. They continued the Lambayeque introduction of making metal copies of ceramic shapes, particularly stirrup-spout bottles. Moche-Lambayeque fine metalwork traditions are exemplified by a Chimú silver stirrup-spout bottle and a pair of golden earspools, both with delicate repoussé decoration.

Below: A fine Chimú rolled sheet-gold, cone-shaped and turquoise bead necklace with gold face bead.

The Chimú silver stirrup-spout bottle is a miniature *audiencia* compound, part of a Chan Chan *ciudadela*. The curiously shaped piece is more like a sealed box surmounted by a stirrup spout. Intricately folded tiny sheet-silver figures decorate the bevelled ends of the bottle: an important official sits in a niche, while attendants stand at the vessel's corners. The flat sides and lower ends are decorated in repoussé, showing designs almost identical to those on the mud-sculpted walls of Chan Chan *ciudadelas*.

The surfaces of the pair of gold-silver Chimú earspools are covered in a story-like vignette in repoussé. At the tops are curious balconied structures, each surmounted by two tiny birds. Below the structure, a crinkled surface represents the sea, within which floats a rectangular raft. Two men on the raft stand back to back and bend over to receive spiny oyster shells from divers. Other divers collect more shells from the seabed. This charming picture must have made these earspools the pride and joy of some Chimú lord or lady!

INCA METALWORKING
Central highland cultures also had long-standing metalworking traditions. Some of the earliest copper working is from the Altiplano. Tiwanaku and Wari metalworkers produced distinctive styles in sheet metals, and their traditions were inherited by the Incas. Innovatively, Tiwanaku architects secured stone blocks with bronze staple-shaped clamps.

Two superlative examples exemplify Middle Horizon metallurgy. A Tiwanaku plaque of hammered sheet gold depicts a block-like face reminiscent of their stone sculptures. The hollowed eyes and mouth probably held stone insets. Fine incised lines around the face mimic the angular patterns of Tiwanaku textiles.

Above: This cast silver Inca male figurine represents an idealized Inca noble, identifiable by earlobes stretched from wearing ear discs. Note inlay gold bands on the hat, face and ankles, and inlay purple stone and orange-pink shell plaques.

A hammered sheet-silver Wari figure represents a warrior. The square-bodied, square-headed fighter wears a four-cornered hat, carries a shield and spear-thrower, and, like the Tiwanaku piece, is incised with fine lines representing his cloth tunic. He was one of a pair, the other being of gold, in characteristic Andean duality.

The great bulk of Inca gold and silver work was destroyed by the Spaniards. The chronicles report that they carried off and melted down 700 loads of gold sheathing from the Coricancha walls! The famous Cuzco garden of life-sized gold and silver plants and animals can only be imagined from remnant examples, such as a gold and silver maize stalk.

Other Inca gold and silver work has been found in provincial and mountain-top *capacocha* burials undiscovered by the Spaniards, such as votive llama figurines and cast-silver human figures. The Incas were fond of pairs of figures in gold and silver. Fortunately, many such figurines have survived, depicting males and females typically holding their hands to their breasts.

Below: Chimú lords, kings and priests used rolled and beaten sheet-gold gauntlets such as these, intricately decorated with embossed patterns and figures of lords or gods, probably in rituals and/or burials.

THE FIRST LOOTERS

Although the Incas honoured the Chan Chan *ciudadela* burial compounds of the Chimú dynasty, after the Spanish Conquest, they were systematically looted by the Spaniards, whose Castilian king established a royal smelter in the Moche valley to insure receipt of the crown's 20 per cent tax.

And there is the sad story of Atahualpa's ransom. Imprisoned in a palace room after his capture by Pizarro, Atahualpa realized that Spanish regard for gold and silver was different from Inca perceptions. He offered to fill his 5 x 6.75m (17 x 22ft) prison room with gold as high as he could reach. Pizarro, exploiting his advantage, also demanded that an adjoining small room be filled twice with silver. Atahualpa agreed, asked for two months for the task, and ordered the collection of gold and silver objects from all over the empire.

This singular episode highlights the different Andean and European perceptions of wealth. As religious symbols, Andean

Above: In conspicuous displays of wealth and power, Chimú and Inca nobles wore ceremonial tunics of fine alpaca wool with thousands of sheet-gold plaques or discs sewn onto them. This Inca example from southern Peru probably formed part of a mummy bundle.

gold and silver represented the essence of the sun and moon, but individual objects could be replaced. Their importance lay in the prestige they brought and in the imagery of the gods they displayed. Spanish interest was purely monetary. They cared neither for the artistry nor for any religious value the pieces held. In Spanish eyes, Inca gold and silver meant wealth and the destruction of idolatrous images.

This sad legacy continues. The unlooted tombs at Sipán and Batán Grande are rare examples of ancient Andean conspicuous consumption of precious metals in their social and ritual contexts.

CARVING AND BUILDING IN WOOD

Wood is rarely preserved in archaeological sites, except under special conditions. Enough has survived from Andean sites, however, to show that it was used in a variety of ways.

PRECERAMIC AND INITIAL PERIOD USES

Early migrants into the New World used wood for spear shafts and *atl-atl* spear-throwers (for big game), and throwing sticks (for small game), and also for stone-tool handles, digging sticks, mortars and fire drills, and for butchering, food collecting and processing.

Below: An Inca wooden coca snuff scoop, with a hand-forearm handle holding a disc scoop intricately carved with mythological figures, presumably representing drug-induced transformation.

Wooden earplugs are known from Preceramic sites. Burial offerings at the Initial Period coastal site of Ancón included a wooden bowl containing feathers, set beneath the head, and a tropical forest *chonta* wood figurine with inlaid shell eyes and articulated arms from a female burial. At Moxeke, a wooden figurine was found in one of the Huaca A platform rooms.

SNUFF TABLETS AND *KEROS*

Tiwanaku and Wari shamans used flat wooden snuff tablets for preparing coca and other hallucinogenic substances. Carved and highly polished, their handles depict animals, beast-headed men and geometric designs, inlaid with stone ornament. Other portable wooden artefacts depicted the Staff Deity.

Elaborately carved wooden *kero* drinking cups were a Middle Horizon speciality, continued by the Incas and into Spanish Colonial times. Many are painted. One carved Tiwanaku example depicts the Staff Deity dressed almost identically to the central figure on the Gateway of the Sun at the Kalasasaya compound.

An exquisite Chimú wooden *kero* comprises a cup, painted with a simple red and black design and black rim, on top of which was a carved figure inlaid with gold, turquoise and shell, standing on a mushroom-shaped pedestal. The grinning figure has a row of rectangular shell teeth, round, red shell eyes and a pillbox hat with shell-inlaid earflaps, and holds a golden cross at chest height.

WOODEN LITTERS

The celebrated Lambayeque-Chimú ceremonial litter is an elaborate frame sheathed with sheet gold. Six main panels and two smaller ones represent small 'houses'. The main houses have central doorways, sloping roofs and dangling gold crescent-shaped eave decorations. Inside stand three Sicán Lord warriors, with characteristic horizontal-comma eyes.

Above: A carved wooden post showing a stylized face, probably part of a thatched roof support, demonstrates Inca carving skill.

Single figures stand in the end houses and between the upper row of houses. Holes indicate that the litter was originally studded with feathers. Such a rich item must have transported a ruler.

The frame of a carved wooden litter was also found in the Lord Sicán tomb at Batán Grande.

IDOLS AND COFFINS

A small, windowless temple atop the main platform at the pilgrimage city of Pachacamac housed a carved wooden idol. It was kept behind a veil, and only priests were allowed to ascend the platform and enter the temple. The figure was carved with human faces on both sides, to represent duality. This idol was destroyed by Hernando Pizarro, whereupon the oracle 'fell silent', but several similar figures, presumed from Pachacamac, are in museums.

Above: Kero *drinking cups were for everyday use and for ritual drinking. Made of wood, pottery and precious metals, this Inca wooden example, depicting an Inca warrior, was probably used by a noble.*

The entryways of Chimú royal *ciudadelas* at Chan Chan were guarded by carved wooden figures standing in niches.

The Chachapoyas stood a row of upright wooden coffins on a rocky ledge at Karajia, on the north-western Inca tropical mountain borders. The 'heads' are carved with full, round beards and wear cylindrical hats, some with human skulls on top. The bodies are painted as clothing. At Los Pinchudos, they built round burial structures with stone mosaic exteriors, above which they placed rows of wooden, highly phallic male figures.

The Moche Sipán Lord was laid to rest on a wooden-slat support and placed in a wooden plank coffin, sewn with cords.

WOOD IN ARCHITECTURE

Rafters of wood supported the thatch roofs of stone and adobe walls. Highland and tropical wood was imported to coastal and desert areas for this purpose, and many adobe walls have insets for beams (for example at Sipán).

Wood began to be imported in the late Preceramic Period. Wooden thresholds at coastal Río Seco are made from trees that grow at 1,450–3,000m (4,785–10,000ft). The importance of these exchange links is revealed by the fact that neither wood nor highland obsidian was essential in the coastal economy, yet they were sought in preference to local materials. At Initial Period Garagay, wooden posts set into lined circular pits supported the roof of the Middle Temple.

The Chimú used wooden moulds to decorate their Late Intermediate Period mud walls.

COMMON TOOLS

A number of Late Intermediate Period Chancay wooden burial masks were found in non-elite graves. With basic features, shell inlays for eyes and often painted red, they appear to be a widespread extension of ancestor cults among citizens.

The Ica-Chincha and other central Peruvian coastal peoples made long, paddle-like objects with delicately carved openwork on the paddle top and along the shaft. One example has a row of long-beaked seabirds and a larger seabird on top of the shaft 'pommel'. Such artefacts are variously identified as ceremonial digging sticks, boat paddles or raft-steering paddles.

Balsa-wood rafts were the standard coastal trading vessels, such as the raft encountered by Pizarro's captain, Bartholomew Ruíz, in 1527 on his second voyage down the north-west South American coast. Laden with Inca gold and silver objects and textiles, the traders were from the Inca port of Tumbes.

Wood was essential in textile weaving for weaving tools and parts. Spindle whorls were ceramic or wood. Backstrap looms required wooden warp beams, shed sticks, heddle rods, bobbins and beating paddles.

Humblest of all, farmers' digging and planting sticks, and handles for agricultural implements, were essential items in planting, tending and harvesting the produce of villages, towns, city-states, kingdoms and empires throughout ancient Andean history.

Below: One of the finest surviving pieces of ancient Andean woodwork is this Lambayeque-Chimú royal litter or palanquin.

STONE, SHELL AND BONE

Ancient Andeans used semi-precious stones, bone and shell for small items of jewellery, on their own or as inlaid work.

OBSIDIAN
The earliest Andean hunter-gatherers used local stone for tools. Obsidian (natural volcanic glass), only available from specific highland locations, soon became preferred and was imported by coastal fishing and farming villages from Preceramic times.

TURQUOISE AND LAPIS LAZULI
Sources of turquoise and lapis lazuli (lazurite) were also rare – turquoise coming from the highlands, lapis lazuli

Below: A Chimú wooden bowl, with inlaid mother-of-pearl, turquoise and spondylus shell representing a wide-eyed sun-god-like face-skull.

from northern Chile. Tiny lapis lazuli beads were found in the hand of the highland Waywaka burial, which also contained the earliest gold foil, *c.*1500BC. Cupisnique burials include shell, turquoise, lapis lazuli and quartz crystal necklaces, and Chavín craftsmen also used exotic stones.

Moche jewellers used stone appliqué extensively, especially finely shaped turquoise chips. Sicán-Lambayeque craftsmen introduced techniques of inlaying shaped and polished turquoise and shell in gold and silver work, and in wood.

One of three gold and turquoise earspools in the Moche Sipán Lord's tomb depicts the lord himself, with two attendants flanking him. All three figures wear headdresses made up of minute turquoise chips. Another earspool has a running

Above: A shell container for lime, used with coca-leaf chewing, whose shape the artisan used to form into a stylized bird, from the Capuli culture of Ecuador.

deer made of shaped turquoise chips and tiny dark stone cloven hoofs, within a gold-bead and turquoise-chip circle.

Wari and Tiwanaku royalty imported turquoise, lapis lazuli, chrysacola minerals and greenstones from distant sources. An elaborate wooden Tiwanaku *kero* cup comprises a cup and 'stem' in the shape of a figure holding a gold cross. His clothing has numerous shell and gold inlays and a turquoise stone in the middle of the headdress. Forty intricately carved, 25mm (1in) figurines of tiny stone and shell chips and gold foil were found at Wari Pikillacta.

The body of the Sicán Lord at Batán Grande was covered in a 10cm- (4in-) thick layer of amber, shell, gold and silver alloy and stone beads (sodalite, amethyst, quartz crystal, turquoise, fluorite and calcite).

Emeralds were imported from Colombia. They were inlaid in Sicán-Lambayeque, Chimú and Inca jewellery.

Quartz crystals were especially coveted by shamans for ritual divinations.

SHELL
Jewellery was made from Preceramic times, mostly as shell necklaces. Shells were abundant at Preceramic coastal villages, and they were exchanged for wood and obsidian with people in the highland regions.

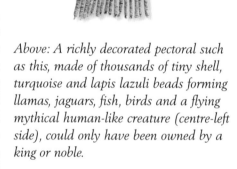

Strombus (conch) and spondylus (thorny oyster; *Spondylus princeps*) shells were especially sought. Shell trumpets were used in religious ritual. One sculptured figure in Chavín de Huántar's circular sunken court, for example, blows a conch trumpet. The dynastic founder Naymlap's royal entourage included Fonga Sigde, 'Blower of the Shell Trumpet', and Pitz Zofi 'Preparer of the Way', who ground and spread shell dust before his ruler.

Spondylus shells were particularly prestigious. They are found only in the warmer waters off the Ecuadorian coast and farther north, and therefore are exotic imports. Preceramic and Initial Period coastal

Below: These five finely carved bone figurines of the Early Intermediate Period Narrio culture of Ecuador might have had shell or stone inlay eyes and were probably temple pieces, possibly fertility figurines.

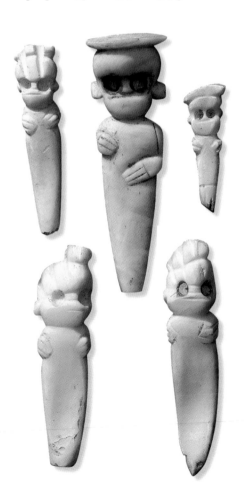

peoples imported them, and Cupisnique people made thousands of shell beads and pendants from local shells and spondylus. They sewed shells to their garments and even made bead skirts.

In the Early Horizon, as well as at Chavín de Huántar and other highland sites, spondylus shells were traded as far south as Paracas in southern coastal Peru. Elite individuals in rich mummy bundle burials wear necklaces of tubular and spondylus shells, thus declaring their high social status.

Sicán-Lambayeque lords and Chimú kings imported thousands of spondylus shells for their craftsmen to shape into jewellery and inlay in gold objects. Fonga Sigde was responsible for importing spondylus shells to Naymlap's court and may have worn earplugs such as the gold pair depicting divers collecting spondylus shells and handing them to men on rafts. Thorny oysters are even depicted and sculpted on Chimú ceramics and sculpted mud walls.

A particularly fine Chimú spondylus shell piece exemplifies the quality of their craftsmanship. Having removed the spines and smoothed the edge of an orange spondylus, the jeweller inlaid dark purple *Spondylus calcifer* into the top portion, to frame two exquisite, darker orange *S. princeps* birds and diamonds. Facing each other in characteristic, symbolic Andean duality, each bird pecks a fish, a typical Chimú motif. The birds and fish have tiny inlaid turquoise eyes, and the whole is highly finished to a uniform smoothness.

Inca craftsmen (or Chimú craftsmen resettled in Cuzco) also worked spondylus. For example, an especially fine necklace of 13 rectangular spondylus plaques was found on the Inca *capacocha* burial of a boy at Llullaillaco. Chachapoyas people included spondylus shell offerings in their round, stone mosaic burial structures.

Above: A richly decorated pectoral such as this, made of thousands of tiny shell, turquoise and lapis lazuli beads forming llamas, jaguars, fish, birds and a flying mythical human-like creature (centre-left side), could only have been owned by a king or noble.

CARVING IN BONE

Bone was also carved from early times. There are bone pins inlaid with turquoise from La Galgada burials, and an amber pendant. Four bone figurines with round staring eyes were found at Cerro Narrio in southern Ecuador.

Carved Chavín pieces include a human finger bone with incised bird motifs, found in the gallery above the Lanzón Stela, a hallucinogenic snuff spatula incised with a snarling feline motif (with traces of red paint) and two carved objects from Shillacoto (rubbed with charcoal).

A pair of highly polished, naked whale-bone figurines from a Nazca grave have square shell headdresses and painted eyes.

A Moche bone spatula is carved as a clenched fist and forearm, incised with intertwined figures and inlaid with turquoise chips.

Incas soldiers used skulls of enemy slain as gruesome victory cups from which to drink *chicha* beer!

FUNERARY ART

Ancient Andean production of ceramics, textiles, metal objects and metal, stone, shell and bone jewellery served multiple purposes. Andean 'art' was not produced for its own sake. Craftsmanship, artistry and aesthetic aspects were important, but the two primary purposes for its production were religious and economic.

POWER, CONTROL AND ARTISTRY

High-quality craftsmanship and artistry were important in producing sumptuary items, to enable individuals of high social status to advertise and emphasize their position. As with other aspects of Andean civilization, much was aimed at demonstrating power and control, and with impressing others with these issues. Much had to do with essence. Dressing in the most elaborate and exquisite garments, wearing the best jewellery and using the best-quality pottery were outward signs that the person wearing and using these items was also of superior quality.

Although the craftsmen and those people for whom the objects were produced cannot have been oblivious to the pure aesthetics of the pieces, they were striving to represent a mindset constantly influenced by religious considerations.

Below: Elite burial masks are thought to represent transformation of the deceased into a deity. This late Moche or Lambayeque gold example represents another 'transformation' and the concept of 'essence', as the gold bears traces of covering paint!

Above: The earliest funerary 'art' is represented in Chinchorros burials (northern Chile from c.6000BC), in which bodies were preserved with salt after removing the viscera and stuffing with straw, then shaped in clay and given facial features.

The social evolution of Andean civilization produced a class of citizens – royalty, nobility and religious leaders – whose purpose was to rule, administer the economy and intervene with the gods on the public's behalf. The entire worldview was governed by the need to maintain balance with divine powers for the welfare of humans and their life on Earth.

RELIGIOUS SYMBOLISM AND ECONOMIC BALANCE

Production of luxury items was to honour the deities and to provide for the redistribution of wealth, however unequally, within Andean society. The deposition of so much sumptuary production in royal and elite graves reveals that the value of the precious metals and other high-quality objects came not from their financial value, but from their worth as demonstrations of power, control, rank and an ability to consume conspicuously. Placing such tremendous wealth in tombs effectively removed it from circulation among humans, but it enhanced the prestige of the tomb's occupant and secured favour from the gods.

Death in the ancient Andean world was only the end of one stage in a cycle of being. Entombment was not necessarily permanent. In many cultures, the mummies (Inca *mallquis*) were regularly 'worshipped', kept in accessible tombs, or in special caves or temples, and brought out on ritual occasions to be consulted,

Above: The burial of an Inca noble, possibly a southern lord, as the text is Aymara of the Titicaca region and the mummy is being placed in a stone chullpa *tower in which an earlier skeleton sits (depicted in Poma de Ayala's* Nueva Corónica, *c.1615).*

entertained and given food and drink. Nazca tombs and *chullpa* burial towers were kinship mausoleums regularly reopened for the deposit of descendants through generations.

The removal of luxury goods from circulation also perpetuated the need for their production and supported continued elite conspicuous consumption, and therefore royal, elite and religious control. The effect was to keep the economy active and healthy. The bulk of the population, engaged in agriculture, supported elite and religious leaders, and the craftspeople necessary to produce sumptuary goods. The exclusivity of Chimú royal compounds at Chan Chan and their massive storage rooms are exemplary in this regard.

The situation can be regarded as an unconscious perpetuation of the Andean cyclical worldview.

CONFIRMING CEREMONY

Funerary art brings together all forms of Andean craft production. Although much of what has been found in burials and tombs was probably worn and used in life, it was also ultimately made in preparation for burial. Religious symbolism was paramount, both in the subject matter portrayed on the objects and in its presentation in the tombs.

Confirmation of the religious rituals depicted on Moche murals, for example, has been found in the Sipán and other elite burials. The principal bodies were dressed in identical regalia to that worn by the priests and priestesses of Moche Sacrifice and Presentation ceremonies shown on walls and ceramics. Their attendants in the tombs were their retainers for the next state of being, and were sacrificial victims, part of Andean religious practice from the earliest Initial Period tombs at U-shaped ceremonial centres.

In Sicán-Lambayeque elite burials at Batán Grande one tomb contained 17 sacrificial victims. And the caches of copper *naipes* suggest both that Batán Grande was the centre for their production and that their value was not only an exchange mechanism in life.

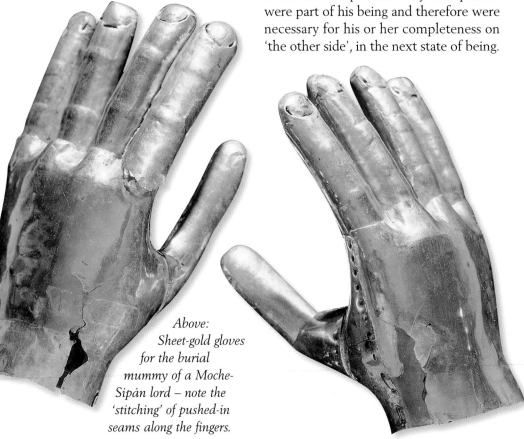

Above: Sheet-gold gloves for the burial mummy of a Moche-Sipán lord – note the 'stitching' of pushed-in seams along the fingers.

JUST FOR BURIAL

The preparation of items specifically for burial is suggested by Paracas and Nazca mummy bundles. Some of the textiles, whose intricate weaving and complex symbolism necessitated great labour over long time periods (sometimes perhaps even a lifetime), are unfinished. This indicates that the individual died before the item could be finished by the maker. Other possible explanations are that the items were being made expressly for the eventuality of burial with the deceased, but that it was also necessary to include them unfinished because they 'belonged' to that person in every sense. Alternatively, some items might have been deliberately left unfinished so that they could be completed by the individual in the next life.

The concept that a set of possessions was specific to an individual may also be the explanation of the deposition of inferior goods in the Sicán Lord's tomb. All items made for and possessed by that person were part of his being and therefore were necessary for his or her completeness on 'the other side', in the next state of being.

GLOSSARY AND FURTHER READING

aclla (or acllyacona) a chosen woman, selected to serve in the imperial cult of Inti
acllahuasi special compounds in which to house *acllas*
adobe mud brick
Altiplano high plateaux regions, especially in southern Andes
amaru mythical serpent-dragon figure
amautas Inca court officials responsible for memorizing Inca history and religion
'Andean Area' sierras and adjacent foothills and Pacific coastal valleys, east to the *montañas* of the eastern Andes and edge of the Amazonian Rainforest, north to south from the present-day Colombian–Ecuadorian border to the northern half of Chile
apacheta special type of *huaca* – a stone cairn at a mountain pass or crossroads
apo Inca official in charge of a *suyu*
apu type of *huaca* – sacred mountain deity
atl-atl spear-thrower used by hunter-gatherers and in warfare
Auca Runa people of the fourth age in Inca creation
audiencia miniature U-shaped temple, sacred compound in a *ciudadela* at Chan Chan
awasca Inca plain, coarser fabric, for ordinary use
ayar legendary Inca ancestor
aylloscas Inca gambling game played by nobles
ayllu community bound in kinship both by blood and marriage, and with territory held in common
Aymara principal Inca language of the southern Andes
ayni Aymara term for *mit'a*

camelids New World descendants of Camedilae family. In the Andean Area these are the llama, guanaco, vicuña and alpaca
capacocha specially selected Inca sacrificial victim, usually noble, often a child
cayman South American freshwater alligator
ceque sacred pathway or sight line in Andean religion, especially from Inca Cuzco. Walked in religious ceremonies and by sacrificial victims
chachapuma puma-headed person/statuary
charqui strips of sun-dried and freeze-dried meat or fish
chasqui Inca imperial messenger/road runner
chicha beer made from fermented maize
chullpa Late Intermediate Period and Late Horizon stone burial towers
chuño the dried pulp left by repeatedly freeze-drying and thawing potatoes
ciudadela huge walled compound of ruling or dead Chimú king at Chan Chan
collcas Inca state storehouses for large quantities of such staples as *charqui* and *chuño*
collectivity Andean idea of corporate thinking:

people undertook activities as co-operative efforts, and considered the group more important than the individual, while the groups looked after the individual
coya official wife of the Inca emperor
curacas local leader or chief, or one of several levels of Inca officials
DWW discontinuous warp and weft
essence Andean concept, related to *transformation*, that the basic nature of an object and its appearance are more important than its actual substance. Applied in art to symbolism and decoration
geoglyph geometric shape or figure from the Nazca Desert and other Andean Area places
hanan upper: applied to one *moiety* of a lineage group (*ayllu*) and to a subdivision of a town or province
Hanan Pacha the Inca world of above
huaca sacred place: natural, man-made, or a modified natural feature
huaqueros in South American archaeology, tomb robbers, looters of archaeological sites; and the pits they left
hunter-gatherers people who live by hunting game, fishing, and gathering wild plants
hurin lower: applied to one *moiety* of a lineage group (*ayllu*) and to a subdivision of a town or province
Inti the sun god; also the Inca emperor
intihuatana 'hitching post of the sun' – Inca rock platform used as a sort of altar for sun observation and worship

Kai Pacha the Inca world of the living
kallanka large rectangular Inca hall used for public purposes
kancha walled enclosure of residential and storage buildings
kero Andean drinking cup, especially for drinking *chicha*
mallquis mummified remains of Inca rulers and nobility
mama female part of the Early Horizon Yaya-Mama cult around Lake Titicaca
manioc low-altitude tropical vegetable tuber
mashwa low-altitude Andean vegetable tuber
mit'a 'tax' obligation to do periodic labour for the state
mitimaes peoples redistributed within the Inca Empire
moiety half division of a lineage group (e.g. *ayllus*). The two intermarriageable family groups of a descent lineage
montaña the forested slopes of the eastern Andes
oca high-altitude Andean vegetable tuber
pacarina a place of origin, the place from which one's ancestors emerged
pachacuti turning over, revolution, a cycle of world events or states of being
pampas extensive temperate, upland grasslands in the south Andean Area
panacas Cuzco imperial *ayllus* comprising the descendants of each Inca emperor
plazas hundidas 'hidden' open courts, semi-subterranean
pukarás Late Intermediate and Late Horizon hilltop fortresses
puna Andean sierra basin or valley, a high, cold plateau
Purun Runa people of the third age in Inca creation

qompi Inca fine cloth for royal and religious use
Quechua principal Inca language of the central and northern Andes
quincha mud-plastered cane used in Andean house walls
quinoa high-protein grain
quipucamayoqs literally 'knot makers'. Inca court officials responsible for *quipus*
quipus Inca system of knotting wool and cotton strings to record basic economic and historical information
reciprocity Andean concept, linked to *collectivity*, of reciprocal trade over long distances and an acceptance of mutual obligations within social co-operation
Sapa the Inca emperor
selva see *montaña*
shaman ceremonial leader, healer or priest

sinchis warrior leaders of the Later Intermediate Period and Late Horizon who built hilltop fortifications called *pukarás*
stela carved stone ritual monument or statuary
suyu division of the Inca Empire, which comprised four *suyus*, or 'quarters', of unequal size
Tahuantinsuyu 'The four parts' – Inca name for their empire
tambos way-stations on Inca, Wari and Tiwanaku roads to accommodate officials, pilgrims and postal runners
tapia poured adobe or mud on stone foundations, which was carved after it dried
tarwi high-protein Andean grain
transformation Andean concept of alternative or even a procession of states of being.

Applied to humans in their life and death, to altered states and other worlds entered by shamans in drug-induced trance, to objects such as the creation of a textile from the cotton plant, in art as the transformation of imagery from one creature to another, and in religious processions enacting such transformations
tumbaga amalgamation of copper and gold (or sometimes silver)
tumi copper or bronze crescent-shaped knife used for ritual decapitation; ceremonial *tumis* were made of precious metals
tupu large copper pin used by Inca women to secure a mantle. Nobles used *tupus* of precious metals
Uku Pacha the Inca world of below

ulluco Highland vegetable tuber
U-shaped complex Andean and coastal western valley temples comprising a main end platform mound with subsidiary long platform mounds extending from its front corners to form a U shape enclosing a plaza
ushnu Inca stone platform in Cuzco and provincial capitals used for imperial observation and address
Wari Runa people of the second age in Inca creation
Wari Wiracocharuna people of the first age in Inca creation
yanacona selected Inca court retainer or servant
yaya male part of the Early Horizon Yaya-Mama Cult around Lake Titicaca
yuca high-altitude Andean vegetable tuber

FURTHER READING

Bowden, Garth, *The Moche* (Blackwell, Cambridge, MA and Oxford, 1999)
Bruhns, Karen Olson, *Ancient South America* (Cambridge University Press, Cambridge, 1994)
Burger, Richard L., *Chavín and the Origins of Andean Civilization* (Thames and Hudson, London, 1995)
Hemming, John, *The Conquest of the Incas* (Penguin Books, London, 1983)
Janusek, John Wayne, *Ancient Tiwanaku* (Cambridge University Press, 2008)
Jones, David M., *The Illustrated Encyclopedia of the Incas* (Lorenz Books, London, 2007)

Malpass, Michael A., *Daily Life in the Inca Empire* (Greenwood Press, Westport, CT and London, 1996)
Minelli, Laura Laurencich (ed.), *et al.*, *The Inca World: the Development of Pre-Columbian Peru, A.D. 1000–1534* (translated by Andrew Ellis, James Bishop and Angelica Mercurio Ciampi, University of Oklahoma Press, Norman, 1999)
Moseley, Michael E., *The Incas and their Ancestors* (2nd edition, Thames and Hudson, London, 2001)

Quilter, Jeffrey, *Treasures of the Andes: the Glories of Inca and Pre-Columbian South America* (Duncan Baird, London, 2005)
Shimada, Izumi, *Pampa Grande and the Mochica Culture* (University of Texas Press, Austin, 1994)
Steele, Paul R., *Handbook of Inca Mythology* (ABC Clio, Santa Barbara, CA, 2004)
Stone-Miller, Rebecca, *Art of the Andes from Chavín to Inca* (2nd edition, Thames and Hudson, London, 2002)
von Hagen, Adriana, and Morris, Craig, *The Cities of the Ancient Andes* (Thames and Hudson, London, 1998)

Young-Sánchez, Margaret, *et al.*, *Tiwanaku, Ancestors of the Inca* (Denver Art Museum, Denver and University of Nebraska Press, Lincoln and London, 2004)

INDEX

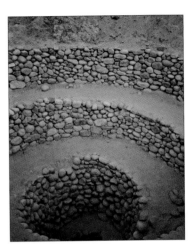

emperor 104, 109

Erizo 200

essence, concept of 57, 63, 71, 80, 90, *246*

F

Fanged God *128*

farming *see* agriculture

featherwork 31, 60, *61*, 85, *108*, 109, 111, 217, 225, *225*, 226–7, *226*, *227*, *238*

fishing *8*, 30, 43, *43*, 58, 60, 84, 85, *86*, 87, 100, 107, 198, 216, *220*, 221

flora and fauna 26, 28–31, 42–3

food *see* diet

fortifications 22, 164–5, *164*, *165*

freeze-drying 101

G

Galindo 156, 160, 163, 164

Gallinazo 49, 206–7

Garagay 95, 144, *146*, 147, 190, 194

geoglyphs 17, 49, *49*, 63, *116–17*, 119, 120, *126*, 140, *140*, 169, *169*, 185

gods 62, 63, *64*, 65, 68–9, 70, 95, 117, 121, 124–5, 186, 187, 209

see also religion

gold 21, 80, 89, 109, 144, 225, 226, 231, 232–41, *246*

gourds 21, 198–9, *199*, 214

guinea pig 21, 31, *31*, 43, 85, 100, 131

Guitarrero Cave 21, 42, 100, 214, 216, 220

H

hairstyles 109

hallucinogens 22, 29, 62, 84–5, 90, 95, 122, *130*, 146, 187, 188–9, *189*, *194*, *217*, *225*, 242, 245

see also coca; San Pedro cactus

Haucaypata 161

housing 69, *99*, 101, 107, 149, 162–3, *162*, *163*, *205*, *210*

Huaca de las Conchas 192

Huaca de los Idolos 21, 142, 200, 222, 228

Huaca de los Sacrificios 21, 122, 128, 142, 156, 221

Huaca del Dragón *53*, 147, *182–3*, *190*, *191*, 193, *193*

Huaca del Higo 192

Huaca del Obispo 192

Huaca Forteleza 160, 163

Huaca de los Reyes 141, 147, 154–5, 158, 191

Huaca Negra 200

Huaca Prieta 21, 43, 62, 122, 162, *195*, 199, *199*, 215, 216, 220

huacas 12, 64, 118–19, *118*, 120

Huanacauri 99

Huancaco 22, 170

Huánuca Pampa *33*, 91, 159, *161*, 178–9, *179*

Huari 22, 23, 50–1, 52, 139, 156, 159, 163, 174–5

Huaricoto 43, 48, 100

Huarpa 49

Huáscar 23, 34–5, 37, 161

Huayna Capac 23, 34, 35, *35*, 37, 70

hunting 31, 58, 85, 87, *87*, *96–7*, 107, 113

I

Ica 53

Ichma 52

Illapa 95, 131

Inca Empire 6, 20, 23, 54–5, 57–71

administration *see* administration

civil war 23, 34–5, 36

decline 23, 69

record keeping 12, *12*

structure 70–1

tax system *see* mit'a tax system

Inca Pisac *152*

inheritance 105

Initial Period 20, 21, 43, 44–5, 46

initiation rites 98–9, 222, 225

Inti 23, 31, 35, 55, 68, 70, 75, 95, *103*, 104, 121, 125, 131, 142, *235*

irrigation 7, *8*, 21, *44*, *45*, 46, 48, 55, 81, 86, 107, 137, 138, 201

J

jaguar 30, 31, *31*, 66, *100*, *126*, 146, 187, *187*, *235*

Jamacoaque *94*, *202*

jewellery *89*, 108, 109, *132–3*, 232, *233*, 238, *238*, 240, *240*, 244–5

Moche *74*, *232*, 236–7, *237*, 244

Jincamocco 22, 51, 68, 159

K

kallankas 149, *158*, 159, *162*, *163*, 178

kanchas *79*, 149, 178

Karajia 243

Karwa 22, 47, 48, 216–17

Kenco *see* Qenqo

kero drinking cups 29, *50*, *52*, 59, *74*, *80*, 81, 88, *96–7*, *100*, 101, *103*, *109*, 188–9, *206*, *239*, 242, *243*

kinship ties *see* ayllus

Kotosh 21, 43, 46, 48, 100, 128, 138, 141, 142, 144, 190, *190*, 194, 200–1, 204, 206

Kotosh Tradition 94, 123, 126, 190

Kuntur Wasi 22, 47, 48

L

La Centinella *118*, 139, 141, 147, 193

La Florida 21, 139, 200

La Galgada 21, 43, 68, 100, 138, 141, 142, 162, 201, 216, 220, 226

La Palma 123

La Paloma 65, 118, 162, 221

La Tolita *120*, *235*

Lambayeque-Sicán 22, 23, 52, *52*, 53, 65, 80, 88, 114, 130–1, 156, 195, 226, 231, 238–9, *238*, *239*, 242, *243*, 244–5, 247

land allocation 78–9, 81, 118

landscape 6–7, *6*, *7*, 19, *24–5*, 26–7

importance of 120, *120*, 137, *138*, *139*, 153, 180–1, 185

sacred sites *see* huacas

lapis lazuli 244, *245*

Las Haldas 139, 154

Late Horizon 20, 23, 54–5

Late Intermediate Period 20, 23, 52–3, 54

law, administration 75, 93, 110–11, *110*, *111*

Lima 17, 23

Lima culture 49

literature 119

litters 83, 227, 242, *243*

ACKNOWLEDGEMENTS

AUTHOR'S DEDICATION
I would like to dedicate this book to Professor Warwick Bray, mentor and friend.

This edition is published by Lorenz Books, an imprint of Anness Publishing Ltd, Hermes House, 88–89 Blackfriars Road, London SE1 8HA
tel. 020 7401 2077; fax 020 7633 9499
www.lorenzbooks.com; www.annesspublishing.com

Anness Publishing has a new picture agency outlet for images for publishing, promotions or advertising. Please visit our website www.practicalpictures.com for more information.

UK agent: The Manning Partnership Ltd;
tel. 01225 478444; fax 01225 478440;
sales@manning-partnership.co.uk
UK distributor: Book Trade Services;
tel. 0116 2759086; fax 0116 2759090;
uksales@booktradeservices.com;
exportsales@booktradeservices.com
North American agent/distributor:
National Book Network; tel. 301 459 3366;
fax 301 429 5746; www.nbnbooks.com
Australian agent/distributor: Pan Macmillan
Australia; tel. 1300 135 113; fax 1300 135 103;
customer.service@macmillan.com.au
New Zealand agent/distributor: David Bateman Ltd;
tel. (09) 415 7664; fax (09) 415 8892

Publisher: Joanna Lorenz
Editor: Joy Wotton
Designer: Nigel Partridge
Illustrators: Vanessa Card and Anthony Duke
Proofreading Manager: Lindsay Zamponi
Production Controller: Steve Lang

ETHICAL TRADING POLICY: Because of our ongoing ecological investment programme, you have the reassurance of knowing that a tree is being cultivated to replace the materials used to make the book you are holding. For further information, go to www.annesspublishing.com/trees

© Anness Publishing Ltd 2010

PICTURE ACKNOWLEDGEMENTS
The Art Archive: /089t, 70b, 90t, 115t, 132–3, 158b, 159t, 191tl; /Gabaldoni Collection Lima/Gianni Dagli Orti: 104b; /Gianni Dagli Orti: 64b, 65t, 66b, 138t, 142t, 143t and b; /Museo Banco Central de Quito Ecuador/Gianni Dagli Orti: 76t; /Museo del Banco Central de Reserva Lima/Gianni Dagli Orti: 123b; /Album/J.Enrique Molina: 163t; /Amano Museum Lima/Mireille Vautier: 41b, 131t, 203t, 227b, 228t; /Amano Museum Lima: 59t; /Archaeological Museum Quito/Gianni Dagli Orti: 47tr, 52t, 53tl, 60, 62t and b, 80t, 86t, 104t, 109b, 112t, 113b, 121b, 122b, 123t, 130b, 157t, 190t, 194b, 203b, 207b, 208t, 209t, 211t, 216t and b, 218t, 219t and b, 222t and br, 223b, 226t, 244b, 245t; /Archaeological Museum Lima/Mireille Vautier: 28bl; /84t, 87t, 91b, 94l, 98t, 101b, 102t, 105b, 107t, 112t, 162t and b, 195b, 205t, 206b, 208b, 211b, 220t, 232b; /Arquivo Nacional da Torre do Tombo Lisbon/Gianni Dagli Orti: 26tr; /Biblioteca Nacional Madrid/Gianni Dagli Orti: 15tl; /Biblioteca Nazionale Marciana Venice/Gianni Dagli Orti: 36b; /Brunning Museum, Lambeyeque, Peru/Mireille Vautier: 238t; /Central Bank Museum Quito Ecuador/Mireille Vautier: 42t; /Central Bank Museum/Mireille Vautier: 200t; /Dagli Orti: 144br; /Daniele Lavallée Collection Paris/Gianni Dagli Orti: 206t; /E. Poli Collection Lima/Gianni Dagli Orti: 198b, 205b, 207t; /Ethnographical Museum Gothenburg Sweden/Gianni Dagli Orti: 113t; /General Archive of the Indies Seville/Gianni Dagli Orti: 036t; /Gianni Dagli Orti: 4.3, 5.3, 16t, 21r, 34b, 46, 53tr, 55t, 56–7, 58t, 63t, 67b, 126b, 129t, 130t, 146t and b, 148br, 149t, 152b, 153b, 155t, 159b, 164t, 165t, 176t, 177b, 182–3, 184t, 185t, 187t, 191tr, 192b, 193b; /Mireille Vautier: 32b, 37t, 101t, 128b, 165b, 202t; /Musée du Nouveau Monde La Rochelle/Gianni Dagli Orti: 37bl, 95t; /Museo Amano Lima: 103b, 200b; /Museo Banco Central de Quito Ecuador/Gianni Dagli Orti: endpaper, 63b, 94r, 95b, 120t, 202b, 235t, 245b; /Museo de Arte Municipal Lima/Gianni Dagli Orti: 89b, 114b, 223t; /Museo del Oro Bogota/Gianni Dagli Orti: 233bl; /Museo del Oro Lima/Gianni Dagli Orti: 61bl, 74b, 80b, 225t, 226b, 232t, 234b, 235t, 237t, 240b, 241b, 243b, 247b; /Museo Guayasamin Quito Ecuador/Gianni Dagli Orti: 204; /Museo Larco Herrera Lima: 48t, 233t; /Museo Nacional Bogota/Gianni Dagli Orti: 15tr; /Museo Nacional de Historia Peru/Mireille Vautier: 65b; /Museo Nacional Tiahuanacu La Paz Bolivia/Gianni Dagli Ort: 209b, 243t; /Museo Pedro de Osma Lima/Mireille Vautier: 33b, 35t and b, 64t; /Museo Regional de Ica Peru/Gianni Dagli Orti: 59b, 194t, 210t; /National Anthropological Museum Mexico/Gianni Dagli Orti: 40br; /Navy Historical Service Vincennes France/Gianni Dagli Orti: 14l; /Olga Fischer Collection Quito/Mireille Vautier: 77b; /Private Collection Ecuador/Gianni Dagli Orti: 44b; /Queretaro Museum Mexico/Alfredo Dagli Orti: 41t; /University Museum Cuzco/Mireille Vautier: 4.5, 74t, 96-7.
The Ancient Art and Architecture Collection: /C.M. Dixon: 129b ; /Prisma: 13r; /J.Sparshatt: 47tl.
Andrew McLeod: 4br, 15b, 23r, 148t, 160b, 180t, 185b, 254t, 254b, 256t.

The Bridgeman Art Library: /Collection of the New-York Historical Society: 111t. /Museo del Oro, Lima: 75r; /Private Collection: 4.4, 37br, 72–3.
Corbis: /© Brian A. Vikander: 5.1; /© Paolo Aguilar/epa: 17t; /Academy of Natural Sciences of Philadelphia: 31b; /Atlantide Phototravel: 145t; /Blaine Harrington III: 40t; /Brian A. Vikander: 134–5; /Brian A. Vikander: 175b; /Charles and Josette Lenars: 186t and b; /Francesco Venturi: 199b; /Gian Berto Vanni: 99b; /Nathan Benn: 40bl; /Richard List: 187b; /The Gallery Collection: 98b; /Yann Arthus-Bertrand: 121t.
Frances Reynolds: 5tr, 9br, 21m, 23m, 43t, 148bl, 149bl, 149br, 164b, 211, 23l, 248, 255b, 256b.
Sally Phillips: 214t, 250t, 252b, 253b.
South American Pictures: 124t; /Anna McVittie: 28t, 50tr, 118b, 174b; /Archaeological Museum Lima/Gianni Dagli Orti: 222t; /Bill Leimbach: 224b; /Britt Dyer: 16b, 84bl, 144bl, 147t, 190b; /Chris Sharp:120b, 170br, 198t, 222bl, 246t; /Gianni Dagli Orti: 177b; /Jason P Howe: 29; /Kathy Jarvis: 33t, 66t, 93b, 156, 157b, 161t, 179bl; /Kim Richardson: 44t, 174t; /Kimball Morrison: 6b, 26br, 83t, 147b, 218b; /Luke Peters: 114t; /Philippe Bowles: 181b; /Robert Francis: 20, 48b, 53b, 139t, 140b, 144t, 170bl, 171b, 177t, 192t; /Tony Morrison: 2, 4.1, 4.2, 5.2, 5.4, 7b, 8tl, 9tl and tr, 12.r, 14r, 17b, 18–19, 22l and m, 24–5, 26bl, 27tl, tr and b, 28br, 30b, 31t, 38–9, 42b, 43b, 45b, 49t and b, 50tm and b, 51t and b, 52b, 54t, 55b, 58b, 61br, 67t, 68t, 69t and b, 71b, 81b, 82t and b, 87b, 90b, 100t and b, 109t, 110t, 115b, 118t, 119t, 122t, 125b, 127t, 136b, 137t and b, 138b, 139b, 140t, 141b, 150–1, 152t, 154b, 155b, 160t, 161bl, 163b, 168t and b, 169t, 171t, 172b, 173t, 175t, 178t, 179br, 180b, 184b, 188t and b, 189t, 191b, 195t, 196–7, 200tl, tr and b, 221tr and b, 224t, 228b, 229t, 237b, 238b, 239b, 242t.
The Werner Forman Archive: /Art Institute of Chicago: 105t; /British Museum, London: 88b, 214b; /Dallas Museum of Art: 1, 5.5, 5.6, 212–13, 227t, 230–1, 241t, 246b; /David Bernstein Fine Art, New York: 47b, 81t, 108t, 217, 225b, 233br, 234t, 244t; /Museum fur Volkerkunde, Berlin:078t, 085b, 086b, 108b, 229b, 239t, 242b; /N.J. Saunders: 4.6, 10–11, 22r, 78b, 79t, 106b, 116–17, 124b, 126t, 127b, 128t, 153t, 154t, 158t, 167b, 169b, 170t, 172t, 173b, 178b, 193t, 220b, 236t; /National Museum of Denmark, Copenhagen: 54b; /Private Collection: 210b, 236b; /Rassiga Collection: 215t; Museum fur Volkerkunde, Berlin: 240t.

p.1 Lambeyeque–Sicán gold burial mask. p.2 The Ponce Monolith, Tiwanaku. p.3 The 'Soothsayer', Poma de Ayala, c. 1615. Above: Machu Picchu. Below: Cuzco.